A History of Homosexuality in Europe (1919-1939) was originally published in France by Editions du Seuil; this is the second volume of the English translation.

Volume I introduced the first glimmerings of tolerance for homosexuality around the turn of the last century, quickly squelched by the trial of Oscar Wilde which sent a chill throughout the cosmopolitan centers of the world. Then, a variety of factors came together in the aftermath of World War I to forge a climate that was more permissive and open. The Roaring Twenties are sometimes seen, in retrospect, as having been a golden age for homosexuals and lesbians; and the literary output of the era shows why.

However, a different dynamic was also taking shape, and the current volume explores how that played out. The Depression, the rise of fascist movements, and a counter-reaction against what were seen as the excesses of the post-war era contributed to a crackdown on homosexuals, and new forms of repression emerged.

What happened to homosexuals during and after World War II has been described in other books; here, Florence Tamagne traces the different trends in Germany, England and France in the period leading up to that cataclysm and provides important background to any understanding of the later events.

TABLE OF CONTENTS

CHAPTER FIVE

BREAKING THE SILENCE: HOMOSEXUALS AND PUBLIC OPINION

Homosexuality was a trendy topic in the Twenties. While it had been taboo until the beginning of the century, in the aftermath of the war there was a virtual explosion of homosexual themes in literature and the arts. More subtle was the emergence of homoerotic imagery in broad sectors of society, especially among young people. Sports events became an opportunity for promoting images of naked bodies strongly charged with erotic connotations, with androgynous appeal, while the proliferation of single-gender organizations and group activities, whether fitness-related or educational, took on a certain homosexual mystique. The public showed an interest tinged with concern; the trend was perceived as representing the new, the modern, a phenomenon that was typical of the post-war period and steadily growing. A few sounded the alarm in the 1920s, complaining of decadence. The image of the homosexual was crafted as a curious mix of old prejudices, new medical definitions and visual stereotypes.

The concept of public opinion is very difficult to define; for our purposes, we will use the term to refer to the expression of the community vis-à-vis a particular phenomenon, and also as the assertion of a prevailing viewpoint within a social group[1]; in fact, it is "neither fixed nor immutable" but, on the contrary, is subject to infinite variations, shifts, and reversals depending on events, external pressures and its own evolution. While public opinion is a collective phenomenon, it is not readily reducible to major entities such as the press, the Par-

---

1. Pierre Laborie, "De l'opinion publique a l'imaginaire social," in *XXe siècle*, n° 18, April-June 1988.

1

liament, associations or any other manifestation that makes such a claim. By the same token, it is not programmatically a function of the social level, demographic origins or religious or political affiliation. However, each one of its elements contributes to shaping and influencing it. Thus, we must be careful, particularly when dealing with a subject as polemical as homosexuality, resonating as it does in the collective imagination, loaded with the weight of judgments from earlier times. Studying public opinion comes under the rubric of the social imagination; it does not reveal what was true about a given era, it only translates the fears and fantasies of the times.

THE WEIGHT OF PREJUDICES

The key question is tolerance, which I will define not as approval of a phenomenon, but its acceptance. The preponderant tendencies in public opinion show that negative prejudices were still common with regard to homosexuality, and were relayed by the principal institutions and the mainstream press, even if there was notable progress compared to the pre-war period. Certain topics, like links between feminism and lesbianism, protecting young people, or fear of foreigners, were used as excuses for promoting homophobic fantasies.

Guardians of Traditional Morals

We can look to what the institutions were saying as a basis for defining what was the standard attitude with regard to homosexuality. As public expressions, they were endowed with historical and political legitimacy; passed on by the major media, they became the bases for much of private discourse. Whether due to indecision, indifference or simple conformity, many people adopt the official line as their own personal opinion and they base their opinion on that of the majority. They pick up the prejudices of their group, be it denominational, social or partisan.

The Churches

The influence of the Churches was still quite strong in the three countries in question during the 1920s and 1930s, even if there was talk of a religious crisis stemming from urbanization, conflicts between Church and State, and the economic crises.[2] In fact, in Western, Christian civilization, the attitude toward homosexuality was above all a function of the religious discourse. Sodomy, a "gratuitous" practice, "unnatural," was unacceptable, as were contraception, sex during menses or pregnancy or while breast-feeding, and masturbation. Religious condemnation was one of the reasons most frequently cited to justify homophobia. However, John Boswell[3] showed that religion is very often only a pretext to justify personal prejudices.

The Catholic Church's position on the question changed very little during the inter-war period. Although it now recognized the legitimacy of sex education (as long as it was handled within the family and in collaboration with the Christian Marriage Association, and recognized two goals in marriage: procreation, but also "the subjective satisfaction of the spouses"), homosexuality was still condemned, as was contraception, in spite of the fact that the "Ogino Method" had been publicized since 1934. This attitude came under the more general disapproval of the quest for physical pleasure, which diverts man from spiritual concerns and endangers the moral environment.[4] Homosexuality is a blatant example of sexuality without any purpose and without any constraint. The Protestant Churches and the Anglican Church did not express much greater tolerance on the subject, although the latter did recognize, for example, the legitimacy of birth control in 1930.

The decline of morals and the "spreading" of homosexuality were much decried in religious publications, Catholic, Anglican and Protestant alike. Claudel's indignation upon learning of Gide's homosexuality in 1924 is indicative of most Catholics' opinion on the subject, as was Bernanos's article in the *Les Nouvelles littéraires* of April 17, 1926, wherein he reproaches Proust's writings for their lack of spiritual concern and religious and moral striving. Medical theories did not show any significant change; one Protestant work notes: "Aversion for the opposite sex, which clearly indicates that homosexuals should be classified as medical cases, and dangerous ones, since they are constantly on the look-out for new partners — particularly women among children — new partners whom they will make abnormal in their turn; but the moral suffering of

---

2. On the influence of the Churches, see Roland Marx, *L'Angleterre de 1914 à 1945*, Paris, Armand Colin, 1993, 175 pages; Dominique Borne and Henri Dubief, *La Crise des années trente, 1929-1938*, Paris, Éditions du Seuil, coll. "Points histoire," 1989, 322 pages; Detlev J.K. Peukert, *La République de Weimar*, Paris, Aubier, 1995, 301 pages.

3. See John Boswell, *Christianisme, tolérance sociale et homosexualité*, Paris, Gallimard, 1985, 521 pages; Peter Coleman, *Christian Attitudes to Homosexuality*, London, SPCK, 1980, 310 pages.

4. Pierre Guillaume, *Médecins, Église et foi*, Paris, Aubier, 1990, 267 pages.

the inverts does merit our compassion."[5] Works published for the use of the various clergies continued to reject homosexuality *en masse* and propagated a particularly retrograde view of sexuality. In his book, *The Problem of Right Conduct* (1931), the canon Peter Green maintained that homosexuality must be dealt with like other cases of insanity (he cited homicidal madness and kleptomania) and punished by law.[6]

Certain religious congregations adopted a more extreme attitude and declared war against the "spreading" of homosexuality, which they had found worrisome since the end of the war. One such case was the German Evangelical Church committee, led by Reinhard Mumm, in association with other groups both lay and religious.[7] Mumm was also appointed to the Reichstag and became a member of the DNVP (German National Peoples Party), which incorporated conservative and far right forces. He conducted an active campaign against "pornography and smut" ("gegen Schund und Schmutz"), and worked to protect youth and to limit abortion, venereal disease, prostitution and homosexuality. The aim was to avoid at all costs any liberalization of the criminal code. The tone was direly pessimistic: "Never was humanity on the brink of such an enormous catastrophe as today!"[8] The cover of one of Mumm's publications, *Das Schundkampfblatt*, depicts St. George slaying the dragon.

The symbolism is clear. "The question of homosexuality took up a lot of these groups' attention, even though it was only one of their concerns. The activity report of the Union of Schleswig-Holstein (July-September 1920) refers to homosexual groups, in particular WhK, and their various initiatives like the film *Anders als die Andern*. It reproaches Hänisch, the Minister for Culture, for his March 1, 1920 visit to Magnus Hirschfeld's Institute, a visit which lasted four hours. It takes issue with the journal *Die Freundschaft*, which dared to publish an article entitled "The Christians among us." Mumm and various associations

---

5. Theodore de Felice, *Le Protestantisme et la Question sexuelle*, Paris, Librairie Fischbacher, 1930, 78 pages, p.73.

6. For greater detail, see Peter Coleman, *Christian Attitudes to Homosexuality, op. cit.*

7. For instance the People's Union for Medical Science (*Verband für Volksheilkunde*) in Essen, The Lay Union for Sexual Ethics (*Laienbund für Sexualethik*), The Schleswig-Holstein Province Union for Public Morality (*Schleswig-Holsteinischer Provinzialverein zur Hebung der öffentlichen Sittlichkeit*) and the Ecclesiastic Social League (*Kirchlich-Sozialer Bund*).

8. For more of Mumm's propaganda and his campaign *gegen Schund und Schmutz*: BAB, 90 MU 3 506-532, Nachl. R. Mumm. This excerpt is from the *Aufruf zum Beitritt in den Laienbund für Sexualethik*, 1924 ("Membership appeal for the Lay Union for Sexual Ethics," BAB, 90 MU 3 506).

launched a petition entitled "Proclamation! The future of the German people is in danger." It particularly took issue with "modern women" and with their masculine way of dressing and doing their hair, and asked the government for a law "against pornography and muck" and for the protection of youth, a stricter application of §184 (on obscene publications), a law on theaters, a ban on "the saxophone, negro dances, [and] nude performances," a crack down on drugs, morphine and cocaine. Similarly, on March 14, 1928 the Kirchlich-Sozialer Bund called for several homosexual publications to be outlawed — *Das Freundschaftsblatt, Die Blätter für Menschenrecht* and *Die Freundin.*[9] The battle "gegen Schund und Schmutz" was a success. On June 19, 1928, most of the homosexual periodicals were registered on the list of "pornographic and dirty writings." In 1928 and 1929, *Die Freundin* was banned for twelve months and in 1931 *Garçonne* was also condemned.

The fight against homosexual movements was waged on all fronts. The magazine *Christliche Volksmacht* ran an article in March 1921 by Primary Education Superintendent Eberhard entitled, "The wave of Inversion." In February 1922, *Deutscher Evangelischer Kirchenausschuss* reiterated its opposition to the abolition of §175.[10] A pamphlet, "Keep §175!" was published by the German Catholic Central Committee Working for the Public Morality (Zentralarbeitsausschuss der deutschen Katholiken zur Förderung der öffentlichen Sittlichkeit). At the same time, the German Women's League (Deutscher Frauenkampfbund) led by Martha Brauer launched a virulent campaign, denouncing homosexual publications and Magnus Hirschfeld: "A manifestly abnormal man cannot advise healthy people in the field of sexual ethics." Leftist parties were also attacked, having become an easy target for the conservatives: "One must particularly bear in mind that it is the protection of the socialist and communist parties that allows this erotic revolution to spread...." Protecting women was an essential part of this propaganda. Women's roles were limited to those of daughter, wife and mother, embodied in the famous "three Ks," "Kirche, Küche, Kinder" (or "church, kitchen and kids"). In 1924-1925, a campaign was waged to have §175 expanded to cover women.

The German Evangelical Church's battle remained relatively isolated; in general, the subject was brought up very rarely apart from polemical pamphlets or in handbooks on sex education. On the other hand, isolated instances illustrate original attitudes or even deviant viewpoints that only underscore the fact

---

9. BAB, 90 MU 3 509, R. Mumm.
10. Potsdam, 90 MU 3 507, R. Mumm.

that, even within the Church, the question of homosexuality remained prob-lematic and ambivalent. The White Cross League, under the Church of England, stepped forward in 1929-1930 to help young male prostitutes in London. The organization, which was already offering support for women prostitutes, sought to address the increase in amateur prostitution resulting from the economic crisis. The League placed the lads in question in receiving centers and tried to find them jobs in order to reinstate them in society. One can also find traces of the cult of homosexuality within the ranks of the Anglican hierarchy. The Oxford Movement (a movement to reform the Church of England, begun at Oxford University in 1833) was accused of homophilia; its leader, John Henry Newman, was known to have romantic liaisons with young boys. By the same token, certain ecclesiastical personalities managed to match their functions with their inclinations; the Reverend E.E. Bradford was, for example, a notorious pedophile poet. Oxford students led by John Betjeman used to go and pay their respects to him, after he retired to his parish; Bradford was of the opinion that his "languid tenderness for the boys/ came to him more from Christ than from Socrates," but he was nevertheless the author of sufficiently explicit poems to be in contradiction with the principles of the Church. These examples were, however, exceptional.

The "public authorities"

Official views on homosexuality, among governments, members of Par-liament, legislature or judiciary, were quintessentially bureaucratic views. They reflected the institution and could not claim to represent public opinion as a whole, even if they were shaped by, and helped to shape, the latter. These views may have reflected the personality of the individuals and their social milieu, but went beyond the personal perspective to become the point of view of the State. Broadly speaking, in the 1920s and 1930s, the public authorities were unfa-vorable to homosexuality, out of concern for protecting morals and ensuring the survival of the population. Male homosexuality was said to weaken the tradi-tional hierarchies, as it encouraged middle-class and working-class men to inter-mingle in the search for a partner. Female homosexuality generally enjoyed a greater tolerance, for it did not undermine the social structure and a woman, under the authority of her father or husband, or under social pressure, could be forced back into line.

In England, the First World War had seen a sharp outburst of homophobia. Thereafter, the English political leaders took a severe line on male homosexuality, while the campaign against lesbianism reached new proportions. Homosexuality was an easier target than birth control or the right to divorce, and thus it made an ideal showcase to illustrate the State's commitment to morality. Moreover, figures who played key roles in the fight against homosexuality had close ties with virtue groups or puritan movements. Sir Thomas Inskip, who served as the Crown's legal adviser off and on between 1922 and 1936, was an ardent member of the evangelical Church. The Director of Public Prosecutions, Sir Archibald Bodkin, had been a member of the board of the National Vigilance Association. Above all, the Minister of the Interior from 1924 to 1929 was the ultra puritan Sir William Joynson-Hicks (Jix); he was behind the banning of Radclyffe Hall's book, *The Well of Loneliness*, and was a party to or a consultant in many lawsuits concerning homosexuals. The fear of homosexuality especially heightened due to the fear of the decline of the Empire, deduced from an erroneous and tendentious analysis in Edward Gibbon's *History of the Decline and Fall of the Roman Empire*: Rome had fallen, other nations had fallen, and if England were to fall in its turn, it would be because of this sin, and its lack of belief in God, and it will be her own loss.[11]

The pressure against homosexuality did not spare the leading elite.[12] In 1922, a liberal deputy, the Viscount Lewis Hartcourt, committed suicide for fear that his homosexuality would be exposed in public. He had made advances to a young man from Eton by the name of Edward James while he was spending a few days at his estate of Nuheham Courtney in the company of his mother. In 1931, Count Beauchamp, a knight of the Order of the Garter, governor of Cinque Ports and leader of the liberal party, suddenly resigned all his functions and left the country. His brother-in-law, the Duke of Westminster, had threatened to reveal his frolicking with the many young fishermen and other farmhands at his property of Walmer Castle. He returned to England only five years later for his son's funeral, after having received assurances that he would not be arrested. George V, when he heard of the scandal, soberly commented: "I did think they were frying their brains."

Homosexuality could also be used for partisan ends. There was a political scandal in France, in late October 1933, after the murder of Oscar Dufrenne, an

---

11. Reverend J.M. Wilson, *Sins of the Flesh*, cited by Jeffrey Weeks, *Sex, Politics and Society*, London, Longman, 1989, 325 pages, p.107. The sin referred to here is masturbation, which at that time was directly associated with homosexuality.

12. See H. Montgomery Hyde, *A Tangled Web, Sex Scandals in British Politics and Society*, London, Constable, 1986, 380 pages.

impresario, director of the variety show "The Palace," a city councilman of the 10th arrondissement and a homosexual. His employees had seen him cozied up in his office with a sailor. Then one of them found his naked body, with the skull smashed to pieces. The culprit was never found. After Malvy gave a funeral eulogy, the Order published a ferocious article stating that: "The spectacle provided by the life and death of Oscar Dufrenne is symbolic: it denounces the corruption of our democracy." Leon Daudet wrote that, "the murderer, a sailor, nephew of a political figure, having had part of his male organs amputated, had been undergoing treatment in a private clinic in Neuilly." In Germany, leftist parties commonly levied charges of homosexuality, in particular against the NSDAP (National Socialist German Workers Party).[13]

The press

A review of the day's press should help in determining more precisely what degree of tolerance there was for homosexuality. As both an expression of public opinion and also the catalyst for new trends, it had a major impact. And in the 1920s, information media developed dramatically. The press expanded considerably and radio and the cinema became widespread. Popular journalism grew rapidly in the United Kingdom, Germany and France and it was backed by considerable capital.[14]

The large national press had little to say on the question of homosexuality. *Le Temps*[15] published on average two or three articles on the subject per annum. The same was true of *The Times*[16] and, in some years, the subject was never brought up at all. The German press was more prolix, primarily because of the debates over reforming the Penal Code and the possible abolition of §175, and because of the militancy of the homosexual movements that were busy holding

---

13. See chapter six.

14. For this study, I systematically perused a wide range of French and English daily newspapers, and I sampled the German partisan press as well. I also drew upon the conclusions of W.U. Eissler, who in his book *Arbeiterparteien und Homosexuellenfrage zur Sexualpolitik von SPD und KPD in der Weimarer Republik* (Berlin, Verlag Rosa Winkel, 1980, 142 pages) systematically surveyed the German socialist and communist press for anything touching on the question of homosexuality, with a special focus on *Vorwärts* and *Neue Zeit*, both of which were organs of the SPD, and *Berlin am Morgen*, *Welt am Abend* and *Die rote Fahne* for the KPD. I also read one satirical review per country. However, clearly, such a survey cannot be comprehensive.

15. *Le Temps*, an evening newspaper, had a print run of 70,000.

16. The *Times*, a conservative newspaper, plateaued at a print run of 200,000.

conferences and sending petitions. There were four rubrics under which one might encounter references to homosexuality: literary and theater criticism, the legal chronicle, reports of parliamentary debates, and polemical articles on the degradation of morals. A fifth category also existed, but it was more of an exception: political articles with polemical overtones, primarily denunciations of opponents who were accused of being homosexual. These various possibilities showed up in varying degrees, depending on the newspaper.

In *Le Temps*, there is generally no sign of homosexuality in the legal chronicle. There is no mention, for example, of Marthe Hanau's lesbianism or Oscar Dufrenne's homosexuality. A brief on December 16, 1928, suggests a homosexual affair. For about three weeks the bank clerk Raymond Bernard had been visiting daily with Mr. Hermann Goldschmidt. When he arrived on the morning of the 15th, the valet showed him into his master's bedroom, as usual. Some time afterwards, he heard the sound of someone falling down. Bernard fired three shots. He was apprehended by the servant, but he committed suicide. The write-up on the 17th read: A wealthy Dutch investor, wounded by his young friend Raymond Bernard, died just a few hours after the tragedy." The circumstances of the drama, like the reference to "his young friend," makes it sound like a falling out between a homosexual and a gigolo.

The question of homosexuality does not appear in the parliamentary debates, either, nor even in articles ranting about modern women or young people. It never comes up in the political arena, except for certain articles on Hitler's Germany.

Thus literary and theater criticism became the main forum for debates on homosexuality. The first article, full of allusions, was on Marcel Proust's *Sodom and Gomorrah I*, which came out shortly after *Guermantes II*. Paul Souday wrote, "I must add that in the final chapter the narrative moves in a direction that is difficult to follow. According to Saint-Simon, there were people in the royal families similar to Mr. Proust's baron de Charlus; but the author of *Memories* borders on suggesting something rather more widespread.[17] The second article was published exactly a year later, when *Sodom and Gomorrah II* came out, May 12, 1922. The third appeared in August of the same year.[17] It is a review of Roger Martin du Gard's *Le Cahier gris*. This is when Paul Souday inaugurated his new way of referring to homosexuality: by reference to Proust. Since blunt references to homosexuality were out of the question, it was hinted at through allusion: "The

---

17. *Le Temps*, 12 May 1921.

Masters thought it was one of those annoying relationships like those of Mr. de Charlus sprinkled throughout the novel by Mr. Marcel Prévost [sic]; it was actually only an innocent but exalted and mystical friendship, with a suspicious-seeming vocabulary the significance of which the naive children did not understand." When Abel Hermant's series on Lord Chelsea was published on February 21, 1924, the allusion took on a new life: "Thus, Lord Chelsea is a kind of English Charlus...or an Oscar Wilde, an aesthete like the one in the story, but just a lord like the baron de Charlus, and not a man of letters." The sense of irritation was already gone: "...The poor things. Couldn't they at least do their business in silence, instead of humiliating themselves publicly? Virtue and vice benefit equally from modesty."

On February 4, 1926, in a famous review of Gide's *The Counterfeiters*, Paul Souday reached the limits of his tolerance. The theater critic Pierre Brisson was next, with his review of *The Captive* at the Fémina theater March 8. The play was performed in the nude, and was characterized as "an extremely remarkable work" on "a bold and strangely embarrassing subject." The subject is actually never specified, for "by spelling it out one is likely to give it that brutal appearance that M. Bourdet has managed to avoid with such fine skill." In the second act, "the discussion broadens, taking on its human significance and all its gravity. Unfortunately that is the precise moment when it becomes most difficult to make any sense of it."

Paul Souday weighed in again on December 23, 1926 with a review of Gide's *If It Die*. "It is far more pathetic than it is pleasant." He was not being coy in order to mislead the readers, who were assumed to be jaded after *Sodom and Gomorrah*: "This is not comparable at all to the adventures of Charlus and the consorts of Marcel Proust, which at least have something picturesque to offer. We have no qualms about Mr. André Gide's private life, and no one is bothering him. Why does he have to hang out his least defensible fantasies for all to see?" Souday followed up on November 17, 1927, with a piece on *Le Temps retrouvé*. The second half of the novel especially upset him: "Any hack novelist could have churned this out." On September 25, 1931, André Thérive, a literary critic who replaced Souday, wrote a few lines on Leon Lemonnier's biography of Oscar Wilde. He makes no explicit allusion to his homosexuality, but mentions "the almost innocent curse from which he suffered," some "appalling details" and "an excessive liberalism when it comes to morals." Then on October 23, 1931 when Ernest Seillière's monograph on Marcel Proust and Ramon Fernandez's on André Gide were published, Thérive wrote a long paragraph on Proust's and

Gide's homosexuality, but again without using explicit terms. "And of course, I will pass over an even greater flaw, which makes it possible to explain almost everything that is inexplicable about this writer." The negative tone dominates, especially in the following paragraph, which compares Gide with Proust: "It is not for us to dwell on such an awkward subject, essential as it may be. It is enough to know that the Proustian pessimism is answered by Gide's Nietzschean optimism, and Proust sees in his confreres a sign of dark and Saturnian predestination, while his second is keen to see that they are the ones who are normal and in good health....Which is the more dire propagandism? The latter, I think." At least, the topic of homosexuality, even if it was not mentioned outright, was being discussed.

In fact, the articles touching on the subject of homosexuality became more frequent in the early 1930s. Theatrical output encouraged it. The Champs-Élysées Comédie staged Roger Martin du Gard's play *Un taciturne* (*The Silent Man*) November 2, 1931. Pierre Brisson described it as "one of the most scabrous of plays" in which "the author's greatest skill lies in his ability to avoid the actual subject of the debate." On January 11, 1932, *Le Mal de la jeunesse* (*The Pains of Youth*) by Bruckner was produced at the Theatre du Marais; and on June 20, 1932, *Jeunes filles en uniforme* ("Girls in Uniform") was put on at the Studio of Paris. October 10, 1932 was the first time *Le Temps* used the words "invert" and "homosexual," talking about *La Fleur des pois* (*The Snobs*) by Édouard Bourdet that was playing at the Theatre de la Michodière. Brisson found the play disappointing: "I do not reproach Mr. Bourdet for a second for having written a play in which, in the presence of the abnormal beings that he brings to the stage, he avoids expressing any condemnation. Not only do I not reproach him, but I congratulate him for his generosity of spirit. I find moralistic theater, so-called 'right-thinking' theater, thoroughly distasteful in principle, futile, and soon out of date. What I do reproach him for is having reduced so perilous a subject to the trivial fun of anecdotic dialogue."

André Thérive came up with a positive review on March 24, 1932 for Colette's book *Ces plaisirs* (*Those Pleasures*), underscoring that it was "dangerous for the weak" but "useful for those who are strong." A corner had been turned: on February 25, 1935, Maurice Rostand's play *Le Procès d'Oscar Wilde* (*The Trial of Oscar Wilde*) was shown at the Théatre des Arts and, in spite of circumlocutions, this time Pierre Brisson used the expression "Uranian love" and Dorian Gray is described as the "patron saint of sodomy, apostle, confessor and martyr of his faith."

However, this was the last review concerning a play or novel with homosexual themes to appear until 1939. The abrupt hiatus can be attributed to the drop in public interest in homosexuality. The media turned its attention to the crisis, international tensions and the threat of depopulation.

Meanwhile, *The Times* stayed resolutely impersonal. Homosexuality was generally mentioned only in the context of legal notes. The description of the facts is concise, to say the least. For example, on January 11, 1919, in a brief criminal note we read — January 10. Before Judge Rentoul, William Frederick Gammon, 38 years old, gardener, was found guilty of having committed an act constituting a serious moral offense and was sentenced to twelve months in prison by the second division. — Still, this kind of *entrefilet* is rare and is negligible among the number of sentences pronounced annually.

Apart from these chronicles, there was a bit more press reporting on the lawsuit over Radclyffe Hall's *The Well of Loneliness*. Here again, the newspaper maintained a strict neutrality and merely retranscribed the debates, almost in their entirety.

Lastly, homosexuality was also touched upon in connection with Hitlerian Germany, at the time of the assassination of Röhm and the raids against the gay bars. The word "homosexuality" is never employed. Röhm's proclivities were evoked as "unfortunate tendencies," and the bars were said to have "a certain reputation." Thus we can see that major media made little effort to familiarize the reader with homosexuality. By comparison, the satirical press was far less reticent to mention it. Still, significant differences existed between the three countries.

Homosexuality was clearly visible in the German satirical press, as can be seen in the German weekly magazine *Simplicissimus*. Many homosexual caricatures had already been published in *Simplicissimus* before the war, during the Eulenburg affair and in connection with the activities of the WhK. Then there were no more until after the war, when they gradually began to appear again. In the period 1919-1939, one may find fifteen homosexual caricatures. The majority appeared between 1924 and 1929, which corresponds to the apogee of the Berliner homosexual subculture. There was none in 1919, and there are no more after 1933. The last was published on May 15, 1932. Most of the caricatures depict lesbians and the Berliner homosexual scene. For instance, September 24, 1924, a Bubikopf girl is lounging on a settee; her mother says to her: "How shall I put it, my child — you are now at an age, Paula, where men start to...." "Stop right there, Mom, I'm a pervert...." On February 20, 1928 a famous drawing by Jeanne

Mammen was published: "She is representative." A very masculine-looking young woman says: "Dad is a lawyer and Mom sits on the regional court. I am the only one in the family to have a private life."

There are a few homosexual caricatures. One dated April 1, 1921, referred to Hirschfeld, under the title "Hirschfeldiana." It shows the homosexual leader with his young and very effeminate Secretary: "Please, take down the following, Miss: As we rebuild our economic life, which is completely stagnant, the imperatives of the day require the immediate abolition of §175." Another, dated September 12, 1927, is entitled "Confusion of feelings" in direct reference to Stefan Zweig's books. Two prostitutes are shown, with a sailor approaching. One says to the other: "Say, Bella, do you think that sailor is a customer or the competition?" On January 28, 1929 there was a caricature of a homosexual ball and, in the center, a young boy dressed as an angel is the object of everyone's attentions. The caption is a little poem:

> Max als Amor war ein grosser Schlager
> Und er bracht' – die bravsten Männer in Gefahr –
> Ja man munkelt, dass von andern Lager
> Magnus Hirschfeld selbst zugegen war
>
> Mutter Nagel schützte Max – als Griechin
> Eine treubesorgte Ballmama
> Und so wagte sich an ihn kein Viech hin –
> Wie gesagt: auch Hirschfeld war ja da![18]

The caricatures in *Simplicissimus* are not actually hostile to homosexuals but rather poke fun at them, and at many others. Hirschfeld's battle is exaggerated and comic and the flappers are absurd, but in the end they are all just symbols of the post-war period; they have the taste of modernity. Rather than any real homophobia, the newspaper's irony reflects the public's distress at the growing visibility of homosexual.

In comparison, *Fantasio*[19] comes across as far more hostile, and there are far more homosexual caricatures there, too. The majority concern lesbians and were

---

18. "Max was a great success as Cupid/ And he placed the hardiest men at risk/ They say that in the other camp/ Magnus Hirschfeld himself was present//Max was Mama Nagel's protégé — in the Greek sense/ a very attentive guardian/ So that not one of those beasts dared approach him/ As it was said: even Hirschfeld was there."

19. This light, satirical magazine was created by the cartoonist Roubille in 1906. It came out every 15 days. In the mid-1930s it lost readership to bolder and more modern papers featuring erotic photographs.

published in the period 1922-1928. Fantasio also made homosexual allusions in its gossip columns and its leading articles. An example from December 1, 1922, is a vengeful article published under the title: "L'hérésie sentimentale; ces messieurs dames" (*A Sentimental Heresy; those Lady-Gentlemen*).

A drawing from May 1, 1923, shows girls dancing together under the caption: "Belles of the ball, but the men will never know." On October 1, 1923, Abel Hermant is sketched in academician's garb and powdering his face, under the legend: "Saint-Simonette." A cartoon from March 1, 1924 shows a series of women with shorter and shorter hair, captioned: "Careful, Ladies! Go any farther with your hair and you'll end up looking like old men." September 15, 1925 had a cartoon like the ones in *Simplicissimus*, showing two girls dancing together. The caption quips,

> Dormez, bonnes vieilles chansons,
> Qui faisiez danser, sans façons,
> Les filles avec les garçons!
> Dans les bars chic qui les rançonnent
> En des poses qui s'abandonnent,
> Ce ne sont plus que... des garçonnes!

On May 1, 1926, André Gide was caricatured under the title, "La fleur du male." The publication of François Porché's book *L'Amour qui n'ose pas dire son nom* (*The Love That Dares Not Speak Its Name*) occasioned a vicious article and a caricature:

> May we say that this protest comes right when it's needed? For they have started to go at it a little too strongly, these 'little friends'! Free to have their fun, and to the play around in the dooryard, and at the back door.... But they are starting to make so much propaganda and to puff themselves up with their special morals that there is bound to be a reaction.... Will the book we are talking about signal that the time has come?... At a time when everyone is talking about cleaning up Paris, perhaps someone will give a clean sweep to certain milieux.[20]

April 1, 1932 brought a new attack, signed Melitta and baptized "Lesbos." "They were no beauties, these captives, with their eyebrows shaven so close their eyes resembled those of young calves, their faces sallow in the yellow light of the lamps, their thin arms sticking out of their pyjamas." In the same vein one finds in *La Vie parisienne*[21] of June 11, 1938 a caricature entitled "The Clever One," showing a man and two women, one of whom is a flapper dressed in a strictly-

---

20. *Fantasio*, 1-15 August 1927, p.311-312.

tailored suit, cigarette on her lip. The caption says, "I'll bet, Marquise, that you're planning to spend your holidays on an ancient Greek island."

Fantasio promoted itself as the ambassador of the "French spirit" and, for that reason, posed as a defender Gauloiserie. That meant that its sales relied on exploiting the most popular current prejudices. The new visibility of the homosexual scene and the rise of homosexual literature reinforced this basic tendency and served as a pretext for the re-assertion of heterosexual love, which was supposedly under threat. Whereas *Simplicissimus* depicted homosexuality as a phenomenon of modernity, *Fantasio* took it as a sign of decline.

Punch, like *The Times*, reveals the extreme prudishness of the British press. There is hardly one homosexual caricature in the period 1919-1939; the only suggestive drawings are those of girls with very short hair, but who are never comparable to lesbians. One cartoon in particular shows the evolution of fashion, starting with a girl with long hair, then with it cut in a bob, then *à la garçonne*, then an Eton crop; then the cartoon shows where it all was headed — the "Dartmoor shave" — and the progressive return to the shoulder-length hair.[22] Another cartoon, on February 1, 1922, shows two young women in the foreground and two very effeminate young men in the background. Hostess: "What a bother, my dear, we are short one man." Guest: "Don't worry; I've brought along two cuties."

Lastly, in the German press one can distinguish nuances in how homosexuality is treated by different political groups.[23] Most of the German newspapers touched on homosexuality mainly in the parliamentary context. A few homosexual scandals, like the Röhm letters in 1931, started an avalanche of articles in the press. Lastly, homosexuality was mentioned in articles ranting about the decline of morals in the post-war era.

Deutsche Zeitung,[24] an organ of the DNVP, represented the interests of the Junker and the ultraconservative business world. The DNVP was anti-Semitic

---

21. Like *Fantasio*, *La Vie parisienne*, inaugurated in 1869, was a light satirical paper that began to decline in the mid-30s.

22. *Punch*, 17 October 1928.

23. To evaluate how political allegiances influenced the approach to homosexuality in France and in England, one would have to go through virtually all the party newspapers for the entire period. That would not be an easy task. Unlike in Germany, there were no outstanding events upon which to focus one's analysis in such a survey.

24. The *Deutsche Zeitung* was founded in 1896; it went out of business 31 December 1934 with the claim of having "the glory of having directly prepared the way for the glory of the Third Reich."

and hostile to the Weimar Republic. Its goal was to restore the monarchy. It was part of the government since 1925. *Deutsche Zeitung* was, throughout this period, savagely hostile to homosexuals and lumped them together with pacifist and androgynous youth, modern women, abortion and sexual liberation — a product of Russia and the Jews.[25] It took up the fight against "pornography and smut" led by Reinhard Mumm, a member of the DNVP. On November 12, 1920, it made a reference to "the pervert doctor" Magnus Hirschfeld. An article from March 25, 1921, attacks the homosexual floorshows: "The danger in these men with their unfortunate proclivities against nature is their desire to propagate their wrong understanding of friendship." On January 7, 1922, under the title "A Champion of Homosexuality," the paper denounced the propagation of indecent writings, in particular the magazine *Der Eigene*. The interest in new medical theories is seen in a number of articles, but the newspaper deliberately chose those least favorable to homosexuals. Thus, February 10, 1924, an article was published entitled "Sexual life and Hereditary Flaws," which maintained that heterosexuality is innate and that homosexuality, like masochism or sadism, is perverse. An alarmist article was published May 10, 1928 under the rubric, "Suicide of the Race"; it denounced "the masculinization of women, the effeminacy of men and the attenuation of the natural contrasts."

This extremely negative attitude may be contrasted to the position of the *Berliner Tageblatt*[26], a democratic daily newspaper. The *Berliner Tageblatt* published an advertisement on September 4, 1919 for Magnus Hirschfeld's Institut für Sexualwissenschaft as well as the Institute's program and the topic of the main conferences given there. The information is handled objectively.

One of the best ways to compare the reactions of the two newspapers is by focusing on the abolition of §175 that was decided by the Commission to reform the Penal Code on October 16, 1929.[27] *Berliner Tageblatt* had been publishing the Commission's reports since October 8. On October 17, it ran an article entitled: "A cultural projection: The End of §175." The newspaper welcomed this decision and gave credit particularly to Wilhelm Kahl, then an octogenarian, president of the commission and member of the DVP (German People's Party),[28] who had

---

25. See for example the 20 February 1921 issue.

26. Le *Berliner Tageblatt*, founded in 1871, disappeared 1 January 1939. When the Nazis came to power, the management and the editorial staff of the magazine were purged. In the Twenties, it had a distribution in the range of 350,000; it fell to less than 35,000 in the Thirties.

27. See chapters six and seven, as well.

voted for the abolition of the paragraph against his own party and whose influence rocked the vote: "If all his friends were as young as him, things would be much better." On the other hand, for several days *Deutsche Zeitung* had been equating "the decriminalization of sodomy" with the deleterious actions of the SPD (German Social Democratic Party) and the German Communist Party (KPD), saying: "A victory for the criminals of the people: impunity for infringing §175." Magnus Hirschfeld and his disciples must now triumph ... We can only hope that the deliberation and the final decision in connection with this article of law fall to another Reichstag than the last, whose majority, it is increasingly apparent, decided to ruin the German people from a moral point of view, too." They also attacked Kahl, who was more or less accused of treason. Kahl answered those charges on October 25, 1929 in *Vossische Zeitung* and justified his position, which he said was based not on tolerance for homosexuality, which he regarded as a vice and a calamity, but on practical reasons: repression encourages blackmail and the propagation and dissemination of homosexual propaganda in society. So we see how the German treatment of homosexuality could vary according to political persuasions. What for *Deutsche Zeitung* was another sign of the decline of Germany was, on the contrary, interpreted by the democratic newspaper as a projection of history.

After Hitler's advent to power, such distinctions are no longer seen. Thus, the elimination of Röhm was treated identically by *Deutsche Zeitung* and *Berliner Tageblatt*, which had been "purified" of its Jewish and liberal editors. Their July 1, 1934 articles simply reproduced the official version as it was expressed by Goering at a press conference.

In conclusion, according to examples studied, the press played different roles in different countries. In Germany, the problem was publicly discussed and the terms "homosexuality," "inversion" and variations thereon were acceptable usage, for they now bore the imprimatur of science. In England, the press followed the prevailing code of silence and did nothing to acquaint the public with homosexuality. In France, the press was more loquacious, but remained extremely prudent. Certain scandal sheets may have used homosexuality to bolster sales, but they ran the risk of being fined. In July 1935, the director of *Détective*, Marius Larique, was given a three-month suspended sentence and a 1,000-franc fine, the manager Charles Dupont got one month with suspended

---

28. The DVP was the party for big business; it had monarchical tendencies, and was tactically allied with the Republic in 1920.

and a 500-franc fine, but the reporter Marcel Carrière was let go. The newspaper had published a photograph of the corpse of a young homosexual who was strangled under unknown circumstances. His naked body had been found on a couch. The picture was captioned, "Playing House."[29]

Greater Tolerance?

The public's reactions with regard to homosexuality are formed by many factors, including the family setting, education, religion, personal prejudices, and general trends in public opinion. In the absence of opinion polls or any other means of querying the population, it is very difficult to analyze how attitudes on this question evolved. Nonetheless, by collecting testimony and by weighing the information sources, one can draw an overall and modulated picture of the public's views on homosexuality.

Homosexuals would run into very different situations depending on what circles they traveled in. Bohemian homosexuals living in a European capital would only occasionally meet with any hostility. Thus we have B., a lesbian, who lived the life of an artist in the 1930s. "It wasn't easy to live freely as a homosexual at that time, the way I did, because I was in an artistic world where it was very common. The artists really didn't give a damn about it and in fact considered it a sign of originality." N., a lesbian who fraternized with anarchists, was also accepted by her peers.[30]

Conversely, an anonymous subject who lived in the provinces was likely to face real rebuffs if her peculiarity came to light: "People were getting used to seeing women in what used to be men's places, used to the cigarettes, to the sometimes crude language, to loud laughter in public. But, outside the big cities, they found us, we the 'emancipated,' arrogant, vulgar and dangerous all at the same time. Bad examples for girls whose parents thought they were still untainted."[31] There were some exceptions, of course. Eleonor, a woman farmer, says: "And it was a different problem, for we were already dressing like men. Jodhpurs, especially, because they were the only thing one work in. I wore them

---

29. AN, BB18 6178 44 BL 402.

30. Testimony from B., born in Paris in 1910, an apprentice dressmaker, and from N., recorded by Claudie Lesselier, *Aspects de l'expérience lesbienne in France, 1930-1968*, from a post-graduate dissertation in sociology, University of Paris-VIII, under the direction of R. Castel, November 1987, 148 pages, p.73-75.

31. Germaine, cited by Dominique Desanti, *La Femme au temps des années folles*, Paris, Stock, 1984, 373 pages, p.46.

all the time. I would have, anyway, of course; my lover was living with me. But I don't think the owners of the farm thought much about it. They never mentioned it. I don't think they cared, really."[32]

The reactions differed considerably according to where one was. In Berlin, as in the other capital cities, tolerance was greater than in the provinces — although it might be more accurate to call it "indifference." At the same time, other areas of Germany were famous for their homophobia, especially Bavaria. And Hans Blüher, with his theories on homosexuality in the youth movements, was stopped from visiting the town of Münster, in Westphalia, for a series of conferences.[33] On March 19, 1921, the Ministry of the Interior received a letter from the president of the regional government. According to the latter, 27 letters of protest, from associations against public immorality in the districts of Westphalia, from the teachers union and the clergy, Catholic youth, the Evangelical Church and many other associations, had arrived at police headquarters, informing them that Blüher's arrival would be prevented all means, even, if necessary, by violence. Something like that had already happened in Munich, where "the president of the pederasts, Magnus Hirschfeld" barely made it out alive.

Most people, while rejecting homosexuality, simply never spoke of it. "At that time, nobody talked about homosexuality. Not the slightest allusion. I don't think that was apparent to me at the time; I was only eighteen, twenty years old. At that age, I probably didn't realize the significance. I was satisfied just to be it [homosexual]. But I thought marrying was the right thing to do, even if I had already had different experiences."[34] Similarly, Quentin Crisp explains why he did not tell one of his friends that he was homosexual: — She wouldn't have believed me, because in those distant days, a homosexual was never somebody whom you actually knew and seldom somebody you had met.[35]

People didn't know much about homosexuality, in any case. Crisp summarizes the stereotypes in vogue: — It was thought to be of Greek origin, less widespread than socialism but more dangerous, — especially for children.[36]

---

32. Eleonor, testimony recorded in Suzanne Neild and Rosalind Parson, *Women Like Us*, London, The Women's Press, 1992, 171 pages, p.34.

33. GStA, I.HA, Rep.77, Tit.435, n° 1, vol.1.

34. Gerald, in *Between the Acts. Lives of Homosexual Men, 1885-1967*, edited by K. Porter and J. Weeks, London, Routledge, 1990, 176 pages, p.6. See also *ibid.*, Norman, p.23, and Sam, p. 99.

35. Quentin Crisp, *The Naked Civil-Servant* [1968], London, Fontana, 1986, 217 pages, p. 24.

36. *Ibid.*, p.25.

But the greater visibility of homosexuality in the 1920s did not necessarily go hand in hand with increased acceptance. Many were indignant at this "depravity," but took a more or less fatalistic approach: "Their special cafés are open to the public. Their morals are discussed in songs and at the nightclub, in newspapers, and conversations. All the same, that doesn't mean that this cordiality should evolve into tolerance."[37]

It is was at about this time that Quentin Crisp launched out on his educational crusade in favor of homosexuality:

> — I realized that it didn't make any difference to be recognized as a homosexual in the West End, where vice was the rule, or in Soho, where everyone was an outlaw of one kind or another; but the rest of England was precisely my target area. It was densely populated by aborigines who had never heard of homosexuality and who, when they discovered it for the first time, were frightened and furious. I was going to work on them.[38]

The reactions ran the gamut from frightened curiosity (he often drew crowds) to more or less hostile mockery, right up to sheer aggression. Crisp noted,

> —The most mysterious thing in all these situations is not that strangers, without a word being said on either side, would attack me. It is that they did not kill me.[39]

Such incidents were not rare; homosexuals were always at the mercy of "fag busters" who attacked in groups. Klaus Mann learned about them through bitter experience in Toulon; even so, he received real help from the police.

> I was immediately approached by an insistent young man, small and lacking in charm. I went with him to the red-light district; went to a few bars, talked with a sailor, etc. The little guy managed to lure me into a completely deserted corner. (What incomprehensible stupidity, not to have suspected a thing!) Howls: 'I'll kill you!' — fists; I ran like lightning, they caught up with me, continued to hit me, took everything I had — money (130 francs), my coat, my wallet, etc; streaming with blood, panting, I went to the nearest police station; a police officer took me to the

37. Albert Chapotin, *Les Défaitistes de l'amour*, Paris, Le Livre pour tous, 1927, 510 pages, p. 177.

38. Quentin Crisp, *The Naked Civil-Servant*, *op. cit.*, p.33.

39. *Ibid.*, p.67.

hospital, where I was bandaged up, and back to the police station, where I gave a deposition; I missed the last bus, and had to go back by taxi. An absolutely atrocious incident.[40]

Tolerance may have been making some progress, but it was not widespread. More than educational level, the extent to which one needed social approval may explain the differences in attitude. Broadmindedness was particularly visible at the universities, and in the literary and artistic milieux. The upper classes had had their consciousness raised by the circulation of works on sexology. In the working class and the lower middle class, the stereotypes were very long lived, even if Daniel Guerin claims that homosexuality was more accepted in workman's circles than among the middle class: "I lived the in 20th arrondissement and in the evening one would see, at the little restaurants, guys between the ages of twenty and thirty, all single and not in the least put out if one expressed a certain homosexual desire for them. To them, anything having to do with sex was natural. They were still in the physical world and this world had not been polluted by moral values."[41] In fact, amateur homosexual prostitution, which was widespread during the 1920s, was largely of working-class origin. The middle classed, which harbored a puritan moral ideal anchored in family values, were the most reticent with regard to homosexuals.

In the absence of precise information on the attitude of the farming community, it would be hazardous to emit a judgment about life in the hinterland. Generalizations are not very useful, for they obscure the complexity of the factors in question. To arrive at any serious conclusion on this, one would have to study thoroughly the behavior of a population on the scale of a whole town and its reactions to, for example, a homosexual scandal. Unfortunately, it is difficult by now to pull together sufficient sources for such a study.

Sensitive Topics

The limits of tolerance are reached in some of the debates that came up during this time. Indeed, homosexuality might be tolerated on a day-to-day basis, but would be rejected again as soon as it became something alien. Certain topics remained sensitive during the inter-war period and occasioned feelings of

---

40. Klaus Mann, *Journal. Les années brunes, 1931-1936*, Paris, Grasset, 1996, 452 pages, 10 May 1936, p.345.

41. Cited by Gilles Barbedette and Michel Carassou, *Paris gay 1925*, Paris, Presses de la Renaissance, 1981, 312 pages, p.47.

irrational hostility and panic. Three topics recur throughout the period: the link between lesbianism and feminism, the need to protect young people, and foreign threats.

It's the feminists' fault

The lesbian question was directly linked to the feminist movement in the inter-war period. Particularly in England and Germany, the feminist movement was seen as a Trojan Horse used by the lesbians to recruit or seduce new followers and to pervert young women and to lure them away from their homes and their husbands. These charges became louder and louder, culminating in Germany in the Nazi era. Feminists were also held responsible for the alleged increase in male homosexuality, for they were considered to have made men disgusted with women by their demands and their independent ways. However, the feminist movements in the inter-war period were not, in the main, open to lesbianism, and were more likely to be frankly hostile. Far from detecting any complicity between the movements, a researcher is struck by the absence of solidarity and the distance the feminists strove to maintain between themselves and the lesbians, which partly explains the disorganization of the latter.

Sheila Jeffreys produced an admirable study of the English feminist movement in *The Spinster and Her Enemies*. Created at the end of the 19th century by several well-to-do and well-educated women, its leaders were morally irreproachable: Josephine Butler was married, Emmeline Pankhurst and Millicent Fawcett were widowed, Francis Cobbe and Christabel Pankhurst were unmarried. Their campaign was primarily political; they demanded voting rights, the right to practice the liberal professions, and access to higher education. They had no complaint about the family as an institution *per se*, but were concerned with property rights for women, and to limit the husband's legal power over his wife. The suffragettes claimed that maternity should not be imposed, which implied birth control; they also called for the prevention of the venereal diseases and the denunciation of male sexual appetites. Among the solutions they proposed were complete chastity, periods of abstinence and, sometimes, contraception. In fact, what the feminists were asking for above all was to be able to use their bodies freely. They saw men as a threat to this freedom and called for them to conform to the "higher" moral standards of women. The slogan on the eve of the war was: "The vote for women and chastity for men."

In this context, the 1920s and 1930s' myth of the castrating woman who hates men and wants to impose a matriarchal society is more easily comprehensible. The dominant male society tended to ball together all the demands of modern woman into a threat to its supremacy. Far from calming spirits, the war reinforced men's fears and hatreds. Some saw the great massacre as the sacrifice of young men to save the women, who stayed safely behind and took advantage of the situation by seeking to emancipate themselves. The feminist movements were held responsible for this domestic rebellion. Very soon "the New Woman" was attacked as a manifestation of all that was wrong, a symbol of degeneracy. The question of unmarried women led the press to call for useless women to emigrate in order to contribute to the settlement of the colonies.[42] This was a total inversion of perspective: whereas the "old maid" had formed part of the British traditional landscape, she sudden became a threat to society; in every unmarried woman, a lesbian might be hiding.

Carefully meting out counsel and warnings, information on female sexuality began to be disseminated, especially in the 1930s, a sign of the tighter morals in the wake of the crisis. J.M. Hotep, in *Love and Happiness, Intimate Problems of the Modern Woman* (1938), explains that homosexuality is "a sorcerer's trick" that transforms the external appearance of boys into girls, and vice versa, but that one could overcome it by fighting it from the very start. T. Miller Neatby, in *Youth and Purity* (1937), notes that "the experience of the post-war period has taught us that homosexualism [sic], especially among women, was more and more common."[43] Since the war, women "are brought together in broad and dangerous intimacy, at work, at leisure and at home." The only way of rooting out homosexuality is "total and immediate abstinence"; parents and tutors must take care to immediately put an end to any friendships that become too intense. In *Approaching Womanhood, Healthy Sex for Girls* (1939), Rennie Macandrew writes — The woman who is never interested in the opposite sex, but only in her own, is retarded at the lesbian stage. This was undoubtedly partly the cause of the suffragette movement before the war of 1914-1918. Some of its leaders hated men."[44]

---

42. The 1851 census in England had already disclosed a surplus of 405,000 women in British society. This surplus carried on after the war.

43. T. Miller Neatby, *Youth and Purity*, London, British Christian Endeavour Union, 1937, 27 pages, p.24.

44. Rennie Macandrew, *Approaching Womanhood, Healthy Sex for Girls*, London, The Wales Publishing Co, 1939, 93 pages, p.29.

The most complete work is that of Laura Hutton, *The Single Woman and her Emotional Problems*, going back to 1937. The author distinguishes the initiator, the true lesbian, masculine, already identifiable in childhood due to her boyish tastes, and the seduced woman who is not homosexual but falls into the clutches of one who is, out of simple ignorance and sexual frustration. The danger to the latter is in giving in to the "excitation" and no longer being able to do without such unnatural caresses. She is then likely to become a neurotic, since she will never enjoy complete pleasure and will not find her natural satisfaction in maternity. As for the true lesbian, she is likely to sink into alcohol or drugs, for she realizes that she does not constitute a satisfactory substitute for her conquest. Nevertheless, considering the shortage of men, Laura Hutton speculates as to whether it would not be wiser to let these women be, since there was nothing better offer them.

The most virulent attacks associating lesbians and feminists came in Germany.[45] In 1925, 35.6% of the women were working, compared to 31.2% in 1907. Girls had also achieved a place in education: in 1931-1932, 16% of students were girls. Women had also succeeded in gaining a certain political influence: between 1919 and 1932, 112 women were elected to the Reichstag, and they were also well represented in local institutions.

But the feminist movement was divided. There was a political feminism, which demanded equal rights, embodied by personalities like Clara Zetkin and Helene Stöcker. The socialist feminists were often disappointed, for they received little support from their political comrades. Radical organizations like Bund für Mutterschutz (League for the Protection of Mothers) were isolated in their battle for contraception, abortion, and divorce reform; the majority of women's groups feared the masculinization of women and praised honesty, self-abnegation, and idealism as essential female virtues.

There was an alarmist line of talk during the 1920s, accusing women of being on strike as far as childbearing and of being responsible for the collapse of family values. Some authors called the modern woman a castrator who deprived the man of his job. Bund Deutscher Frauenvereine (The Federation of German Women's Associations) or BDF, which counted 500,000 members in 80 women's groups, did call for better work conditions and better education for women, but

---

45. Claudia Koonz, *Les Mères-patries du IIIe Reich*, Paris, Lieu Commun, 1989, 553 pages, and Renate Bridenthal, Atina Grossmann and Marion Kaplan, *When Biology Became Destiny, Women in Weimar and Nazi Germany*, New York, Monthly Review Press, 1984, 364 pages.

it stick strictly to the traditional view of women's role. Certain women's organizations were even antifeminist, like the Protestant Federation (with nearly 2 million members), Catholic associations (approximately 1 million members), the Red Cross volunteers (750,000 members) and the Queen Louise League, 130,000 members strong.

With come writers, antifeminism could take the form of a homophobic attack. While no movement had taken up the cause of lesbians, feminism was accused of serving as a cover for a great campaign of homosexual seduction. Anton Schücker, in *Zur Psychopathologie der Frauenbewegung* (1931), produces a systematic attack on modern women. According to him, feminist leaders were a breed apart, that of the masculine woman, with broad shoulders, a deep voice, and a hint of a moustache. They also had a tendency to cross dress. He attributed the fight for emancipation to various factors: social distress, the significant albeit temporary surplus of women, and "the activation of mechanisms of psychopathic reaction and neuroses"; these are homosexuals who, from the first days of the movement, sought to pursue their own personal goals, through the "mass suggestion of normal women" transformed into an army for the feminine cause. The feminist movement "not only accelerated the collapse of the family cultural circle, but encouraged it, without thus far having come up with anything better to put in its place. It has thus contributed to mixing up the sexual characteristics."[46]

E.F.W. Eberhard's *Die Frauenemanzipation und ihre erotischen Grundlagen* (1924) was the major work in Germany; according to Eberhard, most feminists are "virile women," belonging to "the intermediate sex" and exhibiting "many masculine features"; they are not "real women." As a consequence, feminist movements were in fact camouflaged lesbian movements. Of course, most of the members were heterosexual, but the leaders of the movement were homosexuals seeking to appease their fantasies of domination and to wield their magnetism to control other women. By their influence, female homosexuality was spreading, and had by now become more common than male homosexuality. In conclusion, Eberhard called for laws punishing lesbianism in order to arrest the moral degeneration of the country.

In France, the subject seems to have been less explosive, but that does not mean it was missing from the public discourse. Already in 1908 Theodore Jorau

---

46. Anton Schücker, *Zur Psychopathologie der Frauenbewegung*, Leipzig, Verlag von Curt Kabitzsch, 1931, 51 pages.

was playing with the confusion between feminism and lesbianism: "Feminism, which was at first a monomania for equality, became an apology for the liberal instinct. It exudes the ambiguous odor of lust. Didn't one of our more shameless feminists, a certain Renée Vivien, in a book of bad verse that women recite when they've lost their heads, call herself the modern priestess of lesbians loves? This Sappho is always mixing feminist declarations with her 'lyricism.'"[47]

Given these emotional outbursts, it is wise to look to the feminists themselves and to compare the reality of their viewpoint with the fantasies that grew up around them. In England before the war, feminists never mentioned the lesbian question and later it was examined only with the greatest prudence, even if the increasing attacks against unmarried women goaded them to react. In 1913, 63% of the members of the Women's Social and Political Union (WSPU) were unmarried and many others were widowed. Several of them proclaimed the need to create a new class of single people, whose political influence should improve the female condition.[48] Lucy Re-Bartlett went further, affirming that modern woman instinctively liked other women, her sisters, and preferred them to men. Cicely Hamilton rejected the idea that marriage was obligatory; however, although she had some female liaisons, she never mentioned them in her autobiography. In fact, before the war, no feminist openly acknowledged being lesbian; such an admission was sure to compromise her politically.

Moreover, these women did not regard themselves as lesbians.[49] The First World War was a major turning point in relations between feminists and lesbians. The feminist movement was on the wane.[50] Right after the war, the femi-

---

47. Cited by Christine Bard, *Les Filles de Marianne. Histoire des féminismes en France, 1914-1940*, Paris, Fayard, 1995, 528 pages.

48. Cicely Hamilton, *Marriage as a Trade* (London, Chapman & Hall, 1909, 284 pages). Similarly, *Life Errant*, London, J.M. Dent & Sons Ltd, 1935, 300 pages.

49. See Lilian Faderman, *Surpassing the Love of Men*, New York, Morran & Cie, 1981, 496 pages; Sheila Jeffreys, *The Spinster and Her Enemies: Feminism and Sexuality, 1880-1930*, London, Pandora, 1985, 282 pages, p.102-127; and in *Hidden from History* (Martin Duberman, Martha Vicinus and George Chauncey Jr. [dir.], London, Penguin Books, 1991, 579 pages), the articles by Martha Vicinus, "Distance and Desire: English Boarding-School Friendships, 1870-1920" p.212-229 and Esther Newton, "The Mythic Mannish Lesbian: Radclyffe Hall and the New Woman," p.281-293.

50. Emmeline and Christabel Pankhurst's *Women Social and Political Union* (WSPU) rallied to support the war effort from the first days of the conflict; the pacifists quit the organization and joined other groups like the International Womens League for Peace and Liberty. The WSPU transformed into the ephemeral Women's Party before disappearing.

nists were first of all respectable women; they steered clear of violent demonstrations and the flamboyant declarations and instead formed special interest groups within the Parliament.

The torch of sexual reform had been taken by two women, Stella Browne and Marie Stopes. These two pioneers did nothing to help the lesbian cause. Marie Stopes authored *Married Love* (1918), a bestseller promoting eugenics and offering advice on sexuality. Stella Browne was a member of The British Society for the Study of Sex Psychology; she was a socialist feminist who campaigned in favor of abortion and birth control from 1914 until the mid-1930s. The two shared a heterosexual ideal that included stigmatizing lesbians. For Marie Stopes, sapphism was a threat because women who had experienced a homosexual relationship would prefer that form of sex and would give up their families: "If a married woman goes through with this unnatural act, she will be increasingly disappointed with her husband and he will lose any ability to play his traditional role.... No woman who attaches any value to the peace of her home and to the love of her husband must give in to the maneuvers of the lesbian, whatever the temptation."[51] Stella Browne, too, believed that a woman has a physical need for a man. In a report from 1924 entitled "Studies in Feminine Inversion," which she presented before the BSSP, she declared: — The woman who has neither husband nor lover, and who is not devitalized nor sexually defective, suffers mentally and physically — often without knowing why she suffers; nervous, irritable, feeble, always tired or upset over a trifle; if not, she has other consolations which make her alleged chastity an unhealthy imposture.[52] In this memorandum, she describes five cases of sapphism. However, some of the subjects were not in sexual relationships and did not regard themselves as homosexual. Browne defines them as lesbians according to rather strange criteria, independent of any physical or sentimental attraction towards women.

By thus exaggerating their number and their seductive power, feminists made lesbians a tangible threat to the family, and especially to young girls. By drawing up a rigid separation between masculine lesbians and pseudo-homosexuals, they made sure there would be no progressive assimilation of lesbians into society. To preserve the purity of romantic relationships, they denied "real"

---

51. Marie Stopes, *Enduring Passion* (1928), in Sheila Jeffreys, *The Spinster and Her Enemies, op. cit.*, p.120.

52. Stella Browne, "Studies in Feminine Inversion," in *Journal of Sexology and Psychoanalysis*, 1923; cited by Sheila Jeffreys, *ibid.*, p.117.

lesbians the right to love and to be loved in return, and definitively categorized them as deviants.

The conflict between lesbians and feminists was also visible in France. Here, it focused in particular on the question of dress. The *garçonne* style appealed to only a minority of feminists, among the most radical. Even so, the arguments were above all very practical: it was healthier to go without a corset, the length of the skirt caused accidents; and especially, wearing masculine garb discouraged girl-watchers and other importunate creatures, and directly called into question traditional social divisions. Cross-dressing could even be seen as a political gesture; that is how Madeleine Pelletier presented it. The gesture was not always well received, even in leftist circles. In Germany, Rosa Luxemburg and Clara Zetkin wore dresses and long hair in order to avoid criticism. In France, cross-dressing had picked up a few fans, notably George Sand and Rosa Bonheur, but they remained exceptions. Rachilde occasionally dressed as a man, but that was not associated with any lesbian tendency. In the 1920s, she even attacked flappers in her satire, *Why I am not a Feminist* (1928). Even at the heart of the movement, the most militant were hostile to cross-dressing. The Olympic champion Violette Morni, who had won the Gold Bowl in automobile racing and established the world record in the discus and shot put, was removed from the Sporting Federation of France in 1928 for looking too mannish. She wore her hair cut very short, with a suit and a tie. Rumor had it that she had had her breasts reduced, to help her driving. She filed suit against the Federation, but lost. The Federation's two lawyers, Yvonne Netter and Juliette Weller, notorious feminists as they were, decided that Violette Morni was a deplorable example for sportswomen. This is a clear case where the presumed homosexuality of the plaintiff (even if it was never mentioned) was the real reason for rejection and it counted more than her sporting performances.[53]

Madeleine Pelletier (1874-1939), a Communist who participated in libertarian groups and positioned herself as a theoretician of the virile woman, was a lightning rod for criticism. The first woman psychiatrist in France, she claims "to have special morals and she is represented in the circles she frequents as an Amazon.[54] Repudiated by the feminists, she was reduced to silence. It seems however that her masculine appearance was more the expression of a general

---

53. Cited by Christine Bard, *Les Filles de Marianne, op. cit.*
54. According to a police report cited by Christine Bard, *Les Filles de Marianne, op. cit.*, p.197.

distaste for sexuality than any homosexual tendency. She rarely mentions sapphism and, in her utopian novel *A New Life* (1932), she even imagines a future when she could disappear. In her mind, it is clear that homosexuality was a makeshift solution, certainly preferable to subjection to a man but far from satisfactory. Her description of homosexuals even flirts curiously with the medical prejudices and clichés of the time. Madeleine Pelletier ended up deeply disappointed by the French feminists, with their low necklines, too feminine for her taste: "What we have is, fundamentally, a feminism that is full quasi-prostitutes."[55]

One finds parallels in the fate of Arria Ly (Josephine Gordon's pseudonym). She developed the idea of virginal feminism; sexual relations sully the woman, and so one must avoid any contact with men. Her revulsion for sex originated in an extremely puritanical education. Her rejection of men did not impel her toward women, either; when a journalist accused her of being lesbian, in 1911, she challenged him to a duel. It seems that Madeleine Pelletier experienced a flush of attraction for her; it was quickly stifled. She wrote back, saying: "Herewith my portrait, as a man ... above all, do not fall in love; that would be just the moment they would start hollering about Lesbos. The trip to Lesbos does not appeal to me any more than the trip to Cythera."[56] Madeleine Pelletier spoke of her in the masculine and, like Gertrude Stein, she sought a new language, one that would free her from sexual stereotypes. In various texts, she expounded her theory on masculinization: "My clothes say to the man, 'I am your equal.'" And, "if it is the ones who have short hair and shirt collars that have all the freedom and all the power, then, very well — I will wear short hair and shirt collars."[57] She wrote to in Arria Ly: "If I had an income, I would adopt a masculine identity and I would make my way in the sciences or in politics." She was aware of her limitations, however, admitting that: "I am short and stout, I have to be careful, and fake my voice; in the street I have to walk fast to go unnoticed."[58] On the eve of the Second World War, she was convicted on abortion charges; declared mentally incompetent, she ended her days in a psychiatric asylum.

---

55. Cited by Charles Sowerwine and Claude Maignier, *Madeleine Pelletier, une féministe dans l'arène politique*, Paris, Éditions ouvrières, 1992, 250 pages, p.130.
56. *Ibid.*, p.142.
57. *Ibid.*, p.144.
58. *Ibid.*

Meanwhile, French feminists were trying to stakeout a position between tradition and modernity. The members of the UFSF (French Union for Women's Vote) were republicans: their first priority was to show that they were good citizens, not to be confused with the right-leaning Catholic feminists and the Socialists. They led a puritanical crusade for the abolition of prostitution and for respect for women. Concerned with respectability and with maintaining the differences between the sexes, they were very careful not to stir up antifeminist reactions through any provocation.

Lesbian society appeared vulgar in comparison. When the Club du Faubourg organized a debate on the Charles-Étienne novel *Notre-Dame-de-Lesbos*, the feminist Marguerite Guépet denounced them as "some kind of perverted women destroyed by keeping bad company."[59]

In fact, the feminists were not in the avant-garde in matters of sexuality; they only dealt with contraception and the prevention of the venereal diseases. Radical feminists like Madeleine Furrier and Arria Ly stuck to their defense of chastity and steered clear of the lesbians, with whom they had no wish to be associated. Placing themselves at the forefront of the criticism of lesbians, the feminists sought to avoid any danger that public opinion might shift its reproaches onto women in general. By keeping lesbians out of the feminist movement, by refusing to accept them as women at all, by accusing them of actually being women's enemies, they ensured their own safety and their leaders were protected from any unsavory allegations.

Protecting young people

Sex education manuals for young are good illustrations of the evolution in the institutional approach to the subject, at least as far as boys were concerned. If there were any handbooks for girls, they were fewer in number and they seldom touched on the question of homosexuality, no doubt because there was no wish to give girls any ideas about lesbian relations: "a girl's natural instinct was chastity, and the task of sex education was simply to maintain her in this natural chastity. Excessive moral restrictions, however, would risk exciting curiosity and lead girls to revolt against this natural instinct."[60]

---

59. Cited by Christine Bard, *Les Filles de Marianne, op. cit.*, p.197.
60. Oswald Schwarz, *The Psychology of Sex and Sex Education*, London, New Education Fellowship, 1935, 33 pages, p.21.

Given the advances in medical theories and the renewed interest in sexuality that appeared after the war, handbooks on sex education proliferated. Most were just 20 pages long, but some ran to 100 or 200 pages. They were written by doctors, priests, principals of preparatory schools or public schools, and the leaders of conservative moralistic associations. The majority of these works were intended for young boys, six to fifteen years old, and aimed to give them all the sexual baggage necessary to adapt to school life while heading off possible homosexual fancies. Some, however, like *Youth and Purity* by T. Miller Neatby, were addressed to older people, fifteen to thirty years old, which shows that the concern for instilling morals and awareness extended to age groups which might have been thought to be emancipated.

The French, German and English handbooks were quite different from each other. The English manuals were outstanding for their retrograde, alarmist views and they are loaded with prejudices. The question of masturbation is omnipresent and is treated in a most caricatured way. Teen homosexuality is clearly denounced. French works only rarely touched on that question. The warnings were mostly about prostitutes, venereal diseases and vice in general. The German works rather took the form of thick medical treatises, meant to inform parents or teachers. The problem of homosexuality came up fairly frequently, but in scientific terms. After 1933, the topic disappeared completely and sex education was recruited to the service of the "German race." There were a few recurring topics. Most of the works, especially the British, begin with recommendations on personal grooming, nutrition, sleep, everything that one must do to be a "happy, healthy boy." Personal hygiene and the regular practice of sports are emphasized. Such counsels are interspliced with moral or religious precepts, intended to engrave in the child's mind the link between purity of body and purity of mind. The German works also devote considerable space to advice on hygiene; moral purity goes hand in hand with physical purity: "Bodily precautions imply abstinence, a hard bed, cold showers, exercise, a diet low in albumin, white clothing."[61] Moreover, they generally devote a chapter to the description of the sexual functions; sometimes these explanations were very detailed, full of technical terms and thus very confusing for young and uninformed children. Two works by F.H. Shoosmith, *The Torch of Life, First Steps in Sex-Knowledge* (1935) and *That Youth May Know* (1935), are good examples. The first comprises twenty

---

61. Friedrich Niebergall, *Sexuelle Aufklärung der Jugend: ihr Recht, ihre Wege und Grenze*, Heidelberg, Evangelischer Verlag, 1922, 25 pages.

chapters, nineteen of which discuss flowers and animals and the final one touching very briefly on human sexuality. The second consists of four chapters; the first two are devoted to plants and animals, the third to "Puberty and Adolescence," and the fourth to a sermon!

Masturbation is closely related to the question of homosexuality. It is vilified at length; it is difficult to determine when the term is used in a strict sense and when it is meant in the broad sense, including homosexuality, for, in the authors' minds, solitary masturbation must lead to mutual masturbation. Onanism in itself was already strongly condemned and the number of the defamatory terms used to indicate it would be too long to count; it is referred to as a "shameful and degrading vice," a "sacrilegious mania" leading to "premature decrepitude."[62] On this topic, the English, German and French works are unanimous and almost indistinguishable from each other. On the other hand, the English books are characterized by the precision of their instructions. They all advise sleeping on one's side, as sleeping on one's back facilitates nocturnal emissions and sleeping on one's stomach causes friction that leads to erections;[63] the hands must be kept outside the bedclothes. There are precise rules on grooming, as well: "Except when washing yourself, you should never hold your genitals."[64] Every action is described in such a way as to minimize contact; the bad habit of putting one's hands in his pockets is particularly stigmatized.[65] In Germany, the famous liberal Hirschfeld suggested moving the pockets to the back of the pants to avoid Onanism. The Alliance of Honour, a puritanical association, provides a list of the harm that will befall the child who gives in to this vice: — Touching your body, or even just having dirty thoughts, sets off a nervous shock which is spread throughout the body, brain included. This excitation is dangerous, for it causes the exhaustion and the relaxation of the entire body. The boy becomes morose and timid, his performance at school goes down. The nervous system becomes very fragile, his health deteriorates until any recovery becomes impossible. The heart becomes weak, the voice becomes low, blood has difficulty cir-

---

62. Dr Jean Pouÿ, *Conseils à la jeunesse sur l'éducation sexuelle*, Paris, Maloine, 1931, 29 pages.

63. William Lee Howard, *Confidential Chats with Boys*, London, Rider & Co, 1928, 144 pages; F.V. Smith, *The Sex Education of Boys*, London, Student Christian Movement Press, 1931, 15 pages; A. Trewby, *Healthy Boyhood*, London, The Alliance of Honour, Kings & Jarcett, 1924, 63 pages.

64. A. Trewby, *Healthy Boyhood*, op. cit., p.19.

65. Edwin Wall, *To the Early Teens or Friendly Counsels to Boys*, London, The Portsmouth Printers Press, 1931, 120 pages. Cutting out the bottom of one's trouser pockets in order to be able to masturbate without giving oneself away was a common practice in the schools.

culating, the hands are damp, the complexion loses color, the muscles are soft, the sight dims."[66] In France, Dr. Jean Pouÿ informs readers that masturbation may lead to tuberculosis, cause weight loss, retardation and stupidity; according to him, there were brilliant young men of fifteen and sixteen years who had perished because of this vice.[67]

However, by the 1930s, it is rare to find authors who support the notion that masturbation could cause serious illness. The Alliance of Honour's new work, *Personal: To Boys* by T. Miller Neatby, which came out in 1934, ten years after *Healthy Boyhood*, admitted that masturbation did not produce any disease; they did, however, condemn it as a "bad habit" which makes the child "egocentric."

There were still plenty of religious arguments and the best way of dissuading children was still to hold up the threat of damnation: "The fact of touching certain parts of one's body is not in itself a sin. But this act often causes a desire which, except within marriage, is sinful, and thus it is banned as something that leads one to sin."[68] Patriotic and social arguments are also brought in that one might have thought out of place in such a discussion. "Solitary pleasure" endangers social unity and the masturbator is in fact a rebel: "The egoistic, sad and solitary masturbator allows his social qualities to atrophy."[69] Sex education was aimed more at fostering the development of men who would be integrated into society without threatening the prevailing values than at providing sex information: "The premature exercise of one's sexual functions often makes the adolescent an imperfect adult."[70] The child masturbator thus faced a fourfold condemnation: religious, medical, moral and social. The adolescent who experimented with homosexuality was subject to the same judgments, only stronger.

In the English handbooks, homosexual temptations are taken for granted:
— Masturbation is, of course, an abnormal form of sexuality, and thus a perversion, but the next most common perversion is homosexuality, which has

---

66. A. Trewby, *Healthy Boyhood, op. cit.*, p.19.

67. In *Conseils à la jeunesse sur l'éducation sexuelle, op. cit.*

68. Christian Marriage Association, *L'Église et l'Éducation sexuelle*, Paris, Aubin, 1929, 201 pages.

69. Dr Laignel-Lavastine, *Vénus et ses dangers*, Paris, Ligue nationale contre le péril vénérien, 1925, 14 pages, p.10.

70. Dr. Jean Carnot, *Au service de l'amour*, Paris, Éditions Beaulieu, 1939, 256 pages, p.26.

increased greatly in recent years.[71] Nevertheless: — Not everyone who feels homosexual impulses goes as far as to practice this unnatural vice.[72]

However, homosexuality is almost never mentioned clearly and a young boy could very well finish reading the book without understanding just what it was talking about. Boys are exhorted not to socialize with boys who are older than them, nor with vicious boys (those who talk about or who do "dirty things").[73] All the authors agree in expressly prohibiting sharing one's bed with another boy, even for reasons of convenience.[74] — Never sleep with another person, whether a man or a boy ... sleeping with another person releases an uncomfortable heat under bedcovers, which affects the genitals; it causes the blood to rise in them and causes a feeling of attraction inside these delicate organs. That often ends up leading to into an emission which is not natural, due to heat and not to an effort to empty the little overloaded sacs. Moreover, many boys will be tempted to play with each other. The boys may be innocent and naïve, at first, but in the end they find themselves masturbating.... [75]

The link with masturbation is constantly evoked: — Finally, with regard to friendship, in the life of a boy there is first of all interest in himself, and the development of masturbation has already been discussed. Then comes an interest in his own sex, through the worship of the hero — which should be a real help and an inspiration. If that slides into sentimentalism or unhealthy emotionalism in any physical form, it runs a great risk of evolving naturally into the heterosexual phase.[76]

Marie Stopes, the muse of sex education in that period, summarizes the era's trends. After having denied the frequency of masturbation, which she compares to taking drugs or poison,[77] she creates a causal link between the two "defects," saying, — Those who practice mutual masturbation are in many ways more dangerous than those who indulge in solitary masturbation, because digital masturbation ... can very well lead to greater and more abominable defects, which I do not wish to evoke in this book, but against which a warning

71. Violet Firth, *The Problem of Purity*, Rider & Co, 1928, 127 pages, p.107.

72. *Ibid.*, p.108.

73. A. Trewby, *Healthy Boyhood, op. cit.*, p.33.

74. See *The Education of Boys in the Subject of Sex, Confidential Chats with Boys, Healthy Boyhood.*

75. William Lee Howard, *Confidential Chats with Boys, op. cit.*, p.94.

76. Reginald Churchill, *I Commit to Your Intelligence*, London, J.M. Dent & Sons Ltd, 1936, 137 pages, p.14.

77. Marie Stopes, *Sex and the Young*, London, The Gill Publishing Co, 1926, 190 pages, p.41-43.

is not superfluous, nowadays when there is practically a cult of homosexual practices.[78]

Starting in the 1930s, a medical discussion of homosexuality often took the place of the customary warnings. Gladys M. Cox admits that she does not know whether it is a matter of internal secretions or arrested sexual development. Leslie D. Weatherhead, in *The Mastery of Sex through Psychology and Religion* (1931), distinguishes acquired homosexuality and innate homosexuality, and discusses narcissism and treatment by hypnosis. Many authors quote Havelock Ellis or Freud, and the notion of a homosexual phase in adolescence is raised, albeit with reservations: "Adolescent homosexuality marks a stage of development; but this stage is abnormal and only a small number of boys experience it."[79] This idea was enthusiastically adopted by English authors, for it justified the homosexuality that was prevalent in the public schools and reassured parents about their children's future development: — When answering the question: are homo-sexual practices bad?, one should exclude those concerning boys between the ages of thirteen and fifteen and girls between twelve and fourteen. At these ages, the sexual instinct is not yet settled in the sexual organs and it would be unjust to take these practices between children as seriously as the problem merits when it occurs in adulthood."[80]

Havelock Ellis's book on sex education[81] is striking in its broad outlook: he underscores the early appearance of sexual manifestations in the child, and he pleads for uncensored readings and nudity, which he considers hygienic. On the other hand, taking after Magnus Hirschfeld in Germany, he is less forthcoming on the treatment of masturbation and homosexuality. The latter is not even men-tioned, whereas, among the testimony of four young people provided in the appendix, the second concerns a boy who frequently masturbated, who had had sexual experiences (fellatio) with his peers since the age of five, was in love with many boys during his adolescence and who now intended, at twenty-five, to become a pastor!

Certain authors considered that homosexuality was becoming an increas-ingly widespread phenomenon. Journalists, novelists, authors of light plays and,

---

78. *Ibid.*, p.44.

79. Oswald Schwarz, *The Psychology of Sex and Sex Education, op. cit.*, p.18.

80. Leslie D. Weatherhead, *The Mastery of Sex through Psychology and Religion*, London, Student Christian Movement Press, 1931, 249 pages, p.153.

81. Havelock Ellis, *Études de psychologie sexuelle*, t.VII, *L'Éducation sexuelle*, Paris, Mercure de France, 1927, 220 pages.

the innovation of the period, talking movies, are denounced as agents of immorality — the bugbears of the leagues of right-thinking people. And it wasn't only the moralists who condemned homosexuality: R.H. Innes, in his masterpiece *Sex from the Standpoint of Youth* (1933), which favors free love and birth control, vigorously condemns adolescent homosexuality. Described like monsters on the prowl, hiding behind every door and every face, homosexual adults are presented as the very epitome of abjection and human degradation: — There are things in trousers called men, so vile that they wait in hiding for innocent boys. These things are generally elegant, polished, too polished, in fact, and pass themselves off as gentlemen; but they are skunks and rattlesnakes. They traipse around the tourist hotels, rental homes and townhouses where families live ... don't go for a walk with these things, for all they have in mind is to teach you to masturbate or other things that are dirtier still ... at the first word, at the first abnormal action, smite it, smite it so hard that it will bear the scar for all its life. Do not be afraid, these skunks are all cowards.[82]

In the French works, the warnings are primarily against the reading of pornographic magazines, prostitution, divorce, and the "rising flood of turpitudinous libertinage."[83] Moral discipline and chastity are celebrated for "a prolonged childhood is a saved childhood."[84] However, the authors never lose sight of the function of reproduction, the only reason for their study; for them, "individuals are above all seed-bearers" and "celibacy and marriage without children are abnormal states."[85]

Only two works mention homosexuality; the first is a book by Dr. Henri Drouin, *Counsels for Young People* (1926). He spends two pages on "the deviation of the sexual instinct." According to him, homosexuality is less widespread than it is said to be, and true "inversion" is an anomaly and not a perversion.

The second work is Dr. René Allendy and Hella Lobstein's *Sexual Problems at School* (1938), which is more a treatise on childhood and adolescent sexuality than a sex education manual, even if the advice with which it is so replete makes it fall into the rubric of this study. Homosexuality is granted a whole chapter (fifteen pages) in the traditional context of school friendships. While Allendy is

---

82. William Lee Howard, *Confidential Chats with Boys, op. cit.*, p.95.

83. Dr Jean Pouÿ, *Conseils à la jeunesse sur l'éducation sexuelle, op. cit.*, p.25.

84. R.P. S.-J. de Ganay, Dr Henri Abrand and abbé Jean Viollet, *Les Initiations nécessaires*, Paris, Éditions familiales de France, 1938, 47 pages, p.4.

85. Dr Sicard de Plauzoles, *Pour le salut de la race: éducation sexuelle*, Paris, Éditions médicales, 1931, 98 pages, p.37.

opposed to reactionary works (he is particularly hard on the book *Venus and Her Dangers*) and frequently quotes Freud, even Hirschfeld and Ellis, his conclusions are far from clear. He considers adolescent homosexuality a crucial question: "After masturbation, the major sexual problem in schools is homosexuality."[86] However, he does not see it as the product of precocious sexuality but rather the result of naivety, of sexual ignorance: "and how many little boys became homosexual for candies from a good-looking man, met one day on the way home from school?"[87] And, "The horror attached to sexuality leads some boys to such severe forms of timidity in front of women, and to more or less complete impotence, if not toward homosexuality."[88]

Homosexuality was seen as proof of extraversion (masturbation representing introversion), a way of being in touch with the real world, of externalizing one's feelings. This gives rise to the surprising conclusion: "Provided that the child does not get stuck at this infantile mode of satisfaction, homosexual activity may be preferred to Onanism which might lead the child to a state of morbid fantasies or schizoidism."[89] In fact, in a society where early heterosexual relations are not encouraged, homosexuality is granted a social role. Relations between boys might be the least dangerous way for them to appease their sexual instincts, without fear of contamination (at the brothel) nor of degeneracy (by masturbation). There is a distinct air of hypocrisy in a society that denounces homosexuality but is ready to tolerate it as a means of avoiding greater dangers, and that accepts homosexual relations "of convenience" while condemning heterosexual relations and free love.

The German works can be clearly dated to the context of the post-war period: "The sexual distress of our day is great, perhaps greater than ever before."[90] The buzzword was *Verwahrlosung*, the depravity of a younger generation with no moral compass. Book titles were often suggestive: *Jugend in Geschlechtsnot* (*Youth in Sexual Distress*), *Die sexual Gefährdung unserer Jugend* (*Sexual Dangers Confronting Our Youth*), *Die Jugendverwahrlosung und ihre Bekämpfung* (*The Depravity of Youth and How to Fight It*). The destabilizing influence of life in the city,

---

86. René Allendy and Hella Lobstein, *Le Problème sexuel à l'école*, Paris, Aubier, 1938, 253 pages, p.165.
87. *Ibid.*, p.54.
88. *Ibid.*, p.130.
89. *Ibid.*, p.176.
90. Klaus Steigleder, "Die sexualpädagogische Frage der Gegenwart," *in* J.P. Steffes, *Sexualpädagogische Probleme*, Münster, Münster Verlag, 1931, 231 pages, p.177.

family difficulties stemming from the war, the economic crisis and the feminist movements, psychoanalysis, the proponents of sexual liberation and those who were exploring homosexuality — especially Hans Blüher, who contributed to popularizing the notion of adolescent homosexuality as a positive force — were constantly under fire. Unlike in England and France, the criticism was aimed at and the responsibility was shared by the younger generation and the society as a whole. Periodicals easily qualified as pornographic, novels, theater, modern dance, and modern fashion that freed the body and revealed the form in an indecent way were roundly condemned.

Tihamer Toth, in *Queen Jugendreife* (*A Pure Puberty*, 1931), exhorts young people "to fight the dragon" of modern civilization. As in England, masturbation and homosexuality are closely linked: "It is not Onanism as such, but excessive Onanism, or Onanism practiced by others and on others, which is the real problem and which must be countered by teachers' organizations."[91]

Heinrich Hanselmann devotes several pages to this subject in *Geschlechtliche Erziehung des Kindes* (1931). He distinguishes "true homosexuality" from adolescent homosexuality. The latter is normal "and temporary; the young boy experience vague sexual tensions, and it need an object on which to transfer his thirst for love."[92] Many specialists claimed, moreover, that modern young men were interested less in women than the preceding generations; the danger of homosexuality was all the greater if he preferred exclusively male company, at school or in youth groups. It was especially important to protect boys from "real homosexuals" who could prey upon them during this period of sexual indecision, exerting their influence and corrupting the younger fellows: "Homosexual adults simply approach young people in an inoffensive way, at first, possibly offering little gifts and services in order to gain their goodwill and affection. They also try to get into organizations that offer them leadership positions over young people."[93]

The most virulent tomes, like *Die sexuelle Gefährdung unserer Jugend* (1929) by Erich Zacharias, explicitly attack the homosexual movements. This happened

---

91. Dr Heinrich Schulte-Hubbert, *Um Sittlichkeit und Erziehung an höheren Schulen*, Münster, Verlag der Aschendorffschen Verlagsbuchhandlung, 1929, 62 pages.

92. Dr Oswald Schwarz, *Sexualität und Persönlichkeit*, Vienne-Leipzig-Berne, Verlag für Medizin, 1934, 205 pages, p.73.

93. Wilhelm Hausen, "Die Gefahren sexueller Verirrungen in der Pubertätszeit und ihre prophylaktische Behandlung," *in* J.P. Steffes (dir.), *Sexualpädagogische Probleme*, Münster, Münster Verlag, 1931, 231 pages, p.105.

mostly in Germany, because these groups were most visible there. Some teachers compared the homosexual movements to organizations of propaganda and corruption, seeking to destroy Germany's younger generation. "The doctrines of the so-called inversion are nothing less than a very dangerous and premeditated contamination of our youth, which is particularly receptive to such influences at the age of puberty. It bears within it the danger of homosexual poisoning, i.e. of a premeditated perversion of our youth."[94]

The medical vocabulary of contagion and infection is everywhere. In *Schützt unsere Kinder vor den Sexualverbrechern!* (1931), E. Dederding calls for castration for child rapists. Liberal German sexologists, who were writing mainly on the question of sex education, curiously neglected the topic of homosexuality. Hirschfeld left it out of his work for young readers, *Sexualerziehung* (1930).

The education system became a subject of debate as proponents of a homosexual pedagogy, copied on the Greek model, vied with advocates of traditional education. Germany is the only country where such calls for teaching with homosexual content were explicitly expressed. Kurt Zeidler, in *Vom erziehenden Eros* (1919), and Siegfried Placzek, in *Freundschaft und Sexualität* (1927), studied the role of the loving relationship in teaching. Zeidler, who made references to Hans Blüher and Stefan George, gave a scathing criticism of German society, which he said was incapable of appreciating the educational potential of inversion. He claimed that the prevailing moral climate imposed limitations on teachers that hindered their ability to teach for, properly used, their powers of seduction could bring about miracles.[95] However, homosexual relations would have to be restricted to a very spiritual level: a pat on the head, a squeeze of the hand, a hug and a smile should be the limits as far as the teacher's affection for his pupil.

Placzek summarized this view with a shocking formula: "Pedagogy is the right field for the pederast."[96] He acknowledged that a homosexual teacher might spare his pupil some sexual missteps by explaining the nature of his feelings to him. However, once the pupil was past adolescence, he must turn to women. He also warned parents against dangerous homosexuals, the "seducers,"

---

94. Heinrich Többen, *Die Jugendverwahrlosung und ihre Bekämpfung*, Münster, Aschendorffschen Verlagsbuchhandlung, 1922, 245 pages.

95. Kurt Zeidler, *Vom erziehenden Eros*, Lauenburg, Freideutscher Jugendverlag Adolf Saal, 1919, 39 pages, p.18.

96. Siegfried Placzek, *Freundschaft und Sexualität*, Berlin-Cologne, A. Marcus & E. Weber's Verlag, 1927, 186 pages, p.66.

those who forget their duties towards the child and take advantage of their position to satisfy their instincts.

Fascinated by the cultural and aesthetic aspect of the love of boys, sexually inhibited, frustrated due to the moral condemnation of society, the advocates of homosexual education were searching for a way to validate a utopian model of platonic love between adults and adolescents. Their prudish and at the same time exalted tone attracted suspicion from critics and parents and led to many scandals involving teachers. The most famous German reformer was unquestionably Gustav Wyneken (1875-1964), founder of the experimental co-educational school of Wickersdorf[97] and a writer on Eros. Wyneken and Paul Geheeb opened the free school community of Wickersdorf on September 1, 1906. There were separate dormitories for boys and girls; after 9:00 PM, they were kept apart. The classes were shared and decentralized, but Wyneken was the principal leader. This was an elitist school: its aim was to form a new youth, raised to respect the body and the mind. The program included philosophy (Plato, Kant, Schopenhauer, Nietzsche), music (Bach and Bruckner), religion, meditation and mathematics together with physical culture, dance, bodily expression and theater. Wyneken fell victim to a denunciation campaign in 1910: Wickersdorf supposedly exerted a deleterious religious influence on the children. Wyneken had to retire, but he returned in 1919. After six months, a new scandal came out — he was accused of touching two young boys. He was sentenced to one year in prison and had to give up the management of the establishment.

Wickersdorf was organized on a profoundly original basis: the pupils were grouped in friendships, each one with a "chief of friendship" at its head. The latter was the keystone of the unit, responsible for taking care of each pupil, monitoring his progress and maintaining social bonds, creating an *esprit de corps*. The pupils often became very attached to their chief, whom they respected and admired enormously. Emotional relations (Eros) were regarded as advantageous, for they personalized the school relations, encouraged more attentive supervision of the pupils and better comprehension between group members. "The most serious and the most solid friendships which I could observe were always between pupils and teachers."[98] Wyneken very clearly distinguished homosexu-

---

97. Wyneken had worked as a teacher in Hermann Lietz's experimental school. He then became a part of the movement for pedagogical reform that was gaining currency in Europe at the time, like Cecile Reddie in England and Edmond Demoulins in France. In 1919, he briefly worked in the Ministry of Culture under an SPD government.

98. Gustav Wyneken, *Wickersdorf*, Lauenburg, Adolf Saal Verlag, 1922, 152 pages, p.58.

ality from pederasty, or Eros. For him, pederasty was the erotic bond that links a mature man with a young boy. He was highly critical of those who considered it a medical problem: love, he noted, cannot be reduced to a matter of secretions.

In his essay *Eros* (1924), Wyneken explained the erotic relations between Masters and pupils at length as the natural evolution of a major emotional tie, a pure and noble attraction: "The love of the young boys is more austere and more powerful. Man and woman are opposites, neither one fully understands the other. The man lives in a spiritual universe identical to that of the young boy. Most of the things which a woman will never understand, an intelligent and noble young boy will be able to formulate."[99]

Wyneken had watched the Wandervogel movement closely and had studied the troubled relations between the leaders and their admirers. He was fully aware of the revolutionary implications of his education system. Even more than his homoerotic theories, it was his idea of separating the child from his family group and his traditional influences that led to his being persecuted by the legal and moral authorities of the time. "Here is what we call the youth culture (Jugendkultur), and such a youth culture can obviously be carried out only by truly isolating the youth, who should be kept away from the socially and economically conditioned influence of the family, the classes and the parties, as well as dishonesty of conventions."[100] Wyneken intended to free young from ser-vitude, to organize them in an autonomous, free, anarchistic community: "Socialism must reach for youth, just as youth itself is revolution and the future..." A disciple of Nietzsche, he understood that youth represented power and renewal. His thinking was elitist, antibourgeois, and anticlerical, but Wyneken was not a nationalist. He expressed anguish at the manipulation of youth for militarist ends and the abuse of special ties (homoerotic) for authori-tative purposes. He was quite isolated in his position: his elitism and his homo-sexuality alienated those on the left, while the right rejected his libertarian and pacifist model.

In sum, the question of adolescent homosexuality was a matter of consid-erable concern in the inter-war period, particularly in England. Fantasy played a part in this; medical information often gave way to talk that was more moral and religious in tonality, repeating the worst superstitions and propagating a false image of sexuality. However, even this kind of talk was not entirely unam-

---

99. Gustav Wyneken, *Eros*, Lauenburg, Adolf Saal Verlag, 1924, 72 pages, p.46.
100. Id., *Revolution und Schule*, Leipzig, Klinkhardt Verlag, 1921, 74 pages, p.13.

biguous: there were some who favored same-sex romances to premature sexual intercourse with women, or who accepted relations between Masters and pupils that might, as in ancient Greece, foster the boy's development.

The stranger among us

A final sign of the fear that homosexuality inspired in the public was the assimilation of the homosexual with the stranger. The homosexual was always seen as being different. Since the Eulenburg affair, homosexuality in France had been called "the German vice" while the Germans called it "the French malady."[101] Each side defended the morality of its own country, saying things like: "Homosexuality is rare in France."[102] To admit that there were homosexuals at home would mean casting the whole population under suspicion. By contrast, accusing a neighboring country on this ground was an easy way to strengthen national unity. Examples from abroad were used as wake-up calls to warn the population against any such signs of decadence.

In *La Débauche mondiale*, Jean Violet (1927), British homosexuality is granted eighteen pages and vitriolic articles ran in *Fantasio*. The August 1, 1927 number claimed that fully one-quarter of Englishmen were homosexual. But the Germans were the principal target, with comments like "More than here, vice is making devastating inroads in Germany."[103] An article dated November 15, 1919, published in *La Presse de Paris*[104] and symptomatic of this trend was entitled, "Life in Berlin." It seems to refer to the film *Anders als die Andern* and denounces the immorality that reigns in the defeated country: "The cinema allows itself to be used for every sort of aberration; it pleads extenuating circumstances for inverts of both sexes and for meetings on end the National Assembly discusses these insane events which, apparently, cannot be prohibited." Fantasio noted on November 1, 1922 that, "While unfortunately there are too many dubious night clubs in Paris where the oddest 'boys' and 'girls' hang out, it is nothing compared to Berlin, where sentimental heresy prevails with cynicism."

---

101. In the 16th an 17th centuries it was called the "Italian vice," in the 18th, the French and English vice, and since Frederick II the German vice; in the 19th century, it was referred to as "the Arab way."

102. Dr G. Saint-Paul, *Invertis et homosexuels, thèmes psychologiques* [1895], preface by Émile Zola, Paris, Éditions Vigon, 1930, 152 pages, p.142.

103. Ambroise Got, *l'Allemagne à nu*, Paris, La Pensée française, 1923, 248 pages, p.94.

104. This was an issue put out by several Parisian newspapers working in collaboration, including *Le Temps*, in response to a printers' strike.

The Haarmann case, about a German homosexual serial killer, inspired a long article tinged with Germanophobia in *Le Temps*: "They try to compare him to Landru. It is absurd. What a gulf between the reasons, the method, the attitude after the crime! Between the perfect accountant, smiling, fascinating, a really superior degenerate, and the bloodthirsty madman, the aboriginal from the Saxon forests.... As different as the Seine and the Leine!"[105] Lucky France, with its high-quality assassins.

In fact, articles associating Berlin and Sodom had become too numerable to count. Willy, in his work on *The Third Sex* (1927), starts by expounding on the German example: "How can we even speak about pederasty without thinking at once of Germany and its extraordinary organization of vice, which pullulates more there than in any other country in Europe?"[106] Among the other exemplary works of this type, one may cite *Vertus et vices allemands* (first edition, 1904) by Oscar Méténier, *L'Allemagne à nu* (1923) by Ambroise Got, Gabriel Gobron's *Contacts avec la jeune génération allemande* (1930), and Louis-Charles Royer's *L'Amour en Allemagne* (1936). Posing as interested pseudo-scientific analysts, the authors delight in tarring yesterday's enemy with charges of decadence, degeneracy and the cowardice which they associate with homosexuality.

Hitler's accession to power did nothing to improve the status quo in France. On February 15, 1933, insolence is still the order of the day: under the headline, "Charming Adolf," *Fantasio* published a fake interview by Andre Négis presenting Hitler as a raving queen. In July 1934, shortly after Röhm's assassination, *La Vie parisienne* ran a cartoon showing a baker posting various notices in his window, one of which says, "Furnished room for rent, for two men only. Ladies need not apply. We must respect local values in Hitler's Germany."[107] The same year, the magazine published a piece on the homosexuals of Berlin.[108] There is an obvious disparity between the article by Guy de Téramond, who goes on describing the Berliner subculture as it was at the height of Weimar, and the reality that the homosexual scene had been destroyed in 1933. In September 1937, *Le Crapouillot* still ran a report on the "Modern Conceptions of Sexuality" with photographs of Berliner transvestites.

In France, the "Night of the Long Knives" touched off a large anti-homosexual campaign directed against Germany. While the French newspapers used

105. *Le Temps*, 2 October 1924.
106. Willy, *Le Troisième Sexe*, Paris, Paris-Édition, 1927, 268 pages, p.39.
107. *La Vie parisienne*, 1934, p.1019.
108. *Ibid.*, p.1733.

the same terms as the Germans, they amplified their criticism with personal remarks. *Le Temps* of July 2, 1934 vigorously denounced Röhm's homosexuality and welcomed Hitler's initiative: "Although they refer to facts known to everyone, these commands are remarkable in the frankness and the firmness of the tone. Any infringement of §175 in the Code (relating to homosexuality) will be punished most rigorously and will entail at the least expulsion from the storm troopers and the party." *Le Populaire* (SFIO) was more circumspect. It viewed was not sure what to make of the event. The idea of a Nazi Germany that was still a homosexual paradise was curiously entrenched in the minds of French journalists. It is hard to tell whether that was due to ignorance or provocation. The desire to ridicule the Nazi regime and the ambitious Hitlerite seems to have helped keep alive this fable which, in hindsight, appears so out of place.

By comparison, *The Times* was strikingly prudent. The English daily noted that the purpose of the operation was primarily the elimination of "the second revolution," and the rest was just a pretext. Homosexuality was not emphasized, and there are none of the insinuations found in *Le Temps* as to Röhm's offenses. Also in contrast to *Le Temps*, *The Times* published several reports of raids on homosexual bars.

The homosexual might not necessarily be a foreigner in the strictest sense, but was often seen as an intruder in society. Working under cover and in underhanded ways, he knew how to make himself invisible while undermining the national morals. This paranoid vision is the most dangerous: it justifies every kind of excess, and fosters a psychosis within society. It is also the most difficult to dislodge, the more so as it was sometimes corroborated by homosexual themselves.

Proust, in *La Recherche*, talks about the notion of foreignness in regard to the character Albertine. When the narrator discovers that she has had relations with other women, he sees her as "a different person, a person like them and speaking the same language; and by making her their compatriot, rendered her still more foreign to [him]. Her secret, kept for so long, made her a 'spy,' and even worse, 'for those mislead only as to their nationality, whereas with Albertine it was her deepest humanity, the fact that she did not belong to humanity in general, but to a strange race that mingled with it, hid there and never did blend in."[109]

---

109. Marcel Proust, *A la recherche du temps perdu*, Paris, Gallimard, coll. "Bibl. de la Pléiade," 1989, t.IV, 1707 pages, p.107-108.

The theme of the hidden enemy had the most success in Germany; the Nazis latched onto it with a vengeance. Hansjörg Maurer's pamphlet, *§175, Eine kritische Betrachtung des Problems der Homosexualität* (1921), precisely prefigures the Nazi themes of safeguarding the race and homosexuality's threat to German civilization. "What they [those who defend homosexuality] want is nothing other than to scramble, confuse and corrupt as much as possible the moral notions and conceptions of the German race.... They want.... to sap our morality, and that means neither more nor less than destruction of the race! Then they will be completely victorious![110] Further on, he mixes anti-Semitism and homophobia: "And there lies the terrible danger, that these Jewish professors of a foreign race and these itinerant preachers of homosexuality have the right, with their science, to make bodies into carrion, in order to destroy and to break the hearts and the bodies of our German compatriots."[111]

HOMOSEXUALITY AND THE WINDS OF FASHION

During the 1920s, homosexuality was all the rage. Writers, artists, caricaturists all used homosexuals and lesbians (as eccentric, decadent sensualists) symbols of the Roaring Twenties. While this phenomenon produced a reaction — rejection and the impression of increasing immorality — it also contributed to greater tolerance. Having become a standard item, even banal, the image of the homosexual became less shocking, and the sports, nudist and youth movements all contributed to the widespread image of the androgyne as an emblem of modernity and thus spread, not always in conscious ways, homoerotic themes in society.

Popular Fears and Fantasies: The Homosexual and the Lesbian in Literature

The best-known aspect of the homosexual fad in the inter-war period is the way it took over literature. While it was not in itself a new phenomenon, it took on new proportions, especially in France.

---

110. Hansjörg Maurer, *§175, eine kritische Betrachtung des Problems der Homosexualität*, Munich, Willibald Drexler, 1921, 62 pages, p.41-42.

111. *Ibid.*, p.43.

Homosexual and Lesbian Archetypes

Representations of inverts did not change much during the inter-war period. The myth of the homosexual as a corrupter of youth, a satyr or a criminal gained new life, however, in the wake of several sex scandals that erupted in Germany. First there was Fritz Haarmann (1876-1924), who escaped from the asylum and perpetrated sadistic crimes on several young teens. This was a big story and deeply shocked the international public. Theodor Lessing retold the story in 1925 under the title *Haarmann, Story of a Werewolf* (!). Between 1918 and 1924, a large number of people disappeared in Hanover under unknown circumstances, especially boys between the ages of fourteen and eighteen. The remains (bones, skulls) of at least twenty-two boys were found in the Leine, the river that runs through the city. Fritz Haarmann was arrested on June 23, 1924. Pegged as a homosexual, he already had been convicted on several occasions and had been working since 1918 as a police informant. This scandal created a sensation in Germany as well as abroad; 168 newspapers covered it. *Le Petit Parisien*, with its print run of a million copies, sent the journalist Eugene Quinche to Hanover to cover the trial; he later wrote a book, *Haarmann, The Butcher of Hanover*.[112] He described the highly charged atmosphere of the hearings, the way the journalists quizzed the witnesses and Haarmann's neighbors in search of sensational details, and the public's fascination for the character. The book gives a good idea just how laden public opinion was with anti-homosexual prejudices. A few years later, a similar crime wave hit Adolf Seefeld (1871-1936), a vagrant and a religious fanatic, was found to have poisoned a dozen young boys. He was executed in 1936. It is not hard to imagine the impact such affair s must have had on the public. This all reinforced the caricatured image of the diabolical pervert and intensified the already severe psychosis about the dangers to young people.[113]

The image of the lesbian in the inter-war period did change somewhat. Three prototypes can be identified. There was the morbid lesbian, a product of decadent literature and Symbolist painting that was still evoked by certain authors.[114] The image was often melded with that of the prostitute,[115] as it was

---

112. Eugène Quinche, *Haarmann, le boucher de Hanovre*, Paris, Éditions Henry Parville, 1925, 182 pages.

113. *Le Crapouillot* dated May 1938 published a report on "Crime and instinctual perversions" in which we learn that homosexuality is particularly prevalent among criminals.

114. Jean Desthieux, *Figures méditerranéennes: "Femmes damnées,"* Paris-Gap, Ophrys, 1937, 135 pages.

common in those days to imagine that a woman who was selling her body to men all day and night would prefer, on her own time, gentler and more caring caresses. The image of women living together was a staple in depictions of the prostitution underworld. The lesbian was often depicted as a superior lover, a Don Juan subjecting women to her pleasure. This behavior was immediately associated with the prostitute, the only woman able to assert a completely uninhibited sexuality. Sometimes, the lesbian was even shown in the role of the teacher, the one who prepared the woman to accept male attacks and taught her how to make her husband appreciate her. In same vein, prison inmates were also shown as lesbians. In *Dans Les Dessous des prisons de femme (The Underworld of Women's Prisons)* Robert Boucard relates how each new arrival is raped by everyone in the dormitory; each dormitory had "a queen" and each queen had her "favorite." In *Prisons de femmes*, Francis Carco devotes several pages to sapphism. An actual lesbian rite was developed by the prisoners; couples were formed according to the heterosexual model and sentiments were exaggerated: "At Clermont, I saw of five of them die after being separated from their friends. I can give you the names, if you want. Think of it. It's full of couples in there. Some are 'men' and some are women. I was a man. I would pin together the hem of my skirt to make it into trousers. All of those who were man did the same."[116] Some even saw the prison as a refuge: "Every one of us," declared Didi-the-queen, "if we weren't in the lock-up, we could have been preyed on by men."[117] In Saint-Lazare, lesbianism reigned supreme, and the guards did nothing to stop it. From the dungeons to the rooftop, they scrawled gigantic hearts with arrows, and three letters: MFL, which meant Mine For Life, or MUD: Mine Until Death. "Martha loves Sharon," "Bertha is gonna get Irma for stealing Georgette."[118] Still, some discretion was required; any concrete proof would entail severe punishment. In the central prison of Rennes, it was three months in solitary for exchanging notes:

> In the beginning these notes were going around all over the place: 'My dear little wife...' Well, I made them cut that out right quick, they didn't dare try that anymore. If they jump on each other in the night and do nasty things, there's nothing

115. Alexandre Parent-Duchâtelet, in *La Prostitution à Paris au XIXᵉ siècle* (1836; texts presented and annotated by Alain Corbin, Paris, Éditions du Seuil, 1981, 217 pages), had a passage devoted to tribads.

116. Francis Carco, *Prisons de femmes*, Paris, Les Éditions de France, 1933, 244 pages, p.5-6.

117. *Ibid.*, p.7.

118. *Ibid.*, p.31.

we can do about it, that's nature; but to go around boasting about their affairs and creating rivalries, quarrels, fights... that had to stop.[119]

This image was also bolstered lesbians with literary pretensions, like Liane dePougy.[120]

Like the "decadent" lesbian, Claudine embodies a lesbian archetype that is quintessentially French. Born before the First World War, she was still quite popular in the 1920s. Played on stage by Polaire, she launched a whole new fad and many women sought to imitate her. However, while the comic and off-hand style with which many ambiguous situations were treated surely contributed to the increasing acceptance of lesbianism among the general public, it also shows the limits of this type of representation. The marriage of Claudine and Renaud in *Claudine in Paris* shows Claudine's lesbian inclinations in their true light: Claudine is not a lesbian in the modern sense of the term, she is not even a liberated woman: "My freedom weighs upon me, my independence exhausts me; what I had been seeking for months — even longer — was beyond any doubt, a master. Liberated women are not women."[121] — The representation of Claudine as lesbian is only an erotic pretext: "Because of my short hair and my coldness towards them, men say themselves: 'that one's for women.'"[122]

What Claudine embodies is not so much the lesbian as the idea of the lesbian in the inter-war period, in that trendy world where it was considered stylish to appear emancipated and blasé. The French elite, which would have not tolerated militant and aggressive lesbians, was perfectly comfortable with sexual fantasies that did not exceed the bounds of intimacy and excited their imagination, without calling into question male superiority: "It is not the same thing [as male homosexuality]... You can do anything, you others. It's sweet, it doesn't matter."[123] At the same time, the relationship between Claudine and Rézi is placed under the tender, protective wing of the husband who, as an accomplice, encourages their get-togethers and even places an apartment at their disposal, with a goodwill that smells of voyeurism. The very idea of a lesbian relationship

---

119. *Ibid.*, p.145.

120. Liane de Pougy, *Idylle saphique* [1901], Paris, Lattès, 1979, 272 pages.

121. Colette, *Œuvres complètes*, Paris, Gallimard, coll. "Bibl. de la Pléiade," 1984, t.I, 1 686 pages, p.364.

122. *Ibid.*, p.447.

123. *Ibid.*, p.453. Renaud, in an earlier discussion of his son's homosexuality, wrote: "These stories give me such a horror." Claudine herself told Marcel: "Those little playthings there are called 'pensioner's toys,' but when it comes to 17-year-old boys, it's practically a sickness" (*ibid.*, p.253).

existing as such, as a viable alternative for love and sex, is tarnished by the coarse outcome when Rézi gives herself up to Renaud's embrace. Finally, what does Claudine bring to the representation of the lesbian? Rachilde, in her review of *Claudine at School* in the *Mercure de France* (May 1900) stresses that, "This is the first time that one dares to speak ... of these unnatural idylls as some form of natural paganism."[124] But the lightness of the literary treatment, which follows Willy in seeking "to spice up the narrative a little by adding some of the slang, some of the playfulness, some of the atmosphere of lesbianism,"[125] keep Claudine from being an example of the emancipated lesbian, who has no remorse over her tastes in love.

In the same type as Claudine we have the Proustian lesbians, Albertine and her friends, Rosemonde, Andrée, the whole troop of girls in flowers, the lesbians of operettas, puerile fantasies of naughty woman-children sharing guilty secrecies, tasting dirty pleasures, and making fun of men. These girlish games show a mixture of naivety and perversity very similar to the passions of Claudine and take place in a context of male permissiveness that recalls Renaud. Marcel suffers over Albertine's absence and her infidelity, but it is just this secret and her lack of scruples that make her so unique and dear to him. If Albertine had not "been with women," he probably would not have been interested. In his treatment of lesbians, Proust joined the decadent tradition, exploring unknown worlds, as when the narrator surprises Miss Vinteuil and Albertine in a stereo-typical scene of lesbian sadistic fantasy. In fact, whereas the waywardness of Charlus and his ilk are analyzed with clinical precision, the lesbian world remains ethereal and insubstantial. Proust's lesbians are familiar to the public: fallen women, lost women who give themselves up to their instincts with a natu-ralness that endears them to men. And once they give in, they are eaten up by remorse, the just punishment for their pleasures. In fact, they only hope (the ultimate male fantasy) to be saved by a man whom they could love. It goes full circle; Albertine follows Claudine, lesbians do not exist: "But Albertine suffered dreadfully, afterward.... She hoped that you would save her, that you would marry her. In the end, she thought that it was some kind of criminal madness, and I often wondered whether it were not after something like that, having caused a suicide in a family, that she had committed suicide herself."[126]

---

124. Cited by Herbert Lottman, *Colette*, Paris, Gallimard, coll. "Folio," 1990, 496 pages, p.69.

125. *Ibid.*, p.67.

126. Marcel Proust, *A la recherche du temps perdu, op. cit.*, p.180-181.

The third archetype is specific to the inter-war period. This is the "masculine" lesbian derived from the "New Woman," so clearly embodied by Radclyffe Hall and her heroine, Stephen Gordon.[127] However, the public had trouble distinguishing this model from the flapper, the garçonne, the Bubikopf. Featured in many novels, this version is presented as a congenital invert, a victim of fate at best, and at worst as a *femme fatale*, a vampire, a demon who devours her victims and then rejects them without scruple. Such novels had much to do with popularizing these archetypes.

A Raft of Novels

Novels presenting homosexuality as a modern subject seem to have been most numerous in France.[128] Many such novels hinted in their subtitles: "A Modern Story," "A Novel of Contemporary Morals," etc. Some of these were written by homosexuals, but many were written by heterosexual authors.

In fact, the interest in male homosexuality as the subject of a novel dated back to the very beginning of the century in novels like *Monsieur de Phocas,* by Jean Lorrain, when it was just one facet of the decadent enthusiasm for bizarre practices and sexual deviations. Male homosexuality was considered in the same vein with sadism, cross-dressing, and drug taking among men who were craving for new sensations and artificial stimulants. England experienced this passion for homosexuality through aesthetic movements: Oscar Wilde's *The Portrait of Dorian Gray* is one of the best examples of this school, together with all of Ronald Firbank's works. In the inter-war period, vestiges of an ironic and precious treatment of male homosexuality can be found in E.F. Benson,[129] but his descriptions of aging "queens" and inverts from good families knitting and taking tea have more to do with caricaturing and poking fun at high British society, austere and moralistic, than with any hearkening back to the good old days when white lilies were thrown on the tombs of gorgeous young opium addicts.

These literary effects seem artificial and passé in the 1920s. The new trend was inaugurated in France by Lucien Daudet with *Le Chemin mort: roman contemporain* (1908). The hero, Alain Malsort, followed the tragic destiny of a young

---

127. See chapter four.

128. The titles mentioned herein are hardly exhaustive. They were chosen on the basis of their value as examples rather than for their literary motifs.

129. See for example in E.F. Benson, *Snobs*, Paris, Salvy, 1994, 217 pages, and the Mapp and Lucia series.

"invert." Protégé of a wealthy middle-class man, he was forsaken when his looks began to fade and he ended up dying after a scene with his former "friend," crushed by a tram. The homosexual social drama was born.

One year later, Gustave Binet-Valmer wrote *Lucien*, a novel that became an immense success and influenced Proust, among others.[130] The story became a model for many imitators and similar tales were published throughout the period: a biography is drawn up incorporating as many as possible of the "invert" traits defined by doctors, and relating his trials and tribulations as he lives out his destiny as a homosexual who, no matter what he does, cannot escape the inevitable condemnation of society and his own moral qualms. By accentuating the marginality of homosexual, such novels brought society together around common values and fostered an artificial a sense of unity. *Septembernovelle*,[131] Arnolt Bronnen's very pessimistic experimental novel (1923), tells the tragic tale of a married man, father of a child, who falls in love with a young man named Franz. This love is completely liberating for him; he discovers pleasure, exaltation, he loses all sense of prudence. Finally, the wife kills the boy, then commits suicide; Huber commits suicide in turn. *Tu seras seul* (*You Will Be Alone*), by Alain Rox (1936), was a turning point in that it featured a young man who was well integrated into the Parisian homosexual scene.

In another style, the homosexual cycle by Willy and Ménalkas, *L'Ersatz d'amour* (*Ersatz Love*) (1923) and *Le Naufragé* (*The Shipwrecked Man*) (1924), cleverly shifts romantic conventions and is striking for its knowledge of the homosexual milieu and its lack of prejudices. Still, it is not a militant work, and is not free from contradictions. For instance, while the introduction to the *Substitute for Love* tries to sound scientific (quoting Freud, Havelock Ellis and Krafft-Ebing), the authors hasten to add that they believe that "woman is better than the Substitute" and that the history which is about to follow was inspired by the experiences of a friend. In each of his novels Willy closely follows the currents of the day and modulates his racy themes so that they are close to what, in the end, are the rather conventional expectations of his readers. The story takes place on both sides of the Great War with a young Frenchman, Marc Renneval, who discovers homosexuality in Germany, in 1913, with a young officer, Carl von Rudorff. When war is declared, Carl deserts out of homosexual fidelity and his

---

130. See J.E. Rivers, *Proust and the Art of Love*, New York, Columbia University Press, 1980, 327 pages, p.25.

131. Arnolt Bronnen, *Septembernovelle* [1923], Stuttgart, Klett-Cotta, 1989, 65 pages.

friend dies at the front. *The Shipwrecked Man* follows Carl in 1918. Now an active, militant homosexual, he cannot stop thinking of his lover, who he does not know has died. He hears the news while traveling in France, and commits suicide on his tomb at Verdun.

Generally speaking, French works were characterized by a taste for sordid descriptions with seedy bars, washed up male prostitutes, and drug addicts. Homosexuality is just a sub-plot, titillating to the reader. The sensational theme keeps the readers' interest but the conservative moral tone leaves the reader within his comfort zone. In the work of Charles-Etienne, *Les Désexués: roman de mœurs* (1924), the hero, Sandro, "pretty as a woman" and musically gifted, had his sexual initiation during childhood in the arms of a comrade, then was corrupted by a school official: "Never would this intellectual ... have claimed that the body is a holy temple which no one has the right to desecrate, that sensuality destroys the mind and that to upset a human's equilibrium is a crime as great as murder itself."[132] Sandro goes from one disaster to another as a prostitute in the "unsettling world of the sidewalk" and the public urinals, becomes an opium addict, a cocaine addict. A friend from his village arrives in Paris and she, too, descends into prostitution; she is initiated into sapphism. Approaching the age of forty, they decide to marry, but soon fall back into old ways; adopting a young girl could bring them redemption; but she, too, is seduced and is given to a brothel-keeper. Sandro kills his protector and ends his days in a psychiatric asylum; his wife dies and the girl goes on as a prostitute. On the topic of the homosexual downfall and the difficulty of redemption through marriage, Francis de Miomandre produced *Ces petits messieurs* (1922) and *Henry Marx Ryls: Un amour hors la loi* (1923). Even more ridiculous was *Amour inverti*, by Jean de Cherveix, which is nothing but a long, wild fantasy on the idea of a man transformed into a woman. A better effort on the same topic was *La Femme qui était en lui* (1937), by Maurice Rostand.

Homosexuality was not always the novel's principal theme. Many authors merely embellished their works with a few dashes of homosexuality. Sometimes a little dose of homosexuality was enough to raise a tale of adultery above the usual banalities. One example would be *Le Jeune Amant* (1928) by Paul Reboux, in which Helene Joussin, a young widow, meets Marcel Target, a young homosexual actor, at a Lenten ball. In another example, youthful fancies still allow the hero, if the story goes beyond adolescence, to revert to normal tastes without any

---

132. Charles-Étienne, *Les Désexués*, Paris, Curio, 1924, 267 pages, p.46.

risk. In *Classe 22* (1929) by Ernst Glaeser, adolescent homosexuality is chalked up to the war, paternal absence, and lax supervision by overwhelmed mothers. Similarly, in Joseph Breitbach's *Rival et rivale*[133] (1935), the war is used as the backdrop for a generalized scene of corruption. Sometimes, the title is catchy but one may in vain seek in vain any allusion to homosexuality in the novel; *Sodome et Berlin* (1929) by Jean Goll is a case in point.[134] Michel George-Michel's novel *Dans la fête de Venise* (1923), pretending to present a tableau of wild goings-on in Venice, tosses in an obligatory passage on homosexuals. One has the impression that a homosexual character has become essential to any novel that is in the least bit risqué, like the adulteress, the cocaine addict and the negro dancer.

Homosexuality always does not appear so explicitly. Generally, quality literary works show a reluctance to incite a scandal. In *La Confusion des sentiments* (1926), Stefan Zweig tries to sprinkle his pages little by little with openly homosexual references that gradually have the effect of allowing one to understand, without it being mentioned in so many words, that his character is an "invert."[135] In fact, it is the love relation, more than the homosexuality, which is at the center of the novel. Thomas Mann's works are also very rich in homosexual insinuations.[136] The famous *Death in Venice* (1912), largely autobiographical, shows an aging writer falling in love with the androgynous beauty of young Tadzio, a hopeless quest for youth and artistic purity which leads him to his death. In *Tonio Kröger* (1903), inversion is only suggested through a teen friendship, but homosexuality was already being used as a metaphor to express the sense of difference and exclusion, and to speculate on the fate of the artist. In *The Magic Mountain* (1924), Thomas Mann avoids a frank treatment of homosexuality: the homosexual attractions of Hans Castorp survive his adolescence only in a disguised fashion; the woman whom he loves corresponds to the same physical

133. The title of the German original is *Die Wandlung der Suzanne Dusseldorf.*

134. "Sodom and Gomorrha were recreated in Berlin. Drug-taking was no longer hidden, mysticism and belief in the paranormal were popularized, and despite $175, homosexual and lesbian leanings were expressed in public" (Jean Goll, *Sodome et Berlin*, Paris, Émile-Paul frères, 1929, 250 pages, p.139-140).

135. The professor had a bust of Ganymède and a Saint Sebastian; he read Shakespeare's sonnets and Whitman's poems and, in his thesis, the most scorching passages are reserved for Marlowe.

136. For a complete study of homosexuality in relation to Thomas Mann, see Gerhard Härle, *Männerweiblichkeit, zur Homosexualität bei Klaus und Thomas Mann*, Frankfurt-am-Main, Athenäum Verlag, 1988, 412 pages; and Karl Werner Böhm, *Zwischen Selbstsucht und Verlangen, Thomas Mann und das Stigma Homosexualität*, Wurzbourg, Königshausen & Neumann, 1991, 409 pages. See also chapter four.

ideal as the boy with whom he was in love at school, and she repeats the same seductive scenario. Furthermore, one notes that there is an abstraction in both cases that enables Castorp to go on without wondering about his sexual identity. Thomas Mann reinstates homosexuality as a private matter. At the same time, his eagerness to deal with the subject is a reflection of his inability to accept his own homosexuality.

Lesbianism enjoyed a bit of a boost during inter-war period, particularly in France and England. The lesbian, sometimes scarcely differentiated from the flapper, was an exemplary modern subject. She was treated quite differently in literature than male homosexuals. First of all, the subject was more eroticized. The lesbian already had a long history.[137] As a fantasy character in men's literature, she was always used to inject additional erotic overtones into light novels. Unlike male love scenes, which must, thinks one, repulse the reader, one can vary *ad infinitum* the scenes of kisses and Sapphic caresses which seem suggestive yet unthreatening.

The work of Gustave Binet-Valmer, *Sur le sable couchées* (1929) is an excellent example of this new genre. The insignificant plot is only used to set the scene for somewhat naughty amorous relations. An American lesbian, Mabel Waybelet, rich, beautiful and masculine, sets to work seducing a fairly androgynous French girl, Martine. The conclusion is a triumph for a certain idea of morals, when the perverted girl returns to her mother, who has been reminded of her family duties, and the lesbian curiously leaves off her morbid inclinations when a virile man takes her in hand. Suzanne de Callias, a friend of Willy, published *Erna, jeune fille de Berlin* in 1932. The work attempted to be a digest of German modernity; with slender Erna in her short hair, working as a journalist, goes through all the milieux that are "representative" of decadence: Berlin's Eldorado, the Paris Club de la Faubourg, Vienna's psychoanalytical circles. She meets a crowd of homosexual of both sexes and notes of an acquaintance: "The other day he declared that he was not for men. Nowadays, you can be arrested for that."[138] Unhappy Erna finishes her career by marrying a young man on the far Right, who obliges her to stay home. In this sense the novel seemed to presage in late 1932 the approaching collapse of the homosexual myth and the return to the traditional moral order. *Notre-Dame-de-Lesbos* (1914), Charles-Étienne's block-

---

137. We could cite at random Diderot's *La Religieuse*, Baudelaire's "Femmes damnées" and numerous decadent novels: Charles Montfort, *Le Roman d'une saphiste*, Adrienne Saint-Agen, *Amants féminins...*

138. Ménalkas, *Erna, jeune fille de Berlin*, Paris, Éditions des Portiques, 1932, 254 pages.

buster, inaugurated the genre of the lesbian novel with documentary overtones. The old story of a love that can never be is the pretext for running through all the fashionable lesbian hotspots and talking about female homosexuality. In the novel, pseudonyms are used but famous lesbians are depicted.

Sometimes the more subtle lesbian novels took the form of contemporary works pretending to illustrate how morality was evolving. In *Garçonne* (1922), Victor Margueritte gives a none too flattering portrait of his heroine of the moment: bisexual, constantly on the make, opium addict, heroin addict, cocaine addict, but never satisfied. The flapper, as the term *Garçonne* indicates, aspires to being a man, and especially when it comes to love.[139] It would be an error, however, to think that Margueritte is for women's liberation; the "garçonne" is heading for a fall. "A proud joy buoyed her up, at the thought of her double unfolding. 'Men!' She smiled scornfully. Just by wanting to, she had become physically, and morally, their equal. And however, there was no point in avoiding it, she had to admit that somewhere, in the bitterness of her revenge, was a vague uneasiness... Loneliness? Sterility? She couldn't feel its movement, yet, but an invisible worm was there, in the very magnificence of the fruit.[140] Here is an example of the dominant male notion, which supposed that the woman who evaded her marital and maternal functions was incomplete and unhappy. Moreover, the novel's conclusion brings a just reward: the *garçonne* falls in love with a man who saves her life, and she marries him. Here again, this novel which was such a scandalous success in the inter-war period, can be read as a metaphor of the evolving views on the woman's place, in particular the homosexual woman's, during that era: the return to order, presented as the "natural order," rehabilitating all the "deviants" into a single and undifferentiated social body. In fact, the novel was made into a film in 1923, and it was banned as "a deplorably distorted view of the character of French girls."[141] When the play was performed at the theatre de l'Alhambra in Lille, on February 26, 1927, it caused a riot; two agents were wounded and four students arrested. It took a group of gendarmes to restore order.[142]

Many novels were more clearly hostile to female homosexuality, and the British ones in particular attacked it with irony and derision. The two best-

---

139. Victor Margueritte, *La Garçonne* [1922], Paris, Flammarion, 1978, 269 pages.
140. *Ibid.*, p.135.
141. Cited by Georges Bernier, *"La Garçonne,"* in Olivier Barrot and Pascal Ory (dir.), *Entre-deux-guerres*, Paris, François Bourin, 1990, 631 pages, p.161.
142. *Le Temps*, 27 February 1927.

known works are Compton Mackenzie's novels *Vestal Fire* (1927) and *Extraordinary Women* (1928), set in the homosexual and especially lesbian community that grew up in Capri (Siren, in the novel).[143] This decadent and frivolous world already seemed dated in 1927, but Mackenzie contributed to making it the symbol of homosexuality in the English style, smart and dilettantish. *Vestal Fire* is mostly about male homosexual relations. The hero, Marsac, is given to every excess; he goes after the young shepherds of the island, smokes opium, writes verse and even a novel. All his weaknesses are excused: after all, he made his studies at Oxford. "Ten years before, while he was a student, he had been a major figure in the hottest decadent cliques at Oxford."[144] At "Siren," the ancient taste dominates. Marsac published a well-named literary review *Symposium*, with a photograph of a young boy in a bathing suit on the cover, his thick hair falling in a fringe about his face and cut in the middle to form the shape of a heart. This is the world of before the First World War; carefree, esthetist, it seems to have stepped straight out of a play by Oscar Wilde or an Aubrey Beardsley engraving. In *Extraordinary Women*, Capri discovers the war and the changes that came with the 1920s. The island becomes above all a haven for lesbians. The novel is just a succession of adventures in love, festivals, quarrels and reconciliations against a background of small jealousies; lesbian love, according to Mackenzie, is not based in reality, it is just a distraction for fashionable young ladies or disturbed artists, and will end with the first man they meet: "All summer he said that these poor women were running each other only because there was a shortage of men."[145] The intelligence of the women also seems questionable: "Oh, you should read André Gide. I am mad about André Gide. I don't understand a word he writes."[146] However, each character is based on a famous lesbian and the novel, beyond the caricature, is an accurate depiction of the trends of the time. Frivolity

143. At the turn of the century, Capri became a favorite holiday resort for homosexuals; some of them moved there permanently after the trial of Oscar Wilde in order to escape scandal or to feel more free in expressing their sexuality. Among the famous visitors was the baron d'Adelswald-Fersen (Marsac, in the novel), Somerset Maugham, E.F. Benson, J.E. Brooks and his wife Romaine Brooks, Natalie Barney, Scott Fitzgerald, D.H. Lawrence, and Norman Douglas. Willy described the Isle of Capri as: "a miniature capital of sodomy, the Mecca of inversion, a Geneva or a Moscow of the future internationalism of homosexuality" (*Le Troisième Sexe, op. cit.*, p.67-68).

144. Compton Mackenzie, *Vestal Fire* [1927], London, The Hogarth Press, 1986, 420 pages, p.92.

145. Id., *Extraordinary Women* [1928], London, The Hogarth Press, 1986, 392 pages, p.298.

146. *Ibid.*, p.261.

prevails and the worship of beauty is omnipresent.[147] These lesbians sacrifice to the male fashion and give each other men's names, like Rory, who does not go out without her bulldogs and dines in a tuxedo.

Modeled on Natalie Barney, Olimpia Leigh refuses to adopt new conventions: — I like women who are profoundly and ineluctably women. It is their femininity which I find attractive. Really, in a certain sense, I prefer an effeminate boy to a masculine girl.[148] She severely judges the butch who denies the values of femininity: — Poor Freemantle is obviously one of those women with exaggerated sexual tendencies who never had much luck with men ... Her natural inclinations are, I am sure, absolutely normal, but discovering that men remained like marble when she danced with them, she gave up on them.[149]

It is interesting to note that it is the feminine Olimpia Leigh who embodies lesbian militancy and the rejection of men in the most radical way: "She imagined a race of homosexual men and women who would exhaust the physical expression of sexuality by the repetitive futility of the sterile act. The instinct of sublimation would then be refreshed, and finally one would obtain a race of creative spirits which would have completely mastered the body.[150]

Two pure parodies can be added to the list, inspired by contemporary events in Britain: *The Girls of Radclyffe Hall* by Adela Quebec[151] and *The Sink of Solitude* (1928) by Egan Beresford,[152] a lampoon on Radclyffe Hall and her book *The Well of Loneliness*, accompanied by a series of satirical drawings in decadent style, representing lesbians as satyrs. The lampoon has no moralizing intention; on the contrary, it makes fun of all those who were indignant at the Radclyffe Hall book and in particular at the legal proceedings brought by Hicks.[153]

There were also a few works that sought to explore the nuances of homosexuality in a less commonplace way, and, ignoring the equivocal effects, created lesbian novels supported by medical information. This type of work expressed a more sympathetic tone, taking a gentler and more pitying attitude toward the lesbian, victim of an inclination she did not choose and of a society that rejected

---

147. *Ibid.*, p.38.
148. *Ibid.*, p.251.
149. *Ibid.*, p.252.
150. *Ibid.*, p.231.
151. See chapter three.
152. Egan Beresford, *The Sink of Solitude*, "Series of satirical drawings occasioned by some recent events performed by Egan Beresford to which is added a preface by P.R. Stephenson, and a Lampoon Verse composed by several hands," London, The Herness Press, 1928.

her, as she bears her cross until death. In *Bonifas*, (1925) by Jacques de Lacretelle, the heroine Marie Bonifas is ugly and masculine. Her early loves were unhappy. At the age of twenty, she finds herself orphaned; a rich girl in a small provincial town, her refusal to marry wins her a bad reputation. Soon, her love for Claire gives rise to lies; when her friend dies of consumption (!), Marie goes wild: she smokes, rides a horse, and takes to wearing "typically lesbian" clothing, including men's boots and a cane.[154] Threatening letters started to arrive, the windows were smashed, outrageous graffiti appeared, and insults came from all sides. The war offered redemption: Marie distinguishes herself by her organization and her courage; she saves the city. At the end of the war, her legend was spread throughout France, "the heroine of Vermont." But she remains sad and lonely. Marie's fate is sealed. She cannot know happiness; it is unattainable for women of her kind. Lacretelle is not optimistic; the solution which he proposes is the rational use of the lesbian's social qualities. To be forgiven for her "vice," she must devote herself entirely to society and make her virile strengths (usually a handicap) into an asset. Of course, it is clear that social acceptance on these terms requires abandoning any idea of sexual gratification and life shared with a woman.

Rosamund Lehmann's novel *Dusty Answer* (1927) was a big hit;[155] it contrasts romantic friendships with adult homosexuality. The heroine, Judith, who has been in love with a boy, Roddy, since childhood, is attracted by one of her classmates at Cambridge, Jennifer. The climate in the dormitory is poisonous, Jennifer's beauty and her popularity turn the other girls against Judith. Roddy, who is also at Cambridge, is going through the same thing in a special friendship with his comrade, Tony. Jennifer is soon seduced by an older woman, Geraldine, an affirmed lesbian with all the stereotypical traits: she "smoked like a man,"[156]

---

153. It ends with a long poem recapitulating the affair as a parody, roughly — Sing on, O worldly muse, Radclyffe Hall/ And as she wrote a story that was bound/ to fall like a ton of bricks on those narrow-minded souls/ Crushing James Douglas and Sir Joynson Hicks/ [...] The Greek isles where Sappho burned/ We will analyze them through the lens of Freud and Jung/ As Sappho burned with her own special flame / God understands her; we must do the same/ Saying, of such eccentricities, / It's true, poor thing, she was born that way" (a literal translation).

154. Jacques de Lacretelle, *La Bonifas* [1925], Paris, Gallimard, 1979, 338 pages, p.201.

155. In *La Bâtarde*, Violette Leduc tells how deeply the book moved her: "Two teenage girls as lovers, and a woman dared to write it. [...] Jennifer. I was obsessed with the name. Do you love Jennifer? Do you prefer Jennifer over the others? Do you find her a little too fresh, Jennifer? Oh, no! Wild? You think Jennifer is too wild? Not Jennifer" (*La Bâtarde*, Paris, Gallimard, 1964, 462 pages, p.159).

and was masculine and sensual in appearance. Her broad and heavy-featured face and thick neck, tanned skin, how could Jennifer be so lacking in taste! ... — Oh no, it was not true. In spite of all that, she was beautiful; she exerted a disturbing fascination.[157] Jennifer is distracted from Judith and devotes herself to what one can guess must be a voracious sexual relationship with Geraldine. She is lost forever for her friend who does not understand this attraction and who, exiting college, quite naturally turns to men.

In fact, while the English literature of the inter-war period was rich in lesbian characters, the "noir" treatment of sapphism was generally preferred. The lesbian was depicted as a woman who was hard, authoritative, but with a disquieting charm, on the lookout for girls or innocent wives in order to steal them from society and to submit them to a tyrannical yoke.[158] Generally, the seduced young woman is saved and the "real" lesbian expiates her sin, rejected by all. In Francis Brett Young's *White Ladies* (1935), Arabella, a seventeen-year-old girl, falls for the charm of her school director, Miss Cash, a heinous and egocentric lesbian. She soon recognizes her error and leaves her friend for a boy. Naomi Royde-Smith had two extremely depressing novels on female homosexuality. In *The Tortoiseshell Cat* (1925), a young teacher (a recurring stereotype) falls in love with one with her neighbors, a very beautiful woman with black hair, Victoria Vanderleyden, called Victor by her friends. Victoria fools around with many women and has fun seducing men, whom she leads to suicide. Here again, the young woman discovers the "real" nature of her partner in time, and leaves her. *The Island, A Love Story* (1930) pushes the storyline a bit farther. Goosey, a neglected young redhead, has hated men since one of them rejected her. She goes after a girl her own age, Flossie (known as Almond), who is vain, feminine, and ravishing. After Almond gets married, Goosey, who has become a fashion designer, sets up shop on an island, Rockmouth. She refuses an invitation to marry and her reputation suffers from her various manias. When Almond leaves her husband and returns to Goosey, it only excites the local ill will. The two women live together for a few years but continual arguments and jealousy bring their friendship to an end. Almond ends up remarrying whereas Goosey ends up alone, scorned by all, an old maid who is half mad. In *Unnatural Death* (1927) by Dorothy Sayers, the

---

156. Rosamund Lehmann, *Dusty Answer* [1927], London, Collins, 1978, 355 pages, p.188.
157. *Ibid.*, p.197.
158. For another example of a lesbian school director who corrupts and exerts her influence over the students and teachers, see Clemence Dane, *Regiment of Women* (1917; London, Greenwood Press, 1978, 345 pages).

lesbian becomes the quintessential criminal. Under cover of a police intrigue, the story promulgates the worst homophobic prejudices. The old maid, Miss Climpson, who conducts the investigation with Mr. Winsey, is used as a foil to highlight the depravity of the modern woman in contrast to the traditional English correctness, without however tarring all the unmarried people in England with the same brush. But the message is clear: you'd better learn to tell the difference between the old maid and her demoniacal double, the lesbian.[159]

The criminal lesbian and psychopath came into vogue in the inter-war period. The most famous example is by the writer and neurologist Alfred Döblin, *Die beiden Freundinnen und ihr Giftmord (The Poisoning)* (1924), which is based on a news item from the time. The terse style, the way the intrigue is examined all contribute to fixing in the reader's mind the image of two female neurotics, not very intelligent, so dominated by their mutual passion that they lose sight of any elementary rules. Lesbians come across as deformed beings, bordering on crime and abnormality just through their sexuality. The two heroines, Elli Link and Margarete Bende, are in Berlin, married to husbands whom they do not love. They seduce each other, and begin writing back and forth. To a large extent their relationship is based on hatred of their husbands, which they use to justify themselves, masking the reprehensible bizarreness of their love which they themselves consider guilty and criminal.[160] The connection finishes in the drama. Elli poisons her husband with arsenic. With its death, the autopsy reveals the murder. She is arrested, along with her friend. At the trial, the medical experts testify. One of them insists they are intellectually retarded, another directly blames their homosexuality: "The cause of this profound hatred is in particular the homosexual inclination of these women who found it intolerable to live with the demands of their husbands and who, at the same time, in their aspirations to be together were guided, as Link said, only by one obsession: to be free."[161] Elli Link was sentenced to four years in prison, Margarete to eighteen months.

As these kinds of writings became fashionable, not to mention the considerable number of homosexual works and stories of boarding-school romances, they had a decisive influence. Homosexuality was treated in a tragic or heart-rending fashion to encourage readers to be more tolerant, to have pity and under-

---

159. Dorothy Sayers, *L'autopsie n'a rien donné* [*Unnatural Death*, 1927], Paris, London, Morgan, 1947, 253 pages.

160. Alfred Döblin, *L'Empoisonnement* [*Die beiden Freundinnen und ihr Giftmord*, 1924], Arles, Actes Sud, 1988, 108 pages, p.50.

161. *Ibid.*, p.89.

standing. However, the very concept of fashion suggests that this was just one in the continuous series of transitory passions and casts doubt on the notion that public attitudes had really changed much.

The Homosexual as a Symbol of Modernity

In the Twenties, homosexuality became a symbol of modernity, mainly in the artistic and literary fields. *La Vie parisienne* describes the "modern girl" as someone who "has read *Lady Chatterley's Lover*. She knows how children are made and how not to make any. Natural history is not foreign to her, nor anecdotal history, nor the various ways that animals and people make love in their various postures. For a long time now, it has been acceptable to say anything in front of her, and she will understand more than you say. She has seen licentious paintings and obscene photographs, she is not unaware of reality. She knows by science and, to a fairly large degree, by experience. She has slept and not slept with a cherished girlfriend."[162] The term "modern" is used to indicate a great freedom of morals. Thus when the police in Toulon arrested a young man, Giovanni Conforti, he retorted that he was "a modern man who loves people of both sexes."[163]

Homosexuality had become synonymous with the rejection of conventions; it was a means for artists to express their rejection of traditions, middle-class values, and the world from before 1914. It was associated with revolt, vital energy, pure sex, and also with intellectualism, vice, and a way to erase the memory of the horrors of the war in a burst of pleasure. Many avant-garde heterosexual painters in the Twenties were pre-occupied with representations of the homosexual scene. Rudolf Schlichter made a specialty of fetishistic representations. Homosexual bars were featured in *La Petite Chaumière* by Georg Grosz, in 1927, and Otto Dix's *Eldorado*. The screaming colors advertise the harsh makeup of transvestites. Dix was interested in unusual figures from the Bohemian fringes of society; in 1923, he produced a portrait of the homosexual jeweller Karl Krall, whom he represented in a very ambiguous way, in costume, hands on his hips, with his waistline drawn in and a feminine-looking chest. Sometimes irony prevails, as in *Le Dieu des coiffeurs* (*God of the Hairdressers*), a watercolor from 1922, showing a naked, very effeminate young man with very glossy hair and moustache, floating in the foreground amid the instruments of his profession.

---

162. Éryximaque, "La jeune fille moderne," *La Vie parisienne*, 1934.
163. AN, F7 13960 (2), Toulon, 14 September 1932.

For Grosz, the vice and criminality of Berlin were just a prolongation of the horrors of the war. His drawings are also the reflection of his revolutionary engagement. In his *Ecce homo* (1923), he denounces the erotic obsessions of the bourgeoisie, drawing a sinister picture of a world that has been cast adrift. Christian Schad specialized in the genre depicting mores of the times. He published illustrations, for example, for Curt Moreks' *Guide du Berlin débauché* and many lithographs of homosexual bars, like *Adonisdiele* (1930) and *Bürger-Casino* (1930). In the painting that bears his name (1927), Count Saint-Genois of Anneaucourt is arrayed between a transvestite and a woman, who seems to fear competition from the intruder. The count's latent homosexuality is revealed by the discrete placement of the characters in the background.[164]

The "New Woman" is constantly evoked, as the very image even of modernity. *Sonja*, a portrait by Christian Schad from 1928, is the prototype: the model, dressed in black, with short hair, a cigarette-holder in hand, sits alone at a table in a restaurant. *Burbot* (1927-1928) uses similar elements. The dour young woman, eyes circled in black against a livid skin, wears short hair and a dark tuxedo over a white shirt. She too is alone in a bar or a nightclub whose lights are reflected in a mirror in the background. Then there is the vitriolic portrait of the journalist Sylvia von Harden, by Otto Dix (1926), showing the powerful personality of the model but in blood-red tones. Here again we see the cigarette, the monocle, the cocktail, underscoring the independence of the woman. *Les Deux amies (The Two Friends)* by Christian Schad (1928) shows two women with immense eyes, short hair, and a distracted air, each on masturbating, showing the slippery slope from "New Woman" to "lesbian."

In the literary field, Hans Henny Jahnn's experimentation in *Perrudja* (1929), rest on a set of bisexual themes and an exaltation of the androgynous.[165] The subversive character of the work was very quickly detected by the critics. *Völkischer Beobachter* of June 9, 1923 reacted to his play *Der Arzt, sein Weib, sein Sohn* while talking about the "Zionist mentality" and perversion: "What this play is about, unfortunately, is a homage to child abduction, pederasty, divorce, sodomy, incest, sadism and assassination."[166] Reaction to *Perrudja* was violent and in particular it was described as "the disgusting outpourings of a sick mind."[167] The symbolic weight of homosexuality was perceived early on by

---

164. Sergiusz Michalski, *Nouvelle objectivité*, Cologne, Taschen, 1994, 219 pages, p.47.

165. Hans Henny Jahnn, *Perrudja* [1929], Paris, José Corti, 1995, 802 pages, p.234.

166. Cited by Friedhelm Krey, *Hans Henny Jahnn und die mannmännliche Liebe*, Berlin, Peter Lang, 1987, 458 pages, p.14.

Thomas Mann who, in his book *On Marriage*, legitimates inversion because of its artistic and aesthetic potential: "One may justifiably qualify homosexuality as the erotic of esthetics.... It is 'free love,' in that it implies sterility, a dead end, a lack of consequences and responsibility. Nothing happens as a result of it, will not form the basis for anything, it is art for art's sake, which on the aesthetic level can be a very proud and free attitude, though without any doubt immoral."[168] Homosexuality is art for art's sake; in this formula Thomas Mann summarized the topicality of the phenomenon; homosexuality was modern, a symbol of the gratuitous act, just like the murder of Lafcadio or the poems of Kurt Schwitters. A whole generation murdered by the war was recalled in this useless, irresponsible and sterile act.

This interpretation of homosexuality as modernity was primarily a German phenomenon. Not everyone in the avant-garde granted homosexuality such a place of honor. The Surrealist movement expressed particularly negative opinions on the subject. Research on sexuality conducted by the surrealist movement from January 1928 to August 1932, in twelve meetings, with a varying cast of characters participants, is edifying in this respect.[169] The worst homophobic prejudices are stated there, and rare are the voices that defend the "pederasts." Furthermore, René Crevel was notably absent; he undoubtedly would have been extremely isolated in the debate. At the very first meeting, January 27, 1928, homosexuality was attacked very brutally. Raymond Queneau was the only one, with Prévert, to express tolerance. Pierre Unik said, "From the physical point of view, pederasty disgusts me as much as excrement, and from the moral point of view I condemn it." Breton exploded: "What pederasts are proposing to human tolerance is a mental and moral deficit that shows signs of becoming systematized and of paralyzing all the institutions that I respect." Many surrealists, like Breton, would not even hear about it: "I absolutely oppose the discussion continuing on this subject. If this is turning into an advertisement for pederasty, I am leaving." The debate could not go on, for the reactions were too strong and irrational. Hatred for pederasts[170] was expressed in the strong,

---

167. Paul Fechter, *Die neue Literatur*, January 1931, cited *ibid.*, p.15.

168. Thomas Mann, *Sur le mariage* [1925], bilingual edition, Paris, Aubier-Flammarion, 1970, 191 pages, p.55-57.

169. Surrealism Archives, *Recherches sur la sexualité*, January 1928-August 1932, Paris, Gallimard, 1990, 212 pages.

170. André Breton corrected Ilya Ehrenburg and others on this point when they said that the surrealist movement was a bunch of pederasts.

insulting language reserved for those from whom one wishes to separate oneself absolutely, those with whom one cannot have any "relationship." "For these people I feel only antipathy, deep and organic. There is no common moral ground between these people and me." (Marcel Noll).

Sapphism did not elicit the same response. André Breton regained his equilibrium as soon as his integrity as a male was no longer under threat: "I find lesbians very interesting." Yves Tanguy acknowledged his "indifference" on the subject. Albert Valentin responded, "Very favorable to relations between women. I like to help out, even with the woman whom I love. Pederasts disgust me more than anything in the world." Here we find the traditional male attitude; he feels attacked in his virility by any sign of pederasty, yet finds nothing reprehensible in female relations, especially when he can look on. On the other hand, he is adamantly against the masculine lesbians, who compete with him on his own turf. Paul Eluard responded, "The greatest hatred for masculine lesbians, the greatest weakness for lesbians who remain women." In spite of the so-called worship of the woman celebrated by Breton and Eluard, the sexuality of a surrealist is first and foremost a masculine sexuality, concerned with masculine desire and pleasure.

Women's voices did not advance the debate very far. Katia Thirion was traditional: "Between two men, the idea disgusts me completely. I have no desire to visualize these relations. Between two women, I might; but I have never done it, myself." Simone Vion affected a great sexual freedom: "That does not disgust me at all, I have had very good friends among the pederasts and this idea would not bother me. No representation. I literally turned down several women because [I] did not [desire them], but my turn must be coming, soon." Only Mme. Léna acknowledged a marked lesbian inclination: "For men, I don't mind it at all and find the thought exciting. Two men caressing each other — but not doing each other up the ass. I would love to see it. I have no problem as far as women, I am completely [in favor] of these relation. I have had sixteen women." The resigned attitude of these women is surprising, they do not seek in any way to affirm their right to an autonomous sexuality or to question the chauvinist myths proposed by their interlocutors. In the final analysis, the surrealist position on homosexuality appears traditional, conservative, even reactionary, typically middle-class, respectful of convention and rife with prejudices. The artistic avant-garde was not always the sexual avant-garde.

A Vague Homoeroticism: Youth and Androgyny

Homosexuality in the inter-war period cannot be dissociated from the topic of youth: the homosexual erotic ideal was that of the young lad, one's friend at school, the German friend with a fit and muscular body and such an insouciant air that any compunctions were easily overcome. Homosexual sexuality, in the Twenties, was often seen as an adolescent sexuality, irresponsible, uninhibited. Sachs summarized it as follows: "Furthermore, it may be that what keeps me going in loving boys, as much and more than the pleasure is that climate of almost childish complicity which I find more charming than the exercise of full virile force."[171]

Youth movements really took off in the Twenties and Thirties.[172] In these movements, there was an emphasis on contact with nature, and a preoccupation with hygiene. Boys, sorted by age brackets, wore shorts and shirts with open collars. They learned autonomy and a sense of responsibility, on their own. The camp was a kind of leadership school, which imparted a paternalist ideology. At the same time youth inns were introduced in France by Marc Sangnier,[173] the founder of Sillon, following the German example. And it was in Germany that the Jugendbewegungen, of which the Wandervogel was the most famous example, made their greatest strides. In 1926, 4.3 million out of 9 million young people were members of a youth association.[174] Of this number, the "confederated" movement (bündisch, emanating from the Wandervogel) had only 51,000 members, but its influence in society was particularly strong (even if Detlev J.K. Peukert doubts its real impact in the daily life of young people).

---

171. Maurice Sachs, *Le Sabbat* [written in 1939, published in 1946], Paris, Gallimard, 1960, 298 pages, p.167.

172. In England, the number of Boy Scouts went from 152,000 in 1913 to 438,000 in 1938, and Baden-Powell became one of the best-known names in the country. In France, scouting took root just before the First World War, first among the Protestants. The Catholics were more reticent; they founded scout troops in 1920 and guides in 1923. In 1933, France had more than 50,000 scouts (boys), 12,000 French "éclaireur unionists" and 6000 "éclaireurs" (scouts).

173. Sangnier founded the Ligue française des auberges de jeunesse (League of youth hostels) in 1929-1930. The lay Center for Youth Hostels (CLAJ) was founded in 1933, for youngsters of the left.

174. That is more than one out of every two boys and just under one out of two girls; of the total, 1.6 million youngsters belonged to sporting associations and 1.2 million to religious groups. The young workers' movement had 368,000 members (not to mention the thousand or so young communists). See Detlev J.K. Peukert, *La République de Weimar, op. cit.*, p.98.

Founded in 1895 by Karl Fischer and Ludwig Gurlitt, in the beginning Wandervogel was made up of high-school pupils and educators who wanted certain reforms. After the war, its promotion of nationalism was reinforced around the principle of the chief and it developed a myth of youth as the regenerative force of the German people.[175] The war had encouraged the rise of this myth, propagated in particular by the book with powerful homoerotic overtones by Walter Flex, *Der Wanderer zwischen beiden Welten*, published in 1917. It went through twenty-nine editions, with 250,000 copies printed in less than two years. Flex met Ernst Wusche in the spring of 1915, on the Eastern front, but in August Wusche was killed, leaving Flex, who had seen him as the future savior of Germany, in despair. He wrote his book in homage to Wusche's memory, giving an idealized image of his friend, a symbol of the patriotic youth that gave its life for Germany. There was a striking similarity with the myth of Rupert Brooke, which developed at the same time in England.[176]

Youth was set in opposition adult world, which was seen as the world of official authoritarianism, and enacted its own rules, its own values and its own way of life. It was often perceived as a danger and delinquency was seen as a growing problem. The purpose of many of the political or religious organizations was to rein in young people and reintegrate them into a more structured environment. Wandervogel encouraged experience of new lifestyles and was at the avant-garde of the sexual reform. It developed a homoerotic ideology based on male supremacy. Under Weimar, there were no independent leisure organizations for girls, and while they were accepted in certain youth movements they were mostly confined to the family sphere, without having the occasion to develop relationships autonomously.

The great theorist of homoeroticism was Hans Blüher[177] who, in his book *Der Wandervogel als erotisches Phänomen* (1912), asserted that homosexuality was the bond that gave the movement cohesion and contributed to its success. According to Blüher, the youth movements were secretly governed by erotic relations (generally sublimated) between the adolescents and the team leaders.

---

175. On the myth of youth, see the very complete work by Thomas Koebner, Rolf-Peter Janz and Frank Trommler (dir.), *"Mit uns zieht die neue Zeit." Der Mythos Jugend*, Frankfurt-am-Main, Suhrkamp, 1985, 621 pages.

176. See Robert Wohl, *The Generation of 1914*, London, Weidenfeld & Nicolson, 1980, 307 pages.

177. See chapter six. In 1912, Blüher was 24, and was himself a member of the first *Wandervogel*.

Much of the leadership in Jugendbewegung were homosexuals, for (according to him) they were the only ones ready to devote themselves to young people. Blüher's book had enormous repercussions He made homosexuality a symbol of adolescent revolt against bourgeoisie family morals, and a response to the impossibility of living a completely free heterosexual life in a puritan society.

In 1908-1909, after the Eulenburg affair, anti-homosexual hysteria also struck the youth movements. Several leaders, like Wilhelm Jansen (1866-1943) who was part of Gemeinschaft der Eigenen, were forced to resign and Wandervogel was divided into two distinct groups. In November 1910, the Jung-Wandervogel was founded, apart from Alt-Wandervogel. The new movement aimed to be more radical and asserted friendship (as it was defined by Blüher) as a founding principle, even if Otto Piper, one of the cofounders, noted that the group had no more homosexuals in it than other movements.[178]

And indeed, ties between homosexuality and youth groups were not restricted to the back-to-nature movement and the sports associations or, for that matter, movements on the far Right. In Curt Bondy's 1922 book *Die proletarische Jugendbewegung*, a chapter is devoted to the question of sexual "inversion" in the working-class youth movements. Although he was in opposition to Blüher, he did not deny that homosexuality existed in the proletarian movements but insisted rather that these were merely adolescent attachments. Moreover, he saw the homoerotization of the youth movements as a direct consequence of the pressures of middle-class values which inculcated in young men a fear and contempt for women. Bondy concluded by noting that there was no fundamental difference between the middle-class movements and the proletarian movements, but that the latter would have to make an effort not to encourage the development of "inversion" within their own ranks.

In the youth movements, homoeroticism took the form of ardent friendships: "Hand in hand, I walked back home with Hans. Inside of us, [our hearts] sang and palpitated, and while we were in the dark entryway hanging up our things, he rested against the wall and took my head in his hands and looked at me for a long time, and finally he hugged me. 'And now, we eat!' he sang, and then I brought him back to train, and I ran back to the house to discharge my joy."[179] The ideal was to keep this friendship pure; but the struggle between physical

178. See Ulfried Geuter, *Homosexualität in der deutschen Jugendbewegung*, Frankfurt-am-Main, Suhrkamp, 1994, 373 pages.

179. Excerpted from a note in an anonymous boy's sketchbook, 1917, cited by Ulfried Geuter, *ibid.*, p.125.

attraction and desire for purity tore at the boys who did not know how to face these contradictory needs: "We looked for friends and we found them; we trembled in shame before the kisses and the embraces, we dreamers and enlightened boys; and we noticed one day that we were no longer children: puberty had caught us in its spell! We suspected and we saw Sex everywhere, yes, even in Schopenhauer; we even found sex in a warm handshake! And sex, which we feared, seemed disgusting to us."[180]

Ulfried Geuter, who made a systematic study of sexuality in the youth movements, noted that genital sex was taboo in the Wandervogel. The movement's own press and the boys' journals carefully concealed any sexual intercourse, especially any relations between boys and leaders or boys of the same age. He supposed that homosexuality was neither less nor more widespread there than in the German schools. Like the colleges, the youth movements developed a homoerotic mythology that favored complete homosexual relations. On the other hand the Wandervogel, even if it was not specifically homosexual, contributed to disseminating in public the image of a younger generation of ambiguous sexuality, undifferentiated, free in its body.

Body worship is one of the essential elements of the inter-war symbolism.[181] Esthetic references to the combined topics of sun, water and nudity were common, with the naked, muscular, young, androgynous body embodying all that was modern, healthy and athletic. This worship of the body and of youth, which was also felt in France and England, was especially heightened in Germany. In the Twenties, nudity was still associated with the liberals,[182] with the explosion of pleasure associated with the Weimar Republic and the apogee of Berlin. The erotic and particularly the homoerotic value of these representations was very powerful. The painter Fidus (Hugo Höppener) made a name for himself with illustrations in the Munich weekly magazine *Jugend* and his representations of naked young men worshipping the sun. More and more, photography turned to images of nude bodies, and taken not in the studio but in the great outdoors. The group of friends that created the Photo Alliance in France expressed the *joie de vivre* of the Popular Front through the liberation of the body. Cecil Beaton's photographs and, even more, those of Herbert List and Horst P.

---

180. Rudolf B. to Alfred Kurella, letter dated 1920, cited *ibid.*, p.130.

181. See George L. Mosse, *Nationalism and Sexuality, Respect and Abnormal Sexuality in Modern Europe*, New York, Howard Fertig, 1985, 232 pages.

182. Thus the socialist song: *Brüder, zur Sonne, zur Freiheit* ("Brothers, toward the sun, towards liberty").

Horst illustrate the triumph of the male body, and are charged with a powerful homoerotic force. Nazi Germany made the "perfect" body the illustration of the merit of the race.

The German notion of beauty in the inter-war period was primarily androgynous. As it was under Weimar, so it was thereafter, under the Third Reich: fair bodies, bronzed, with long and tapered limbs, with the hair slicked back embodied a timeless and almost asexual ideal. Already Thomas Mann noticed the new trend among youth: the lack of differentiation, the will to create a new kind of beauty that was disengaged from sexual stereotypes:

> — He verged on that idea of the androgyne that the romantics revere in friendship between the sexes, being equals on the human level.... It is no coincidence if their incipient capabilities coincide with the psychoanalytical discovery of the original and natural bisexuality of human beings. And if our young people — and we congratulate them! — experience a more serene and calmer attitude with respect to sexual problems than former generations were able to achieve, if this field is stripped of its most terrifying taboos, it all has to do with, and is in harmony with, the fact that the new generation is more detached and familiar with the homosexual phenomenon, and are more tolerant. As Blüher, our conscience, establishes a psychological link between this element and at least one manifestation of the youth movement, the Wandervogel. Without any doubt, homosexuality, the loving tie between men, sexual friendship, enjoys a certain favor today due to the climate of the times and it no longer appears to cultivated minds solely as a clinical monstrosity.[183]

The androgyny of bodies is fraught with strong homoerotic connotations. The evolution of representations of the body in the 1920s and 1930s shows two contradictory but complementary trends: the "masculinization" of the woman, and the "feminization" of the new generation of males. This fashion as most evident among apolitical youth, those who were Americanized and eager to attain the society of leisure, and who thus emphasized a break with the generation that had dragged the world into war. This category was visible really only in the Twenties, just until 1928-1929, before the Crash.

The topic of the androgyne was not just a fixture in artistic representations; it was also very seriously discussed as a basis for a new society, a response to the crisis of humanity as a whole. Camille Spiess developed this line of thought in writings that are now thankfully quite forgotten, but which enjoyed a certain vogue at the time. His example reveals very clearly the philosophical, political, sexual and racial fantasies that developed in tandem with the concept of androgyny and which, far from being neutral, could be used to convey dan-

---

183. Thomas Mann, *Sur le mariage, op. cit.,* p.53-55.

gerous and reactionaries ideas. Spiess was born in Geneva in 1878; he studied medicine and specialized in zoology. He was a disciple of Gobineau and also a follower of Mme. Förster, Nietzsche's sister. Of Nietzsche he retained primarily the theory of the superman (called "genius," in his work). His references were often many and contradictory: he quoted Plato, Stirner, Goethe, Whitman, Freud and Carpenter. He was savagely hostile to Magnus Hirschfeld, whose theory of a "third sex" he vigorously disputed. On top of all that he added a jumble of esoterica including readings of the Upanishads, the Kabala, theosophic writings, the thought of Lao-tse and Leibniz, Jakob Böhme and Jean-Paul, the poetry of Stefan George and astrology, including the advent of the Age of Aquarius, androgyne *par excellence*. His political choices are rather difficult to define; he published *L'Inversion sexuelle* at Éditions de l'En-dehors — which usually produced rather anarchistic texts; he was violently opposed to Action française, whose nationalist choice he disapproved: according to him, the true fatherland is not the nation but the race. In 1932, he wrote an open letter to Romain Rolland, denouncing "the bloodless humanitarism of contemporary idealism." On the whole, he could be defined as an anarchist on the right, with dubious ideas but with the logorrhea of an avenger, who tried to formulate a personal model on the fundamental themes of the era — race, sexuality, power — which he pompously dubbed psychosynthesis.

The Spiess œuvre is characterized above all by its hermetic, obsessive style and rigor. All his reflection is centered on the worship of the androgyne as the future of mankind and the higher form of humanity: "One must develop in oneself both the female and male powers of the flesh and the Spirit, childhood and adolescence, to build our liberation which is the erotic renaissance, the indestructible childhood of the human heart, born in the human conscience.[184] According to Spiess, the original man was an androgyne (he refers to Platonic myth), complete and perfect in form, and he aspired to become that again. The question of androgyny together with that of the improvement of the race encompassed the elimination of "impure" races." He found in androgyne the solution to the "Jewish problem," the embodiment of divine man, Dionysian or super-Christian in contrast to Israel, the mongrel, the fallen man with his clipped sex. In the same vein, the exaltation of the androgyne goes hand in hand with a con-

---

184. Camille Spiess, *Éros ou l'Histoire physiologique de l'homme*, Paris, Éditions de l'Athanor, 1932, 280 pages, p.36.

tempt for women, considered as the lower form of humanity; the improvement of the race could, according to Spiess, take place only with men as the basis.

Spiess associated androgyny with adolescence (which is not, in itself, original). On the other hand, he builds upon that a very complex theory aimed at showing that man passes through all the genders in the course of his life: first he is a woman (body, childhood), then a man (heart, adolescence), then both at the same time. As a result a man may become a woman (inversion), a man (version), or a genius, i.e. an androgyne (aversion). For Spiess, the genius is pederastic, while the invert is homosexual or is a degenerate. The pederast has as his ideal the body of the man, but his high spiritual aspirations bar him from the sex act. The declamatory style shows that homosexuality is severely condemned as a lower form of humanity: "Regeneration, asexual bisexuality, poetic, pederastic or parthenogenetic, the genius, unique and platonic love which is at the foundation of the Androgyne, of the normal, complete man, whose heart is in his head, of the man who never leaves his own milieu — this is not generation, the heterosexuality of those who are off balance, nor is it degeneracy, the homosexuality of those who are off balance — cuckolds and degenerates. In short, and to conclude, Pederasty is not homosexuality and the pederast is not a homosexual and never will be.[185] To arrive at genius, the man must be reborn from his on mind at the moment of puberty. No more sex act, no more contact with the other. The man generates himself. All the while celebrating eroticism and Dionysian forces with lengthy sentences, Spiess in fact expresses a rejection of the sexual as a whole. He is aiming for the formation of a race of geniuses, removed from all impure elements (women, homosexuals, Jews), who would be self-generating and who would dominate the world by their higher intelligence.

The theory of the androgyne was full of racist and totalitarian suggestions; it was founded on a pessimistic view of society and a desire to regenerate by a system of exclusion. It is a mystical form of eugenics, which may appear harmless since it is so unrealistic. However, such wild rantings found echoes in extremist milieux and could easily be coupled with traditional racist theories like those of Gobineau and all the antidemocratic and antimodernist critics: "The great merit of psychosynthesis is to prevent the evil of sexual or Jewish senility of the race (whose very name shows its incurable character), and to destroy the libidinous and heinous doctrines of Freudian pansexualism, from which stems the insanity of our life (money, interest, general stupidity, religion), because the selfishness of

---

185. Id., *Pédérastie et homosexualité*, Paris, Daragon, 1917, 68 pages, p.36.

the human heart or the sexual prostitution of love is a Jewish pollution on the scale of hatred, war and death....."[186] Spiess' work was included and analyzed in various collections of the time, which shows that his theories had a certain influence. Louis Estève in particular, in the *L'Énigme de l'androgyne*, defends his doctrines: "We have only to await the day when Han Ryner's Craftsmen of the future, adopting the principles of sexual selection, will allow the application of the theories of Camille Spiess and, through the universal androgynat, will establish on earth the reign of the genius — the dawn of Culture, Wisdom and Humanity — harbingers of the end of the world."[187] Estève found political and social finality in the esoteric jumble that was quite close to the theories of Hans Blüher studied above. The androgyne is the new man, called to found a world that is perfect, masculine, combatant, victorious, and the exact opposite of the society born after the war. The androgyne is a utopian genetic plan based on criteria for the purification of the race, fantasies of power, and a will to eradicate the female from the human.

This reactionary glorification of androgyny shows the ambiguity surrounding this concept. Whereas androgyny was initially a youthful reaction against traditional values, it was also used as a basis for the theories of the far Right. Androgyny represented at the same time an erotic ideal — that of the healthy, athletic body — which was presented as an example, and the sign of a major upheaval of sexual roles, which some perceived as a symptom of decline. In the Thirties, this vague homoeroticism disappeared from creative representations but it continued to be present, in a deformed way, in the esthetics of the Männerbund, the groups of virile men marching in uniform, in the exaltation of sports competitions, and all of Nazi mythology. In fact, the crisis of masculinity ran through the entire inter-war period. Characterized at first by a retreat of the masculine to the benefit of feminine values (themselves modified by male experiences), it then took the form of an over-investment of virility, in an ultimate effort to rediscover the traditional guideposts. Both attitudes illustrate the essential place of the male body in the social imagination of the inter-war period, and its origin may be found in a certain eroticization of the war. The ambient homoeroticism within the society explains why the figures of the homosexual and the lesbian were casualties in the storm of the Thirties. Objects of both

---

186. Id. *Éros, op. cit.*, p.88.
187. Louis Estève, *L'Énigme de l'androgyne*, Les Éditions du monde moderne, 1927, 161 pages, p.32.

desire and fear, they held up a mirror to the fantasies of the population, which was not ready to recognize its own duality.

* * *

A marked shift in sexual behaviors followed the First World War. The public, agitated by conflicting and antagonistic currents, had difficulty choosing between a moralistic backlash and a reformist liberation. Homophobia remained a very hot topic throughout the period, for it was debated by the leading institutions, churches, public authorities, and the press. As a new and fundamental fact, homosexuality became a fashionable topic which had to be discussed, analyzed, romanticized. The literary coverage was extraordinary.

Despite all of that, tolerance remained very limited. The inter-war period constituted a turning point in which popular fears and aversions contended with scientific advances and the claims of homosexuals themselves. However if, in the mid-Twenties, one might have believed there had been a long-term triumph for the forces of progress, it was clear by 1931-1933 that the embryonic shift was not supported by a real desire for change nor by a large-scale acceptance of modern values.

CHAPTER SIX

HOMOSEXUALS AS POLITICAL CHIPS

> Un caprice du temps, arbitre en toute chose,
> Proclame l'amour, et non la mort des amis.
> Sous la voûte d'azur, le soleil des athlètes,
> Ils sont trois, nus: le nouvel Allemand bronzé,
> L'employé communiste et moi, qui suis anglais[188]
>
> A caprice of time, arbiter of all things,
> Proclaims love, and not the death of friends.
> Under the azure vault, the sun of athletes,
> They are three, nude: the tanned New German,
> The communist employee and me, an Englishman

For Guy Hocquenghem, homosexuality was political; indeed, it was revolutionary. Homosexual relations carry within them the seeds of the destruction of the middle-class society; they undermine its very foundations: the family, authority, masculinity. Homosexuality is a corrosive factor that strikes at its very heart. It saps the certainty of the moral structure and creates new relationships, which can override existing hierarchies. In the 1920s and 1930s, the politically astute recognized this potential. Whether they tolerated or detested homosexuals, they were all frightened by this anarchistic force, which could hardly be subsumed in the program of any party. As committed activists, homosexuals' support would always be welcome; but they did not pull enough weight to force any of their claims onto the agenda. As enemies, opponents, they were

---

188. Stephen Spender, *Le Temple* [1929], Paris, Christian Bourgois éditeur, 1989, 310 pages, p.310.

the ideal target, the perfect scapegoat, and as such attracted all sorts of insults and guaranteed candidates the support of the public.

HOMOSEXUALS IN THE POLITICAL ARENA

Is it possible to believe that there is a link between sexual preference and party allegiance? It would be hard to come up with any answer on that, and there is little in the way of hard evidence from which to judge. Indeed, when political parties collected statistics about the background of their voters, they have not asked about sexual preferences. Neither have homosexual organizations sought to analyze their members' political inclinations. The German movements, which were best organized, presented themselves as being apolitical, even if events showed that they were close to the SPD and the KPD, at least in the leadership echelons. That however does not imply that all the members voted on the left, even if the movement encouraged them to do so. Neither can we rely on testimony from well-known figures, primarily intellectuals, the majority of whom came from the middle and upper classes, as a guide to the political persuasions of homosexuals in general. However, the large majority of homosexual intellectuals did throw themselves into the parties of the left, the Socialists and especially the Communists. Of course, political involvement is the product of several factors, and sexuality is only one variable among others. Nevertheless, these intellectuals particularly insisted that their homosexuality played a part in the choice of their engagement.

The Fantasy of the Working-Class Lover

The workingman fantasy is a major topic at many homosexual the period; not only was it an essential aspect of the homosexual erotic imagination of the 1920s and 1930s, but it also led to the political awakening of many homosexuals. This phenomenon was particularly widespread in England, but one finds traces of it in Germany and France. Stephen Spender poses the problem in an interview he granted some years ago.[189]

---

189. Françoise du Sorbier (dir.), *Oxford 1919-1939*, Paris, Éditions Autrement, "Mémoires" series, n° 8, 1991, 287 pages.

— There was a very strange bond; and it was undoubtedly proper to England, although it could also have existed in other countries, between homosexuals and the working class. It took the form of a deep attraction for young workingmen.[190]

This remark is corroborated by all, both the intellectuals and the nameless homosexuals: "Homosexuals in those days crossed the social barriers with an ease unknown in the other sectors of society."[191] It was a kind of fetishism; the working boy, or one engaged in manual labor, was endowed with an intense erotic charge. This is striking, for example, in Marcel Jouhandeau's *Mémorial IV, Apprentis et garçons*, where he evokes the tensions of his youth in the company of the butcher's assistants and apprentices who worked in his father's shop. Similarly, "Christopher Isherwood suffered from an inhibition, which was then not uncommon among higher class homosexuals; he could not find sexual release with a member of his own class or from his country. He needed a foreigner from the working class."[192]

There were two distinct beliefs: first, the conviction that only the working class could respond to the physical and love-related needs of homosexuals; second, the certainty that homosexuals, solely by virtue of their sexuality, could escape their class and to come into contact with boys of any background. This idealization was typical of the inter-war period, as if there was something special about the young workers of those days: "In those remote times, young men from the outskirts had a heart of gold."[193]

It is very difficult to explain the upper and middle class fascination for working-class boys, which was mostly mythological and was full of ambiguity. Daniel Guerin, in his *Autobiographie de jeunesse (Autobiography of Youth)*, obligingly describes his many meetings with young workmen: "The dialogue was completed in the crude room he had, as an apprentice; without any ill thoughts, without making me beg, he covered me with mad caresses and gave up to me his lovely beardless body."[194] Reading such passages, one has the impression of a perfectly liberated working class, the model of the sexual revolution, not acting out of self interest (there is no question of remuneration for services rendered), depoliticized (the workmen sleep with boys from good families without any

190. *Ibid.*, p.51.

191. George Mallory, in *Between the Acts. Lives of Homosexual Men, 1885-1967*, edited by K. Porter and J. Weeks, London, Routledge, 1990, 176 pages.

192. Christopher Isherwood, *Christopher and His Kind* [1929-1939], London, Methuen, 1977, 252 pages, p.10.

193. Daniel Guérin, *Autobiographie de jeunesse*, Paris, Belfond, 1972, 248 pages, p.165.

194. *Ibid.*, p.164-165.

objection), devoid of any prejudices and inhibitions. This idealization of the working class is a curious phenomenon. It leads one to suppose there was a high degree of tolerance for homosexuality amid the working class, which is difficult to prove, for little testimony was left by homosexuals of modest background. Many writings however do the workmen's indifference to homosexuality: "Homosexuality was not regarded as dishonourable if one did it for money."[195]

> —Homosexuality always was completely accepted in the districts east of London. In my youth, we regularly went to one of the pubs in the East End where our parents were regulars. And they called the boys by their working names, "Hello Lola, darling. How are you, sweetie? Will you sing us a song?" The East End was full of families piled together cheek by jowl in tight little lanes; everyone was always at each other's houses and they knew all about their sons and accepted it.[196]

The topic of the working class as an object of pleasure was already widespread at the end of the 19th century and fed the scandals of the Victorian Era.[197] Oscar Wilde described the pleasure of "feasting with panthers" while Edward Carpenter settled in Millthorpe with his working class lover, George Merrill, and influenced Bloomsbury deeply. However, whereas the Victorian taste was for very young boys, even for pedophilia, and practically amounted to a trade, the 1920s and 1930s developed the theme of the workman as the "ideal friend,"[198] the companion with whom one could perhaps "live all his life," defying conventions. This ideal of course was comparative: most homosexuals had many casual flings with boys, even if they also had ongoing relations with two or three regulars. Ackerley wrote that he had between two hundred and three hundred lovers in his life and Guerin describes his unrestrained search for pleasure: — I only thought of multiplying, of piling up, of adding, of collecting, of counting the adventures on my fingers.[199]

Some young workers were sharply disappointed when they realized they were only a pleasant pastime.[200] Nevertheless, the myth of a stable relation with a working class friend was seriously entertained; E.M. Forster's novel *Maurice* represents a Utopia where homosexuals could live freely, independent of moral

---

195. George Mallory, in *Between the Acts, op. cit.*

196. John, son of a worker, and kept as a lover, *ibid.*

197. This theme amy be compared to the heterosexual relations that men of good family might entertain with housemaids, seamstresses, cooks, florists and others of the working class.

198. J.R. Ackerley, *My Father and Myself* [1968], London, Penguin, 1971, 192 pages, p.109-110 and following.

199. Daniel Guérin, *Autobiographie de jeunesse, op. cit.*, p.166.

repression and social differences. Maurice finds in Alec, the gamekeeper, the friend whom he has always wished for, and he declares he is ready to turn his back on society to preserve this love. But if in *Maurice* the two boys manage to find happiness and are never separated (although one has no idea on what, and how, they will live from now on), real situations were harder to work out. It is often difficult to tell the difference between sincere love and camouflaged exploitation of young people who need money and are ready to give in to the advances of wealthy men. It seems nevertheless that good faith prevails, with much naivety, for many homosexual intellectuals liked to think, like Pygmalion, of educating and reorganizing the life of their protégés, raising them by their love above their social condition. — I do not rule out education but I do not wish it, I can help him myself,— declared Ackerley, for example.[201] Sometimes, they even envisioned a real equality which would transcend the social classes, by the miracle of homosexuality alone: "The man had not called him Sir, and the omission flattered him. 'Hello, Sir,' would have been the most natural greeting to a foreigner of mature age, and what is more, the guest of a rich client. However, the vigorous voice had shouted, 'Hello, beautiful day!,' as if they were equals."[202]

It is the same belief in an equality of circumstance that inspires Guerin when he reports his relations with young workmen: "We became real pals."[203] According to him, he developed a genuine complicity with these boys. One of them took him around to meet "other ornaments of Piazza d'Italia," another tipped him off as to which guy to go with and which to avoid. While there was certainly a commonality of interests, we are still far from a real friendship based on confidence and mutual comprehension.

We should nevertheless try to elucidate the nature of the bonds that linked homosexuals with the working class during the 1920s and 1930s. J.R.

---

200. Such was the case, for example, of Ivan Alderman, who met Ackerley in Richmond Park when he was just 15. He immediately fell head over heels in love; for him, this was Prince Charming, a rich homosexual, very handsome, cultivated, driving a sports car and who would pick him up in his neighborhood and take him to chic parties. Sixty years later, he still looked upon him as the greatest love of his life. He only gradually came to discover that what he saw as a lasting relationship was nothing more than one episode in Ackerley's very long series of romantic adventures. The breakup was very painful. See Peter Parker, *A Life of J.R. Ackerley*, London, Constable, 1989, 465 pages, p.94-95.

201. J.R. Ackerley, *My Father and Myself, op. cit.*, p.109.

202. E.M. Forster, "Arthur Snatchfold," in *Un instant d'éternité et autres nouvelles*, Paris, Christian Bourgois éditeur, 1988, 306 pages, p.149.

203. Daniel Guérin, *Autobiographie de jeunesse, op. cit.*, p.165.

Ackerley gives his own analysis of the phenomenon in these terms: — If my research led me out of my own class, toward the working class, i.e. toward that innocence which I was never able to find among members of my class, it was in order to spare myself the culpability that I felt with regard to the sexuality of my social inferiors.

This idea was widespread: homosexuals of the upper classes often had had a puritanical education that condemned pleasure in sex, and of course any deviant sexuality. They were persuaded that only they were persecuted in their sexuality; in the working class, they felt, sexuality must natural, without constraints and prejudices. Here again, we can discern a mythical concept: homosexual intellectuals did not observe that working class men were freer sexually, they assumed it, *a priori*. This idealized notion was supported by their ignorance of the new environment in which they were acting:

> — With even more curiosity than concupiscence I precipitated toward these strapping men that were no longer separated from me by an opaque barrier. Their way of life was simplified to the extreme, their picturesque and masculine garb, their ripe language, which was sometimes somewhat hermetic for me, their skin tanned by the great outdoors, their muscular strength, their honest and natural animality that was not slowed or dimmed as yet in those days by any factitious inhibition, any petit-bourgeois prejudice (and they were, what is more, less monopolized by the girls than today), all that took me by surprise, metamorphosed me, enchanted me.[204]

This sense was all the more marked since, as for Auden, Spender or Isherwood, the exoticism of the place was added to the difference in class; Christopher Isherwood felt — a marvelous freedom in the company of [these boys]. He, who only could make veiled allusions in English, could now crudely ask for what he wanted in German. His limited knowledge of the language obliged him to be direct and he was not embarrassed to pronounce foreign sexual terms, which had no connection with his life in England.[205]

Thus, for Isherwood, England represented heterosexuality and erotic inhibition and all he could think about was being abroad. The photographer Humphrey Spender, Stephen Spender's brother, noted that Heinz, Isherwood's young German lover, an unemployed worker, was "the decisive factor in his life," the reason for all his wanderings from country to country.[206]

---

204. *Ibid.*, p.167.

205. Christopher Isherwood, *Christopher and His Kind, op. cit.*, p.110.

206. Cited by Paul Fussell, *Abroad, British Literary Travellers between the Wars*, Oxford, Oxford University Press, 1983, 246 pages.

It seems that there was a feeling of humility and perhaps of guilt in homo-sexuals' attitude toward the working class. Ashamed of their material wealth that enabled them to keep the boys, they tried to get closer, to deny the barriers between them. The relationship might venture into sadomasochistic terrain. Marcel Jouhandeau liked to fantasize about being humiliated by young workmen: he would invite workers, even criminals, to his room and only ask them to let to him cut their nails; or he might bathe the feet of a plasterer. Rela-tions between Auden and several of his German companions degenerated to the point of blows. Even when the threats were only virtual, it is striking how eager a number of British homosexuals were to go out with police officers, the very people whom they ought to seek out the least. Virginia Woolf had earlier been astonished by this paradoxical passion for the police force, which she found with Plomer, Walpole, Spender, Forster, Auden and Ackerley.[207]

And however, the relations were more complex. The boy was not just a sexual plaything, he was a physical incarnation of the homosexual ideal. During a time that saw the rehabilitation of the body, the fantasy of the strong and healthy workman was a staple in the homosexual middle and upper classes that had been raised in contempt of the body and physical values. Often of weak con-stitution (E.M. Forster, Lytton Strachey, Brian Howard), they looked for manual workers whose bodies were clearly shaped by exercise: — I found [the ideal friend] rather quickly. He was a sailor, a robust sailor, a boy from the working class, simple, normal, no education... He was a famous light-weight boxer in the navy; his silk skin, his muscles, a perfect body, like that of a beautiful young man from Crete, was a delight to be contemplated.[208]

The working boy often played his role gladly; proud of the admiration he attracted, he might further cultivate the muscular look, becoming a narcissistic being only concerned about the beauty that brought him the attention of well-born young people. It was a double fascination. While the homosexuals were worshipping the workers, the latter became more self-conscious and sometimes lost the naturalness that was their principal charm:

> [Maurice] embodied exactly that physical type to which I was attracted. He had a trunk of athlete, and a hard face. He excelled at swimming and water polo. He was not elegant, for his massive body did not look good in clothes, which are a good mask for malingerers but vain tinsel for the strong. He had the body-builder's well-

---

207. Letter from Virginia Woolf to Quentin Bell, 21 December 1933.
208. J.R. Ackerley, *My Father and Myself, op. cit.*, p.10.

known narcissism. He liked to show off his muscles, his beautiful muscles, his pride and his capital, whose magic effect he was well aware of.[209]

These relations that were based in virility, physical superiority, the opposition between the "strong" and the "weak," often turned to wrestling, to a fight between boys, measuring their strength against each other and going right up to the sex act:

> Fighting that transformed into sex seemed perfectly natural to these German boys; in fact, it excited them, too. Perhaps because it was something that one could not do with a girl, or at least not on the level of physical equality; something they liked as an expression of the aggression/attraction that exists between two men. Perhaps also this moderately sadistic game was a characteristic of German sexuality; many of them liked to be beaten, not too hard, with a belt.[210]

The body exerts a magical attraction and its power is without limits. In "Dr. Woolacott" by E.M. Forster, an invalid believes he finds strength in the arms of his lover, a farm hand: — He opened his arms to him, and Cleasant accepted the invitation. Cleasant had often been proud of his illness, but never, never of his body; it had never occurred to him which he could elicit desire. This sudden revelation upset him, he fell from his pedestal, but he was not alone: there was somebody to whom he could cling, with broad shoulders, a tanned neck, lips which half-opened in caressing him.[211]

The working boy seems to live a mythical world where the values are reversed, where all that was prohibited is finally allowed, where happiness is accessible: Come to me, and you will be as happy as I am, and as strong."[212] A certain magnetization occurs between the two classes and never achieves equilibrium, for they are separated by the invisible barriers of wealth, social access and culture. Happiness is thus almost impossible to attain, especially since the attraction for working boys goes with a desire to have "normal," heterosexual boys. Auden describes the impossibility of reconciling the two aspirations with a certain bitterness: — There are two worlds and one cannot belong to both at the same time. If one is part of the second of these worlds (that of the refined intellectuals), one will be always unhappy, for one will always be in love with the first world (that of the nonintellectual athletes), although despising it at the same time. The first world, on other hand, will not return your love, for it is in its nature to love only that which is like itself.[213]

---

209. Daniel Guérin, *Autobiographie de jeunesse, op. cit.*, p.172.
210. Christopher Isherwood, *Christopher and His Kind, op. cit.*, p.30.
211. E.M. Forster, "Dr Woolacott," in *Un instant d'éternité, op. cit.*, p.136.
212. *Ibid.*, p.134.

The fascination for the working class is tinged with a kind of dislike for the middle and upper classes, as if sex could not be spontaneous and natural within a class considered to be too respectable and moralistic: — I found that boys of the higher classes were a little too untouchable and not physical enough. We were all too strait-laced and were a little uptight in a way or another. That all needed to be loosened up.[214]

The worship of the body led in parallel to a depreciation of intellectual values. The working culture was attractive at first as a new, pure and preserved world: — The boys of the working class were less reserved and less contemplative, and their friendship opened to me with interesting fields of the life, which otherwise would have remained unknown to me.[215]

But soon, this desire to extirpate oneself of one's own background grew into a militant anti-intellectualism that was quite unwelcome among professional intellectuals; for the homosexual wishing to prove to his friend that he was now on "his side," it was no longer enough to share his concerns; now he agreed to disavow his own culture and all signs of his past: — He had a primitive class instinct, a bitterness. For him, I was never anything but the son of a family, a bourgeois, on whom he had to take his revenge. Since he was impecunious, he made me sell a priceless edition of *Les Jeunes filles en fleurs* by Marcel Proust, abundantly corrected in the hand of the author, and I made this sacrifice, without hesitation, delighted to give him such a proof of love, while he, inciting me to do it, showed a wicked anti-intellectual joy.[216]

Forster's novel *Ansell* is presented in the form of a parable of this confrontation between the classes. Edward, a young man who intends to go into a university career withdraws to the countryside to write his dissertation. There, he finds his childhood friend, Ansell, the gardener,[217] whose strength and independence of mind he envies. In an auto accident all his books and notes for the thesis fall into the river; only one or two are saved. Thanks to this sign from fate, Edward understands that real life is in nature, at Ansell's side, and he gives up any intellectual pretensions. This example is particularly emblematic of the

---

213. Cited by Humphrey Carpenter, *W.H. Auden, a Biography*, London, Allen & Unwin, 1981, 495 pages, p.260.

214. Christopher Isherwood, interviewed in *Gay News*, n° 126.

215. J.R. Ackerley, *My Father and Myself*, *op. cit.*, p.110.

216. Daniel Guérin, *Autobiographie de jeunesse*, *op. cit.*, p.174.

217. As a child, Forster felt his first homosexual emotions for the family gardener, whose name was Ansell.

process of identification that homosexual intellectuals were undergoing. Initially attracted sexually by the boys of the working class, they went on to envy their lifestyle, their lack of education, their freedom. Intelligence then becomes synonymous with frustration and inhibition.

This identification soon leads to a rejection of their own class. Rupert Brooke was the first to protest: "I hate the upper classes!"

Christopher Isherwood explained that his attraction for this type of boys came from his hostility to the bourgeoisie, which led it consciously to seek not only its opposite, but whatever would be most shocking to middle-class values.[218] W.H. Auden expressed the same feeling when he was in Germany: — The German proletariat is sympathetic, but I do not like much the others, therefore I spend most of my time with Juvenile Delinquents [sic].[219]

Stephen Spender went even further when he explained: "My revolt against my family's attitude also led me to rebel against morality, labor and discipline. Secretly I was fascinated by outlaws, the despicable, the depraved, the lazy, the strays; and I wished to offer to them all the love that was denied to them by respectable people.[220]

It is interesting to note that one finds exactly the same terms and the same justifications coming from Frenchman Daniel Guerin: "Part of my taste for young fellows 'of the people' came from a sense of rebellion against the established order, against my family."[221]

Sometimes the two generations of homosexual intellectuals did manage to enjoy a real empathy with the popular classes. Behind the boys who were the objects of their desire, homosexuals learned to see a whole world which was unknown to them; and as they loved the sons, they came to love the families, and soon all their milieu as such: "The differences of class and interest between Jimmy and me provided certainly elements of mystery which almost corresponded to the difference between the sexes. I was in love, in fact, with his origins, his soldier's trade, his working-class family."[222]

---

218. Christopher Isherwood, interviewed in *Gay News*, n° 126.

219. Cited by Humphrey Carpenter, *W.H. Auden*, op. cit., p.90. Capitalization as per Auden.

220. Stephen Spender, *World within World* [1951], London, Faber & Faber, 1991, 344 pages, p.9.

221. Daniel Guérin, *Autobiographie de jeunesse*, op. cit., p.175.

222. Stephen Spender, *World within World*, op. cit., p.184.

Becoming familiar with their lovers' financial and family difficulties, homosexuals from the well-off classes discovered the distress of the workers struck by the economic crisis in England and the destitution of the German proletariat. Their political opinions and their social ideals were transformed:

> —Thanks to Walter, I imagined ... what it was like to be unemployed. I imagined, I suppose, that something that in my mind I started to call 'the Revolution' would change his fate and I felt that as a member of a wealthier social class I had contracted a debt towards him. If he had robbed me, I would have understood that he could never take away from me the advantages which society had given me over him: for I was a member of a class whose money automatically enabled me to benefit from the institutions of theft, to automatically assume the guise of respectability. Then I understood that there were two classes of robbers: the social one and the antisocial.[223]

The very essence of homosexuality is equality. Through the sex act, the two partners forget their last differences, of origin, class, and race, until there is nothing but two lovers linked in the same destiny, "— for in this romantic, anachronistic life, the ambassador is the friend of the convict...."[224]

The miracle of the confluence of the bourgeois and working-class homosexuals is specific to the inter-war period; it was the coming together of two groups excluded from society, misfits, scorned, looked down upon. "I could speak with law-breakers because I was one, myself," acknowledged Stephen Spender.[225]

Beyond the differences in class, it was the same struggle that united them. This partly explains the alliance of homosexuals and the leftist parties, ambiguous as it was.

Homosexual as Leftist Activists

In the 1920s, homosexuality became a means of rocking respectable opinions and of shaking up the Establishment. What better way to declare one's hostility towards the official morals of society than to go and spend some time with the homosexuals? Homosexuality gave the same thrill as drugs nowadays and the pleasure of being certain to outrage the older generation.[226]

---

223. *Ibid.*, p.118.

224. Marcel Proust, *Sodome et Gomorrhe* I, in *A la recherche du temps perdu*, Paris, Gallimard, coll. "Bibl. de la Pléiade," 1988, t.III, 1934 pages, p.19.

225. Stephen Spender, *World within World*, *op. cit.*, p.119.

226. Noel Annan, *Our Age: English Intellectuals between the Wars: A Group Portrait*, New York, Random House, 1991, 479 pages, p.113.

This attitude was not limited to England, where homosexuality was repressed by law; in France, for a boy from a good family to come out as a homosexual was a political act and sometimes it was hard to tell whether homosexuality had led to political engagement or the inverse: "When I first got involved in the social struggle, I was both a homosexual and a revolutionary, without being able to clearly distinguish how much this came from the intellect (readings, reflections) and how much from feelings (physical attraction toward the working class, rebellion, rejection of my old middle-class background)."[227]

As a "deviant" form of sexuality, homosexuality justified taking a counter-current position: "By receiving [Marcel], I was up to something that was more than sentimental: there was already a certain appetite for social transgression. I was launching a challenge to my class."[228]

To be a homosexual is to be on the outside; to choose an extreme political position is to push that exclusion to its logical end, to retaliate for society's charges that the homosexual is a potential danger. "The homosexual, whether or not he knows it or wants it, is potentially asocial and therefore virtually subversive."[229]

Lastly, by participating in revolutionary parties, the homosexuals hoped to advance their cause. Enthusiasm for the working class, and the hopes raised by the formation of the Soviet Union, supported the idea of a natural communion between homosexuality and revolution; Michel de Coglay writes of the naive enthusiasms of certain homosexual for the communist cause. In a Montmartre café he met, for example, "a young draughtsman with a certain type of nose, who bellowed his faith in Hirschfeld and in Moscow, which he supposed, quite imprudently, to be hallowed ground for free pederasty and free democracy."[230]

The myth of a working class favorable to the homosexual justified a belief in an egalitarian proletarian revolution that would bring tolerance for all minorities: "Homophobic prejudice, hideous as it is, will not be thwarted merely by means that I would qualify as reformist, by persuasion, by concessions to the heterosexual adversary, but will be definitively extirpated from people's consciousness, just like racial prejudice, only by an anti-authoritative social revo-

---

227. Daniel Guérin, *Homosexualité et révolution*, Paris, Utopie, coll. "Les Cahiers du vent du ch'min," 1983, 66 pages, p.11.

228. Id., *Autobiographie de jeunesse, op. cit.*, p.167.

229. Id., *Homosexualité et révolution, op. cit.*, p.17.

230. Michel du Coglay, *Chez les mauvais garçons. Choses vues*, Paris, R. Saillard, 1938, 221 pages, p.159.

lution,"[231] declared Daniel Guerin. Thus it was that in the 1920s homosexuals discovered that their sexual preferences could be a political weapon.

Pacifism

Already during the First World War, Bloomsbury had been characterized by its pacifist stand. The second homosexual generation took up the torch in the 1930s.

The friendship of many well-bred English homosexuals for working-class boys, especially German, was seen as a provocation. To have a German lover after the war was to betray all those who had died in the trenches, in the name of pleasure and of perversion. It was tantamount to announcing oneself as a criminal, to siding with the enemy. — Public hatred engenders private love. Love your enemies! My God! I love the English![232]

This fraternization with the enemy was partly the consequence of the extraordinary guilt which they felt for not having fought in the war: "Like most of those of my generation, I was obsessed by a complex of terrors and desires related to the idea of 'war.' 'The war,' in its purely neurotic sense, meant the Test. The Test of your courage, your maturity, your sexual prowess. 'Are you really a man?' Unconsciously I believe, I wanted to be subjected to this Test, but I also feared failure. I feared Failure so much — in fact, I was so sure that I would fail — that, consciously, I denied my desire to be tested. I denied my devouring morbid interest in the idea of 'war.' I claimed to be indifferent. The war, I would say, was obscene, not exciting, just a bother, an irritation.[233]

The pacifism shown by the homosexual intellectuals in the first half of the inter-war period was the product of this fascination intermixed with hatred. "At the height of our pacifist campaigns of the early 1930s, we were in fact almost in love with the horrors which we denounced," acknowledges Philip Toynbee.[234] Stephen Spender regretted there were no great causes for which he could fight. At Oxford, like those of his generation who had not known war, he acknowledged having been jealous of the veterans of the Great War, as if he had been robbed of the opportunity to prove that he was a man and of the glory of victory. However, at college, like Auden and his friends, he presented himself as an

---

231. Daniel Guérin, *Homosexualité et révolution, op. cit.,* p.15.

232. Stephen Spender, *Le Temple, op. cit.,* p.41.

233. Christopher Isherwood, *Lions and Shadows,* London, Methuen, 1985, 191 pages, p.46-47.

234. Cited by Françoise du Sorbier, *Oxford 1919-1939, op. cit.,* p.49.

ardent pacifist, overwhelmed with hatred for the OTC (Officer Training Corps), the obligatory military drive still in force in the public schools. The myth of the war, the horror of the trenches, honor and disgust all intermingled for this generation that had no past to assert and which felt solidarity only over the cruel awareness of having missed the main event.

Homosexual life in the 1920s and 1930s thus often resembled a parody of the war, with its passion for uniforms including those of the soldiers of the Guard, sailors, and the police. E.M. Forster noted that any uniform at all would do, even if it was only a bus driver's.[235]

The political implications of these attitudes toward the war and toward the German working class boys were of utmost importance. Christopher Isherwood is sincere when he acknowledges his political hesitations: — It is so easy to make fun of all this homosexual romanticism. But the leaders of the fascistic States did not laugh; they understood and used precisely these fantasies and these desires. I wonder how I would have reacted at that time if one of the English fascistic leaders had been intelligent enough to serve me his message in a form suitably disguised and pleasant? He would have converted me, I think, in half an hour."[236]

From their special relationship with the German working class, English homosexual intellectuals learned to love Germany and some would never be able to fight it, like Auden and Isherwood who left England for the United States in 1939. Auden and Spender, however, had already overcome the pacifist option and had supported the International Brigades in Spain. But even if they militated actively against Fascism, taking in political refugees and participating in activities for conscientious objectors, they could never fight Germany with weapons. In *Christopher and His Kind* Christopher Isherwood explains that, as long as his friend Heinz, as a homosexual, had been a target of the Nazis, he had felt an unconditional hatred for them. But Heinz was soon constrained to don the uniform and join the German army. Isherwood's reasoning at that point sheds light on the role of homosexuality as a dimension of one's conscience: — Let us suppose, says Christopher, that I now have a Nazi army at my mercy. I can destroy them all by pressing a button. The men of this army are known to have tortured and assassinated civilians — all except one, Heinz. Would I press the

235. Cited by Valentine Cunningham, *British Writers of the Thirties*, Oxford, Oxford University Press, 1988, 530 pages, p.55.

236. Christopher Isherwood, *Lions and Shadows, op. cit.*, p.48.

button? No. Now let us suppose that I know that Heinz has taken part in their crimes. Will I press the button, then? Of course not; and that is a purely emotional reaction.... Now, let's suppose that the army attacks and suffers one loss, Heinz himself. Will I press the button and destroy his criminal companions? No emotional reaction this time, just a clear answer which one cannot escape: once I have refused to press the button because of Heinz, I will never be able to do it again. Because any man of this army could be Heinz to somebody else, and I do not have the right to play favorites. Thus Christopher was forced to acknowledge himself a pacifist — even though it was the consequence of a line of reasoning that he found repugnant.[237]

Communism and the far left

Homosexuality, by putting certain intellectuals of the 1920s and 1930s in touch with the working class, was a considerable factor in determining their political perspective. In his autobiography, Daniel Guerin establishes a relation of cause and effect between his attraction for working class boys and his political involvement. He was from the middle class himself, and it was through his intimate relations with working boys that gave rise to his social conscience. He discovered misery, and barely-disguised prostitution; the money he gave the boys is a form of restitution, in recompense for the culpability which he felt over having been born in better circumstances: "I did not find any displeasure in the so-called venal love affairs... And what is more, my partners were young workers who were overexploited or unemployed, and soldiers receiving pathetic remuneration, and with them I corrected the wrongs of society and the army."[238]

Guerin came up with a symbolic phrase to illustrate this situation: "I came to socialism via phallism."[239] Conscious of his singularity, he reflected at length on the relationship between homosexuality and revolution. He says of his political progression, "My shift in the direction of socialism was not objective, intellectual in nature, but rather subjective, physical, and driven by the heart. It was not in books, it was in me, initially, because of the years of sexual frustration, and because through my contact with oppressed young people I learned to hate the established social order. Carnal pursuits led me to cross social bar-

---

237. Id., *Christopher and His Kind*, op. cit., p.249-250.
238. Daniel Guérin, *Autobiographie de jeunesse*, op. cit., p.169.
239. Id., *Homosexualité et révolution*, op. cit., p.44.

riers. More than the seduction of bodies, hardened by the work, I sought friendship. And that is what I hoped to find, a hundred-fold, in socialism."[240]

To choose the revolutionary path is, to some extent, to be adopted by the working class. Guerin sounds sad when he speaks of that "fraternity of the son of the people, from which always life always excluded me."[241] Guerin notes that his social origin and his sexual preferences were always obstacles to his political integration — one way or another, he never fit in. "Some ... to distinguish me from the authentic proletarians, would contemptuously call me an idealist. Others when they got wind of my sexual dissidence, would insult me."[242]

Homosexuality as a motivation for political engagement is, of course, suspect. It is difficult to take seriously somebody whose behavior seems dictated by emotions, whose least action may be attributed to his sexual rather than political inclinations. Just as for the homosexual, whose sexuality is already, by virtue of being "dissident," a political act, so for the Communist — there are all kinds of incompatibilities. Guerin was fully aware of this: "I resolved to employ my particular form of eroticism, hitherto uncontrolled, wasted, more or less asocial, and subordinate it to the highest end: the liberation of all, which would at the same time be mine. Those whose adhesion to socialism took different forms would no doubt have trouble to understand mine."[243]

The visceral intolerance for homosexuality that was found within the revolutionary groups is symbolized by Henri Barbusse's article in the magazine *Les Marges* (March 15, 1926): "I figure that this perversion of a natural instinct, like so many other perversions, is a measure of the social and moral decline of a certain part of contemporary society.... [the complacency of the decadent intellectuals] can only reinforce the contempt that the healthy and young popular force experiences for these representatives of morbid and artificial doctrines, and all of this will hasten, I hope, the hour of wrath and renaissance." Guerin tried to hide his homosexuality until 1968:

> What people of my kind suffered from most, in those days, was the constant fear of losing the respect, of bringing on the contempt or even loathing, of those of our comrades who might catch us in *flagrante delicto* expressing our homosexual inclinations. One had to keep quiet at all costs, to dissimulate, to lie, if necessary, to preserve a revolutionary respectability whose value could be measured only in com-

240. Id., *Le Feu du sang: autobiographie politique et charnelle*, Paris, Grasset, 1977, 286 pages, p.13-14.

241. Id., *Autobiographie de jeunesse, op. cit.*, p.205.

242. *Ibid.*, p.209.

243. Daniel Guérin, *Le Feu du sang, op. cit.*, p.14.

parison with the abjection into which one was likely to fall if one dropped the mask.[244]

Homosexual engagement could take a more radical form. The best-known example is that of the Soviet agents Guy Burgess, Anthony Blunt and Donald Maclean.[245] Schooled at Eton, Burgess entered Cambridge in 1930 and soon became known for his charm and his eccentricity. A very active homosexual, he formed a friendship with Anthony Blunt, who had made his studies at Marlborough where the cult of homosexuality was strong. At Trinity College in Cambridge, he was classified among the esthetes and he developed several homosexual relations, but more discretely than Burgess. It was Blunt who brought Burgess into the Apostles. Burgess then caught the attention of Maurice Dobb, an economics professor in Pembroke College and one of the first British academics to join the Communist Party to; he introduced Kim Philby to him. Burgess, like many other homosexual intellectuals, was then attracted by boys of the working class, with whom he liked to discuss the problems that they met in their daily life, whether economic problems or political; he had some flings at every social level and spent time with skilled laborers, truck-drivers, workmen, students and professors alike. From 1933 to 1934, he began a thesis entitled "The bourgeois revolution of England of the 17th century." Blunt joined the Party under the influence of Burgess, with whom he was passionately in love. Burgess brought along Donald Maclean by the same lure; he was, at the time, undecided as to both his sexual and political leanings.

In 1934, the process accelerated. Philby's visit to Cambridge was decisive. Burgess became enflamed and Philby recruited him for the Soviet secret service. Burgess then spent the summer of 1934 in Germany perfecting his political education, then he left for the USSR with Anthony Blunt. In 1935, he became the parliamentary assistant of a homosexual young deputy on the far Right, Jack MacNamara, a member of the Anglo-German Fellowship, an association for Nazi sympathizers. Burgess gained the confidence of MacNamara and they organized a series of sex-tourist trips abroad, especially to Germany where MacNamara had ties within the Hitler Youth. Burgess managed to be in touch with a number of highly placed homosexuals like Édouard Pfeiffer, the chief private secretary of Édouard Daladier, War Minister, an agent of the 2nd French Office and of MI6. MacNamara and Burgess were invited on several occasions to pleasure parties at

244. Id., *Homosexualité et révolution, op. cit.*, p.39.
245. See Yuri Ivanovich Modin, *Mes camarades de Cambridge*, Paris, Robert Laffont, 1994, 316 pages.

Pfeiffer's or to Parisian nightclubs. It is interesting to note what role Burgess's homosexuality might have played in his joining the Communists, and then in his espionage activities. Burgess followed the typical trajectory of the British homosexual intellectual of the 1920s: public school, Cambridge, attraction for working-class boys. However, he was also a product of the 1930s; his discovery of the working class translated, on the political level, to joining the communists, in parallel with an increasing tendency toward the red at Oxford as well. In the field of espionage, his homosexuality would have been able a handicap. Philby regarded inversion as a disease and never brought it up with Burgess; and Yuri Ivanovich Modin, Burgess's Soviet contact, was rather hostile: "There was an enormous unvoiced comment between us, but I think that that facilitated our relations in a certain way."[246]

It seems that this tacit tolerance was based on the effectiveness of the homosexual networks, the famous "Homintern." By virtue of his homosexuality, Burgess had the most varied doors opened to him; it enabled him to gain access to State secrets, to slip in and out of very different political milieux. Homosexual solidarity was very important; seductive and skilful, Burgess could manipulate his informants and his handlers, or deceive them completely. After the war, this success on the part of the spies of Cambridge set off another homophobic campaign based on fears of national treason and the enemy within.

Communist involvement did not always take such extreme forms: W.H. Auden, Christopher Isherwood and Stephen Spender flirted with Marxism throughout the period. Stephen Spender ended up joining the Party in 1936, before leaving for Spain. His lover Hyndman joined soon thereafter.[247] Spender recalls that his friends were shocked: "We looked at that as an extraordinary act. Communism was for us an extremist cause, almost *against nature* [my emphasis] and we had difficulty to believe that any of our friends could be communists."[248]

Spender's commitment was mainly emotional; he was all for the German working class and he disavowed his own people: he was haunted by a deep guilt feeling over his social background, his culture, his privileged situation. For Spender, homosexuality and politics were inextricably interwoven: in 1935, in his poem "Vienna," he expresses his indignation vis-à-vis the elimination of the Viennese Socialists by Dollfuss, and at the same time he evokes his love for

---

246. *Ibid.*, p.86.
247. See the testimony of David, an English teacher, in *Between the Acts, op. cit.* After spending two years in Germany, 1929 and 1930, he rejoined the Communist Party.
248. Stephen Spender, *World within World, op. cit.*, p.132.

"Jimmy." — I wanted to show that the two experiences were different but dependent. For both were intense, emotional and personal, although one was public and the other private. The validity of the one depended on that of the other: for in a world where humanity was publicly trampled, private affection was also sapped."[249]

The war in Spain revealed several contradictions underlying Spender's commitment. In 1936, he not only joined the English Communist Party, but he also published a book of political reflections, *Forward from Liberalism*, which was selected as Book of the Month by the Left Book Club. And, he left Hyndman and got married. This brutal change left him quite uncomfortable. When Hyndman joined the Party, then signed up with the International Brigades, he felt responsible. Hyndman very quickly regretted his engagement. Spender then accepted an offer from the *Daily Worker*, which wanted him to report on a Soviet ship run by the Italians in the Mediterranean. He found Hyndman, who begged him to get him out of the Brigades. Spender got him relieved from combat duty, but Hyndman deserted. When he tried to plead his case, the game was up and the British Communists let their homophobia show clearly: "I think I know exactly why you do not admit the lack of valor in this comrade in particular," they retorted to him; and the following remark sounds like a warning: "You know too many boys for your good." Finally, Hyndman was saved and repatriated to England. Spender returned to Spain in the summer of 1937, as a deputy to the Congress of Writers which was held in Madrid. The meeting disappointed him considerably, and he never went back to Spain. Auden, too, was deeply marked by his sojourn among the "Juvenile Delinquents," among whom he ran into several members of the German Communist Party (KPD). Under the influence of Gabriel Carritt and Edward Upward, his interest in Communism grew. In August 1932, he published the poem, "A Communist to Others," which starts with the apostrophe, "Comrades!," soon followed by "A Handsome Profile" in September 1932. In April 1933, he had an article in the *Daily Herald* entitled "How to Become Master of the Machine," preaching the introduction of a socialist state. His interest in Marxism remained primarily romantic, however, and in the autumn of 1932 he wrote to Rupert Donne: "No. I am a bourgeois. I will not join the CP."[250]

---

249. *Ibid.*, p.192.
250. Cited by Humphrey Carpenter, *W.H. Auden, op. cit.*, p.133.

Sympathies for Communism died out soon after it became known that homosexuality had been made a criminal act in the USSR in 1934. Gide is an instructive example. Gide had built his reputation as a writer on a work exalting pleasure and freedom. His *Nourritures terrestres* (1897) was a guide for a whole generation. His denunciation of traditional morals and social conformity, his assertion of homosexual rights, also led him to question French politics in the 1920s. In *Voyage au Congo* (1927) and *Retour du Tchad* (1928), he denounced colonialism. In 1932, Communism began to seem like "a doctrine of liberation for man, allowing him to flourish in every way, far from bourgeois hypocrisy."[251]

In the *Nouvelle revue française*, he declares his desire to see "what a State without religion can give, a society without cells."[252] Gide believed more in morals than anything else, and militant engagement was repugnant to him. It was Hitler's advent to power that led him to side with the Communists. He became a "fellow traveller" and participated in various militant actions. He was on the board of *Commune*, the review of the Association of Revolutionary Writers and Artists; he chaired meetings and went to Berlin with Malraux to plead the cause of Dimitrov, who was jailed after the Reichstag fire.[253] In 1935, he chaired the opening session of the International Congress of Writers for the Defense of Culture in Paris. His enthusiasm quickly waned. His visit to the USSR in 1936 was a great disappointment, although he was greeted with many honors. Soviet reality was very different from what he had hoped for, and man was no freer from convention than elsewhere. The repression of homosexuality also must have played a part in his disillusionment. In *Return from the USSR*, Gide touched on that subject only in a note:

> Still, is this law [against abortion] justified in a certain sense? It leads to very deplorable abuses. But what are we to think, from a Marxist point of view, of that older one, against homosexuals, which equates them to counter-revolutionaries (for non-conformity is pursued right up to and including sexual questions), condemns them to deportation for five years with possible extension, if being exiled has not cured them.[254]

---

251. Serge Berstein, *La France des années trente*, Paris, Armand Colin, 1993, 186 pages, p.99.

252. Nicole Racine, "André Gide," in Jacques Julliard and Michel Winock (dir.), *Dictionnaire des intellectuels français*, Paris, Éditions du Seuil, 1996, 1264 pages.

253.   Serge Berstein, *La France des années trente, op. cit.*

254. André Gide, *Retour de l'URSS*, Paris, Gallimard, 1936, 125 pages, p.63.

Christopher Isherwood also relates that he tried to play down the importance of this news, alleging to his friends that England and the United States, like most capitalist countries, had similar laws. But the socialist myth was shaken, for the new society that Marxism had supposedly generated could not be better than the others if it excluded homosexuals:

> — For, if the Communists claimed that their system was more just than capitalism, didn't that make the their injustice towards homosexuals even less excusable and their hypocrisy all the worse? Christopher understood that he now had to dissociate himself from the Communists, even as a fellow traveller. He could, on certain occasions, accept them as allies, but he could never look upon them as comrades. He must never again yield to confusion, never deny his tribe, never apologize for existence, never think of sacrificing himself in some masochistic way on the altar of the false totalitarian god, the sacred voice of the Majority whose priests alone could decide what was "good." — [255]

The homosexual identity was now clear. It had become strong enough to influence political choices, it had become powerful enough to change class behaviors, and above all it had become strong enough to guarantee its own survival. When Hitler came to power in 1933 and Stalinism was installed in the USSR, two profound threats faced homosexuals and put an end to their hopes for greater international emancipation. In 1933, choices were made and the homosexual cause took precedence from now on over other allegiances, political, social or intellectual:

> — As a homosexual, Christopher had hesitated between embarrassment and mistrust. He was embarrassed to assert his egoistic demands at a moment when collective action was needed. And he was wary of using the attitude towards homosexuals as the sole criterion by which any political government or party was to be judged. Yet his challenge towards each one of them was: "OK, you talk about freedom of expression. Does that include us, or not?"[256]

A Fascistic Fascination?

Not all homosexual intellectuals took up with the left. Some were fascinated by the fascistic model, which corresponded to an aesthetic and political ideal that was in vogue in certain homosexual circles. The attraction of fascism seldom took the concrete form of joining the party; it was more a matter of being sympathetic, of some vague alliance. Curiously enough, it found an echo in the Parisian lesbian community. Here, too, one must be careful in analyzing what part homosexuality played, since party affiliation was influenced even more so

---

255. Christopher Isherwood, *Christopher and His Kind*, *op. cit.*, p.248-249.
256. *Ibid.*, p.248.

by other factors such as class. Nevertheless, we may ask what was the attraction of political movements that were in principle hostile to the homosexual.

An élitist and aristocratic homosexuality

One faction of German homosexual activists proclaimed a nationalist and racist ideology. Hans Blüher, the theorist of the Männerbund, thought that a men's state would be the ideal political form. He was also a member of Gemein-schaft der Eigenen, Adolf Brand's homosexual movement, whose ideology was aristocratic, antifeminist and inegalitarian; it was the opposite of the WhK, which was close to the socialists. Brand and Blüher were not Nazis, but neither were they worried during the 1930s, when they were visible representatives of the German homosexual community. The poet Stefan George (who had founded a nationalist club with poetic and aristocratic overtones around the cult of a teenager, Maximin, who died at sixteen years), was also courted by the Nazis but rejected any compromise: he died in exile in Switzerland. Thus, we must be careful: the elitist tendency of German homosexuals was founded on a romantic notion of the days of yore, and was more similar to the völkisch than the fascistic trend. Even if their ideals might have brought them closer to Nazism, they did not have anything to do with the NSDAP (National-Socialist Workers Party). It seems that it was the populist component of Nazism, more than its attitude with regard to homosexuality, that kept them away. Many of the aristocratic homo-sexuals saw the Nazi party as a bunch of rough and uncouth thugs — so it could never serve as the source for the rejuvenation of German society.

Many of the more visible lesbians of the 1920s and 1930s also took posi-tions close to Fascism. The question divided the small community of lesbian intellectuals in Paris, which split into two quite distinct camps. The liberals included Djuna Barnes, Sylvia Beach, Colette, Hilda Doolittle, Janet Flanner, Adrienne Monnier and Virginia Woolf. On the other side were Romaine Brooks, Radclyffe Hall, Lucie Delarue-Mardrus, Liane de Pougy, Alice Toklas, Una Trou-bridge, Gertrude Stein and Natalie Barney. There were several factors behind their paradoxical choice: most of the latter group were characterized not only by their considerable wealth but also by their vague anti-Semitism. These women paradoxically replicated the dominant male ideology; by cozying up to the fas-cists, they expressed a certain misogyny, a homophobia, and they projected onto the Jew the fear of "the other."[257] Instead of rising up against an ideology that would oppress them, they identified with the reactionary forces. They tacitly aligned themselves with a fascistic program that was hostile to them, in the belief that their economic privileges, their social class, even their religion, would protect them.[258] They imagined that the war to come would put an end to Western civilization as they knew it and that they would then be able to go on again with their former way of life under the aristocratic and cultural regime that Fascism, in their view, would establish.

The example of Radclyffe Hall is emblematic: as we have seen, she identified with men and thus, in fact, with the male cause; the lesbian model she contributed to creating is largely based on traditional values. Radclyffe Hall was no feminist: her view of the evolution of woman's fate was pessimistic and unpleasant. A minority of women would manage to secure their independence and occupy of positions of responsibility, but the majority would always prefer to restrict themselves to their role as wife and mother. In every field except that of sexuality, Radclyffe Hall embodied the conservative middle-class values of high English society. She was rich, and was allied with the conservatives, defending her class interests and the Establishment. When she was on trial, she was shocked to see that only the Labour party defended her book. At the end of the 1930s, she settled in Florence and nourished a certain admiration for Mussolini and the fascists. After a dispute with a tradesman who had tried to swindle her, she appealed to the local fascists, saying: — In cases like this, the Party is really a source of consolation.[259]

The deterioration of the international situation seemed to her a direct consequence of the treaty of Versailles and the Jewish influence. Her anti-Semitism and anticommunism were increased by her contact with her friend Evguenia Soulina, a Russian exile: — Jews. Yes, I really begin to be afraid of them; of course not the two or three dear Jewish friends I have in England, but Jews in general. I believe they hate us and they want to cause a European war, then a world revolution, in order to destroy us completely."[260]

---

257. For a discussion on this subject, see Shari Benstock, "Paris Lesbianism and the Politics of Reaction, 1900-1940," in Martin Duberman, Martha Vicinus and George Chauncey Jr. (dir.), *Hidden from History*, London, Penguin Books, 1991, 579 pages, p.332-346.

258. Liane de Pougy was a Catholic; Radclyffe Hall and Alice Toklas converted to Catholicism.

259. Letter from Radclyffe Hall to Evguenia Soulina, 15 March 1939, cited by Michael Baker, *Our Three Selves: A Life of Radclyffe Hall*, London, Hamish Hamilton, 1985, 386 pages, p.329.

260. Letter from Radclyffe Hall to Evguenia Souline, 22 March 1939, cited *ibid.*

In the same way, Gertrude Stein's affiliation with the right was only the logical consequence of her antifeminism and anti-Semitism. The couple she formed with Alice B. Toklas was a caricature; it rested on a strict division of roles and, while Alice was confined to "feminine" pursuits, only Gertrude received intellectual praise. — Heterosexist society is scarcely threatened by a relationship which is so culturally determined. Stein wrote and slept while Toklas cooked, embroidered and typed... " She was not a radical feminist. She was Jewish and anti-Semitic, lesbian and scornful towards women, ignorant of economics and hostile to socialism.[261]

Some of these people were strikingly blind. A friend of D'Annunzio, Romaine Brooks spent the Second World War in Florence, fully confident in Mussolini. When his arrest was announced on July 25, 1943, she wrote in her journal: — With the imprisonment of Mussolini, the dream of a unified Europe collapses, that is what the fascists say and the nightmare is reinforced by the steady advance of the Bolshevik army.

Natalie Barney also settled in Florence, recreating there a little court and living in total obliviousness to outside events. Gertrude Stein, who remained in France, translated documents into English for the Vichy regime. Colette's attitude was also ambiguous: some of her writings appeared in serial in *Gringoire*, including "Bellavista" in September 1936. *Ces plaisirs* (*These Pleasures*) were to be published there in 1931; only the first parts came out, December 4 to December 25. In one issue of *Gringoire*, she denounced Leon Blum for his non-French origins, accused Salengro and reported on the annual gathering of Nuremberg by indicating Hitler as an authentic friend of France.[262] While she signed the declaration of rightist and leftist writers for the unity of Frenchmen along with Aragon, Malraux, Maritain, Mauriac and Montherlant, during the war she continued to publish apolitical texts in collaborationist newspapers like *Le Petit Parisien*. *Julie de Carneilhan* appeared in *Gringoire* in 1941. In November 1942, she sold an article on Burgundy to *La Gerbe*; Herbert Lottman, her biographer, notes that the newspaper then presented Burgundy as an old German province, and transformed Colette's text into a piece of propaganda. It is not clear if she was tricked; but there was certainly a superficiality on the part of the writer who never took a clear position on political questions. Her publications, which gen-

---

261. Blanche Wiesen Cook on Gertrude Stein, cited by Shari Benstock, *Women of the Left Bank, Paris 1900-1940*, Austin, University of Texas Press, 1986, 518 pages, p.19.

262. See Herbert Lottman, *Colette*, Paris, Gallimard, coll. "Folio," 1990, 496 pages.

erally remained very far removed from ideological problems and the war, attest that she did not realize how much was at stake.

Other intellectuals simply chose tacit collaboration. In Germany, A.E. Weirauch, the author of the lesbian best-seller *Der Skorpion*, continued to be published under Third Reich. She did not join the Nazi party, but became member of the Nazi writers' organization, Reichsschriftumskammer.

Obsessed by their privileges and the concern for protecting their own little world, many lesbians closed their ears to Virginia Woolf's analysis, as affirmed in *Three Guineas:* that feminism is opposed to Fascism, which rests on a patriarchal view of society. If the lesbians taking refuge in Paris were able to express their sexuality freely, it was because of their social and financial advantages; they were bound by these privileges to the same institutions which oppressed them; and therefore they did not seek to oppose an ideology which corresponded to their deepest convictions.

Erotic and aesthetic appeal

More difficult to grasp is the aesthetic and erotic attraction which Nazism exerted on certain homosexuals. In *Kangaroo*, D.H. Lawrence associates the power of persuasion of the masses with latent homosexuality. Thus Kangaroo, leader of an Australian fascist movement, attracts disciples as much by his intense powers of seduction as by his political ideas. The hero, Richard Evans, albeit a socialist sympathizer, allows himself to be swept along for a moment by an almost carnal attraction for Kangaroo. Political combat and the workingman's fraternity combine in a kind of Männerbund that sees friendship as the basis for direct action.

For other homosexuals, the fascistic fascination seems more like a quest for self-destruction. Having internalized the prejudices of society, they endeavor to prove how abject they are. Self-hatred, vice, betrayals, these are the stations of the cross that they see as inevitable. Maurice Sachs is a good example. Sachs was born in 1906; his real name was Ettinghausen. He was Jewish but refused to admit it. Even as a child, he wanted to be a girl. He studied in a self-managed school inspired by the English model. There was a lot of sports activity there, and the boys made special friendships. Sachs became the victim of certain pupils, was tortured and perhaps raped.[263] He had several homosexual experiences. His

---

263. See Henri Raczymow, *Maurice Sachs ou les Travaux forcés de la frivolité*, Paris, Gallimard, 1988, 503 pages. See also chapter three.

novel *The Sabbath* talks about this period of especial debauchery which ended with the expulsion of a great number of pupils in 1920. Thereafter, Sachs spent time at trendy clubs and met famous homosexuals: Abel Hermant, Jean Cocteau. Then he met Albert Cuziat. In 1926, he entered the Carmelite seminary, but fell in love with a fifteen-year-old American, Tom Pinkerton. The scandal ended his religious career. From there on out, he lived a very chaotic life. In 1936, although he had hitherto been adamantly against Stalinism, he signed a contract for *Maurice Thorez et la Victoire communiste.* Just about then, Gide returned from the USSR, and Sachs seemed to be politically off-balance. After 1940, he was living on the fringes. He got involved in the black market, traded with war profiteers, signed up for dirty work of various kinds, but did not get involved with the Germans. Then he suddenly left his apartment in 1942, and his trail became enigmatic: in November 1942, he was in Hamburg; but he was Jewish, homosexual, and did not speak German. It is possible that since 1942 he was in the Gestapo in France. In Germany, he was a voluntary worker in a camp. He met a homosexual doctor, anti-Nazi, for whom he translated the evening news from London Radio. Then, he met another homosexual doctor, a Nazi, who named him a French deputy to the executive committed of the camp. At the end of April 1943, he wanted to get out of that but still wanted to make himself useful to Germany. He worked for the secret service of the Wehrmacht, while continuing to pursue a very active homosexual life. November 16, 1943, he was arrested with his friends for reason homosexuality, pursuant to $175. He was interned at the Fuhlsbüttel prison, north of Hamburg, and died there in April 1945, one day before the British arrived, lynched by his cellmates. An absolute outsider, like Genet he made disloyalty his rule. Nietzschean, influenced by Gide and his theory of the gratuitous act, he planned his own descent into hell, like the necessary sanction for a sin that can never be expiated.

MISUNDERSTANDING OR BETRAYAL? THE LEFT SHIFTS BETWEEN PURITANISM AND OPPORTUNISM

In the 1920s, many homosexuals were inclined to support the left. Since the end of the 19th century German social democracy had expressed interest in the homosexual cause. The Russian revolution fostered the idea of a left that was favorable to sexual minorities, determined to grant the individual the right to his own body, against hypocritical and conservative middle-class morals. However,

the attitude of the left was ambiguous and unstable, and then it became radicalized in the 1930s.

The Soviet Illusion

The establishment of the Soviet Union seemed to be an important mile-
stone for English and German homosexuals. In 1918, the Russia Bolshevik
decriminalized homosexuality,[264] which placed it at the avant-garde of the
sexual reforms of the 1920s and earned it the recognition and the admiration of
European homosexuals.[265] By easing the legal penalties for homosexuality, the
Bolsheviks embodied the forces of progress. They seemed to be promoting a new
system of sexual morals, based not on false respectability but on the rehabilitation of the body and on equality of exchanges in love. However, in 1934, homosexuality as a "fascistic perversion" become a crime again in the USSR.

In fact, the Marxist position with respect to homosexuality was never very
clear. The basic text on the subject is Friedrich Engels' *The Origin of the Family,
Private Property and the State* (1884). The division of labor between men and women
is not questioned and heterosexuality is presented as natural. The topic of homosexuality is touched upon only incidentally, in connection with ancient Greece,
and in the most negative manner possible: "But the depreciation of women was
paralleled by the degradation of men, and went so far as to make them fall into
the repugnant practice of pederasty and to dishonor themselves by dishonoring
their gods by the myth of Ganymede."[266]

Engels was known to detest homosexuality, "the abominable practice of
sodomy" which he called "a shocking vice and against nature," the sign of a
sexual failure and a degradation of women. After Karl Marx sent him a pamphlet
by Karl Ulrichs, in June 1869, Engels responded: "This is a very curious 'Uranist'
that you've sent me here. These are really revelations against nature. The pederasts are starting to add up and discover that they represent a force within the

---

264. In tsarist Russia, homosexuality was a crime: according to article 995 in the
criminal code of 1832, which was derived from various German penal codes, *muzhelozhstvo*
(anal relations between men) was interdicted and could be punished by a loss of all rights
and by exile to Siberia for four to five years. In cases of rape or seduction of minors or
mentally retarded persons, article 996 recommended a sentence of ten to twenty years
forced labor (Simon Karlinsky, "Russia's Gay Literature and Culture: The Impact of the
October Revolution," in *Hidden from History, op. cit.*, p.347-364).

265. It remained a crime in Georgia, Azerbaidjan, Uzbekistan and Turkmenistan.

266. Friedrich Engels, *L'Origine de la famille, de la propriété privée et de l'État* [1884], Paris,
Éditions sociales, 1971, 364 pages, p.64.

State. They only lacked an organization, but, according to this text, it seems that they already have one.... How fortunate it is that we personally are too old to fear that when this party wins any of us will have to pay a bodily tribute to the victors.... But just wait until the new penal legislation of northern Germany adopts the *droits du cul*,[267] and things will change considerably. For us poor people out front, with our puerile attraction for women, it's going to become very difficult."[268]

Thus it is clear that the sources of Marxist thought give no hint of tolerance for homosexuality. The charge of intellectualism reinforces the myth of an innocent working class, "naturally" inclined toward the good, and safe from all sexual perversions. From the point of view of homosexuality, this prefigures the concept of "fascistic perversion": a "deviant sexual behavior can be the product only of the decadent classes; a homosexual workman obviously must have been corrupted by a bourgeois. In the same way, a lesbian is an inactive woman, who seeks to while away her days; a good revolutionary cannot be a lesbian, she cannot even be a feminist: "I would not bet on the reliability and perseverance in combat of any of these women whose personal love life is inextricably intermeshed with political activity. Nor for that of those men who run after every skirt.... No, no, that is all incompatible with the revolution!"[269] Youth is not spared, either: "The youth movement does not escape this disease, either — the concern for being 'modern' and allocating a disproportionate place to the question of sex .... As many have reported to me, sex is the number one topic among youth organizations .... It can very easily lead one or another to *sexual excesses, ruining the health and strength of young persons*[270] .... Ultimately, sexuality and revolution do not seem compatible: [the revolution] does not tolerate orgiastic excesses like those which are normal for the decadent heroes and heroines of D'Annunzio. The dissolute sexual life is bourgeois, it is a manifestation of decadence."[271]

Certain writings did maintain the myth of a USSR that was liberal on the homosexual question. Dr. Grigorii Batkis, director of the Institute for Social

267. In French in the original.

268. Letter dated 22 June 1869, cited by Hans-Georg Stümke, *Homosexuelle in Deutschland, eine politische Geschichte*, Munich, Verlag C.H. Beck, 1989, 184 pages, p.20.

269. Lenin's response to Clara Zetkin in 1920, published in 1925, cited in Clara Zetkin, *Batailles pour les femmes*, Paris, Éditions sociales, 1980, 444 pages, p.192.

270. Lenin, *ibid.*, p.188. My emphasis.

271. *Ibid.*, p.192.

Hygiene in Moscow, wrote a pamphlet *The Sexual Revolution in Russia* (1923) and it was published in Germany in 1925. He affirmed that the Soviet State did not interfere in sexual questions as long as there was no violence and no one was injured. The article "Homosexuality" which appeared in the first edition of the Soviet Encyclopedia, volume 17, in 1930, is also evocative. It cites Hirschfeld and Freud to justify the non-criminalization of homosexuality, but says that while homosexuality is not a crime it is still, in the view of Soviet legislation, an illness. Also, even if the change in the law encouraged homosexuals to breathe more freely, it was no guarantee of a shift in attitudes. Admittedly, during the period when homosexuality was legal, no one was persecuted; Soviet representatives were sent to the congress of Magnus Hirschfeld's World League for Sexual Reform in 1921, 1928, 1929 and 1930; he was even hosted for a visit to the USSR in 1926. It was also anticipated that the fifth congress of the League would take place in Moscow, but it was finally held in Brno, in Czechoslovakia. Nevertheless, Simon Karlinsky noted that compared to the tsarist period, which was very repressive by law, and the revolutionary era, which was only superficially liberal, there was a greater tacit tolerance during the first Soviet period. Homosexual Soviet writers like Mikhaïl Kuzmin (1875-1936) were not mentioned in the Soviet press; they were never criticized directly for their sexual orientation, only on the basis of their social origins. Many artists married in order to protect their careers. Sergei Eisenstein presents a particularly striking example of the confusion in Western Europe as to the situation of homosexuals in the USSR. In the USSR, he had tried to repress his homosexuality; it seems that he was influenced on this subject by the Party line: "If it weren't for Marx, Lenin and Freud, I would have become a new Oscar Wilde," he revealed to the critic Sergei Tretiakov.[272] Finally, during a trip to Berlin and Paris he got over his fears — the ultimate paradox when we realize that German and French homosexuals at that time thought of the USSR as a model. After a scandal in Mexico, under threat from the Soviet government to reveal his private life and stop him from making any more films, Eisenstein had to go home and agree to marry.

The hostility to homosexuality in the press and within the government never did wane. Gorky declared in *Pravda* and *Izvestia* that the new law of 1934 ensured "the triumph of proletarian humanism" and that the legalization of homosexuality had been Fascism's principal cause.[273] He penned the shock line,

---

272. Cited by Simon Karlinsky, "Russia's Gay Literature and Culture...," *loc. cit.*, p.361. 86*Ibid.*

"Wipe out homosexuality and Fascism will disappear."[274] The press launched a homophobic campaign comparing homosexuality to "a degeneration of the fascistic bourgeoisie." It was not just a crime against morality, but a crime against the State, "a social crime" lumped together with banditism, counter-revolutionary activities, sabotage, espionage, etc. It became grounds for three to five years in prison in "benign" cases, and from five to eight years if one of the partners were dependent on the other (articles 154a and 121). According to Wilhelm Reich, there were cases of homosexuality with the state security agencies. In January 1934, there were multiple homosexual arrests in Moscow, Leningrad, Kharkov and Odessa, including many artists. Homosexuality was equated with a rejection of socialism; it was said that a member of the working class could never be homosexual.

However, while homosexuals were looked upon with severity and contempt, they were not systematically persecuted; as long as they remained discrete, as long as they married, they were generally left alone. The enthusiasm of many homosexual intellectuals for the Soviet example thus rests primarily on a misunderstanding. Marxism retained a puritanical outlook on sexual questions, quite apart from any general liberalization of morals. Homosexuality was rejected by most theorists of Marxism and homosexuals were barely tolerated in the USSR. Fundamental progress, in the form of the de-criminalization of homosexuality, was only a temporary concession.

Support from the Anarchists

During the inter-war period, a certain anarchistic faction came to support the homosexual cause. However, due to their low numbers and their lack of organization, their influence on public opinion was negligible.[275] Individualistic

273. Excerpt from an article from 1934, "L'humanisme prolétarien," translated in France in 1938.

274. Indeed, the anarchist movement was quite diminished after World War I, with the exception of Spain where it played a very significant role in the civil war. Anarcho-syndicalism, especially, had failed by the tie of the war to bring to fruition the notion of the "general strike." In France, the Union Anarchiste had some 3000 members in 1938. French anarchists were opposed to the State, to capitalism, to state institutions such as the school and the army. On questions of sexuality and family, they proclaimed themselves against the family and marriage and in favor of free unions instead. See Jean Maitron, *Le Mouvement anarchiste in France*, t.II, *De 1914 à nos jours*, Paris, Maspero, 1983, 435 pages.

275. *Ibid.*, p.174.

anarchists, in particular, were interested in the sexual question. Eugene Armand gives a definition of individualism: Any group or association which seeks to impose upon an individual or upon a human community a unilateral concept of life, economic, intellectual, ethical or different, is not individualistic anarchy; that is the touchstone of anarchistic individualism.[276] The anarchistic individualists were especially inspired by the philosophy of Max Stirner and his disciple John Henry Mackay.

Stirner's individualism could be used as a basis for a defense of homosexuality. Indeed, his philosophy, by developing the viewpoint of the individual released from the constraints of society, allows sexual minorities to flourish and supports the assertion of personal singularity. Stirner questions morals that result directly from the dominant classes: " 'Crime' and 'disease' are two nonegoistic points of view, in other words they are judgments which do not come from me, but from another, whether the injured thing is the law, a general concept, or the health of an individual (the patient) or of a body (society). 'Crime' is treated without pity, 'disease' with a 'charitable gentleness,' 'pity,' etc."[277]

This passage can easily apply to homosexuality, which was considered as a crime and at the same time a disease, and was judged with severity or commiseration depending on the point of view. Stirner also shows that the general consensus dominates the moral framework; the homosexual, like any "individual," i.e. men who think for themselves and defend their rights to be "different," is only a scapegoat, a unifying force for the rest of society: "The people furiously set the police on everything that looks immoral or even just improper, and this moralistic popular rage protects the institution better than the government could ever do."[278]

Stirner's followers expressed a great tolerance with respect to homosexuals. Unlike the Communists or Socialists, whose views were changeable and ambiguous, the individualistic anarchists defended homosexuals with constancy and clarity. In France, various works published under the direction of Eugene Armand at the Éditions de l'En-dehors clearly express their sympathies for homosexuality: "The attitude of the anarchistic individualists with regard to homosexualism is not about prejudices, or taking sides; it reconciles the scien-

---

276. Max Stirner, *L'Unique et sa propriété*, Lausanne, L'Age d'homme, 1972, 437 pages, p.283.

277. *Ibid.*, p.284.

278. Eugène Armand, *L'Homosexualité, l'Onanisme et les Individualistes*, Paris, Éditions de l'En-dehors, 1931, 32 pages, p.19.

tific point of view with an absolute respect for personal freedom."[279] This liberalism is expressed in several works dealing with homosexuality, but also in the friendly support lent to the homosexual magazine *Inversions*. There is a danger of over-generalizing, however; the tolerance displayed by the anarchist leaders was not always shared by the base. *Inversions* was the subject of a quite a debate among the readers of *L'En-dehors*.[280]

This anarchistic thought presents two arguments in favor of homosexuality: the first is its provocative value in questioning established values, the powers that be. Homosexuality eats away the patriarchal society from within. Armand points out an aphorism from the anarchist Isaac Goldberg: "Sexual perversities are to love what anarchy is to bourgeois conformity."[281] The second, based on individualistic values, argues in favor of minorities of all kinds; the homosexual, just like the partisan of free love, has the right to live out and express his difference. "From the standpoint of pure liberty, it is obvious that one cannot restrict an individual from using his body as he likes. If not, and this applies as well to homosexualism as to masturbation or prostitution, it's a small step to arbitrariness and inconsistency."[282]

However, this tolerance must not be equated to proselytism. Armand was clearly heterosexual, he did not wish for homosexuals to take over, he did not think that homosexuality was a higher form of love — which explains why he criticized Corydon and those who sought to establish distinctions between "inverts" and "pederasts." Simply, he felt that everyone had the right to do what he liked and that it was not right for others to judge: "[Let's have] freedom to practice love, each one as he likes — but keep the door closed!"[283]

---

279. Dr Choubersky, who wrote in the 12 March 1925 issue, was indignant. To him, homosexuals were sick and inversion was a "congenital defect." The homosexual act was ignoble and "would represent *the normal coïtus of a drunken brute with a brood female* as idyllic." Homosexuals knew nothing of the true meaning of love, they were fated never to know anything but substitutes for normal men or women. Other readers showed somewhat more understanding, but were shocked by the elitist tone of the writings and the pretensions of some of the inverts who seemed to believe themselves superior to the others. Even so, the tolerance did not go as far as approval: homosexuals were still abnormal.

280. Eugène Armand, *L'Émancipation sexuelle, l'Amour en camaraderie et les Mouvements d'avant-garde*, Paris, Éditions de l'En-dehors, 1934, 23 pages, p.2.

281. Eugène Armand, *L'Émancipation sexuelle, l'Amour en camaraderie et les Mouvements d'avant-garde*, Paris, Éditions de l'En-dehors, 1934, 23 pages, p.2.

282. *Ibid.*, p.4.

283. Eugène Armand, Vera Livinska and C. de St Hélène, *La Camaraderie amoureuse*, Paris, Éditions de l'En-dehors, 1930, 32 pages, p.31.

The individualist arguments inscribe the defense of homosexuality in the register of minority rights but they are also based on a clear knowledge of the homosexual milieu and the problems that homosexuals meet. Armand quotes Carpenter, Ulrichs, Ellis, Krafft-Ebbing, Féré, and Moll. He researched the state of the law towards homosexuality in France, Belgium, Holland and Italy. He was familiar with the newspapers of the German militants, *Der Eigene* and *Die Freundschaft*. However, the conclusion of the French anarchists, while it is liberal, is biased. Rather than defending homosexuality on the basis of individualism and a questioning of social prejudices, they fell in line with the tradition of educating the public by presenting homosexuals as victims and by expanding the medical dialogue. Still, they did maintain a firm and positive position:

> The cases of congenital inversion regard homosexuals themselves; those who are really ill, if it is proven, are pathological and not disciplinary cases. [The anarchistic individualists] recognize homosexuals' right to associate, and to publish newspapers, magazines and books to expose and defend their case, and to invite into their groups latent uranists. [They] do not make except inverts of either sex.[284]

An example more representative of the influence of the individualistic anarchists in the defense of homosexuality can be found in J.H. Mackay (1864-1933). He was a homosexual and a disciple of Stirner, and wrote a biography of the latter; he had ties to Adolf Brand's Gemeinschaft der Eigenen. Under the pseudonym of Sagitta he operated as a homosexual activist. For Mackay, the defense of homosexuality is part of a general anarchistic fight against any oppression of the individual. However, by refusing to offer any justification for homosexuality, he placed himself in an extremely marginalized position, not well suited to the German society of the inter-war period. While it was eminently creditable, his action did nothing to further the progress of homosexual liberation or the education of the public. The individualistic philosophy carried to its logical conclusion seems more like a romantic ideal than a political action. One realizes this in the reading of his novel *Der Puppenjunge* (1926), which recalls the adventures of a fifteen-year-old boy, Günther, from the provinces, who goes to Berlin to find work and sinks into prostitution. The novel is interesting for its description of the shady side of Berlin and for his original presentation of homosexual relations, detached from any medical reference and any attempt at justification. He denounces above all the system where money dominates, and which is supported by established family men, who make a point of satisfying their desires in anonymity and impunity.

---

284. *Ibid.*, p.20.

Lastly, one may ask what was the influence of the philosophy of Nietzsche, as the basis for a critique of morals and a rehabilitation of homosexuality. Nicolaus Sombart says that Ludwig Klages, a homosexual known to all of Munich, who gave lectures to young boys, expressed boundless admiration for Nietzsche; he tried to bring him back to life by staging ecstatic dances of young boys. Indeed, there are several arguments in Nietzsche's philosophy that legitimate sexual deviance. For him, morality was only the sum of the conditions necessary to the conservation of a poor, half- or completely-damaged species.[285] He reproaches the Church for fighting passion by "castratism." "For, to attack the passions at the root is to attack life at the root: the practices of the Church are hostile to life.... "[286] And that is the morality that is "against nature," that is, "almost any morals that are taught, preached and advocated even now, rise on the contrary against the instincts of life," and they are a condemnation, sometimes secret, sometimes open and insolent, of these instincts...."[287]

Such assertions questioned all the bases of the traditional society and reversed the roles. They made those who were "immoral" into a life-affirming force. From Nietzschean philosophy, certain homosexuals built a theory of elitist homosexuality and deduced from it that the homosexual is an aristocrat, a member of a higher class, above the common laws and affirming his difference as a kind of glory. One finds traces of these ideas in Adolf Brand, Gustav Wyneken and Hans Blüher.

The Confused Line of the German Left

The German left was very closely associated with the debate on homosexuality in Germany and therefore we can analyze developments from that perspective.[288] Conversely, the French and English parties never had to draw any conclusion about the question in a public debate and thus it would be difficult to draw any conclusions there.

---

285. Jean Granier, *Nietzsche*, Paris, PUF, coll. "Que sais-je?," 1982, 127 pages.

286. Friedrich Nietzsche, *Le Crépuscule des idoles*, fragments, Paris, Hatier, 1983, 95 pages, p.74.

287. *Ibid.*, p.74-75.

288. See W.U. Eissler, *Arbeiterparteien und Homosexuellenfrage zur Sexualpolitik von SPD und KPD in der Weimarer Republik*, Berlin, Verlag Rosa Winkel, 1980, 142 pages; and Friedrich Koch, *Sexuelle Denunziation, die Sexualität in der politischen Auseinandersetzung*, Frankfurt-am-Main, Syndikat, 1986, 223 pages.

The SPD and the KPD, allies of the homosexual movements

The interest of the German Socialists in homosexual rights goes back to the end of the 19th century. While the party remained extremely noncommittal on the question, certain individuals decided in favor of homosexuals, like Ferdinand Lassalle, Eduard Bernstein and August Bebel. Under Weimar, the German Social-Democratic Party (SPD) was the leading German party.[289] While it always seems to have been one of the principal supporters of the homosexual struggle, it engaged in less visible ways alongside the militants. However, several eminent Socialists signed the WhK petition, like Rudolf Hilferding, who was a Minister for Finance and editor of the organ of the Independent German Social-Democratic Party (USPD), *Die Freiheit;* Gustav Radbruch, who was a Minister for Justice; Friedrich Stanpfer, editor of *Vorwärts,* organ of the SPD; the president of Reichstag Löbe and Hermann Müller, who was a chancellor of the Reich later on. The SPD stood up on several occasions against the repression of homosexuality. At the congress of Kiel, for example, in 1927, it adopted a resolution asking for the abolition of laws against divorce and homosexuality. Nevertheless, the SPD was not noteworthy in the 1920s for its militancy on the question, and it appears even on this point to have been in retreat compared to the pre-war period.

The German Communist Party (KPD) was founded in January 1919.[290] It immediately became interested in the homosexual cause. Articles on the question were published regularly, in particular in *Berlin am Morgen* and *Welt am Abend* under Willi Münzenberg. Nevertheless, no names of known Communists are found on the WhK petition. The links between the KPD and WhK were close, however, since Richard Linsert was at the same time a member of the Party and Secretary of the WhK. At the same time, Felix Halle, the legal expert of

---

289. It had a million members, 203 newspapers, and was related to the General Confederation of German Workers. As part of the government, until 1923 it was part of the center-left coalition which comprise, in addition to the SPD, *Zentrum* and the German Democratic Party (DDP). In the 1919 elections, SPD received 45% of the votes, but only 21% in May 1924. It regained some ground after that, with 30% of the votes in 1928, but showed a net decline in 1932 with 20%.

290. It came out of the Spartakist movement, which was badly shaken up after the deaths of Karl Liebknecht and Rosa Luxemburg on 15 January 1919. It quickly became a mass party with 350,000 members, 30 dailies and by 1932 more than 15% of the electorate. Even more than the SPD, the KPD recruited among young people jeunesse and the peasantry. Since 1923 the KPD, having shed the "leftist" elements, became a well-disciplined party that followed Moscow's direction.

the KPD, had participated in drafting the legislative counter-proposal for the WhK. Moreover, as a communist representative, he was present at the congress of the World League for Sexual Reform that was held in Copenhagen in 1928.

The KPD's position on homosexuality is specified in the book by Halle, *Geschlechtsleben and Strafrecht* (1931): "The proletariat, conscious of its class, detached from the ideology of property and liberated from the ideology of the Churches, approaches the question of sex and the problem of homosexuality with an absence of prejudices attained thanks to a comprehension of the social structure as a whole... In consonance with the scientific advances of modern times, the proletariat looks upon these relations as a special form of sexual gratification and expects the same freedoms and restrictions for these forms of sexual life as for sexual relations between the sexes, i.e. the protection of sexual minors from attack,.... control of one's own body and, finally ... consideration for the rights of third parties.[291]

Halle published several articles aimed at drawing the attention of the communist readership to the sexual question. Thus an article appeared in *Die Internationale* on November 1, 1926 entitled "Reform of the Penal Code on Sexual Matters and the Proletariat," where he expounded his theories. The leading class used the Penal code to satisfy its sadistic instincts; it is in its interest to control the sexual life of the popular classes and thus to keep the proletariat in check. According to Halle, it was grotesque to condemn homosexual prostitution at a time when a million young people were unemployed and thrown out on the street. Lastly, he recalled that in the USSR, homosexuality was not condemned by law. Here we see an original approach to defending the homosexual cause: the proletariat must show solidarity with homosexuals, for both are victims of the ruling class which seeks to retain control of the individuals in order to keep them docile and underpaid. Homosexuality was dependent on social conditions. Male prostitutes were not necessarily degenerates, but were forced into it by poverty. By linking homosexuality and the working class, Halle reprised a topic that was dear to the intellectual English homosexuals, but which was counter to received opinion: for a long time, homosexuality had been regarded as vice of the decadent rich and aristocrats.

The SPD and the KPD had to express their positions during the various debates on the reform of the Penal Code. The SPD, now a part of the government,

---

291. Cited by James D. Steakley, *The Homosexual Emancipation Movement in Germany*, New York, Arno Press, 1975, 121 pages, p.83.

declared itself open to compromise with the bourgeois parties.[292] Gustav Radbruch, socialist Minister for Justice from October 1921 to November 1922, decided in favor of decriminalization, but his draft law, which abolished §175, was not retained. In 1929, the SPD voted for the depenalization of homosexual acts between consenting adults, but it sided with all the other parties (except the KPD) on the repression of homosexual acts involving dependents, minors and male prostitutes.

Unlike the SPD, the KPD would not hear of collaborating with the bourgeois parties. Thus it was the party in the Reichstag most in favor of homosexuals. It asked in particular that the law not treat homosexuality any differently from heterosexuality: no harsher penalties for homosexual prostitution, no higher age of sexual majority, no broadening of the concept of indecent exposure. These goals matched exactly those of the WhK. Thus the KPD succeeded it as the best defender of the homosexual cause, and its ties with the militant movements were reinforced. In June 1924, it announced itself at the Reichstag in favor of the abrogation of §175 and in favor of an amnesty for all those already convicted or whose lawsuits were pending. In 1927, during discussions of the governmental draft law at a plenary session, the communist deputy Koeren asked for the removal of the paragraph. He based his argumentation on the example of the States of the South of Germany which, until 1871, had not condemned homosexuality. In 1929, the Communists were the only ones to vote for the depenalization of homosexuality, whatever the conditions. On October 8, opening day of the debates of the commission on the reform of the Penal Code, the communist deputy Alexander voted for the total suppression of section §21 of the Penal Code which concerned incest, bestiality, rape, sexual intercourse with minors and indecent writings, in addition to homosexuality. His proposal was not adopted. At the time of the Reichstag debates in 1932, the communist deputies expressed their support for the homosexual cause once again.

Deputy Maslowski stressed the inconsistency of the legislation, underscoring in particular the fact that neither lesbianism nor was Onanism condemned. However, in spite of their efforts, neither the SPD nor the KPD turned out to be definite allies for the homosexual cause.

---

292. *Zentrum* was opposed to decriminalization.

Homosexuality at the heart of party politics

The SPD and the KPD adopted a two-faced approach to homosexual politics. On the one hand, they supported the homosexual movements and called for the abolition of 175, on the other, they took advantage of the homosexual scandals to tarnish the political bourgeoisie and their opponents, and did not hesitate to launch homophobic campaigns themselves. In 1902, *Vorwärts* published an article revealing that Alfred Krupp, the wealthy industrialist and arms manufacturer, had entertained young men at his villa in Capri. The scandal led Krupp to commit suicide. The Eulenburg affair was also exploited by the SPD for political ends. In July 1924, the Haarmann case[293] was the pretext for a new campaign. *Rote Fahne*, a communist newspaper, described Haarmann on July 17, 1924 as a very serious criminal, a sadistic homosexual well known to the police and the courts. The communist press now started referring to police brutality as "Haarmann's methods," and demanded that "cops be purged of their sadistic, homosexual, criminal, monarchist and fascist elements."[294] These abuses led Bund für Menschenrecht to publish a protest, in number 24 of *Blätter für Menschenrecht* of 1924, which is highly illustrative of the confusion and disappointment of the homosexual organizations.

However, the most serious scandal was that which broke open in 1931 and 1932 around the figure of Ernst Röhm. The first phase started in 1931. In fact, that year, Röhm was at the center of a major homosexual scandal.[295] A first suit was brought against him and several of his friends; it opened on June 6, at the court of Munich. The waiter Fritz Reif gave a deposition against Röhm. Few before Christmas 1930, he had been led by one of his friends, the hotel employee Peter Kronninger, to a room in a building on Barerstrasse. There lay a man named Ernst, naked on a bed; a few days later, Kronninger indicated that it was Ernst Röhm. Ernst, after having stripped him, embraced him and masturbated him. Then he turned to Kronninger, who had also been undressed, and continued. Kronninger had promised Reif money for his services; days passed without the payment arriving and Reif sent a note, threatening to reveal everything to the police if he did not get 25 RM at once. Via Kronninger, he accepted just 8 RM. Kronninger and Röhm denied the whole thing. Kronninger had known Röhm for

---

293. See chapter five.

294. *Die rote Fahne*, 26 July 1924, cited by W.U. Eissler, *Arbeiterparteien und Homosexuellenfrage...*, *op. cit.*, p.105.

295. BAB, R 22/5006.

two years, there had never been anything sexual between them. Röhm, for his part, admitted that, "from a sexual point of view, he was abnormally inclined." He admitted to having engaged in some lesser offenses but said he had never committed any infringement of §175.[296] The cases were eventually dropped for lack of evidence.

However, on April 14, 1931, the socialist newspaper *Münchner Post* published an anonymous letter from a former Nazi, who accused Röhm of being homosexual. In June, the newspaper published several letters which reiterated the same assertions. The June 22 bore a spectacular headline: "A Hot Fraternity in the Brown House. The sexual life of the Third Reich." On June 24, 1931, *Völkischer Beobachter*, organ of the party Nazi, denied the charges and accused the newspaper of having fabricated the documents. The affair gained steam in 1932. March 7, 1932, in the midst of an election campaign, *Münchner Post* published letters from 1928 and 1929 addressed by Röhm to a friend, Dr. Heimsoth. Röhm was then in Bolivia and he expressed his regrets at not finding any companions. He missed the young Berliners. The socialist press began to describe Röhm's homosexuality in the horrified and hysterical tones usually reserved for the cheapest newssheets. The June 22, 1931 *Münchner Post* speaks about "fornication of the kind referred to in §175, to make your hair stand on end." The March 10, 1932, *Vorwärts* ran a headline about young SA "in the clutches of M. Röhm." The Communist Party, in *Rote Fahne* of March 11, 1932, joined in: "The Hitlerian party is a nest of informants and spies, of intrigues between the leaders and the most horrible corruption!" *Welt am Abend* talked of "Intrigues and sexual Hypocrisy around §175 in Hedemanstrasse," and "Captain Röhm abuses unemployed young workmen." The campaign sought to reveal the hypocrisy of a party that was claiming it wanted to restore the virtue of the German people and which railed against homosexuality as a Jewish and Bolshevik plague. Leftist parties particularly hoped to upset parents whose children were involved in Nazi movements.

The campaign had disastrous effects on public opinion for it equated homosexuality with corruption and Fascism. The WhK was extremely anxious, and sent the head office of the SPD a long letter demanding an explanation and questioning the reality of the party's support for the homosexual movement.[297] The SPD answered positively: "The social democratic party has not modified its concept of homosexuality ... the social democratic press used the Röhm affair

296. Under §175, only acts "resembling coïtus" were punishable.
297. Cited by W.U. Eissler, *Arbeiterparteien und Homosexuellenfrage...*, *op. cit.*, p.111.

only because the adherents of national-socialism support the repression of homosexuality and we would like to call attention to the hypocrisy of a party that seeks to label homosexuals as criminals and yet leaves one of them in a position of authority....the party does not intend to throw opprobrium on homosexuals nor to insult them. We will discuss this matter at the appropriate time and hour with the representatives of our party press."[298]

The campaign must have seemed good politics for the leadership of the SPD, but it was completely incompatible with the commitments the party had made with regard to homosexuals; moreover, they used the same means as those which it intended to fight. Kurt Tucholsky, a journalist at *Weltbühne* and Communist fellow traveller, took violent exception to the casual insults made by left with regard to homosexuals:

> For quite a while now, the press of the radical left has been disseminating accusations, jokes, and wounding remarks about Captain Röhm, a member of the Hitlerian movement. Röhm is, as we know, homosexual ... I regard these attacks as completely indecent.... Above all, one should not go spying on his adversaries in their beds. The only thing which is allowed is the following: to call attention to remarks made by the Nazis about 'the vices of the East' and the post-war period as if homosexuality, lesbian love and similar things had been invented by the Russians and had been infiltrated inside the German people, noble, pure and intact. If a Nazi says this kind of things, and only then, it is permitted to say: you have homosexuals in your own movement who admit their inclinations, who are even proud of it — so keep quiet!....— We fight the scandalous $175, everywhere we can, therefore we must not join the choir of those among us who want to banish a man from society because he is homosexual.[299]

In fact, at the very center of the Communist Party, there were differences of opinion concerning homosexuality. Certain remarks linked homosexuality and capitalism, and an article published in *Rote Fahne* October 28, 1927 described homosexuality as "non-proletarian." Starting in 1934, homosexuality was clearly labeled as "a fascistic perversion."

The delicate alliance between Communism and sexuality were well illustrated in Germany by the difficulties encountered by Wilhelm Reich. He started out as a member of the Austrian social democrat party in 1927; he joined the KPD in 1930 and persuaded it to link the various movements for sexual reform into one organization, the Deutscher Reichsverband für Proletarische Sexualpolitik (or Sexpol), which called for the abolition of $175. For Reich, who sought to reconcile Marxist theory and psychoanalysis, the social revolution would have to

---

298. *Ibid.*, p.112.
299. Ignaz Wrobel (*alias* Kurt Tucholsky), *Die Weltbühne*, n° 17, 26 April 1932.

encompass a sexual revolution as well. At the end of 1932, his relations with the Party deteriorated and he was thrown out in February 1933. The same year, he left Germany for Denmark, before emigrating to the United States in 1939.

Thus, the relations between the German left and the homosexual movements were thus complex. If the SPD and the KPD were the WhK's best potential allies in obtaining the abolition of §175, they also used homosexuals as a political football. Most of the homosexual leaders, who supported the left, whether they were in the WhK, Gemeinschaft der Eigenen or the Bund für Menschenrecht, were bitterly disappointed by the attitude taken by their allies. If it seems excessive to call it a betrayal, at the very least it was insincerity and opportunism.

GENEALOGY OF A CRIME: HOMOSEXUALITY AS A FASCISTIC PERVERSION

"Totalitarianism and homosexuality go together."[300]

After 1934, the Communist Party defined homosexuality as a fascistic perversion. Furthermore, several authors, at various times, evoked the close linkage between Nazism and homoeroticism.[301] However, the repression that hit homosexuals in 1933 shows clearly that Nazism was basically hostile to homosexuality. Therefore it is advisable to clarify the Nazi position on the question.

For a long time homosexuality was a minor subject within the Party: no punitive measures were envisaged, for example, against Nazi homosexuals. In fact, two mindsets were in conflict: that of the Männerbund, defended by Hans Blüher, and that of hysterical homophobia, represented by Himmler. Hitler took a pragmatic approach for quite a while, without clearly taking sides. If he finally went for repression, it is because this solution was only logical in the racist and demographic political context.

---

300. Theodor Adorno, *Minima Moralia*, Paris, Payot, 1980, 230 pages, p.43.

301. Klaus Theweleit, *Male Fantasies* [*Männerphantasien*, 1977], Minneapolis, The University of Minnesota Press, 1987-1989, 2 vol., 517 pages. George L. Mosse, *Nationalism and Sexuality, Respect and Abnormal Sexuality in Modern Europe*, New York, Howard Fertig, 1985, 232 pages.

The Myth of the "Männerbund"

Hans Blüher (1874-1945) authored two works that had a great impact in Germany early in the century: *Die deutsche Wandervogelbewegung als erotisches Phänomen*, in 1912, and *Die Rolle der Erotik in der männlichen Gesellschaft*, published in two volumes in 1917 and 1919. Hans Blüher was close to the Irregulars and certain socialist circles, and he was a member of Gemeinschaft der Eigenen. His first work introduced Blüher's name to the general public by affirming the homo-erotic component of the youth movements. In his fundamental treatise, *Die Rolle der Erotik*, Blüher went further in trying to establish an overall theory of the virile State, starting from the associative base.

Blüher borrowed from Plato the term of Eros, which was also employed by Gustav Wyneken, and by which was meant adhesion to an object (a man) inde-pendent of its value.[302] The State, according to Blüher, was not the city, but the mass society of the turn of the century, authoritarian and in crisis. The historical Männerbünde which he cited as examples are quite telling: the order of the Tem-plars, Knights of Malta and cadet schools. Each was of a strictly hierarchical nature, with military discipline. He used Sparta as a reference more than Athens. Blüher borrowed from Freud the idea of bisexuality, repression and sublimation. But he rejected the idea of homosexuality as a fixation, an inability to change one's object of desire, for that notion was in contradiction with his intention of making inversion the optimal form of sexuality, both necessary and desirable. In fact, Blüher falls in line with Gemeinschaft der Eigenen. St. Ch. Waldecke pub-lished an article in *Der Eigene* entitled "Männerbund und Staat,"[303] in which the Männerbund is described as a higher form of organization, a countervailing power to the State which brought together the elite of the nation in a never-ending fight for liberation. The goal of the Männerbund is not equality, the prayer of the weak, but freedom, the desire of the powerful. Blüher wanted to found an elitist, aristocratic society, a cultural State joining together young men of valor, linked by the invisible bonds of their love: "The young boy falls in love with an older man after being detached from his mother and his first female bonds." Those who are not destined to govern must obey; such is the function of people as redefined according to an erotic and cultural hierarchy. The enemies of the Männerbund are clearly identified: women, the family (the male State must

---

302. Hans Blüher, *Die Rolle der Erotik in der männlichen Gesellschaft*, Iéna, Eugen Dieder-ichs, 1919, t.I, 248 pages, p.226.
303. *Der Eigene*, 1 October 1920.

"break the principle of the family"), the school, and age groups that confined adults and adolescents to separate worlds.

The Männerbund — "male association" — was the fundamental structure, and the model for others. The State must be a kind of global Männerbund, establishing a homoerotic society. "The masculine society is the sociological means used by inverts to protect themselves from social death." Only homosexuals (sublimated ones, for Blüher is extremely reticent when it comes to complete sexual intercourse) will be able to reach the top levels of the State. The theory of the Männerbund as conceived by Blüher seeks be an alternative to both liberalism and Marxism.

What impact did Blüher's thought have on Nazism? Hitler read his books; he quoted him in his *Tischgespräche*. His idea of the Männerbund was especially applicable in SA and the organizations derived from the Freikorps. It provided the basis of the Nazis' ideology of power — they were supposed to embody the German elite, a political aristocracy called to dominate the inert masses. Alfred Rosenberg took up this idea in *The Myth of the 20th Century*: "The order of the Teutonic knights, the templars, freemasonry, the Jesuit order, the rabbinical society, the English clubs, the German student corporations, the German Irregular forces after 1918, SA, the NSDAP, etc., are all examples which prove, irrefutably, that a political, social or religious model, as different as it may be in the forms that it takes, almost always ends up as a society of men and their civil education."[304]

Blüher's theory inspired a great many discussions; it was became the basis for a whole meditation on the organization of adolescent groups and in particular it showed that homoeroticism played a part in the power of the team leader. In fact, as Nicolaus Sombart explained, a male, elitist, aristocratic and cultural association seemed a natural German alternative to the Weimar Republic, which was liberal and democratic. It was particularly well received in a number of extremist groups, which proliferated after the war. These movements developed a nationalist and reactionary ideology, and rejected the republic as a daughter of disaster, the fruit of treason.

Sombart himself was part of a youth group inspired by the example of the Irregular forces and the myth of the Männerbund. He described it as a "cult of

---

304. Alfred Rosenberg, *Le Mythe du XXe siècle* [1930], Paris, Éditions Avalon, 1986, 689 pages, p.465. However Blüher, who at first was in high regard, soon saw the regime banning his books; he lived in retirement with his family until 1945. He seems to have been accused of not sufficiently vaunting his nationalism, and of not having specified that his *Männerbund* was German and nothing but German.

virility, friendship and fidelity ... this [was a] community bound by a pact and whose secret was male eroticism or, to express myself plainly, homosexual relations between the members of its basic team, at the center of which was the charismatic leader, Männerheld, the hero of the men."[305]

Nazi mythology falls into the same rubric.[306] It picked up the imagery of the left — the naked body, free and sportive, and distorted it into something rigid and violent, the imagery of combat, fighting, destruction. The seductive allure that emerges is always violently homoerotic, but it takes on a sadistic nuance that is only found in the images of Weimar. As Klaus Mann observed, afterwards:

> In those days, certainly, in that era of political innocence and erotic exaltation, we had no idea of the dangerous potentials and aspects of our puerile mystique of sexuality...[We did not see] that our philosophy based on "the significance of the body"...was sometimes used or exploited by elements that were not very sympathetic.[307]

The Nazi movement certainly exploited homoerotic imagery. Hitler very clearly associated beauty and the "Aryan race," and ugliness and the "Jewish race." Beauty is an infallible criterion for recognizing a healthy person; thus it must be made into a fundamental value, a goal to be attained. The "artists" of the regime, like Arno Breker and Joseph Thorak, represented the German ideal, the incarnation of the superiority of the race. Their ideal of beauty was derived from the ancient model, but was reduced to a few clichés: muscle, monumentalism, male superiority. The man's body became a symbol of the body of the German nation. Its virile force, its will for power announced the regeneration of the society, whereas the democracy was associated with the body in putrefaction, such as it is represented in expositions of "degenerate art." This representation was eminently narcissistic and rejected abnormality, defects, all that is "unhealthy" as a danger, a disease which risked infecting the entire body. The homoerotic connotations tied to worship of the body and to the will for power also appear very clearly in the treatises of Hans Suren, a Nazi officer who preached physical culture as means of safeguarding the purity of the race and exalting the size of the German people. In one of his works, *Gymnastik der Deut-*

---

305. Nicolaus Sombart, *Chroniques d'une jeunesse berlinoise, 1933-1943*, Paris, Quai Voltaire, 1992, 369 pages, p.26.

306. Ulrike Aubertin and Annick Lantenois, "La grande exposition de l'Art allemand et l'Art dégénéré," in *Art et fascisme*, Bruxelles, Complexe, 1989, 260 pages, p.139-154.

307. Klaus Mann, *Le Tournant* [1949], Paris, Solin, 1984, 690 pages, p.162.

schen, rassenbewusste Selbsterziehung (1935), physical exercises are abundantly illustrated with photographs of the author, nude, muscular, his body oiled. The athletic poses are also suggestive and aims to create a desire in the reader for the perfect body thus exposed. Admiration and desire are intermixed with other feelings, aggravated by calls for virile friendship.

The ideal of the National-Socialist hero, with powerful homoerotic connotations, is also eminently visible in the films produced under the Third Reich. Action films like *Hitlerjunge Quex, Juniors, D3 88* and *Crew Dora,* exploit the themes of heroism, virile beauty, and friendship between comrades to stimulate interest.[308] Leni Riefenstahl's propaganda documentary *The Gods of the Stadium* also uses homoerotic esthetics to exalt the regime. Just as it took over the liberation of the body for its own conservative purposes, Nazism built on the notion of the younger generation as the regenerative force of the nation; it celebrated its independence and enthusiasm. This ardent youth became the pillar on which it would build its State: "Youth is its own State, it holds up to the adult a kind of front of solidarity, and that is quite natural."[309]

Nazi mythology was also based on memories of the First World War.[310] Nazism touted itself as the extension of the friendship of the trenches and it kept alive the memory of those who fell in combat in order to fan the enthusiasm of the new generation. Thus, in the *Horst Wessel Lied*, the SAs do not march alone, they are accompanied by the invisible presence of the patriots who died "at the front." During the ceremonies at Nuremberg, a list of those who had died in service to the party was read out, and at each name, a member of the Hitler Youths appeared.

It is undeniable that Nazism was based partly on a homoerotic esthetics, but even so it should not be deduced that it was a pro-homosexual movement. Like other male movements, it attracted some homosexuals, in particular in the SA and the Hitler Youth, but that was only a marginal phenomenon and was not the aim of the leaders. There were probably no more and no fewer homosexuals

---

308. See Richard Grunberger, *A Social History of the Third Reich*, London, Weidenfeld & Nicolson, 1971, 535 pages.

309. Adolf Hitler, *Mein Kampf* [1925], Paris, Nouvelles Éditions latines, 1934, 685 pages, p.415.

310. George L. Mosse, "Souvenir de la guerre et place du monumentalisme dans l'identité culturelle du Nazisme," in *Guerres et cultures (1914-1918)*, Paris, Armand Colin, 1994, 445 pages.

within the NSDAP than in other parties. On the other hand, the NSDAP was characterized very early on by a virulent homophobia.

Hysterical Homophobia

Himmler expressed the principles of the Nazis' fundamental hostility to homosexual very clearly in a speech addressed to the general SS on February 18, 1937.[311] Himmler's speech is typical of the discourse on homosexuality in the inter-war period; it was not very original. Himmler presented himself in the form of a specialist on the question: "No service has accumulated as much experience in the field of homosexuality, abortion, etc., as the Gestapo in Germany." According to him, homosexuals were, first of all, a demographic danger. According to estimates, homosexual associations had signed up between two and four million members, but in his view there were only one or two million: "Not all those who were part of these associations were really homosexuals." This notion agreed with the opinion of many doctors who distinguished between "inverts" (or "real" homosexuals) and "pseudo-homosexuals," those who had been seduced and were likely to be recuperable. However, "If the situation does not change, our people will be destroyed by this contagious disease." This idea was not new: we have seen that it was one of the pet theories of the discourse on decadence in the inter-war period. Himmler immediately established a link between the contagion and the body of the nation: "But this is not about their private life: sexual activity can be synonymous with the life or death of a people, with world hegemony or a reduction of our importance to that of Switzerland." The German people must be numerous in order to conquer its vital space.

The second threat posed by homosexuality was the risk of a secret homosexual organization at the heart of the State: "If you find a man in a given position who has a certain penchant and if this man has decision-making power, you can be sure to meet in his entourage another three, four, eight, or ten individuals or more who also have this predilection." Himmler believed that homosexuals looked out for each other. Thus, if ministerial adviser X was homosexual, he would select as his associate not a qualified person, but a homosexual like him. The homosexual leader cannot operate rationally in the professional arena but would follow his instinct. Moreover, you cannot trust a homosexual: he is sick, loose, dishonest, irresponsible, and disloyal. He is "an ideal target of

311. Heinrich Himmler, *Discours secrets*, Paris, Gallimard, 1978, 255 pages.

pressure," with "an insatiable need for confidence." This is a compendium of the most banal prejudices with regard to homosexuals, all woven together into a notion attesting to the extreme danger of allowing homosexuals to function at the higher levels of the State.

After these various warnings, Himmler went to the heart of the matter: homosexuality in the SS. For Himmler, this was a fundamental contradiction: the SS were to be the elite of the German nation, intended to regenerate the country, and therefore could hardly harbor perverts and cowards. Himmler entertained the myth of an original Germany, Nordic, pure and brutal, which would have not known homosexuality (since that was a consequence of the mixture of the races). He found traces of it in the rural areas, which according to him were free of this plague.

To regenerate the race, concessions would have to be made. Himmler's Puritanism allowed for some curious compromises. He declared himself in favor of prostitution, "for one cannot want, on the one hand, to prevent all young people from falling into homosexuality, and on another hand to close off all outlets."[312]

He favored early marriages and tolerated illegitimate births. Young people in the cities, corrupted by the atmosphere of depravity that characterizes large cities, would be brought back to normality by discipline, order, sport, labor and by being restricted to camps. To limit the risk of spreading homosexuality, Himmler was ready to modify the operation of the State at a profound level, to ward off the ill effects of tradition and bourgeois morality. He wanted to stop the "masculinization" of girls, and to remove the advantages of male associations. Boys should stop being ashamed of loving girls and should stop giving greater value to male friendships. Himmler also took a swipe at Blüher for having spread these ideas. Young German must be knights, "men who are make themselves the champions of women."

To legitimate his ideas of fraternization between the sexes and sexual freedom, Himmler inevitably had to step away from Christian morals. In 1937, the great wave of denunciations of Catholic priests and monks had already begun. "We will prove that the Church, at the level of its leaders as well as of its priests, is in large part an erotic association of men that has terrorized humanity for one thousand eight hundred years now, requiring society to provide it with

---

312. *Ibid.*, p.87-88.

an enormous quantity of victims, and which in the past has shown itself to be sadistic and perverse."[313]

Himmler's ideal was that of a pagan, Dionysian society cloaked under puritan and idealistic emblems: "I consider it necessary to ensure that boys of fifteen to sixteen years should meet girls at dances, parties and other occasions. Experience shows that at the age of fifteen or sixteen the young boy is in an unstable position. If he develops a crush on a girl at a dance or has a little puppy love, he is saved, he moves away from the dangerous place. In Germany, we do not need to fret about putting boys and girls together too early and possibly encouraging them to have sex..."[314] In this, Himmler pulls together several influences, one of which is a traditional contempt for homosexuality, which is expressed among the common people as well as in the leadership circles and which is based on a series of clichés. Another is racist, pagan, Nordic: brandishing the specter of depopulation and of degeneration, he preached the destruction of the enemy within and the renewal of the race through orgiastic procreation and community. The last item was unique to Himmler: he was hysterically homophobic. His unreasoned fear and disgust made homosexuality an obsessive concern. His Puritanism almost verges on a certain voyeurism and a pleasure in governing and controlling the sexuality of others. This conjunction of traditional, historical and personal prejudices explains the scope of his discourse. As the organizer of large-scale repressions, he would live out his fantasies of purging and purification.[315]

By comparison, other Nazi leaders who expressed themselves on the question appear defensive or redundant, whether we look at the SS lawyer Karl-August Eckardt, author of an article entitled "The Unnatural Vice Merits Death," in *Das schwarze Korps* of May 22, 1935, or Alfred Rosenberg who, in *Der Sumpf* (*The Swamp*) and in *The Myth of the 20th Century*, violently attacks homosexuals and lesbians as "symbols of the cultural decline and the ruin of Europe."

However, generally, Nazi theoreticians considered sapphism to be less offensive than male homosexuality. It was thought to be less widespread, and it was thought that "pseudo-lesbians" were more numerous than "real ones." And especially, the Nazis considered female sexuality only as "passive" and "dominated" — nothing special in that.

313. *Ibid.*, p.93. On this subject, see chapter eight.
314. *Ibid.*, p.94.
315. Himmler frequently repeated his discourse on the homosexual menace, notably during a radio broadcast on the occasion of the police congress in 1937 (BAB, NS 19/4004).

Pragmatism and Scapegoats

The Nazi policy with regard to homosexuality, as it was defined by Hitler, was above all very pragmatic. Hitler was not a partisan of the Männerbund, even if he was conscious of the homoerotic tendencies at work within the movement. Neither was he an hysterical homophobe: he could, when necessary, tolerate homosexuality within his own party. His sexual policy was guided by a single factor: need for the survival of the race.

Racism and sexuality

In *Mein Kampf*, Hitler developed the principal theses of his sexual theories. The links between sexuality and race are constantly noted: "The sin against blood and race is the original sin of this world and marks the end of humanity if we indulge in it."[316] The dangers which threatened the race were primarily syphilis and the Jews, who embodied the degeneration of the individual. For him, as for the Church, the only goal of the sex act was procreation. This primary concern led him to reject any constraints that could weigh on the sex act and thus Christian and bourgeois morals: marriage was not an aim in itself — adultery, and childbirth out of wedlock contribute just like the others to the supreme goal.[317] However, it was essential that sexual energy not be dispersed vainly. In the same way that the British pedagogues encouraged the practice of sports to moderate sexual heat, young Germans were subjected to a military discipline which hardened them, exhausted them sexually and constrained them to chastity. The difference is constantly spelled out between healthy, procreative sexuality, useful for the State, and depraved sexuality, lust, and perversion. Those who are not healthy, physically and morally — and who thus have no social value — are guilty, and so are those who refuse to give a child to the community. The greatest sins are sterility, bodily infirmities, and giving primacy to the intellect over the physique. The homosexual is registered as guilty, even if this is not directly said.

In Nuremberg, September 8, 1934, the Führer defined the role of the woman in the National-Socialist State. The emancipation of women is "a formula invented by Jewish intellectuals." If "the world of man is the State," "the world of the woman is smaller: indeed, her world is her husband, her family, her children and her home," and "each child that she brings into the world is a battle won for

---

316. Adolf Hitler, *Mein Kampf, op. cit.*, p.247.
317. *Ibid.*, p.409.

the nation."[318] In the same way, Joseph Goebbels described women in his inaugural speech at the exposition on "Woman," on March 18, 1933, not as having "lesser qualities" but "different qualities."[319] And again, emphasis was laid on the need to increase the birth rate.[320] Under these conditions, marriage was no longer a private affair but a political responsibility. To raise children became a national duty.[321] The image of the woman was that of the "angel of the home," guardian of love and peace, and without political opinions. Consequently, it was important that she possess a "feminine allure." In his book *Die Wende der Mädchenerziehung* (*On Education for Girls*, 1937), Frank Kade describes the physical aspect of the German girl: "'The ideal of beauty' in the recent past, which exalted little painted dolls with small breasts and narrow trunks has been shaken. People are looking for powerful feminine figures, full-blossomed, exuding a natural health, a type of German woman whose proud beauty both mental and physical embody sacred fertility and the German will for life.[322]

Is Hitler's sexual theory a reflection of his private life? The question has been asked many times. Biographers have made much of Hitler's sexual frustrations, and his misogyny. Others, on the contrary, have said that he was a great success with women. Generally speaking, his sex life remains largely obscure and it would be risky to lend credence to the theories claiming he was a repressed sadist or homosexual. These charges, formulated by certain newspapers and then by German émigrés and the Communists, have more to do with efforts to discredit him than with any known facts. In fact, discussions of Hitler's sexuality do not shed any light on his sexual policies. Hitler was not

---

318. *Le Temps*, 10 September 1934.

319. Cited by Claudia Schoppmann, *Nationalsozialistische Sexualpolitik und weibliche Homosexualität*, Berlin, Centaurus, 1991, 286 pages, p.18.

320. With the Treaty of Versailles, Germany lost more than an eighth of its territory and about 10% of its population. In fourteen years, the population of Germany went up by more than 5 million to attain 65 million in total. The German population kept on going up but, between 1910 and 1933, the proportion of those under the age of 20 diminished. The drop in birth rates before the war was aggravated by the War itself. In the first three years after the war, they began to catch up again, then the birthrate began to decline again and fed fears of an eventual loss of population.

321. In 1938, a new law permitted divorce in case of a refusal to have children or of sterility. Divorces went up quickly, from 49,497 in 1938 to 61,789 in 1939. In 60% of the cases, the woman was blamed. See Claudia Schoppmann, *Nationalsozialistische Sexualpolitik...*, *op. cit.* By the same token, it was forbidden to publicize contraceptives, and abortion and sterilization were interdicted. In 1943, abortion merited the death penalty.

322. Cited in *Hidden from History*, *op. cit.*, p.74.

much concerned about homosexuals. He tolerated them in his entourage when they were useful. He may have been a misogynist, and built the Nazi State in the style of the Männerbund, with powerful homoerotic connotations. But his politics of power and conquest rested required an elevated birthrate: and according to that criterion, the homosexual was antisocial.

The hostility of the NSDAP was expressed very early and very publicly. The attack on Magnus Hirschfeld in Munich in 1921 occasioned rejoicings in the nationalist press. Thereafter, spiteful articles multiplied, while at the Reichstag, the NSDAP maintained an unambiguous position on the reform of the Penal Code. On September 15, 1927, Dr. Frick, NSDAP deputy to the Reichstag, expressed his party's opinion on the abolition of §175: "We are of the contrary opinion, that these people of the §175, i.e. unnatural sex acts between men, must be fought with all our might, because such a vice must lead the German people to ruin.... Naturally it is the Jews again, Magnus Hirschfeld and those of his race, who act as guides and as initiators, at the moment when all of Jewish morality is indeed devastating the German people." On May 14, 1928, in Munich, the NSDAP publicly expressed its opinion on the question: "It is not necessary that you and I live, but it is necessary that the German people live. And it cannot live unless it has the will to fight, for one must struggle to live. And it cannot fight unless it behaves like a man....Anyone who is considering a homosexual or lesbian love is our enemy!.... Might makes right, and the mighty will always be against the weak. Today, we are the weakest, but we will make sure we become the strongest again! But we will only be able to do that if we practice virtue. We reject all vice, and especially male homosexuality, because it takes away from us the last possibility of one day freeing our people from the slavery to which it is subjugated today."

The nationalist press indignantly attacked the reform of the Penal Code that was under consideration with the draft law of 1929. *Völkischer Beobachter* of August 3, 1930 was particularly menacing: "We congratulate Mr. Kahl and Mr. Hirschfeld for their success! But do not believe that we Germans will leave this law in force for one day, when we come to power." The homophobia of the Nazis was clearly marked from the beginnings of the movement, but people were late to recognize it. The existence of homoerotic tendencies within the party certainly misled certain homosexual groups that wanted to believe right up until the end that it was possible to find an area of agreement with Hitler.

Several times, during the legislative elections, the German homosexual movements (WhK, Gemeinschaft der Eigenen, Bund für Menschenrecht) sent various parties a questionnaire to test their attitude with regard to homosexuals. Until 1932, the NSDAP did not take the trouble to answer. When it finally did, its hostility was complete and unambiguous: "To your letter of the 14th this month [October] we reply that the subject that concerns you is, to put it bluntly, antipathetic to us in the highest degree."[323]

The Röhm case

The case of Röhm, discussed above, was particularly revealing in regard to Hitler's attitude toward homosexuality. Ernst Röhm was born in Munich in 1887 to a family of civil servants. His childhood was uneventful. At the age of nineteen, h joined the army and, in 1914, he greeted the war with enthusiasm. He distinguished himself there for his talent as an organizer. In 1919, he met Hitler and took part in 1923 in the Beer Hall putsch in Munich. Hitler admired the way he organized the SA,[324] and ignored any allusions to his homosexuality. Röhm did not recognize himself as homosexual until 1924. Then, not being particularly concerned for his reputation, he made no mystery of his preferences and was even a member of the Bund für Menschenrecht. He was a regular on the homosexual scene and had close ties in the Berliner world of male prostitution. In 1925, there was a quarrel (unrelated to homosexuality) between Hitler and Röhm, and he resigned. Then he was implicated in a lawsuit against Hermann Siegesmund, a prostitute who was in possession of compromising letters.[325] He left Germany and accepted a job with the Bolivian army. It was from La Paz that he wrote to the homosexual doctor and astrologer Karl Heimsoth the letters that were revealed by the *Münchner Post*. In 1930, a mutiny led by Captain Walter Stennes nearly destroyed the Sturmabteilung (SA), or stormtroopers, and in 1931 Hitler recalled Röhm, whom he appointed chief of the SA.[326] To keep the organization in line, the idea came up of giving the SA some military role — without anyone having a clear idea what form it could take. Under the effect of the Depression, the SA continued to grow, and had 700,000 men in 1932. Complaints about Röhm's sex life continued to pour in, but Hitler remained impassive. On

---

323. Published in *Das Freundschaftsblatt*, n° 44, 3 November 1932.

324. La *Sturmabteilung* (SA), or "assault sections," were founded 1921. Their purpose was to fight adversaries of the Nazi Party in the streets during political rallies. The SA was originally composed of veterans and members of the Corps francs; later it attracted young men and workers, and many who had been disenfranchised.

325. Richard Plant, *The Pink Triangle*, New York, Holt & Cie, 1986, 257 pages, p.59.

326. The homosexual lieutenant Heines, who was let go in May 1927 for lack of discipline and insubordination, was recalled on the same date.

February 3, 1931, he even defended him in a circular, saying: "The SA is not an institution of religious education for girls from good families, but an association of hardened combatants....The private life of the members of the SA is condemnable only if it reveals principles contrary to the fundamental duties of the Nazi ideology."[327] Until 1933, hitler needed röhm to help him come to power and, in spite of the many scandals caused by his letters, hitler did not withdraw his confidence in him. In December 1933, Röhm was named a member of the government.

Beyond the declarations of the moment, how can we understand the elimination of Röhm?[328] Hitler had long regarded the SA as a means of balancing the old and the new forces within the party. But in 1934, the SA, which had absorbed the Stahlhelm, counted 1.5 million members, most of them from the proletariat. It maintained a campaign of permanent revolutionary: after the "national" revolution, there would have to be a "nationalist-socialist" revolution or "second revolution." Moreover, Röhm wanted to transform the SA into a traditional army that would replace the Reichswehr. This ran directly counter to the political ambitions of the military, supported by Hindenburg, the president of the Republic and supreme chief of the armies. Hitler, for his part, was opposed to any action that might lead to a conflict or competition with the regular army, a supporter of the regime. Moreover, Röhm had made plenty of enemies. Heinrich Himmler, who became chief of the SS on January 6, 1929, hated Röhm, who was his superior since the SS was subordinated to the SA. Since the mutiny of 1930, the SS had been charged with keeping an eye on the SA. But the SS, which had been founded in 1923,[329] still had only 50,000 members in 1932. The power of the SA constrained Himmler's ambitions. This latter, supported by Reinhard Heydrich, chief of the security service, and Hermann Goering, minister-president of Prussia and chief of the Gestapo (Geheime Staatspolizei, or secret police), put the thought in Hitler's mind that Röhm might be planning a coup d'etat, and thus aggravated the tensions within the NSDAP. Warnings against the "second revolution" were multiplying. On February 28, 1934, Hitler announced that the

---

327. Cited by Hans Peter Bleuel, *La Morale des seigneurs*, Paris, Tallandier, 1974, 247 pages, p.100-101.

328. On this point, see Marlis Steinert, *Hitler*, Paris, Fayard, 1991, 710 pages.

329. The origins of the SS go back to 1923, when Hitler founded a pretorian guard to ensure his personal security. This guard received is definite name in 1925: the *Schutzstaffel* ("echelon of protection"), or SS. It was an élite group, apart from the party and the organization.

army would remain the only legitimate military force; Röhm was quite loud in expressing his disappointment, thus lending some credibility to rumors of a plot. Hitler and Röhm had a last interview on February 4. In the meanwhile, Himmler, Heydrich and Goering gathered false documents intended to support the notion that there was a conspiracy afoot.

"Operation Colibri" was launched. On June 29, Hitler went to Munich, accompanied by his close associates and some officers of the SS. Adolf Wagner, the Bavarian Minister of the Interior, had been charged with arming the local SS. The Reichswehr, under the command of Colonel Werner von Fritsch, secretly provided the weapons, ammunition and transportation. Himmler, Goering and Heydrich were responsible for the situation in Berlin. Röhm's successor had already been found: it would be Victor Luze, an SA chief.

Röhm and his friends were vacationing at the Pension Hanselbauer on Lake Tegern, in Wiessee, near Munich. A meeting with Hitler was scheduled for July 1. During the night of June 29 to 30, Hitler arrived in Munich. He had several SA lieutenants arrested, then went to the pension, "riding crop in hand, to confound the traitors there."[330] SS troops raided the hotel. Lieutenant Edmund Heines was found in bed with his driver. Some of the SA were slaughtered on the spot, the rest were taken away to Stadelheim prison. In Berlin, Himmler and Goering directed the repression, which extended beyond the SA circles. Nearly three hundred people were killed, including the organizers of the "leftist plot," Gregor Strasser and the former chancellor Kurt von Schleicher; representatives of the conservative opposition, like Dr. Klausener, head of Catholic Action; and collaborators of Papen, and old adversaries of Hitler, like von Kahr who had caused the failure of "the putsch of brewery" in 1923.[331]

Röhm was not cut down immediately. On July 1, Theodor Eicke, head of the first SS concentration camp at Dachau, showed up in his cell and handed Röhm a revolver. Röhm refused to commit suicide, which would have been an admission of guilt; he was shot by Eicke.

At no moment did Röhm's homosexuality play any part in his elimination. However, it was the main thing pointed out to the public to explain the massacre, with the attempted putsch. The first to promote this version was Goering, in his official statement to the press, which was picked up in the national and

---

330. Marlis Steinert, *Hitler, op. cit.*, p.268.
331. Serge Berstein and Pierre Milza, *Histoire du XXᵉ siècle*, Paris, Hatier, 1987, t.I, 433 pages, p.327-328.

international press. He made much of the morals of the SA and the spectacle that had been found at the pension: "In the next room [to that of Röhm] the Führer found Heines, Breslau's prefect of police and chief of the Silesian attack sections, in the company of a 'joy boy' (Lustknabe)." Röhm was presented as a sick man, trapped by his homosexuality and thus subject to influence: "Röhm, by virtue of his unfortunate disposition, allowed himself to be dragged into affairs that would prove fatal for him. No doubt impelled by his special circumstances, he surrounded himself with a staff of men who led him to feel that he was the strong man of all Germany. Thus was forged the plan to institute a regime led by these morbid individuals."[332]

This fable spread rapidly. Goebbels' report was even clearer:

> They discredited the honor and the prestige of our assault sections [SA]. By their unparalleled life of debauchery, by their display of luxury, and their carryings on, they flouted the principles of our movement, the principles of austerity and personal cleanliness. They were on the point of casting onto the entire leadership of party suspicion of a shameful and disgusting sexual anomaly....Millions of members of our party, the SA and SS are glad of this purifying storm. The whole nation can breathe again, delivered from this nightmare. They have seen once more that the Führer is determined to act without mercy when the principle of propriety, simplicity and public decency is concerned and that the punishment is all the more severe when it has to do with people in high places.[333]

On July 13, Hitler himself gave a speech before the Reichstag at the old Kroll Opera, which was broadcast to all of Germany to justify the "clean-up" operation. "In the SA, sections started to be formed that constituted the core of a conspiracy against the normal concept of a healthy nation and against the security of the State. We noted that people were being promoted in the SA for the simple reason that they were part of the coterie with certain characteristics. ... I gave the order to shoot the main perpetrators of this treason and to cauterize these abscesses that were poisoning us..."[334] Thereafter, Röhm's former friends were eliminated. On October 10, 1934 the Court of Munich opened a suit against Peter Granninger[335] and several other close associates of Röhm, mostly young homosexuals, two of them still minors.[336]

---

332. *Le Temps*, 2 July 1934.
333. *Ibid.*, 3 July 1934.
334. *Ibid.*, 15-16 July 1934.
335. This is probably Peter Kronninger, who was already implicated in the 1931 case. 149.BAB, R 22/5006.
336. BAB, R 22/5006.

The elimination of Röhm had taken on the mask of a crusade against immorality. The image of the Führer personally rousting the traitors and degenerates was engraved in the popular imagination, supporting the idea of a virtuous regime, a defender of family and morals. However, Röhm's homosexuality had been only a pretext and never was a real factor.

* * *

Nazism never displayed a unified vision of homosexuality. The Männerbund types exalted virile friendship and made them one of the bases of the State, but homosexuality was never asserted as such by the regime. On the contrary, certain leaders, like Himmler, developed a hysterical homophobic rhetoric which was used as a basis for repression. In the Nazi Weltanschauung, the world was divided into communities which were not to mix: the races were to remain separate, the sexes were not to mingle. The homosexual crossed the boundaries and nullified the differences. He was an intruder who could not be tolerated.

For homosexuals, the 1920s were years of political disillusionment. Many homosexual intellectuals had worked for the left, but their efforts produced very little fruit. In Germany, the SPD and the KPD were the best defenders of homosexuals, but they too entertained homophobic prejudices, fostering in the public opinion an image of the homosexual as sadistic, bourgeois, debauched and fascistic. For the Nazis, they were a symbol of the corruption of Weimar and the left. Homosexuality was used by all sides as a tool and a weapon.

PART THREE

A Factitious Tolerance: Losing Ground under the Repression of the 1930s

The Homosexual as a Criminal and a Victim

And since, my soul, we cannot fly
To Saturn nor to Mercury
Keep we must, if keep we can
These foreign laws of God and Man.

—A.E. Housman, *Last Poems*

CHAPTER SEVEN

CRIMINALS BEFORE THE LAW

The cult of homosexuality, the bold talk of the homosexual associations, the flamboyance of the "gay" cities, and the fad of homosexuality in literature did not erase the reality of anti-homosexual repression. Male homosexuality was a crime in England and Germany in the 1920s and 1930s. This fact is essential: even if there was more tolerance in some sectors of society, being homosexual always brought shame and social exclusion. In France, on the other hand, homosexuality was not covered by the law. This unique characteristic French situation made a difference: it partly explains the lack of militant movements and the individualism of French homosexuals. Similarly, sapphism was not considered a crime in the three countries concerned: lesbians were therefore not united with male homosexuals, and did not share their concerns.[337] However, the forces of reaction were present throughout the period. They were based on the traditional institutions, the State, the Church, the press, and on the public's latent homophobia. Together they maintained a climate of muted fear, even among the most liberated homosexuals.

---

337. Here we will look at the repression of homosexuality in England during the period of 1919-1939; for Germany, we will analyze only the years 1919-1934 in order to maintain a valid basis for comparison. This is a comparison of forms of police repression under democratic regimes.

REACTIONARY ENGLAND (1919-1939)

> I do not know if this [homophobic] prejudice will one day be overcome by experience, knowledge or reason. It is the last bastion of pure irrationality in society. And England is the guardian and the center of it.[338]

English society in the 1920s was at a crossroads. The hedonism of the Roaring Twenties was denounced by those who wanted to maintain standards, who protested the new liberality and the abandonment of old rules of "respectability." Homosexuality was a crime punished by the law and it was a social sin punished by contempt and a loss of social standing. The homosexual threat was a frequent topic for legislators and judges, and the police took specific actions to root it out. Nevertheless, such efforts were largely ineffective.

The Legal Situation

Legislation on homosexuality went through several stages in England. Sodomy (buggery), a practice described as a "sin against nature," was prohibited between men and women as well as between men and animals and between men, since a law dating to 1533 under Henry VIII. Until 1861, the sentence for this "abominable vice" was death; then it was replaced by sentence that could range from ten years to life in prison. This law was directed against a precise type of sex act and not against a category of people, although it is probable that the majority of executions related to homosexuals. Its goal was primarily to ensure the reproduction of the species by avoiding the dispersion of male seed in acts that could not lead to procreation.[339]

The situation changed in 1885, following the Labouchère Amendment to Criminal Law Amendment Act:[340] — If any person of the male sex, in public or in private, perpetrates or is party to the perpetration, facilitates or tries to facilitate the perpetration by a person of the male sex of any act of gross indecency on a person of the male sex, this constitutes a misdemeanor; upon being found guilty he is liable to a sentence of imprisonment not exceeding two years, with or without forced labor." The amendment is remarkable for the imprecision of its

---

338. Cited by Dennis Proctor (ed.), *The Autobiography of G. Lowes Dickinson*, London, Duckworth, 1973, 287 pages, p.12.

339. See Arthur N. Gilbert, "Conception of Homosexuality and Sodomy in Western History," in *Journal of Homosexuality*, vol.6, n[os] 1-2, fall-winter 1980-1981; Vern L. Bullough, *Sin, Sickness and Sanity: A History of Sexual Attitudes*, New York, Garland, 1977, 276 pages.

formulation, which leaves it open to the most rigid interpretations. While the new law was less repressive than the old one (since it reduced the length of the sentence considerably),[341] it now condemned any form of sex between men. For the first time, the sodomite was no longer just a sinner, but a criminal; and homosexuality was no longer defined as a sexual practice, but as the search for sexual partners of the same sex. Homosexuals were regarded as a separate group from the rest of the population and were given special treatment; meanwhile, lesbians remained outside the purview of the law.

The condemnation of private acts encouraged blackmail. England became the only European country to condemn simple masturbation between men. Moreover, whereas the law of 1861 had rarely been applied, the Labouchère amendment drew attention to homosexuals, resulting in an appreciable increase in convictions. Wilde was one of its first and most famous victims.

In 1898, the Vagrancy Act further toughened up the law by extending it to solicitation for immoral purposes; it applied only to homosexuals. In 1912, the Criminal Law Amendment Act more clearly defined the Vagrancy Act by establishing the penalty for soliciting at six months in prison, with whipping in the event of repetition; this type of offense was tried in summary jurisdiction.

The Organization of Repression

How was the letter of the law applied in day-to-day reality? The simplest means to study that question is through the judgments handed down and the police and legal practices.

---

340. The genesis of this amendment is complex; the *Criminal Law Amendment Act* concerns the origins of juvenile prostitution and aims to protect girls from sexual abuse, by raising the age of consent from 13 to 16. While the bill was under consideration in the House of Commons "late on the night of 6 August 1885," an amendment was proposed by Henry Labouchère, a liberal deputy, with the initial purpose of making the bill fail by rendering it ridiculous. Several deputies were concerned to find that this clause dealt with an entirely different category of offenses than that which the law was intended to address, but the President of the House, Arthur Peel, having declared that "no matter what might be inserted" as an amendment to the law, the amendment would be adopted just one vote short of unanimously.

341. Homosexual acts committed with a minor, with or without consent, remained punishable by ten years in prison and could lead to a life sentence.

Changes in sentencing for homosexuality

Sentencing related to homosexuality varied over the period; and they do indeed seem to reveal trends of repression.[342] First one should note that throughout the period, the number of cases steadily went up. Police statistics show an increase in the number of reported crimes. Obviously, this trend does not necessarily mean that there were more homosexuals, but that the crack down and the methods of detection were more effective. The number of "unnatural offences" ("U") increased by 185% between 1919 and 1938, with the maximum reached in 1938, with 134 cases. The total crimes recorded by the police thus increased by 185%. The number of cases of indecency (I) increased by 155% between 1919 and 1938, the maximum figure being reached in 1936, with 352 cases. The most important figures are found for attempts (A) to commit unnatural offenses; this rather vague term seems to have referred to most of the cases of homosexual acts which were apprehended by the police but which had not yet been consummated; it seems that there was a preference for charging homosexuals for this crime rather than the two others, for it required less evidence. There was a startling increase of 902% in the number of cases, 92 in 1919, but 822 cases in 1938! Thus we perceive, throughout the period, a constant stepping up of repression that was particularly brutal around 1931-1932. It is clear that the police wanted to increase the pressure, and that is translated clearly in the charts and figures. It seems, however, that the increase in arrests was not immediately reflected in an increase in convictions. Thus, whereas 81% of the men arrested for crimes against nature were convicted in 1919, only 55% were in 1938. For public indecency, the figure goes from 88% in 1919 to 40% in 1936, a ridiculous figure. Finally, for attempts to commit unnatural acts, the rate of 81% in 1919 fell to 50% in 1938; and it was only 41% in 1937. Two reasons can explain these sharp drops. If we assume that the judges did not wish to harden the sanctions against homosexuals, that would imply that the police were alone in wishing to increase the repression. That seems rather improbable. It is more plausible that in their zeal, police officers were more and more careless in bringing credible evidence upon which to convict the suspects. Police repression

---

342. Statistical tables in the Appendices indicate the principal trends. The yearly charts have only been presented for 1919, 1933 and 1937. The statistics were published every year from 1919 to 1938; because of the war, the 1939 statistics are not detailed but are grouped with those for the period 1939-1945; I have indicated the 1940 statistics as well (*Parliamentary Papers*, "Accounts and Papers," Judiciary Statistics).

rests as much on intimidation as on punishment; by increasing their raids, by disturbing trysts, by arresting many suspects, the police maintained a climate of panic which led homosexuals to retreat into anonymity and the private sphere. That was probably a sufficient success for the police, since the public space was now in conformity with the prevailing morals. The counterpart was the relative impunity of the various homosexual "crimes."

It is also noted that the increase in the number of trials (+94% for crimes, +409% for attempts and +81% for public indecency) is also not distributed evenly. The vast majority of crimes against nature continued to be tried in circuit court [cour d'assise], whereas most attempts were now tried in correctional, unlike before. Thus, while in 1919 only 49% of the cases were treated in correctional, in 1938, 75% were. This gives the impression that the judges were trying to speed up the processing, to generate more sentences even if it meant reducing penalties (the charges being increasingly thin). This type of procedure was also preferred in cases of *flagrante delicto*. Men arrested for soliciting were also considered in correctional court.

Statistics on this subject were not kept regularly, and we have the figures only for the years 1919-1935. The figures are stable (45 on average) and ridiculously low: one must therefore suppose that most cases of male prostitution were dealt with under other labels (U, A, I) and not specifically.

A refined study, year on year, enables us to identify some broad trends. The number of convictions rose sharply between 1919 and 1938. If we take 1919, 1933 and 1937 as examples, we note that for crimes against nature, 78% of those tried in 1919 were convicted, but 90% in 1933 and 87.5% in 1937; for attempts, we go from 76% in 1919 to 80% in 1933 and 83% in 1937; and, for the public indecency, from 61% in 1919 to 75% in 1933 and 87% in 1937. Thus, the decline in the conviction rate due to the acceleration of police work and the concomitant lack of evidence is counterbalanced by the increased severity of the judges. The cases that arrive before the courts are judged mercilessly. The nature and the duration of the sentences show that clearly: right after the war and until 1923, crimes against nature still merited forced labor and could go up to ten years; from 1924 to 1930, only the prison terms were given; and from 1931 onward, forced labor was again applied, with severity. The age of those sentenced is another interesting indicator; from 1919 to 1929, those convicted were between 30 and 60 years old; in 1929 and especially 1931, they were often between 16 and 21. That might also be a sign of an increase in amateur prostitution, which relates, as discussed above, to unemployment.[343] It thus seems that the sentences were now applied with equal severity to all age groups, without any particular consideration for youth.

Appeals, on the other hand, were very stable: there were very few, and they were almost systematically rejected. Statistics from correctional show similar trends to the circuit courts; the number of trials went up markedly, from 74% in 1919 to 87% in 1933 and 1937.

Finally, we can study the results by district: during the three years under review, the sector of the Metropolitan Police (London) comes in at the top with 62 arrests in 1919, 149 in 1933, 185 in 1937. That seems normal, since the town of London is the center of English homosexual life. Nevertheless, some caution is necessary: in the German statistics, Berlin is not in the lead when it comes to arrests. Repression in the British capital was particularly strong, and case studies confirm it. The other districts that practiced a particularly repressive regime in those years were Lancashire, Southampton and York (West Riding). Certain areas experienced a sudden increase in arrests, which implies that a specific policy was being carried out with regard to homosexuality.

Let us take the case of Cheshire, which saw only 10 cases in 1930, 13 in 1933 and 105 in 1937; then we have Devon, 9 in 1919, 65 in 1933, 53 in 1937; Kent: 12 in 1919, 30 in 1933, 66 in 1937; and Warwick: 2 in 1919, 20 in 1933, 83 in 1937. Certain areas were completely spared, however, either because homosexuals were particularly discrete there, or because the police were not interested. It is difficult to say. But in rural zones like Dorset (0 cases in 1919, 3 in 1933, 2 in 1937), homosexuals probably lived very discretely.

In a general sense, the crimes were distributed throughout a greater number of districts since 1933. The biggest increase in such crimes took place in the large cities and the most industrialized areas, but the number of areas affected kept going up, which leaves one to suppose that the campaign to root out homosexual crimes was being extended across the whole country.

One can draw several conclusions from these statistical observations. First, while the 1920s may have been years of moral liberation, they were not years of legal permissiveness. There was a certain legal relaxation, however, until 1930-1931. The penalties were less severe and the judiciary acted as a brake, limiting the effect of the high number of arrests through the number of convictions.

---

343. The dates coincide: the number of unemployed hit 1,304,971 in 1929, crossed the threshold of 2 million in 1930 and *The Times* headline of 6 August 1931 shows a record of 2,713,350 out of work.

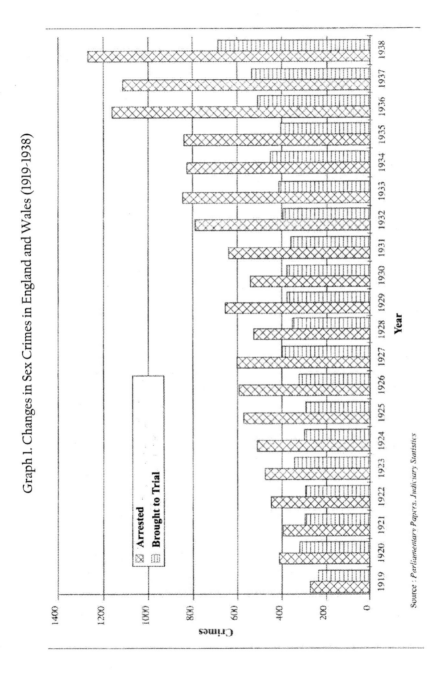

Graph 1. Changes in Sex Crimes in England and Wales (1919-1938)

However, even a light sentence (a fine, deferred prison term), even the threat of a lawsuit, could destroy a career and a family and could mean social opprobrium. After 1931, the intensification of the repression is obvious. We will see that this was not a matter of chance, but was carefully organized.

Police methods

We can hardly expect to come up with a comprehensive picture of all the methods employed by the police, of the social positions of the men they arrested, and the charges made against them; we do, however, have information from many archives[344] that provide detailed information on prostitution by the soldiers of the Guard, soliciting in the London parks, the monitoring of the public urinals, the methods used by the police, the way homosexual crimes were treated by the judges, and the policies the leading authorities followed in dealing with homosexuality.

The attitude of the British police toward homosexuals between the wars was characterized by contempt and a certain lack of concern. The sexual criminal was not very interesting prey and the police preferred to deal with other matters. In the 1920s, homosexuality remained a relatively minor problem, anyway, and the officers were satisfied to apprehend on the fact the male prostitutes and their customers, and to pursue the "queens." The goal was more to frighten them, to chase them out of one neighborhood, to operate arrests in mass: "The uniformed police were not regarded as man-eaters. I did not have the least idea of the rules, but they never chased us; they simply asked us to move on."[345]

In the 1930s, the police activity expanded and the homosexual community as a whole became a target. Throughout the period, the police looked on homosexuals as a particularly cheap kind of criminal. A policeman from those days describes arresting homosexuals in these terms: "The queer [was] treated like an inanimate object with no sensitivity. [The police officers] rubbed his face with toilet paper to provide proof of the make-up, they joked and laughed at him as if he were not there, and always found the same petroleum jelly packet in his pocket."[346] Very often the arrests bordered on the illegal, especially in cases of soliciting. The boy was identified on the basis of his look, his clothing, his make-

---

344. HO 45, HO 144, MEPO 2, MEPO 3, Public Record Office. Nonetheless, most of the documents are off limits for 75 years or are inaccessible. Furthermore, most of the cases seem to have vanished.

345. Quentin Crisp, *The Naked Civil-Servant* [1968], London, Fontana, 1986, 217 pages, p.29.

up. Prof of soliciting was pretty much beside the point: "The attitude of the law was arbitrary — basically, 'F_ you.' Boys who were arrested for soliciting were declared guilty before they ever opened their mouths. If they managed to say anything, the sound of their voice only resulted in increasing their sentence. I think the boys were right in thinking that they were convicted just because they were effeminate."[347]

At the Hammersmith police station, there was a group that "specialized in catching homosexuals."

> — They hardly talked about anything else, and anytime they found someone who would listen to their stories, they would howl with insane stupid laughter and sprinkle their anecdotes with insults — those bastards! — for fear that anybody might think they found pleasure in what about they talked about so much. They would go out in plain clothes and hide in the bushes and the urinals close to the tow path in Putney, and once every fifteen days they would triumphantly bring back a couple of old gentlemen whom they'd managed to surprise together; they'd spend the following month laughing nervously with their friends, remembering the details.[348]

This seems to have been the prevalent attitude. The agents of the Metropolitan Police in London were assigned strategic places for surveillance, mainly the parks and urinals. These officers worked in pairs, for a period of two months maximum. For the urinals of Marble Arch and Hyde Park Corner (two popular sites for male pick-ups) the district police chief called for "the use of two officers in civilian clothes during the week" and pledged, "We will not keep the same men on that job for long periods."[349] This concern not to leave the same officers on the job for too long is a reflection of two concerns: the fear that they would come to be recognized by those who used the urinals, and thus become useless, and the sense that to expose young police officers to such depravity was likely to disturb them psychologically, or even pervert them.[350]

The monitoring of the urinals was an official activity of the police, and it was a mainstay of the repression of homosexuality. The first allusion to such sur-

---

346. Cited by Richard Davenport-Hines, *Sex, Death and Punishment*, London, Fontana Press, 1990, 439 pages, p.145.

347. Quentin Crisp, *The Naked Civil-Servant, op. cit*, p.30.

348. Cited by R. Davenport-Hines, *Sex, Death and Punishment, op. cit.*, p.145.

349. Immorality in Parks and Open Spaces (MEPO 2/3231).

350. The *Times* of 7 December 1921 gives the outlines of an affair that casts a shadow on a policeman; Freeman Howard Carr, 38, who had been an agent in the Metropolitan Police since the age of 18, was sentenced to 9 months in prison for attempting to molest two boys.

veillance goes back to 1872; until 1923, the instruction books for police officers said this:[351] — People frequenting the urinals for evidently improper aims must be threatened with pursuit, and if they continue their practice and if there is evidence to justify their interpellation, they must be apprehended and charged." In 1923 the instruction booklet was modified. $140: — People frequenting the urinals for evidently improper aims must be threatened with pursuit. If they persist and commit an offence, they must be arrested." $141: — Each time that a man is challenged for persistently soliciting or importuning for immoral purposes in a public place (Vagrancy Act, 1898, section 1), every effort must be made to guarantee the independence of the corroborating evidence. The people thus solicited will have to provide their names and addresses and to present themselves at court. If they refuse their assistance, the details will have to be noted by the police officers in their pocket book and will be displayed as evidence." Here is evidence of a change in police practices in a definitely repressive direction. At the same time, there seems to be a growing concern to ensure the success of the operations. To avoid any breakdowns, it was further specified, in August 1937, that no police officer without experience was to be placed in "this delicate situation."

In fact, it was nearly impossible to secure third-party testimony and it seems that, in their fight against homosexuals, the police officers did not always benefit from the support of the population. Convictions were thus very difficult to obtain. Take the case of John Henry Lovendahl, a 67-year-old man who was tried for gross indecency in January 1938. He had been found masturbating, in clear view of passers by, in Crown Passage, North End Road, Fulham. Two policemen in plain clothes who were making their rounds at 12:30 entered a urinal located next to the pub "The Crown." Lovendahl was in the central stall. The first police officer called in his colleague, who confirmed the first officers observation. Lovendahl remained in the urinal from 12:30 to 12:55. Twenty men had come and gone from the urinals during that time and not one agreed to give his name and address to testify. No doubt some of them did not want to contribute to Lovendahl's arrest, but even more so, most of them must have feared that it would tarnish their own reputation. The place had become indissolubly linked to the practice; wasn't entering a urinal, that notorious homosexual hangout, proof of homosexuality?

---

351. MEPO 3/989.

The question of the urinals and soliciting in public was a thorny issue for the police services, which tried on several occasions to beef up their repressive arsenal. Several draft amendments to the instruction booklet were considered, like this one, going back to 1937: "If one observes people frequenting the urinals for evidently improper aims and if there is not sufficient evidence to justify an arrest, the facts must be reported without delay so that special measures are taken to resolve the problem, if that is considered necessary." The monitoring of homosexuals might have been a minor point compared to other crimes, but the police took this aspect of their work mighty seriously. Following discussions on this subject in August 1937, superintendent F. Smith of the Peel House police station observed that at the police academy they analyzed the exact meaning of "loitering" and "frequently" in detail so that students could define their action precisely. On the other hand, he suggested that the warning of the suspects was seldom practiced, for it was not very practical and was dangerous in any event. This indicates that a great deal of thought was given to the repression of homo-sexuality by the English police throughout the period.

Another problem arising from the control of homosexuality was that of plainclothes policemen. The use of plainclothes policemen was controversial, for many shysters extorted money from homosexuals by passing themselves off as police officers. It was proposed several times between 1919 and 1939 that police officers having to deal with homosexuals should go back to wearing their uni-forms; one recommendation by the Royal Commission on Police Powers and Procedure asked in particular that the use of plainclothes police stop being used in arresting homosexuals, and that this measurement be made public in order to prevent the risk of blackmail. A confidential memorandum of June 17, 1929 from the Ministry of the Interior, also asked that the use of plainclothes police be pro-hibited. Nevertheless, no measure was taken.

Several examples testify to the difficulties generated by the use of plain-clothes policemen. On September 26, 1933, an arrest was questioned:

> We received complaints that a certain urinal was used by sodomites. Conse-quently, the men who patrolled in plain clothes focused on this spot, but they were given no detailed instructions as to how to act; the result was that several people were incriminated for indecent conduct. The nature of the evidence that was fur-nished led the magistrate to make very forceful observations — which does not sur-prise me. It is obvious that, if the police act in this way, it can be suggested that, in a sense, they caused the infraction![352]

---

352. MEPO 3/990.

Another note dating to August 1933 reported a quite similar case. A policeman had obtained four arrests in a urinal using a method that at least bordered on provocation: he hung around the urinals waiting to be approached by a passer by. The arrested men had pleaded not guilty; the magistrate condemned the process used and recommended very light sentences: between three months and fifteen days in prison and a minimal fine (5 pounds).

It is certain that this type of technique often misfired. According to Quentin Crisp, a notorious homosexual who was quite familiar with the male prostitute milieux,

> — the professionals very quickly were able to identify a police officer, even in civilian clothes. Those who were caught were homosexuals who only occasionally went to the urinals, and also passers by who were intrigued by the police officer's activity: These were people who had never heard of homosexuality, but whose perfectly natural curiosity was piqued by any strange manifestation of human behavior, and so they were in danger because of police techniques. One may be certain that, even on a good day, simply asking the agent what, in the name of heaven, he was doing, would be enough to get you arrested; on a bad night, a simple glance in his direction would be sufficient.[353]

The arrests generally took place at the exit of the urinals and in the London parks, especially Hyde Park, which was known as a place of prostitution, female as well as male. The counts of the indictments were seldom listed as unnatural offence, i.e. sodomy, but indecency and indecent assault. The latter two terms covered everything form a kiss to mutual masturbation. Professional male prostitutes and soldiers of the Guard were arrested for soliciting.

The London police seemed to be particularly anxious about the high number of crimes recorded in the parks. This is how the case of William Richardson and Charles Pritchard, two young men arrested for indecent assault in Hyde Park, is described in the police report: "It is a strange case, one more example of these extraordinary, really incredible things which are done in the park from the point of view of morals. Here is a young man, apparently very respectable, who pulls in another young man of a social condition distinctly lower than his in Hyde Park at 11 o'clock in the evening, in winter, and suggests they go for a walk; they sit down, and at once he starts to act in an indecent way with a complete stranger."[354]

---

353. Quentin Crisp, *The Naked Civil-Servant, op. cit.*, p.81.
354. 18 January 1926: Prosecution of William A.J. Richardson and Charles Pritchard (MEPO 3/297).

While many civilians were arrested this way, it seems that the soldiers of the Guard remained the authorities' essential concern. They did, indeed, go in for a veiled prostitution in the city's parks as a way to enhance their incomes. A problem of jurisdiction arose, for the soldiers of the Guard were subordinate to the military authorities. However, in the context of the fight against homosexuality, the civil and military authorities were ready to cooperate: "The military authorities are eager to help the Police as much as possible in order to [stop all these unnatural crimes]..., but [they] consider that the civilians are worse than the soldiers, for they offer to them drinks, then take them along in the park and there lead them to [commit such crimes]."[355] Calling civilians the ringleaders promoting military prostitution became quite the fashion — the military authorities demanded that the military police be entitled to arrest civilians who were caught in the company of soldiers. It was even proposed that, like any private person, an officer could grab the citizen and lead him to the police and testify against him. These proposals were not taken up.[356]

Homosexuality was a serious subject of concern for the military authorities, because the repeated charges against the soldiers of the Guard undermined the honor of the army and called into question its role as guardian of the nation. If the civilians were not treated better, it is because homosexuality represented a threat to every form of authority. It developed outside of the usual hierarchical structures, which were always very marked in England in the inter-war period. Thus, hiding beneath the usual charges of vice and perversity were reproaches of a more serious nature; the homosexual was regarded as a particularly dangerous criminal, because he undermined State security and shook the foundations of the society and of middle-class morality.

Case studies

An examination of court records will help us to better understand the circumstances and the methods employed against English homosexuals. First, we will look at the trial of Lionel Perceval, a working class man twenty-one years old, charged with soliciting in Hyde Park, April 1, 1925.[357] The officer who arrested him testified to the audience: "He smiled and looked well-dressed men in the eye." The details of his comings and goings were discussed. Perceval

---

355. Indecency by Soldiers in the Park (MEPO 2/1485).
356. Indecency in Hyde Park: Military Police Powers (MEPO 2/1485).
357. Lionel Perceval (MEPO 3/248).

entered a urinal at Marble Arch, settled in beside an elegant man and smiled at him. He did not use the urinal and came out quickly. Then he went over to Hyde Park, where he entered into conversation with a man, then he took a path while continuing to look behind him as if waiting for the man to follows. The man joined him a little later and both moved toward a sheltered spot where the police officer lost sight of them. He finally found the suspect some time later, at the same place as before, and acting in the same way. At the time of his arrest the defendant said: "I didn't do anything tonight. Let me go. I won't do it anymore and I won't come back here anymore." This testimony is representative of the procedure used in arresting men near homosexual hunting pick-up spots. The police officer observed the individuals engaging in suspicious conduct, deduced their activities from their movements, but did not necessarily wait to catch them in *flagrante delicto*. In the present instance, Lionel Perceval was let go, for the testimony of one police officer alone was not sufficient to prove his guilt.

The following example is particularly interesting, for it shows how questionable police methods could be. Frank Champain, a former boarding school teacher aged 56, made the headlines in 1927.[358] He had been arrested for sexual harassment and soliciting for immoral purposes; he was tried on August 10, 1927,[359] at the police court in Bow Street, by Judge Charles Biron; sentenced to three months of forced labor, he appealed on September 21 and the sentence was overturned. His victory was directly caused by improper police methods, as documents added to the file later tend to prove the defendant's guilt. Champain was arrested after visiting several public urinals several times each; however, the circumstances of the arrest are controversial. Champain was being watch by policeman Hanford.[360] In eighteen months, the latter had already caught twelve homosexuals, eight of them while he acting as witness for another colleague, four of them on his own. But he was acting alone, when he could easily have called in one of his colleagues who worked nearby; and he acted as a "provocateur." Champain, a respectable teacher, had his excuses lined up, and it was the policeman's word against his. Hanford's imprecise testimony worked against him. Champain maintained that he needed the pot of skin cream that was found in his personal effects because he had skin problems, and he produced a medical certificate attesting that a vascular disorder obliged him to use the urinals fre-

---

358. Frank Champain (MEPO 3/405).
359. *News of the World*, 28 August 1927. Champain was captain of a football team.
360. MEPO 3/992.

quently. He emphasized that to offer a cigarette to a stranger was a gesture of simple courtesy and that see oneself followed by a man for an hour would make anyone suspicious. The judge accepted these arguments and discharged Champain.

The press supported the defendant throughout the whole lawsuit, an extremely rare phenomenon; the affair leaves one thinking that it was the freedom of movement of all citizens that was at stake. "Cases of this kind do not happen to big sportsmen like Champain," one may read. "Here is a man who, because he offers a cigarette to a policeman in plain clothes, is hauled before a magistrate and is convicted," noted the *Daily Mail* (September 21, 1927). A letter from a certain J. Chester, September 27, 1927 and appended to the file reflected the public's lassitude vis-à-vis such arbitrary arrests (even if testimony may be tendentious):

> I pray God that a law is voted soon specifying that no arrest can be made unless a member of the public has filed a complaint and given evidence that sexual harassment has taken place....do not misunderstand me, I have no sympathy for the real young degenerates who devote themselves to a kind of prostitution, far from it; but I believe that a great number of innocent young men are in prison today for acts that they did not commit for money ..... I think that I must do what I can until the time returns when one can breathe easily if one happens to be out after midnight in the west of London.

There seem to have been many problems involving police misconduct during such arrests. The case of G.H. Buckingham, which goes back to November 1937, shows however that no real progress was made during the period. Buckingham, aged fifty, single, was convicted for sexual harassment involving a nine-year-old boy. Although the child's testimony was credible and there was a witness, the methods used by the police were so flawed that the verdict was overturned.

Medical theories sometimes influenced the way the police treated homosexuals. Hugh A. Chapman, a sailor, was arrested in 1934. The doctor who examined Chapman at the prison in Brixton found him nervous and very simple-minded. He decided that the defendant's sexual perversion was acquired, probably at sea. He did not find any indication of insanity or mental deficiency. Following this testimony, the charge was lowered to common assault. He was sentenced to two months of forced labor. But he was arrested again in March 1935, for activities around the urinals at Three Kings Yard and Providence Court.

It turned out that he was recidivist, having already been sentenced to six months of hard labor for harassing, in 1931. The reputation of the suspect played a major role in the treatment he received. Chapman, as a sailor and a recidivist, and being not very intelligent, was a perfect homosexual criminal in the sense that he combined so many of the stereotypes.

On the other hand, the example of Mitford Brice[361] shows that the prejudices could be expressed in the contrary direction. Brice was convicted in 1936 on charges of public indecency. He had to pay a fine of 10 pounds. There is a note in his file recalling that he was well known to the authorities and to members of the hunting dog club, and that he was authorized by the late king to compile a book on the royal kennels. Brice was a gentleman, he devoted himself to typically British activities, and he knew the gentry. The charges against him thus became suspect and highly unlikely. To be a homosexual in the police reports is initially to present the standard profile of the sexual delinquent; it is not a "vice" which can affect the elite.

Lastly, a case discussed in the legal chronicle of *The Times* illustrates the fact that the legal machine could experience serious failures. A particularly grave case came before the court of Worthing in 1926. Leslie Buchanan Greenyer was accused of public indecency and indecent assault on five different boys between July 1923 and August 1924. Greenyer gave swimming lessons and organized sports matches. During the holidays, he invited boys to his apartment, where the police found indecent photographs. Witnesses testified to various improprieties. A police officer testified that the defendant, at the moment of his arrest, became pale and said: "But this means absolute ruin, doesn't it?" Neither Greenyer nor his two guarantors showed up for the trial. The judge declared that this case dealt with crimes of the most revolting type, and said he did not understand how the defendant could have been let go on bail; he asked what measures had been taken to prevent his getting away. It is not clear how the matter ended.

The Conference on homosexual crimes of May 7, 1931

During the period 1919-1939, homosexuality became a major concern of the police services. Many homosexuals reckon that the cult of homosexuality started to wane in the upper classes by 1931 and definitely by 1933, and that the consequences of the economic crisis and the international threat of fascism delivered a fatal blow to the movements for sexual reform. The way the fight against "the plague" was intensified and the increasing number of arrests corroborate these complaints.

---

361. MEPO 3/994.

It seems that in 1931 the question of homosexuality became so threatening that, for the first time in England, a conference on homosexual crimes was held in London, at 1 Richmond Terrace.[362] It was intended to officially define an action plan and to coordinate the efforts of the various parties concerned. Present were General B.A. Montgomery Massingberd, General Deedes (director of personnel), General Corkran, Colonel H.D.F. Macgeagh, Norman Kendal, and Brigadier J. Whitehead of the Metropolitan Police, the Public Prosecutor and his assistant N.S. Pence. Questions on the agenda included how to improve the police's methods of detection, disciplinary measures in the army, the possibility of creating a homophobic train of thought within the regiments, protecting the soldier against this kind of crimes and collaboration between the legal and military authorities.

Several points were raised from the very start of the conference. The Public Prosecutor pointed out that his services were not concerned with this type of crimes unless sodomy or public indecency were involved. The majority of cases implicating soldiers concerned the Vagrancy Act and were judged summarily. He could therefore intervene only in the event of blackmail. The press was at the heart of the discussion: many articles had pointed to the brigade of the Guard as the center of male prostitution; the Champain trial (evoked by name) had done much harm: since then, indeed, the police were constantly under attack; they were suspected of being over-zealous, of producing false witnesses; the policemen patrolling the usual meeting places were very unpopular. Lastly, the legal outcome was becoming less and less reliable. The two representatives of the Metropolitan Police brought up the difficulties which they encountered in their work; the proportion of soldiers of the Guard implicated in homosexual crimes was set in its proper context: of 127 cases of soliciting in 1930, only 7 were reported as having to do with guards. The agents employed were absolutely trustworthy and they were used only one month out of two. The police did not think that the homosexual criminals were organized into gangs, even if many seemed to know each other. A young soldier could fall into the hands of such people and be corrupted. As for the recurring question of putting Hyde Park "off limits" for the soldiers, N. Kendal did not think that that would improve the situation. He also specified that he did not want to conduct a "very intensive campaign," in any case not more than what was being done at the time. The military authorities called for a campaign to shift public opinion and some more police

---

362. Homosexual Offences Conference (HO 45/24960).

action in order to demonstrate clearly that this type of crimes would not be tolerated. And they came up with a black list of suspects based on the revelations of a guard in the brigade named Evans. He apparently admitted that other guards had initiated him to these practices and he drew up a list of those who were involved, as well as the rates each one charged. The military authorities gave assurances that they wanted at all costs to protect the young soldiers from "contamination" by any person inside or outside the regiment. Any man who was let go from the Guard should be examined by a special subcommittee. General Corkran added that he hoped to develop a strong feeling of homophobia in the regiment. The young soldiers would be informed upon their arrival of the danger of sex crimes. Colonel Macgeagh stressed that such an "intensive campaign" would only be effective if it were supported by a similar campaign in the police. The real leaders were the civilians who paid the money. The Public Prosecutor proposed that young soldiers attend a conference on homosexual crimes in order to be informed of the reality of these crimes. They would be told what type of people was likely to approach them, the amount of money offered and the disastrous consequences of such practices. Lastly, General Corkran pointed out that, each year, of many suspect guards were returned, and it feared that they do not become recruiting agents.

Thus, the fight against homosexual crimes was now being coordinated at all levels: the police, the military and the legal authorities. The liberation of morals was thus basically arrested from the very beginning of the 1930s.

The Obsession with Lesbians: The Temptation to Repress

According to English law, female homosexuality did not exist. The notion is never mentioned: to conceive of a female form of homosexuality and the "corruption" of one woman by another woman is to consider the possibility of an autonomous female sexuality, independent of the man, and thus of a woman having power. It is impossible in the context of a legislation that was essentially established in the 18th and 19th centuries. Besides, there were no historical antecedents in England.

The inter-war period offered a radically new view of the role of the woman. The constitution of a class of "old maids" that was structural to the society raised the delicate problem of the financial and legal independence of woman, while the obvious subjacent sexual question was modestly overlooked. The idea of a of homosexuality that was contagious by "corruption" impelled the legislative authorities to take measures against lesbians, especially as the increasing numbers of independent women gave reason to believe that the phenomenon was spreading.

The draft legislation of 1921

Concern over the supposed expansion of lesbians practices in England led to a first attempt at repression in 1921.[363] Three conservative deputies, Frederick MacQuisten, Sir Ernest Wild and Howard Gritten, asked that a clause be added to the Criminal Law Amendment Act extending the penalties planned for male homosexuality to cover lesbian acts as well. This clause, entitled "Acts of Indecency between Women) provided that: "Any indecent act between women is a misdemeanor and must be punished in the same manner as any identical act committed by men according to Section 11 of Criminal Law Amendment Act of 1885." To justify this request, MacQuisten noted that such a measure "should have been inserted into this country's criminal code long ago" and he emphasized the propagation and the dangers of the vice of lesbianism: what member of the House of Commons, he asked, had not been informed of this "underground wave of degradation and dreadful vice" which threatened modern society? One of his friends "had been seen ruined by the tricks of one of these women, who had gone after his wife." Citing the risks that such a depravity posed for the Empire, he recalled that, "when these moral failings become commonplace in a country, the fall of the nation is near at hand" and that the clause was intended to "crush a demon that can undermine the foundations of the greatest civilization." Sir Ernest Wild gave his support to this eradication of evil, regretting that they had to "pollute the House with the details of these abominations" and saying that "it would be stupid to deny that many people in our society are guilty" and "not to punish vice when its existence is proven." Sapphism was called a disease and it was said that "the asylums are full of nymphomaniacs and women who were dedicated to this vice. Wild then expressed his worries about the influence of lesbians on society, noting first of all that they inhibit childbirth, "since it is well-known that a woman who devotes herself to this vice no longer wants to have anything to do with the other sex. They waylay young girls and lead them to depression and madness." The lesbian threat was denounced as a

---

363. HO 45/12250; see also Joseph Winter, "The Law that Nearly Was," *Gay News*, n° 79; Richard Davenport-Hines, *Sex, Death and Punishment, op. cit.*, p.151-153; *Hansard, House of Commons Debates*, vol.145, col.1799-1807; *Hansard, House of Lords Debates*, vol.46, col.567-577.

modern and urgent problem; Rear-Admiral Sir R. Hall called it "a combat between men and women." Few voices were raised to oppose the amendment. Colonel Josiah Wedgwood, a Labour deputy, stressed that such a measure would open the door to all blackmailers; and he feared that is adoption would only serve to propagate practices which otherwise most people would never have known about. "I do not believe that there are many members of the Labour party who know what this clause covers," he commented. Colonel J.T.C. Moore-Brabazon was the only other deputy to issue reservations. According to him, fear of punishment had never succeeded in getting rid of homosexuality; there were only three ways to deal with them: "execute them, lock up them in the mad house, or leave them alone entirely." The MacQuisten amendment would only introduce obscene thoughts into the minds of innocent people.

The amendment was adopted by the House of Commons on August 4, 1921 by a vote of 148 to 53, but the House of Lords prevailed: Count de Malmesbury declared at the very start of the debates that the clause had not been studied carefully enough; he was supported by the Public Prosecutor, Lord Desart, who stressed that an amendment of such importance should have been presented by the government itself rather than by a deputy. He found the threat of proliferating lawsuits and the risk of blackmail outweighed the charges of increasing sapphism, the true scope of which he doubted. "We know all those romantic, almost hysterical, friendships that young women experience at a certain time in their lives. Let us suppose that under certain circumstances a young woman who got wind of the [law] thinks: 'How easy it would be to file a complaint.'" He pointed out that no woman of any social standing would be able to face such a charge, as the very hint of it would ruin her. Thus, he believed, "blackmail would not only be certain, but inevitably successful." Lord Birkenhead, Minister for Justice, then made much of the danger of letting women know that such monstrosities existed; according to him, 999 women out of 1,000 had never heard of such practices. The fatal blow was carried by the Archbishop of Canterbury, which said he was convinced that the law was futile. The House of Lords sided with him and the amendment was thus abandoned.

The draft legislation of 1921 was the first (and the last) attempt to make female homosexuality illegal in England. It testifies to the emergence of the woman as an independent social actor. The obsession with lesbians reflects the dominant male class's fear of any attack on its sexual and social prerogatives. "When a woman is bad, she is bad and, if she is bad, she will lead you to hell," quipped Sir Ernest Wild, who in one of his classic poems described the ideal woman as, "feminine, capricious and weak."[364]

The failure of the law was hardly a triumph for lesbians, quite the contrary. The arguments used to criticize the law were its ineffectiveness in doing away with the vice, the risk of blackmail, and especially the fear of spreading sapphism to an even wider audience. Not one person stood up to defend homosexual love. Paradoxically, in abandoning the law, the Parliament still accentuated its contempt for lesbians, whose practices did not even merit punishment as homosexual activity.

The trial of Radclyffe Hall

The draft law had failed, but the fight against lesbianism went on. It took simply a different path. Radclyffe Hall now became the symbol of the dangerous lesbian and her trial was one of the paramount examples of anti-lesbian hysteria in England in the inter-war period. It highlights two essential points: the increasing influence of literature as a means of disseminating information on homosexuality, and the disguised repression of female homosexuality.

An icon of the "congenital invert," Radclyffe Hall's name was well known to the public in 1920 thanks to the poems and novels which she had already published. Her masculine appearance, her severe garb had made her a fashionable celebrity. Scandal struck her first in 1920, when Sir George Fox-Pitt accused her of immorality and of having broken up the marriage of Admiral Ernest Troubridge. Indeed, Una Troubridge had left her husband after meeting Radclyffe Hall, before asking for a divorce. Radclyffe Hall sued Fox-Pitt for slander, and the verdict was pronounced in her favor. After the *The Unlit Lamp* was published, Radclyffe Hall set out to write a book on the fate of the "invert," *The Well of Loneliness*. This 500-page novel was written between June 1926 and April 1928; three publishers turned it down, but Jonathan Cape agreed to publish it and a first edition of 1500 copies came out on July 27, 1928. The book was severe in format and priced rather high. The first reviews were sober, sometimes favorable. The *Times Literary Supplement* applauded the generosity of the writer, but denied the literary value of the book — a recurring reproach, for example, for the works of Leonard Woolf and Vera Brittain, both rather favorable to homosexuals. In August, a second edition of 3,000 was printed. On August 19, 1928, the *Sunday Express* ran a front-page headline: "A Book which Should Be Banned." The editor,

---

364. Cited by Richard Davenport-Hines, *Sex, Death and Punishment*, op. cit., p.152.

Douglas James, found *The Well of Loneliness* "an intolerable work, the first of this genre in the annals of English fiction," and said its distribution could only be harmful, since people of any age could read it. "I would prefer to give a boy or a girl in good health a flask of hydrocyanic acid rather than this novel. Poison kills the body, but moral poison kills the soul," he concludes, "and the book must thus be banned."[365] The *Sunday Chronicle* and *People* followed the example of the *Sunday Express*. The *Daily Herald*, a Labour newspaper, and the *Evening Standard* posed the problem of censorship and accused Douglas of trying to increase sales by fanning the flames of scandal. Amidst all this flap, the publisher decided to send the book to the Ministry of the Interior for a ruling on whether or not the work was obscene. William Joynson-Hicks ("Jix") ordered him to stop the publication on August 21, and the next day Jonathan Cape withdrew the book from sale. The same day, Cyril Connolly published his review of the work in the *New Statesman*; he found it long, tedious and devoid of humor, a sermon on inverts, animal welfare and respect for nature.

In reaction to these attacks, a defense was organized; many readers had been stunned by the vehement assault on the book and claimed that it was overkill. Vita Sackville-West, who was in Potsdam when all this exploded, underscored the difference between relaxed Germany and puritan England: "The *Well of Loneliness* issue causes very violent reactions at home. Not only because of what you call my propensity, nor because I think that it is a good book, either; but sincerely on principle (I plan to write to the Minister to suggest he bans Shakespeare's sonnets).... I nearly exploded when I read the various articles in *New Statesman*. Personally, it would not displease to me to abjure my nationality, to make at least a gesture; but I do not wish to become German — even if, at the nightclub last night, I saw two ravishing young women singing verses that were frankly Sapphic."[366] Radclyffe Hall gained the support of the writer and critic Arnold Bennett, E.M. Forster, Leonard and Virginia Woolf. Forster proposed to write an open letter of protest to be signed by intellectuals. Initially enthusiastic, Radclyffe Hall sabotaged the plan by requiring that the letter be accompanied by an explicit homage to the quality and the moral integrity of the work.

---

365. Cited by Michael Baker, *Our Three Selves: A Life of Radclyffe Hall*, London, Hamish Hamilton, 1985, 386 pages, p.223.

366. Vita Sackville-West to Virginia Woolf, August 1928, in Louise de Salvo and Mitchell A. Leaska (ed.), *The Letters of Vita Sackville-West to Virginia Woolf*, London, Hutchinson, 1984, 473 pages, p.335.

The book went its way in Paris, where it was published by Éditions Pégase and was distributed throughout the world, including Great Britain. Volumes were blocked at customs, bookshops were searched by the police and copies were seized. Jonathan Cape and Leonard Hill, Éditions Pégase's agent in London, were summoned to appear before the magistrates' court in Bow Street, in order to determine whether or not the books were to be destroyed. The defense counsels tried to bring in favorable witnesses. It very quickly became clear that few writers for the general public were prepared to defend the book's literary qualities, and even then the few authors who agreed to testify were themselves homosexual or bisexual. John Galsworthy, president of the PEN-Club and a homosexual, refused to defend the book, as did Hermon Ould, also homosexual and General Secretary of the PEN-Club. Evelyn Waugh did not want to hear a word about it. Havelock Ellis refused to testify, saying that since his book *Sexual Inversion* had been convicted for obscenity he was not a valid witness but on the contrary was likely to aggravate the situation. Arnold Bennett said he was against the rehabilitation of a book that had been legally prohibited and G.B. Shaw called himself too immoral to be a credible witness for the defense. Finally, forty witnesses were collected, including E.M. Forster, Virginia Woolf, Hugh Walpole, A.P. Herbert, Pr Julian Huxley, the deputy Oliver Baldwin, Desmond MacCarthy, director of the *Saturday Review*, Dr. Norman Haire, a sexologist, Lawrence Housman, of the BSSP, the actor Clifford Bax and the novelists Rose Macaulay, Storm Jameson, Sheila Kaye-Smith and Naomi Royde-Smith. Many had been reluctant to testify. Storm Jameson complained to Virginia Woolf that he was afraid he would be called upon to defend *The Well of Loneliness* on its merits as a work of art; Virginia Woolf assured him that that would not be necessary.[367] Virginia Woolf herself was assailed by doubts and describes the dizzying atmosphere in the lead-up to the trial: "Leonard and Nessa [Vanessa Bell] say that I should not go there, that it would cast a shadow on Bloomsbury. All of London is agitated. Most of my friends are trying to escape giving testimony, for reasons which one can guess. But in general they just claim that their father has heart trouble or a cousin has just had twins."[368]

The trial began on November 9. The judge, Sir Charles Biron, was very hostile from the outset, and although witnesses claimed that "there is nowhere an obscene word, a lascivious passage," he accepted the view of the chief

---

367. Michael Baker, *Our Three Selves, op. cit.*, p.236.
368. *Ibid.*

inspector John Prothero, who had supervised the raids on bookshops and who affirmed that "the book is indecent, because the subject is indecent." The case was lost before it began. Biron rendered his judgment on November 16, saying that the book referred to "unnatural acts, to the most horrible and disgusting obscenity"; he rejected the "absurd proposition" that "well-written obscenities are not obscene" and concluded: "I have no hesitation in saying that this is an obscene work...I thus order that the book be destroyed." On November 22, a letter of protest signed by 54 intellectuals, including Arnold Bennett, G.B. Shaw and T.S. Eliot, was published by the *Manchester Guardian*. Attorney General Thomas Inskip confirmed the judgment in appeals, saying that he knew only two literary references alluding to such women: one in the first chapter of the epistle of St. Paul to the Romans, the other in the sixth book of Juvenal. According to him, this book was the "most subtle, demoralizing, corrosive, and corruptive that has ever been written."[369]

Thus, *The Well of Loneliness* was interdicted in Britain,[370] but became a best seller in the United States. It sold a million copies in Radclyffe Hall's lifetime. Nevertheless, the scandal had unquestionably been a blow to the writer, and in 1929 she decided to leave England. Radclyffe Hall and her friend Una Troubridge then set to traveling abroad, and spent long periods in France, where Gallimard published the book. The book's fate was, however, paradoxical. The trial marked the apex of anti-lesbian phobia in England after the First World War. But the attacks on the book were indirectly aimed its author, whose masculine getup and militant sapphism made her one of the most visible figures in London. *The Well of Loneliness* was in fact remarkably discrete about lesbian sex acts, the most explicit sentence in the book being: "And that night, they were not separated."[371] Virginia Woolf and Compton Mackenzie published *Orlando* and *Extraordinary Women* at the same time, without any worries. The book was mainly reproached for not condemning homosexuality.

However, the legal and moral authorities did not want the possibility of a parallel life, independent of the existing social structures, to be evoked. To understand the position of the legal authorities vis-à-vis female homosexuality,

---

369. *The Times*, 31 October 1928, 10 November 1928, 17 November 1928 and 15 December 1928. See also Michael Baker, *Our Three Selves, op. cit.*, chap.18 and 19; and Jean Raison, "Publish and Banned," in *Gay News*, n° 148.

370. It was interdicted until 1949.

371. Radclyffe Hall, *The Well of Loneliness* [1928], London, Virago Press, 1982, 447 pages, p.316.

it is interesting to compare the fate of *The Well of Loneliness* with that of *Extraordinary Women*. The latter was not challenged in the courts, although that possibility had been raised.

"Extraordinary Women"

Compton Mackenzie's *Extraordinary Women* was published in August 1928, in exactly the same period as *The Well of Loneliness*.[372] This novel describes the life of a circle of lesbians living in the island of Capri during the First World War.[373] The book went relatively unnoticed, but received a favorable review in the *Saturday Review* on September 8, 1928. *The New Statesman*, a leftist newspaper whose editor was homosexual, published a very interesting article on August 25, 1928. The book was praised not for its literary qualities, but because it shined a light on the plague of modern society, sapphism; in a few lines the newspaper summarized the public opinion with regard to lesbians:

> Twenty years ago, such a topic would have seemed outrageous and completely unacceptable for a novel; but it is impossible to overlook it in this post-war world populated by girl boys and boy girls. It used to be a problem of psychopaths and less one spoke about it, the better. It is now a relatively widespread social phenomenon that stems, no doubt, from Mrs. Pankhurst's suffragette movement and her hatred of the men, but also from broader causes relating to the war and its after-effects. One can no longer expect the novelist to close his eyes to this aspect of modern life ... and although in 1913 *Extraordinary Women* would have been regarded as a overblown and scandalous work, and may have been censored like *The Rainbow*, we wonder today whether Mr. Compton Mackenzie has not done the public a service....

> This book is more deserving of applause than of opprobrium. It has, at least, the courage to offer a faithful description of a modern social disease — in a sense it is a minor illness, a kind of hypochondria, a factitious passion that will pass like all fashions in our society, since to a large extent it of course is more a matter of fancy than of facts, easily dissipated by the arrival of a man worthy of the name....

> The book is tedious. But its tedium arises from intrinsic monotony of the Sapphic life. If it does not say so outright, it at the very least suggests that women cannot fall in love with other women while remaining healthy and decent beings.

This article reflects three of the recurring themes in the obsession with lesbianism: first of all, an assimilation of lesbians with the feminist trend; then, presentation of lesbians as sick and perverted beings living in sorrow and bitterness; this image allows a salutary contrast with the supposed flourishing of the woman safely ensconced in a proper home; finally, and paradoxically, the

372. See in the Public Record Office: "Compton Mackenzie, *Extraordinary Women*" (HO 45/15727).
373. See chapter five.

actual existence of lesbians is denied, since sapphism is attributed to confusion and the lack of men.

In spite of these favorable reviews, the Minister of the Interior, the House of Lords and the Public Prosecutor received several letters from private individuals who drew a parallel between this book and that of Radclyffe Hall and asked that it be banned. This led to an exchange of letters between Minister Hicks and Judge Biron, which are all the more interesting since they were the two principal figures leading to the banning of *The Well of Loneliness*. The main arguments raised against banning this book were of a legal and moral order. Sir Charles Biron stressed that it was a satire and that the characters see their life and their happiness broken. Whereas *The Well of Loneliness* "seeks to excuse those who give themselves up to vice, *Extraordinary Women* draws a most unpleasant picture of these practices and the degrading condition to which they lead." The minister considers the book "sickening" and is indignant at the moral corruption into which English society had sunk: "It is perturbing to note that these books were written independently of one another; two books on this same subject testify to breadth of what Miss Hall knows, and of what Mr. Mac Quenzie [sic] supposes as for the development of abnormal sexual intercourse; and these two books are not the only ones that have been brought to the attention of the Ministry of the Interior treat of this subject which is ambiguous at the very least. The danger of this category of books lies in the fact that women who do not have a healthy home environment may become interested in this disgusting subject and, out of curiosity, go as far as to put it into practice." However, in a letter addressed to Hicks, Lord Douglas commented that the fact that the characters "are disgusting" did not place the book in the category of criminality. The matter was buried.

Two elements are outstanding: the authorities showed considerable tolerance for embarrassing books, as long as they are likely to dissuade possible homosexual sympathizers, while another book, considerably less explicit but favorable to lesbians, was banned; then, among the letters sent to the minister calling for the book to be banned, two were more or less overtly in the name of homosexuals. The authors of these letters considered Mackenzie's book defamatory and damaging to the image of the homosexual in eye of the public. They underscored in particular that, whereas *The Well of Loneliness* was reserved, by its high price, for a limited and cultivated public, *Extraordinary Women* was addressed to the general public. These arguments were ignored.[374]

The situation of Germany under Weimar is particularly interesting as it constitutes a synthesis of the various trends that were visible in the 1920s — repressive forces on one side, liberal forces on the other. In Germany, homosexuality was not only a private phenomenon, but also a public engagement: there were activist organizations calling for homosexual rights. Government institutions had to face an organized opposition that was seeking the abolition of repressive laws.

The Legal Context

Little is known about the repression of homosexuality in the old Germanic laws.[375] According to Tacitus' *Germania*, "infamous people" were to be buried alive. *Lex Visigothorum* and *Glosse zum Sachsenspiegel* Buch III Article 24 threatened them with castration. The criminalization of sodomy dates back to the Middle Ages. In Schwabia, men found guilty of sodomy had been hanged since 1328. Article 116 of the *Constitutio Criminalis Carolina* of 1532 punished sodomy with death by fire. However, the exact significance of the word "sodomy" is difficult to determine: it could relate to relations between men and women, men, men and animals, on the Sabbath with the devil, heresy, etc. In the century of the Enlightenment (Aufklärung), cruel executions were abandoned. Jurists of the 18th and 19th centuries sought to found a "natural law" that respected human nature. Sodomy was no longer a sin, but became an "unnatural act," for it was counter to reproduction. Thus, in 1794, the Prussian penal code punished "sodomy and the other unnatural sins, which cannot be named here because of their abomination," with forced labor and a caning.[376]

Following the adoption of the Napoleonic Code in France, several German states started to revise their penal codes; in 1751, Bavaria still burned sodomites at the stake, after decapitation; in 1813, it abolished the laws condemning homosexual acts between consenting adults. Wurtemberg did the same in 1839, and

---

374. Several pencil notes from the Minister and the Public Prosecutor suggest that the information about others could be taken from tendentious letters.

375. Such a step backwards was hardly innocuous: by 1935, Nazi jurists were working to prove that the condemnation of masculine homosexuality was an old German tradition.

376. Part 2, title 20, §1069 and later. See Judge Oyen, *Merkblatt betreffend die widernatürliche Unzucht*, 1935, BA, R 22/973.

Brunswick and Hanover in 1840. In Baden, only acts committed in public were punished, and in Saxony, Oldenburg and Thuringe the maximum sentence was one year in prison. This shift did not go far, however; after the unification of the German states, the very restrictive Prussian laws were used as the basis for the German penal code. In the Prussian penal code dating from April 24, 1851, §143 related to homosexual acts: it condemned unnatural sex acts between two men, and men and animals; it was extended to Hanover (annexed in 1867), then to the Confederation of Northern Germany in 1869 (when it became §152). Lastly, in 1872, its provisions were incorporated into in the penal code of the Reich in §175: "Unnatural sex acts (widernatürliche Unzucht) which are perpetrated, be it between persons of the male sex or men and animals, are grounds for imprisonment, and possibly the loss of civil rights." The article was formulated in vague terms, and jurisprudence chose to interpret it restrictively. The unnatural acts punishable by law were "acts similar to coitus" (beischlafähnliche Handlungen). The expression is quite unclear and it led to discussion; jurists wondered whether it implied that the participants had to be naked and whether sperm had to be exchanged. During trials, medical experts were asked to prove that a homosexual act had taken place. Only a restricted number homosexuals were punished under this law, but it was resented as a constant danger because it encouraged blackmail.

Institutional Waffling: Draft Laws Come and Go

The reform of the German penal code took several years to implement; with each preliminary draft, the question of §175 was raised anew. There were many about-faces, with preliminary drafts alternatively proposing the reinforcement or the abolition of the law.[377] This lack of continuity illustrates the contradictory forces that were at work within German society, which was divided between a desire for tighter controls and an aspiration to liberalism. This divide was revealed at even at the heart of the Reichstag, where two camps clashed, one asking for the paragraph to be abolished, the other one calling for it to be retained or strengthened.

Before the war, two drafts had already been proposed. That of 1909, in the context of the Eulenburg affair, would have reinforced the law, in particular in cases of prostitution and relations obtained by force or influence, and it would have extended it to female homosexuality. That of 1911 envisaged, on the con-

---

377. The text of all the draft bills on homosexuality are provided in the Appendices.

trary, removing homosexuality from the list of punishable offenses; that was abandoned in 1913.

The 1919 plan was nearly identical to that of 1913, but the 1925 plan show a turn toward repression. At this time, the "Weimar coalition" (the SPD, Zentrum, and the German Democratic Party, DDP) were replaced by a more conservative government.[378] Among the conservative ministerial functionaries who wrote the draft law was ministerial director Bumke, who had participated in the writing of the 1909 draft. The 1925 draft did not take up the question of lesbianism, but it asked that, "in particularly serious cases," a five-year prison sentence be required and that all unnatural acts fall within the compass of the law." The draft used the same expressions as that of 1909 in denouncing the homosexual threat: "Moreover, it emanates from that that the German opinion conceives sexual intercourse between men as an aberration which has as a characteristic to undermine the character and to destroy moral sensitivity. If this aberration were to spread, it would lead to the degeneration of the people and a reduction of its power."

In response to protests from the homosexual movements, which were campaigning on the basis of the innate nature of "inversion," the lawyers jurists answered that a considerable proportion of homosexuals had been seduced or contaminated: "If §175 were removed, then the danger would exist that these attempts [of seduction and propaganda] would go on even more publicly than today and in particular that young men will be led into temptation not only by direct seduction, but also by an influence reinforced in words and writings. Then homosexual conduct would irrupt in circles which, thanks to current prohibitions, have heretofore been spared."[379]

Something dramatic happened on October 16, 1929.[380] The commission, supported by the Socialists and the Communists, voted 15 to 13 to abolish §175. Among the fifteen were the president of the commission, the very influential

---

378. After the legislature elections of 1924, the government was enlarged twice, thanks to the integration of the DNVP, forming a bourgeois government oriented toward the right, and having a majority (two Catholic parties, *Zentrum* and BVP, the conservative DNVP, the two liberal parties, DDP and DVP). In 1925, the old marshal Hindenburg, the conservative candidate, was elected president; the regime then took off in an ultraconservative direction.

379. Cited by Hans-Georg Stümke, *Homosexuelle in Deutschland, eine politische Geschichte*, Munich, Verlag C.H. Beck, 1989, 184 pages, p.66-67.

380. 1928 was the last year that the SPD made progress, and even became the leading party in Germany; the KPD also gained considerably.

private councilor Kahl, a member of the DVP, two democrats, nine from the SPD and three from the KPD. Voting against were the five members of the DNVP, two from the DVP, one from the Volkspartei, three from Zentrum and two from Wirtschaftspartei (economic party). The following day, however, a coalition of deputies from the SPD, the democrats, Zentrum, and the national-German party, and Kahl, succeeded in creating a new law against homosexuals, under the title of $297, "serious impudicity between men" (which did not, however, cover non-venal relations between consenting adults). Only the three deputies of the KPD voted against, thus showing the fragility of the movement in favor of homosexuals. $297 condemned male prostitution, acts with minors and abusive seduction obtained by authority, influence and threat on people in positions of dependence. This new motion was never put into force, however, as the economic crisis changed everyone's priorities.

The 1933 draft law reprised much of the text from 1925. Thus, by far the majority of drafts that were considered penalized homosexuality. Only the 1911 and 1929 drafts pondered the reduction of penalties for acts between consenting adults. The general line from the early 1920s to the early 1930s was the penalization, and even increased penalization, of homosexual acts.

Real Repression

By studying the evolution in sentencing, the attitude of the police, and several homosexual trials, we will try to see what was the policy actually in practice under the Weimar Republic.

Changes in sentencing

Changes in sentencing for homosexuality convictions entered between 1919 and 1934 did not go in a straight line. The average number of arrests was higher during this period than at the turn of the century, which may perhaps be explained by the greater visibility of the German homosexual community in the 1920s, but which may also reflect stepped up police activity. Between 1902[381] and 1918, the average number of arrests is 380. Between 1919 and 1934, it is 704. In England, the average number of arrests over the same period is only 574 (702 over the years 1919-1939).[382] The German figure is thus particularly high and thus we can be sure the German institutions were not lax.

---

381. The statistics first distinguished between homosexuality and bestiality in 1902.

Certain years show clear evidence of a crackdown. The highest number of arrests was recorded in 1925 and 1926, with 1226 and 1126 respectively — an increase of 32.4% between 1924 and 1925. The process had begun in 1924, when a 69% increase in arrests was recorded compared to 1923! The political situation may have had something to do with this abrupt increase, since it was in 1924 that the "Weimar coalition" fell apart.

In 1928, the number of arrests stabilized between 600 and 750, an average number but higher than it was earlier in the period, when it hovered at around 500. In 1919, the percentage convicted was 71%. In 1925, when the arrest rate was highest, 83% were convicted, and in 1933, 86%. This clearly indicates a lesser degree of legal tolerance during the period. Those arrested had less and less chance of being released or exonerated at the end of their trial. Moreover, more and more often the convicts were recidivists (20% in 1920, 40% in 1933). The majority of those convicted were given prison sentences. The most benign cases got out on bail with a reprimand or a fine. The fine, and the loss of civic rights, might be accompanied by a prison sentence. The loss of civic rights touches affected only a very limited percentage of people: 2.5% on average, throughout the period. On the other hand, fines were more widespread at the beginning of the period (before 1925): approximately 30% received fines, while in 1933, only 12% did. This does not mean that fines were replaced by prison sentences, for in 1919 more than 97% of those convicted received prison sentences versus 85% in 1933. It is more likely that the addition of a fine was gradually abandoned. Moreover, the length in prison terms did not go up.

Only 9% of those who received a prison sentence got more than one year, and 5.2% in 1933. Some 23% of the people imprisoned in 1919 got three months to a year, compared to 29% in 1933. The majority were sentenced to less than three months in prison: 68% in 1919, 65% in 1933. The statistics from Länder enable us to map a hierarchy of the most repressive areas. In 1925, Prussia was far in the lead with 730 cases, followed by Bavaria (207), Saxony (139), Wurtemberg (69), the Hamburg region(48), the land of Baden (46), Thuringe and Hesse (28), Mecklenburg (21), Brunswick (9) and Oldenburg (8).

The conviction rate also reveals variations in legal repression. The rate was only 75% for the Hamburg region, 78% for Prussia and Wurtemberg, 80% for

---

382. Great Britain in those days had 45 million inhabitants; Germany, 65 million. In proportion to the population, the repression was a bit more intense in Great Britain than in Germany.

Mecklenburg, but 87% for Oldenburg, 88% for Saxony, 89% for Hesse, 90% for Bavaria, 98% for Baden, and a whopping 100% for Thuringe and Brunswick. The figures for each city are given in 1930, and they are very indicative. The number of convictions is not proportional to the population, nor to the homosexual community present: in first place was Dresden, with 98 cases, followed by Munich (75), which reflects Munich's reputation for extreme hostility to homosexuality and the strong Nationalist-Socialist influence. Then came Karlsruhe, Stuttgart, Frankfurt-am-Main, Düsseldorf and Berlin tied, followed by Hamburg, Bremen and Lübeck. Berlin, the international capital of homosexuality, counted only 41 cases, and Hamburg, a harbor city notorious for male prostitution, had 24! That explains the relative sense of impunity among homosexual Berliners, and the homosexual flight from the provinces to the capital, as well.

Looking at the age distribution in 1928, one can see that the age bracket most affected was the 18- to 21-year-olds. Most of those arrested were between 18 and 50. The distribution by profession in 1928 is very significant. Most cases relate to workmen in industry or the craft industries (306 out of 804), then workmen engaged in trade and transport (146), then farm laborers (134). The working class is over-represented compared to business owners, foremen or managers, and the liberal professions. One possible explanation would be that the popular classes more frequently resorted to pick-ups in the street, whereas the middle and upper classes had access to more discrete means of finding partners. It is also possible that respectability and influence protected certain people.

The legal statistics thus contradict the generally accepted view: as far as its institutions, Germany did not practice a more liberal policy with regard to homosexuality than England. The difference in perception comes primarily from two phenomena: the continually increased police presence in England, which created a climate of tension in the British homosexual community; and the ambiguous attitude of the German police which practiced a tacit tolerance of the most current homosexual manifestations (balls, clubs, bars, etc.), but which severely repressed homosexual practices: soliciting, pandering in the urinals, sodomy, etc.

The police play disturbing games

As in England, plainclothes policemen were stationed in strategic places (urinals, train stations, parks) and were charged with identifying suspicious individuals. Nevertheless, it was permissible to frequent homosexual meeting

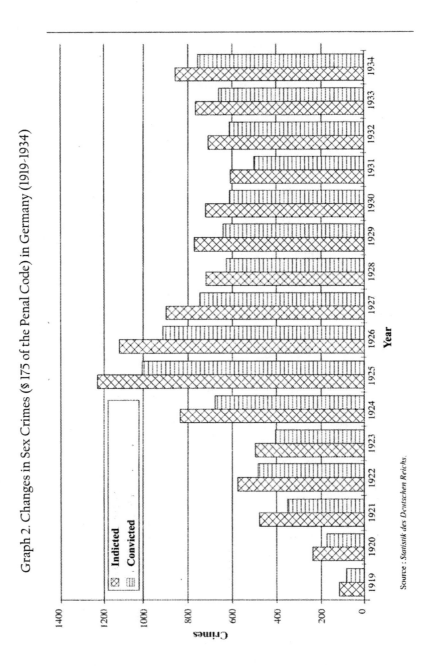

Graph 2. Changes in Sex Crimes (§ 175 of the Penal Code) in Germany (1919-1934)

Source : *Statistik des Deutschen Reichs.*

places, even if the police exerted a discrete surveillance, especially when the masked balls were going on. Dancing between two people of the same sex was tacitly accepted. While homosexual and lesbian clubs were sometimes inspected, the purpose of such proceedings is open to question: — We saw those raids as more of a big joke than a real danger, and nothing much ever happened, anyway. The police wrote down some names, gave us a warning, and left."[383] In the same vein, Christopher Isherwood noted: "The Berlin police 'tolerated' the bars. No customer was likely to be arrested just because he was there. When the bars were raided, which did not happen often, it was only the boys who had to show their papers. Those who did not have any or who were wanted for a crime would dash out the back door or go out a window when the police arrived."[384]

It seems that the purpose of these raids was more to round up suspects than to arrest homosexuals. The *Berliner Tageblatt* of November 14, 1919 and January 23, 1920 talked about raids in homosexual clubs (that detail was not specified by the newspaper), in particular Monbijou and Domino. At this point in time, police chief Hermann was conducting a major campaign against gaming clubs, and raids took place almost every day (with varying degrees of success, for look-outs would keep an eye on the street and alert customers, who scattered to nearby bars). Some 800 people were arrested November 14, 1919. Rather than homosexuals, it must have been the male prostitutes and traffickers who were the targets of such operations. In fact, a tradition of tolerance had been established in Berlin between the police and the homosexual movements since the agreement between Berlin police chief Leopold von Meerscheidt-Hüllesem and Magnus Hirschfeld at the end of the 19th century. Thereafter, police chief Hans von Treschkow also collaborated with the WhK.[385] However, there were files on homosexuals (Rosa Listen) existed, especially under von Meerscheidt-Hüllesem, including the names of several prominent figures. This was enough to enable the police to keep a lid on the homosexual community, but would have been hard to use as the basis for a massive crackdown. And as Hirschfeld noted, "If the police wanted to handle homosexuals the way they do common criminals,

383. Charlotte Wolff, *Hindsight*, London, Quartet Books, 1980, 312 pages, p.76.

384. Christopher Isherwood, *Christopher and His Kind* [1929-1939], London, Methuen, 1977, 252 pages, p.29-30.

385. In his memoirs, *Von Fürsten und anderen Sterblichen* (Berlin, Fontane, 1922, 240 pages) von Treschkow manifests a certain tolerance with regard to homosexuals, albeit not without some prejudice. He felt that $175 made no sense.

given the fact that Meerscheidt-Hulle's list of pederasts includes thousands of names — they would shortly find that the current law is unenforceable."[386]

The lists did have tragic consequences, however, for after the Nazis came to power they were used as a basis for identifying homosexuals.

Certain cities distinguished themselves in their treatment of homosexual infractions. The Dresden police,[387] who had topped the list for the number of arrests in 1930, imposed special sanctions: three days in jail for "staying in the urinals or in proximity of such places without any purpose," "staying in these places in order to prepare or to pursue an intimate relation with a homosexual or to act in a suspicious manner with men," "sheltering homosexuals and spending the night with such people," "roaming about here and there without any purpose or objective, and loitering in the vicinity of the old market, the Post Platz, Wiener Platz, or the station, and exposing oneself without any reason in the same squares and public places," and "soliciting men." The Dresden police were provided with a standard form for apprehending homosexuals and male prostitutes.

The WhK also complained in March 1930 in the *Mitteilungen des WhK* about the attitude of the Munich police. "While the police administration of other German cities keeps a discrete eye on homosexual establishments, in order to control the blackmailers and other elements, the Munich police torment the customers of these establishments with endless raids and investigations." They describe a raid carried out on January the 9-10, 1930. Fifty police officers burst in, goose-stepping. "Nobody move, stay where you are!" they barked. Everyone was asked to show his papers. Those who did not have any were arrested and taken along to the station. The rest had to leave, whether or not they had paid their tabs. Many were mistreated and one man was beaten. They were let go only the following day at noon. Thus, the German police seem to have had a mixed attitude; in many cities, particularly Berlin, tolerance was the rule. Other cities, either because of regional politics or the pressures of public opinion, were far more repressive.

---

386. Magnus Hirschfeld, *Les Homosexuels de Berlin* (1908), Lille, Cahiers Gai-Kitsch-Camp, 1993, 103 pages, p.98.

387. Dr Hans Muser, *Homosexualität und Jugendfürsorge*, Paderborn, Verlag Ferdinand Schöningh, 1933, 184 pages.

Case studies

A number of very complete files exist on petitions for clemency filed under Weimar. They display all the information about the petitioner, a report of the facts, a statement of the principal charges, then the reasoned opinions of the various experts entitled to make a judgment about the legitimacy of the plea. These opinions, when they are detailed, are an invaluable source of information and enable researchers to evaluate how tolerant the judges were with regard to homosexual acts.

Benno Sahmel filed a clemency plea with the court in Tilsit, June 19, 1931.[388] Sahmel was born on December 9, 1905; he was a shop clerk, unmarried, without any assets. He was already convicted, and along with him Kurt Seidler, 48, unmarried, a retired salaried worker, and Heinrich Dumat, 20, apprentice pastry-cook. Sahmel, who is described as of a "homosexual disposition," met Seidler, who was of the same disposition, in 1928. They entertained sexual relations until the end of 1930, "one taking the member of the other in his mouth, until ejaculation." Dumat had relations of the same order with Seidler. Moreover, Sahmel received from Seidler "considerable sums of money," which aggravated his position. Sahmel was sentenced to three months in prison, Seidler was fined 300 RM with an alternative sentence of two months in prison, and Dumat got a fine of 50 RM or ten days in prison. Sahmel, who did not discharge his sentence, filed for clemency; this was rejected without much discussion: he was an individual with a "bad attitude." This was a very simple case: sexual relation between consenting adults, without sodomy. There was, however, an aggravating circumstance: the defendant was more or less paid for his favors. Three months in prison already represents a fairly stiff sentence (remember that more than 60% of those convicted were given less than three months). The other two received considerably lighter sentences, so it is clearly the aggravating circumstance which made the difference. Dumat's minimal sentence also shows that the duration and the number of relations entered into the calculation of the penalties.

Another example is Franz Bartel, who appealed to the regional court of Prenzlau in 1931. He, too, was turned down.[389] Bartel was born on April 23, 1897 in Templin; he installed stoves, unmarried, with no income. On June 2, 1930 he met Lindenberg in an inn. After having had a few drinks and playing at dice, Lin-

---

388. GStA PK, I.HA, Rep.84a (2.5.1), n° 17272.
389. GStA PK, I.HA, Rep.84a (2.5.1), n° 17276.

denberg accompanied his comrade, already quite intoxicated, to his apartment. Along the way, Bartel tried to grab his genitals. In the room, they took off their shirts and lay down on the bed. Lindenberg fell asleep immediately. While he was asleep, Bartel "tried to introduce his member into the anus of Lindenberg." Bartel was convicted during a trial in Prenzlau in 1931 and was sentenced to three weeks. Lindenberg was acquitted. It seems that the state of intoxication did not in this case justify a remission of penalty, apparently because the jury felt that a healthy man, even in a state of intoxication, would not naturally do such a thing. The fact that only an attempt was made probably explains the relatively light sentence.

More serious was the case of Heinrich Kiefer, who appealed to the regional court of Düsseldorf on September 14, 1929.[390] Kiefer was 26 at the time of the incident, unmarried, unemployed, and with dubious means of support. In February 1928, Kiefer was a chef associated with a hotel. At that time he committed indecent assault upon an apprentice cook. The apprentice tried to push Kiefer away, without success. Kiefer also went after the boy in his room and grabbed him again. On April 7, the apprentice lodged a complaint with the police against Kiefer, but during a confrontation the latter rejected any responsibility. The same day, the boy threw himself under a train, leaving his mother a letter explaining that this man had taken his honor and that he could no longer work with him. Kiefer was sentenced to ten months in prison. The sentence could have been even longer, since there was repeated violence. The appeal for clemency was rejected. The public prosecutor and the counsel for the plaintiff both rose against such a request. The lawyer made every effort to get a tough sentence against Kiefer, saying that even if the boy had not committed suicide, he would have been "corrupted and poisoned in his spiritual life by this bestial criminal; and if he had had the strength and the will to resist the moral attacks, the stinking breath of this criminal would have remained with him for the rest of his days."

Leo Romanowski's petition for clemency, presented to the regional court of Königsberg on February 13, 1923,[391] is a large file. Romanowski was a recidivist, a general practitioner, 34, and accused of a series of indecent assaults. His edifying case is described in exhaustive detail. He had pursued adolescent boys, offering cigarettes and pocket money. Romanowski was sentenced to one year

---

390. GStA PK, I.HA, Rep.84a (2.5.1), n° 17245.
391. GStA PK, I.HA, Rep.84a (2.5.1), n° 17209.

and nine months, a particularly heavy sentence, due to the implication of minors and the repetitive assaults. Not only had Romanowski continued his advances on the boys, but he had already been convicted in April, 1922 for exhibitionism (in front of a girl). The request for mercy was well founded. The defendant had twelve brothers and sisters, all "normal." He was "deeply depressed," "by nature perverse" and "obviously also an onanist." He had already fulfilled one year of the sentence, and the rest of it was commuted to three years, suspended. This decision was cancelled on April 11, 1928 because of a new trial. During the summer of 1927, Romanowski had gone after another schoolboy. Romanowski was sentenced this time to six months in prison. This third sentence was fairly heavy, but it is clear that extenuating circumstances played in his favor this time: he had not seduced a minor, since Goltz had already had homosexual relations. It is interesting to note that, according to justice, a young man was "normal" by definition. The first homosexual act, whether it was consensual or not, was always regarded as a seduction and thus an act of violence. However, if thereafter the boy goes in for homosexual acts, he himself is regarded as such. On the petition for clemency, opinions were divided: the legal counsellor (Gerichtshilfe) argued for a prison sentence that took into account the time already served. He recalled that the defendant had tried to fight against his nature and that he had even tried (without success) to have relations with women. He had even contemplated marriage. Moreover, Romanowski had been ruined by the inflation and did not have the money to go to a country where homosexuality was not illegal. His brothers and sisters could not help him. Finally, the defendant also benefited from extenuating circumstances, since the victim was a homosexual. The sentence was useless, since it would not cure the defendant. On the other hand, it would make him lose his job. Lastly, one ought to consider that the new penal code, when it came into effect, would no longer condemn homosexuality. The public prosecutor and the court decided against the remission of sentence and clemency was not granted.

Otto Gerpott, a 27-year-old single general practitioner, came before the regional court of Torgau on April 12, 1929.[392] Six young men appeared with him, they were 16 to 18 years old at the time of the incidents. In 1927, Gerpott had engaged in "unnatural acts" with each one of them. He was sentenced to a year and a half in prison and two years of loss of civic rights. The sentence was very heavy — the unusual duration and the loss of civic rights was extremely rare.

---

392. GStA PK, I.HA, Rep.84a (2.5.1), n° 17257.

This severity may be attributed to the youth of the boys and the number of punishable acts. Gerpott was regarded as "a seducer," the very prototype of the homosexual bogeyman. The request for leniency was of course rejected, for the defendant had shown many times over that he was a danger to youth; his good conduct could not be considered a predictor of his future attitude. Another appeal was filed in November. The lawyer said that the defendant had a job waiting for him in Dresden, and he would be able to open an office again. He came from a good family, he had studied hard, and during the war he served as an army medical officer in the navy. After 1925, his homosexuality was confirmed and he had started to drift. The lawyer thus argued that the rest of the sentence be suspended; and it was. A new appeal was filed in January, 1930, to restore his civic rights and to attenuate the prison sentence. But the situation had deteriorated. The lawyer acknowledged that the conduct of the defendant had changed: he did not show any remorse and he spoke very cynically about his earlier actions. All further appeals were rejected.

Ernst Domscheit represents another case involving a "seducer." The regional court of Königsberg heard his appeal on June 17, 1930.[393] Domscheit, 38, was married and the father of two children. He was on State support. He had fought during the First World War, was decorated, and preserved "the character of a lieutenant." His reputation was good. However, in July 1928, he had assaulted a thirteen-year-old schoolboy, his friends' son. He fondled him again during subsequent visits. After assaulting the child on New Year's Day, he was tried and sentenced to eight months in prison. That was a heavy sentence, but lower than Gerpott's, for only one child was involved. The appeal asked for a suspended sentence, with a fine of 100 RM. Domscheit's reputation worked in his favor, as well as the family's financial situation. But clemency was refused. A new request was filed. The lawyer explained that Domscheit was not a degenerate; and the trial had already destroyed his life — there was no point in adding to his misfortune. Appended to the file was a letter from Elsa Domscheit, his wife, beseeching the Prussian Minister for Justice to bear in mind her tragic position: the children had nothing to eat, they had no winter clothes, and she herself could do nothing but weep day and night. A few days later Domscheit send a petition, himself; but all in vain. A third hearing was held on January 12, 1931; this time, clemency was granted — a suspension until January 31, 1934 and a fine of 100 RM.

---

393. GStA PK, I.HA, Rep.84a (2.5.1), n° 17263.

To conclude, we will look at the appeal filed at the regional court of Wiesbaden on June 30, 1931.[394] The case is complex, for it involves foreign nationals and a notable figure. It also illustrates the methods used by the police. The two accused are Jacob Müller, a tailor, Austrian, born in 1903, and the Czechoslovakian consul in Frankfurt-am-Main, Zdenek Rakusam, born in 1887. The consul general of Czechoslovakia contacted the public prosecutor to ask that the incident be kept out of the press. Rakusam had gone back to his country and did not show up for the hearing; he held a diplomatic passport and there was little chance of obtaining his extradition. The public urinal located close to the Saint-Boniface church at Wiesbaden was a favorite with homosexuals, and therefore it was under constant police surveillance. On the afternoon of June 29, 1931, the police observed that two men had stayed in the urinal for an abnormally long time, "like homosexuals who are trying to establish a contact." Schietinger had been observing the scene for five minutes, when he noted — the wall which enclosed the urinal allowed a view of the occupants' feet — that the two men had changed places and that other men had gone in at that moment. A man coming out of the urinal gestured to him to indicate what was going on in there. The two were arrested. Müller swore that he was not homosexual, and that after being struck speechless by the other man's conduct he had tried to push him away. The court found that story far-fetched, for if Müller had wished to refuse, he could easily have done so, either by struggling or by calling for help. Müller was sentenced to thirty days and a fine of 120 RM. No clemency was granted. The sentence was about average, but on the high side for a case involving only masturbation and fellatio. The incident took place in front of witnesses, which entailed a disturbance of law and order and provocation of scandal.

These reports elucidate several important points. First, they are all extremely precise: the sexual practices are described with great meticulousness. The judges did not condemn all homosexual acts uniformly. The duration and the nature of the penalty was always a function of the act itself: touching the sex organs through the trousers did not merit the same sentence as mutual Onanism or sodomy. The number of times that the act was practiced, and the age of the partner, also played a great part in the evaluation of the misdemeanor or crime (German judges separated the two charges clearly, even if the defendant was often accused of both a misdemeanor and a crime against morality (Vergehen und Verbrechen gegen die Sittlichkeit).

---

394. GStA PK, I.HA, Rep.84a (2.5.1), n° 17275.

As in England, many the cases were based on police surveillance of suspicious places. Agents were assigned to the urinals and other strategic places frequented by homosexuals; they were to catch the men in the act, if possible, or at least to ensure a deposition by a witness so as not to risk a possible defeat in court. Another portion of the arrests resulted from denunciations, especially in the case of children or adolescents who had been victims of violence by an adult. In those cases, the sanctions were much more severe, but they depended more on the age and "innocence" of the victim than on the circumstances of the act. Thus the incident of the apprentice cook and Werner Broschko was viewed as a rape, but still did not entail a sentence as heavy as that of Gerpott, which entailed the seduction of several young people, obviously consensual, or Romanowski, who was certainly recidivist but who limited himself to awkward attempts at masturbation and exhibitionism. And finally, it is possible that, in other cases, the arrest might follow a denunciation on the part of third-party witnesses.

Lastly, we note that the majority of petitions for clemency did not succeed. Several arguments were used in favor of the prisoners: some were traditional, like good conduct, good reputation, first offense; others were more specific: the defendant is manly, he participated in the war effort — or, on the contrary, is a congenital "invert," one who has tried without success to find a remedy for his condition; a prison sentence cannot cure him. This argument was generally counter-productive, as the public prosecutor judged the individual to be all the more dangerous since he could not control himself. Then the financial situation and marital status might be raised: the disastrous consequences of the crisis were often highlighted. Unique to the early 1930s was the pretext of the new draft law showing that, before long, homosexuality would not be condemned. Most of the time, leniency was withheld in the name of morals; the defendant was described as a vicious person and especially dangerous to youth. The commute sentences generally consisted of a probationary period — part of the sentence was suspended or commuted to a fine — and the original sentence could be re-imposed if the defendant did not meet his obligations.

Censorship

A final dimension by which to measure German anti-homosexual repression is a study of censorship. First, one ought to mention that the vast majority of the files preserved by the Prussian police pertaining to censorship of obscene illustrations, writings and representations are unrelated to homosexuality.[395]

The most famous instance of homosexual censorship was the banning of Richard Oswald and Magnus Hirschfeld's film, *Anders als die Andern*. Several homosexual periodicals were also banned, such as *Die Freundschaft* in 1921[396] and *Blätter für ideale Frauenfreundschaften*, a lesbian publication, which appeared on police lists dealing with indecent publications in 1924.[397]

We will look at two cases of censorship to see what factors came into play. In 1928, the December issue of the homosexual periodical *Die Insel* was banned.[398] *Berliner Morgenpost* reported the incident, and explained that the review was condemned for publishing an excerpt from the book by Peter Martin Lampel, *Jugend in Not* (1928). Lampel had done a survey on the life of children on public assistance and in one chapter he talked about their homosexual relations. That was the passage that *Die Insel* reprised. The Attorney General explained in a letter dated February 26, 1929 that the review was registered on the "pornography and smut" list because the publication of the Lampel excerpt was intended to excite the sexual instinct of the reader and to gratify sexual obsessions. The Attorney General did not attack Lampel's book, which was not censored, for he considered that the homosexual passages were there for information purposes whereas, taken out of context, they could only be intended to satisfy the erotic impulse of the reader — especially in a homosexual periodical. Moreover, as the newspaper was available on the newsstand, it could fall into the wrong hands, such as those of adolescents.

On August 31, 1926, the homosexual publisher Friedrich Radszuweit complained to the Prussian Minister for Justice about actions taken against *Das Freundschaftsblatt* with regard to the advertisements which appeared in the newspaper, and which he said the police always interpreted in a negative way. He asked for a hearing in order to clarify the position of homosexuals. The Attorney General responded to a request for information from the Ministry for Justice by explaining that this homosexual periodical was only condemned once, for an advertisement published in Number 7: "Soldier, fired because of his homosexual inclinations..., seeks work of any kind. General Delivery, Potsdam HR24." The newspaper was fined 100 RM on June 25, 1926 because from the majority of

---

395. These are only a portion of the original files, of course, but they are almost entirely devoted to issues of abortion, birth control propaganda, and *Nacktkultur*, especially the theater shows featuring nude dancers and so-called "art photos."

396. GStA PK, I.HA, Rep.84a, n° 5339.

397. GStA PK, I.HA, Rep.84a, n° 5341.

398. GStA PK, I.HA, Rep. 84a, n° 17347.

readers such an advertisement could elicit only obscene thoughts, since the periodical only covered sexual topics. As in the case of *Die Insel*, it is the homosexual character of the periodical that renders suspect the articles or the classified advertisements that are banned.

The police were sometimes alerted by denunciations by private individuals. The Prussian Minister for Justice received a letter from a German national living in Florence, Martin Vogel, in 1931. He complained of finding books that he considered obscene on the display stands of the secondhand booksellers. He quoted several titles, including certain works by Magnus Hirschfeld. An investigation was started. The Attorney General's response was very clear. The work directed by Magnus Hirschfeld, *Geschlecht und Verbrechen*, "can in no event wound the sensibilities of a normal man, because the scientific character of the work underlined first and foremost. Such a book, with its historical overview, is intended to enrich knowledge of the relations between sexuality and crime and has a particular value, especially nowadays."[399]

In fact, censorship was neither systematic nor blind. The judge did not censor any homosexual publication *a priori*, but only those which were disturbing to the law and order. There again, just as there were nuances in the "gravity" of the homosexual act, there were degrees in obscenity.

FRENCH HOMOSEXUALS — OUT ON PROBATION (1919-1939)

> In France, this vice is not grounds for imprisonment, thanks to the morals of Cambacérès [who drafted the civil code under Napoléon Bonaparte] and the longevity of the Napoleonic Code. But I do not accept that I am tolerated. It wounds my love of love and freedom. [400]

France is a special case in this study, since it was the only country not to condemn homosexuality. While the French police used the same methods as the British and German police with regard to homosexuals, French judges had to confront homosexuality only in very special cases. However, behind this theoretical impunity, a practice of monitoring homosexuals developed that was based on a certain homophobia in the legal and police sectors.

---

399. GStA PK, Rep.84a, n° 17355.
400. Jean Cocteau, *Le Livre blanc* [1928], Paris, Éditions de Messine, 1983, 123 pages, p.123.

Was France the Land of Homosexual Tolerance?

France enjoyed an excellent reputation in the inter-war period among the homosexual community, especially the foreigners. Lesbians in particular elected Paris as their international capital and celebrated its moral liberalism: "Paris always seemed to me the only city where one could express oneself and live life his own way. In spite of harmful effects inflicted by foreigners, it continues to respect and even to encourage personality."[401] Klaus Mann evoked Parisian life in these terms: "The florists are teasing two customers. 'Ah, two big flirts!' they exclaim joyfully, and giggle while holding out bunches of red, yellow and blue flowers. One of them, particularly mischievous and playful, asks an impish question: 'Or one big flirt and his boyfriend?' and doubles over in laughter. And even the imposing police officer who threads his way between the baskets observes good-naturedly: "Ah, we do have fun in our Paris."[402]

Beyond these idyllic descriptions, how real was the French tolerance?

Homosexuality Unknown to French Law

Since the revolutionary laws of 1791 and the penal code of 1810, homosexuality was not repressed under French law.[403] Under the *Ancien Régime*, in fact, it was not a question of homosexuality but of sodomy, a term indicating an act and not a category of people, but whose elastic definition could also cover the concept of heresy, without sexual overtones. Royal justice and the canonical law punished both these crimes with burning at the stake. French law, grounding itself on the great revolutionary principles, only punished if there were victims. Consequently, "sexual perversions," if they were voluntarily consented to, did not enter the scope of the law. Lastly, the principal writer of the civil code, Jean Jacques Régis Cambacérès, was homosexual and some have deduced that this accounts for the particular tolerance of French law on this subject.

The judges are interested

Still, just because homosexuality is not mentioned as a crime in French law, that does not mean that the judges had nothing to say about it.[404] The legal institution started to discuss homosexuality in the 19th century, thus going

---

401. Natalie Barney, *Souvenirs indiscrets*, Paris, Flammarion, 1960, 234 pages, p.21.

402. Klaus Mann, *La Danse pieuse* [1925], Paris, Grasset, 1993, 272 pages, p.264.

403. See Jean Danet, *Discours juridique and perversions sexuelles (XIXe-XXe siècle)*, Nantes, université de Nantes, 1977, 105 pages.

beyond its purely repressive role. This discourse was characterized by pejorative and stigmatizing adjectives ("immoral acts", "guilty excesses," "shameful passions") which evaded any attempt to define a perverse act. Precise definitions were only formulated much later. Justice in those days was quite dependent on medical theory, which had been far quicker to come up with definitions and classifications of perversions. The homosexual question could thus be tackled in the context of public indecency and indecent assaults, in particular on minors.

The correctional court of the Seine convicted one Bénard for exciting minors to debauchery.[405] He apparently took two 18-year-olds to a hotel room, and reciprocal activities took place. He gave them money for dinner and cigarettes; the following day, he did it again. The Paris Appellate Court annulled his conviction because the background of two boys clearly contradicted the count of indictment. Both had been soliciting before they met Bénard and, in fact, he could not have been an agent of corruption with respect to them since, being inverts, they already had been earning their living for some time by exploiting their defects; under these conditions, the charge of "excitation of minors to vice" could not be upheld against Bénard.

The legal wording is, as always, important to obtaining a conviction. While the Appellate Court rejected this version of the facts, it did not exclude the possibility of pressing other charges. Bénard was not found guilty only because he was not their first customer; minors are considered guilty when they can no longer be regarded as innocent victims of a corrupter-initiator. Here we find again the distinction made by the German judges.

Another incident involves a minor, Joseph Gilles, 18, who was found "on November 10, 1931, in Paris, wandering on the public thoroughfare, staying in a furnished room and deriving his resources solely from prostitution."[406] Gilles was arrested for vagrancy and placed on probation in the "paternal society of

404. See Jean-Paul Aron and Roger Kempf, *Le Pénis et la Démoralisation de l'Occident*, Paris, Grasset, 1978, 306 pages. Jean Danet's work, *Discours juridique et perversions sexuelles*, sheds light on the tribunals' attitude to homosexuality. He shows that, if the law spells out interdictions and sanctions, the tribunals were not satisfied with strictly applying the penalties. The first half of the 19th century was spent in defining various perversions; the end of the century was a time for public debates on homosexuality and onanism; the period from 1900 to 1939 was above all preoccupied with pederasty.

405. The appeals court of Paris, 11 October 1930 – GP 1930, 2e sem., p.886, cited by Jean Danet, *Discours juridique et perversions sexuelles, op. cit.*

406. TGI Seine, 26 February 1932 – GP 1932, 1re sem., p.778, cited by Jean Danet, *ibid.*

Mettray,"[407] under the guardianship of a trusted person, Mr. Barthélemy. His "seducer" was sentenced to six months and a 200-franc fine.

Like male homosexuality, female homosexuality was not condemned by French law; and there is no sign of any particular desire to fight lesbianism in the inter-war period. The question only came before the judges when minors were involved, in which case the incidents did come under the purview of the law. In the Parrini affair, a woman was accused of corrupting young girls. The records of the Aix Appellate Court (December 6, 1934) state that Parrini had molested several female minors, and concludes by saying that, "If article 334 (334-1) of the penal code does not, in theory, cover acts of personal and direct seduction, the natural physiological manifestations of one sex for the other, this text finds its application when, as in the present case, they are unnatural acts, which must be regarded as acts of perversion, depravity and excitation to vice, acts which make of their author an agent of corruption." *La Semaine juridique*[408] noted that this ruling was not in conformity with the doctrines of the Supreme Court of Appeals. The court in Aix had sentenced Claire Parrini to three months in prison, suspended, and a 25-franc fine. But the Supreme Court of Appeals over-turned it: "Whatever acts of vice they may have committed, only those who have engaged in procurement to satisfy the passions of others are liable under article 334-1; it is only stated in the judgment under discussion that Claire Parrini attracted young partners and engaged in indecent practices on them, without these scenes necessarily occurring in the presence of anyone other than her partners. These statements do not show that the accused engaged in these prac-tices for the satisfaction of other passions than her own; it follows that the appli-cation of art. 334 al.1 is not justified and that, consequently, the judgment lacks a legal basis." Thus, on the whole, the judges' repressive power over homosexuals was very limited. Still, it is important to note that the finer details of the law were applied only reluctantly; and it would be a mistake to think that the system of justice in France was completely indifferent to homosexuality.

Censorship

Even if it was not directly covered by the law, the question of homosexu-ality could still be tackled via obscene and pornographic publications. The leading magazines that were tried were *Frou-Frou* and *Garçonne*, light-weight

---

407. This was the reformatory where Jean Genet was.
408. 1935, p.259-260; document provided by Claude Courouve.

periodicals that were known for their clever classified advertisements. Reports on these magazines do not make explicit references to homosexuality; however, in 1925 the general council of Seine-Inférieure called attention to the proliferation of publications that were an outrage to decency, and to the propagation of "doctrines" that questioned the traditional organization of society.[409] What they had in mind was mainly homosexuality, the liberation of morals, divorce and contraceptive practices. Given that concern, publications which were in no case obscene but which might diffuse subversive ideas, could fall afoul of the censors. As a case in point, the homosexual review *Inversions*. This magazine was very short-lived, for it was immediately attacked for obscenity. However, there were no legal grounds for banning it. This affair is therefore particularly revealing as to how homosexuality was dealt with in France.[410]

In fact, it was an accumulation of complaints, both official and anonymous, that caught the attention of the justice system.[411] The first edition of *Inversions* appeared on November 15, 1924, and complaints poured in immediately: on November 5, 1924 a deputy, Mr. Prévert, gave to the president of the chamber written question no. 1359, asking the Minister for Justice if the legislation authorized a homosexual magazine called *Inversions* to announce its publication by way of advertisements in the press. He was told that indecency charges had already been filed against the manager. Then, on November 26, 1924, the Minister of Justice received a letter from Mr. de Forge, vice-president of the Association of War Veteran Writers, who was indignant that the review would "proudly proclaim its wretched program." De Forge stressed that he wrote as the father of a family, and "if tomorrow my son, attracted by this rag with the eye-catching title, buys it and becomes perverted, what will be your responsibility in the matter? In Germany the police pursue *Die Freiheit* [*sic*, he probably meant *Die Freundschaft*], in obscene journal of the same kind, which is only sold under the table [in fact, it was sold very legally in the kiosks]. *Inversions* is sold on the boulevards, posts its address and is calling for classified advertisements."

After the second edition came out, there were more complaints. The Ministry of the Interior forwarded to the Minister of Justice an excerpt from the *Mercure de France* of December 15, 1924 with an advertisement for *Inversions*, which had been sent in by Louis Coquet, a retired, disabled colonel. The very "moral

---

409. AN, BB 18 6173 (1925).

410. For the entire affair, AN BB 18 6174/44 BL 303.

411. This was frequently the case. Other publications were denounced by individuals as being "bad for morals," for young people, or for France (AN, BB 18 6172/44 BL 228).

fiber" of France was calling for the magazine to be prohibited. This posed a problem, however. The Attorney General advised the Minister of Justice on December 23 that a conference on homosexuality had been announced by the Club du Faubourg and various newspapers, such as *L'Ère nouvelle*. Books like Gide's *Corydon* and Dr. Nazier's *L'Anti-Corydon* would be discussed.[412] The prosecutor's conclusion was simple and indicative: "A subject that is shocking is not in itself punishable." However, he informed the Minister of Justice of the state of the investigations. The publisher, Mr. Mazel, had been contacted: he was away while the magazine was being printed and did not know the nature of the publication. He now offered to break his contract. The address listed for the magazine at 1 Bougainville was only the address of the Bougainville Hotel, where the mail was delivered; it was collected by Gaston Lestrade, 23 years old, who occupied a modest room in this hotel which, "for reasons of economy," he shared with a tapestry maker. The prosecutor's final words are stunning. He had read *Inversions* himself, and considered it to be aesthetic and of quality: "I have not seen any dirty expression or obscene terms in it." He recalled that in its March 25, 1911 judgment the Supreme Court of Appeals, interpreting the laws of 1882, 1898 and 1908 on public indecency, said that there can be no lawsuit if obscenity were not shown. The prosecutor then completed his letter with an edifying about-face: "It is necessary to take account of the manifest change in public opinion, which shows itself to be in favor of the repression of public indecency and the protection of youth from depravity.... This publication, although it does not contain anything obscene, is indeed highly contrary to morality; it is scandalous, it is dangerous." And he thus recommended condemning it for public indecency.

Gilles Barbedette and Michel Carassou relate how the rest of the story unfolded in their book *Gay Paris 1925*. The first judgment declared Beyria guilty of public indecency and Lestrade guilty of complicity. Beyria was sentenced to ten months and 200 francs, Lestrade to six months and 200 francs. Both appealed; the matter came before the Paris Appellate Court on October 13, 1926. The Advocate General asked for the session to be held behind closed doors. The Court pointed out first of all that, "From the very first lines, this publication informs its readers of the spirit in which it is conceived and the goal that it pursues: '*Inversions* is not a review of homosexuality, but for homosexuality.'"[413]

---

412. This conference took place 20 October 1924, at 10 boulevard Barbès; 500 people participated.

413. The minutes of the Cour de cassation are cited by Gilles Barbedette and Michel Carassou, *Paris gay 1925*, Paris, Presses de la Renaissance, 1981, 312 pages, p.269-274.

The Court then developed an implacable line of argumentation, acknowledging that "it is true that the magazine in question is correct in form and that no indecent terminology is found therein," but observing that obscenity may be present by implication and abstraction, without any obscene expression being quoted. Then came the decisive factor, the fact that the publication defended homosexuality: "The law of August 2, 1882, sufficient to repress abuses at the time when it was legislated, at present leaves decency and public morality defenseless against the new forms that pornography (ever skillful at slipping through the tiniest legal cracks) has managed to invent." *Inversions* was thus condemned by the law taken in its broadest sense, that of "flagrant indecency." The Court cited many extracts from the review as examples of attacks on proper morals and concluded "that almost every page of this publication constitutes a cynical apology for pederasty, a systematic appeal to homosexual passions and a ceaseless provocation of the unhealthiest curiosities; that also, in spite of the studious care to avoid any improper language, such articles constitute not only an attack on morals and a propaganda liable to compromise the future of the race through its neo-Malthusian tendencies, and also ventures into obscenity, if not by words, at least by the indecency of some of the topics covered and by the general tenor of the publication." Here, the social question takes the lead: the fear of a generalized perversion of the society is compounded by another, more pernicious, fear of a homosexual plot that could destroy the foundations of the society from within. Quoting a personal advertisement from a reader in Berlin seeking a correspondent in France, the Court asserts that the publication, "in terms that are superficially prudish but transparent enough for those in the know" was serving as a liaison between homosexuals in various countries and consequently was an active agent of propaganda for spreading pederasty, and was thus a "licentious provocation, cunningly inciting readers to the most repugnant of vices." The Court thus could only come to one conclusion: it upheld the judgment and accepted as the only extenuating circumstance the fact that Beyria and Lestrade did not take part in writing the articles, but only accepted submissions and published and sold them. They were thus sentenced to three months imprisonment and a 100-franc fine.

Homosexuals under Surveillance

Why would the police spy on homosexuals, when they were not regarded as criminals? A preliminary answer can be found in the Ministry for Justice observation on the preliminary draft of legislation concerning the prevention of venereal diseases: "It seems that in certain large cities, given the current concern for policing morality, the local authorities actually order a certain number of arrests and detentions on an administrative basis. But these are practices that the law does not cover. The legal basis and the intention of these practices would be highly controversial."[414] In other words, police monitoring of homosexuals was not justified by law. However the government, especially at the local level, found that unacceptable. In fact, the French law was very advanced in its attitudes; any deficiency in this regard can probably be chalked up to the efforts of individuals intent on carrying out a veiled attack on a political opponent.

The Homosexual as an ordinary delinquent

Very often homosexuality, which could not be regarded as a crime in itself according to French legislation, was perceived as an aggravating factor in any criminal event. A suspect wanted for a crime or a misdemeanor that had nothing to do with morals would still be written up as a homosexual in the police report. Édouard Riguet, wanted for drug dealing, was described as frequenting many "pederasts." One may suppose that spending time in this bad company did him no good and would be regarded as aggravating factors when he went to trial.[415] In a similar way yet on a far different scale, Ferdinand, Duke de Montpensier, prince of Bourbon, sixth child of the count de Paris, was listed between 1915 and 1931 as "an inveterate bon vivant," addicted to morphine and young homosexuals. It is not clear whether he was under police surveillance for his drug use or his homosexual activities. "Ferdinand de Bourbon uses narcotics every day; moreover, he indulges in pederasty and his villa "Bellevue" in San Remo is the scene of continual orgies."

Files were kept on the social, cultural and political elite of the country were and information concerning their principal weaknesses was noted. The marquis de Boury, deputy of the Eure, suffered "unfortunately from vice which makes him dependent hand and foot on a band of young men without consciences. He has taken as his so-called Secretary a professional homosexual, Messein (called Messaline), who lives with him in Paris as well as at his château. This individual, who used to have his favors to himself, is now the procurer feeding his wretched vices with little boys or young adolescents."

---

414. AN, BB 18 6186.
415. For this case and the next, see AN, F7 14837.

A close associate Messein, Huguette Despres, was addicted to cocaine and morphine. In 1916, she was signed into Sainte-Anne's, where "she got into scenes of unimaginable orgies between people of both sexes, pederasts and lesbians."

Homosexuals were sometimes the victims of blackmail: "Miss A.S., whom I was called to treat, found herself the easy prey of two inverts who reside at 17 Trudaine avenue. These two individuals ran an opium den." Linking drugs and homosexuality is old hat; people came into the police's sights because of their use of narcotics, but the discovery of homosexual activities only increased the interest of the police. An event a little bit anterior to our period shows how homosexuality and delinquency were linked in the mind of the police. April 19, 1916, an anonymous letter of denunciation drew the attention of the police to a college professor, Marcel Seyrat, claiming that "a certain Marcel Cérat [sic] pursues immoral acts with young men and sells cocaine to all the women of Montmartre."[416] An investigation was opened. A letter from the prefect of police to the Ministry of the Interior dated August 22, 1916 reveals that Marcel Seyrat "goes to Montmartre establishments," such as "the brasserie Leon, 76 boulevard de Clichy," where "he meets drug dealers and pederasts." Furthermore, he had the manners and the style of the latter, and thus it could be that he shared their morals. However, he was "not found in the special files of drug dealers and pederasts" and was described as "a rather timid lad, effeminate, of good character and enjoying an excellent reputation at Pouillac." All this goes to show that the monitoring of homosexuals was a customary procedure; their meeting places, their practices were known; and above all, it shows that special files were kept on homosexuals, even though it is difficult to determine whether that was done in any systematic way.[417] Further reports on Marcel Seyrat detail his relations and habits, including the fact that he was known for "receiving visits from beardless young men rather often." He was "known to be a follower of pederasty" and he lost a job at Serga Concert because of the very particular customers that his presence attracted," but none of these elements apparently led the police to do anything.

---

416. AN, F7 14840.

417. It is quite probable that people who were written up for various misdemeanors (drugs, theft, prostitution, etc.) were also reported as being homosexuals, if they were. In his book *Chez les mauvais garçons* (Paris, R. Saillard, 1938, 221 pages), Michel du Coglay asserts that, of 250,000 homosexuals in the Paris region, the police had files on 20,000 to 25,000. These figures are no currently verifiable, as there are no relevant archives.

All of this applied to lesbians as well as homosexuals. One Grignette, known as Albano, was listed in the police files as providing opium to the courtesan Émilienne d'Alençon. She is designated as a lesbian; little else is noted. Similarly, Mrs. Marie Lesage, a painter and a lesbian (underlined in the police report) and a friend of Jean Guitry, is written up as a regular at Triboulet, on Pigalle St., where she was known to use morphine, cocaine and opium.[418] However, a report from February 22, 1917 describes her as "depraved, lesbian; she has had many [male] lovers and is always going to houses of ill repute." This is perplexing: does the term lesbian have any real significance? The sexual definition seems not to have been very clear; in a police report, the term lesbian seems to have been shorthand for vice and depravity in general.

It is clear that the banker Marthe Hanau's reputation did not play in her favor during her trial. Known for her extravagance, her masculine appearance (strictly tailored clothes, short hair, cigarette-holder), she would show up with her partner Josèphe in the usual places — le Bœuf sur le Toit or le Monocle. An atheist, Jew, divorced, and lesbian, she was a perfect target for the judges when the financial scandal erupted in 1928. Convicted in 1930, she was sent to the women's prison until July 1935.

There are unfortunately few documents to round out these observations. Suffice it to say that the homosexuality of a suspect was regularly noted in police reports, where it was seen as an aggravating circumstance, even if it was not the reason for the police interest in the first place.

Homosexuality and prostitution: military surveillance

The links between homosexuality and prostitution are difficult to analyze, for there are few traces of police surveillance. Female prostitution undoubtedly made up the vast majority of the files because it was regulated and that allows for easier monitoring. The boys mostly worked independently, in the street. They were thus harder to track, especially as many of them were amateurs who only occasionally prostituted themselves.

However, there are some scattered references to male prostitution. For example, on February 10, 1914, the Minister of the Interior sent a note to the prefects "prohibiting any person owning a residential hotel or furnished rooms, a café, cabaret, bar or public house, from allowing into their establishment on a

---

418. AN, F7 14840.

regular basis, for the purpose of engaging in prostitution, girls or women of vice or individuals of unusual morals."[419]

In fact, police surveillance of homosexuals was focused on certain quite precise areas where law and order and state security could be threatened. The archives[420] reveal that very close monitoring, using methods similar to those used by the English police, was in effect in the French ports in order to keep an eye on relations between sailors and civilians. It should be emphasized that homosexuality was only of secondary importance in the monitoring of maritime locales; files were kept on homosexual sailors just as they were on communist sailors, and sometimes establishments suspected of harboring one or the other category are listed together. Unlike in England or Germany, the search for homosexual sailors (and civilians) was not an aim in itself: these individuals were not reproached for a sexual preference which simply exposed them to scorn; rather, like frequenting prostitutes, homosexuality was seen as a sign of poor character. The problem, in both cases, was the habit of frequenting seedy establishments, and soliciting in the streets. Moreover, and this is what mattered most, homosexuals talk: wherever they meet with a partner, in a hotel or on the street, they become chummy and might become chatty. The military authorities were afraid of the sailors saying too much, and giving away state secrets, as well as whatever propaganda their lovers might pass along.

Police reports are available for a period from 1927 to 1932, covering the cities of Toulon, Brest and Lorient — large naval ports and naval bases. The reports were written by the special police station of the city concerned; some were intended to share information with other commissariats in order to coordinate the search for suspects (between Toulon and Cannes, Toulon and Draguignan); some were notes to the naval authorities. In addition, police reports were sent each month to the prefect, who would send them to the Ministry of the Interior under the title, "Surveillance to identify civilian and military homosexuals." Thereafter, the Ministry of the Interior might communicate to the Ministry for the Navy the names of suspect sailors. The reports usually bore similar captions: "Homosexuals," "Homosexuals in the Marines," "Incidents of Pederasty." Most of the monthly reports were made up exclusively of lists of names, distinguishing civilian and military homosexuals, and the suspicions that were entertained in regard to each individual, the place in which he was discovered,

---

419. AN, F7 14663.
420. AN, F7 13960 (2): pederasty in maritime circles (1927-1932).

the charges that could be levied against him. In certain cases, the surveillance work is described and the police officer charged with the report often allows himself to comment on the homosexuality of the suspect and his practices. They were generally categorized as "passive" or "active" homosexuals.

Like the soldiers of the Guard in England, the sailors, the "blue collars," had the advantage of a specific romantic allure. "The glamour of the uniform," a fascination with travel, and sexual availability combined to keep the myth alive. One police report notes that: "The sailor, whether he's a hunk or a little cutie, is particularly sought after and a clandestine industry has developed to exploit this taste."[421] Most of the homosexuals in the military were in the navy, and they took advantage of shore leave to earn a little easy money and various other perks. One report notes that "many sailors from one vessel earned a lot of money in Cannes and Nice, working as 'fags.'"[422] Another sailor, George Baldassi, spent his shore leaves "in the company of notorious homosexuals" from whom he accepted, "as the price of his shameful favors, drinks, food, cigarettes and cash."[423]

The sum received varied between 15 and 20 francs for fellatio or masturbation and 40 to 50 francs for a night. Soliciting might be direct, but some had pimps or received regular customers. Sometimes the scene was just a set-up for robbery, often by pick-pocketing.[424] The prostitution was often not formal: the sailor did not ask for a specific amount of money before leaving with his "customer"; the remuneration was implied and the client would give the sailor money as a gift, not as payment for sexual favors. For this reason, payment was not always guaranteed. Sometimes, moreover, the sailor would not accept money and was satisfied to let his partner pay for a meal, a show and a room. The sailor might even be paid if he refused sodomy or another favor, apparently in order to make sure he kept his mouth shut and to avoid a change of humor, as a sailor who flew into a rage could easily attack his partner. Indeed, none of the sailors claimed to be homosexual, and most explained that they engaged in prostitution solely to make some money.

The quartermaster of the destroyer George Leloup was surprised on May 15, 1932, at 00:30, in Toulon in the company of a known homosexual, and vehe-

---

421. Information report on clandestine prostitution of the State's sailors in diverse establishments in the capital.

422. Report dated 14 March 1928 (Brest).

423. Report dated 14 September 1932 (Toulon).

424. Report dated 23 January 1932 (Toulon).

mently denied the assignation. The police officers saw this as "obviously bad faith, just an attempt to avoid getting his friend in trouble and thus losing his desired and shameful services."[425] Indeed, the police surveillance did make these rendezvous more complicated and the sailors' friends employed various dilatory tactics in order to protect their partners.

Some of the sailors engaged in homosexual acts only occasionally; others made a virtual second job of it and admitted to going out with many inverts, or had one designated friend. Lastly, certain civilians got their names on the lists when they made advances on sailors who were not interested. One German, Alfred Pockrandt, followed an 18-year-old sailor into a urinal in Toulon, and "at the moment when he was urinating, grabbed him..."[426] Shocked, the sailor left, screaming at the importunate one; he, terrified, called to a policeman for help! Pockrandt good-naturedly explained that he detested women, and liked to masturbate."

This shows a clear difference between England and Germany. The homosexual is not perceived as a criminal in power and he calls on the police when he fears he will be attacked. However, it is unlikely that this attitude was widespread, not because homosexuals were afraid of having a police record but because, if they had any social standing, they feared that word would get out.

And the police reports named everyone who was suspect, without always having irrefutable evidence of their homosexuality. One Eugene Boulch thus refused the advances of two civilians, but he was fully cognizant that his own conduct was not beyond reproach: "While denying that he was an active homosexual, [he] admitted to having acted somewhat carelessly in going to Bonavita and Lafitte. He promised to be more circumspect in the future."[427] In fact, any sailor on leave in Toulon was a potential delinquent. Visiting certain places or people of dubious reputation, and showing suspicious attitudes, were all it took to confirm the assumption that he was a homosexual.

Homosexual civilians that were reported by the police do not fall into any one category; every age group is represented, between the ages of about 17 and 50; the suspects' professions are also varied, but most were working class and lower middle-class. The workmen hung out at the same establishments as the sailors and frequently worked at the port, making it easy to establish casual

---

425. Report dated 17 June 1932 (Toulon).
426. Report dated 19 May 1932 (Toulon).
427. Report dated 17 June 1932 (Toulon).

acquaintanceships. These relations were more likely to go unnoticed than those that took place downtown, where a discussion between a sailor and a well-off man, generally late in the evening, would readily catch the attention of the police.

As a case in point, a retired consul initially gave a false name when he was arrested, then "he admitted, not without a touch of humor, to being an invert, but said that above all he had to think of his reputation."[428] These men often preferred to act in a city where they were not known. However, the police regarded certain suspects as "notorious inverts": either well-known men of the city, or men who had already been arrested a few years or a few months before. There was in fact a whole homosexual harbor subculture that barely bothered to hide, whose members knew each other, and many of whom took suggestive nicknames like "Zaza," "Mauricette," "Ramona," "Georgette," or "Loulou."

The January 23, 1932 police report shows photographs of several inverts and transvestites "who enjoyed a vogue in Toulon analogous to that of the great courtesans." For these men, the port (especially that of Toulon) was their hunting ground, a private preserve for homosexual pickups. The police quote, for example, Robert Lafitte, "one of busiest passive homosexuals in Toulon": obliged to operate with more and more discretion and finding increasingly slim pickings, Lafitte fulminated against the police, reproaching them for the destruction of what he regarded as "one of the principal attractions of the city and one of the causes of the hotel industry's success."[429]

Some, like Andre Brissand, far from being shy, accentuated their eccentricities in a bid for attention: he would "purposely exaggerate his effeminate face and cynically glorify in being a passive pederast."[430] In the same way, according to the police report, Christian Bérard, a painter,[431] George David, writer, and many young men would gather at Clos Mayol in the company of young sailors. They were almost open in displaying their vice and would walk the streets dressed in eccentric costumes. They spent the winter in Paris and the summer on the Riviera.[432] They had no trouble admitting to their homosexual proclivities, but they refused to sign any declarations. These almost openly declared homosexuals were not ashamed, but were deeply unhappy with the police procedures:

---

428. Report dated 19 December 1931 (Toulon).
429. Report dated 17 June 1932 (Toulon).
430. Report dated 11 September 1931 (Toulon).
431. Bérard was in Cocteau's circle, which may be what is referred to here.
432. Report dated 11 September 1931 (Toulon).

they resented the surveillance, and often felt their private lives were invaded, and they are sometimes constrained to go down to the station to testify, in a humiliating procedure. Alongside the local Toulon people there were those who were just passing through, who chose Toulon because of its sexual advantages. Andre Chanvril was one of the latter. "This civil servant frequently comes to Toulon, with the sole aim of meeting friends there, to satisfy his perverse instincts."[433] And the port naturally attracted many foreigners, who are well represented in the police reports.[434]

How did these homosexuals recognize one another? First of all, they used the vest or jacket pocket handkerchief to signal their sexual preferences; a handkerchief that was wide and folded over signaled a passive; if it was divided in two parts, it meant equally passive or active; divided into three, it meant active. Then, the simplest mechanism was to go strolling at nightfall, in certain parts of Toulon where sailors congregated, places that were well known to the homosexuals — and to the police. La Place de la Liberté, la Place d'Armes and la Place Saint-Roch were favorite meeting places, but there was also Vauban Avenue and the boulevard de Tessé "between 7:00 and 9:00 pm." Cruising by car, one might try the boulevard du Nord.

Having picked up a sailor, one generally went to a bar in the city, some of which principally served homosexual customers: at the bar Seguin, in Nice, in "the vault," the owner would pass behind the chairs in a certain way to indicate that one could go up to the rooms. The reports emphasize that it was difficult to give a list of these bars for the addresses and the names changed every season. In Marseilles, in the bar Chez Étienne, the owner kept a list of sailors, served as a go-between, and took a commission of 10%. Excelsior and the Café Suisse were also sites for homosexual assignations. In Brest, there were the Café des Pingouins and the Café du Départ. For Toulon, we have an almost exhaustive list of bars: in 1929, there were the Marna bar, Jacky, the de la Rade — "a virtual commodities exchange for naval products," the Cigale, Camille, and the Dubois dance hall; in 1930 the Zanzi-Vermouth, Chez Madeleine, and the dance hall Finimondi (ex-Dubois, so famous that passengers from the English steamers serving the lines to the Far East would go there just out of curiosity); in 1931, the bar Neptunia, the snack bar at the theater, the Regence, the Palace, and the Claridge.

---

433. Report dated 19 May 1932 (Toulon).
434. Four Italians, three English, two Dutch, two Chilians, two Spaniards, a Bulgarian, an American and a German were identified.

Then, the two men would go to a hotel; there again, the same names keep coming up: the Hotel Belvedere, the Terminus (on the boulevard de Tessé), the hotel du Nord, the hotel de France (on place Puget), the Hotel Giraud (rue de l'Humilité), and the Hotel des Négociants (rue de la République). Apparently the personnel there were unusually obliging. They were also closely watched by the police, who frequently raided the rooms. Some ran classified advertisements, in the newspaper *Frou-Frou*, for example.

One could also meet sailors at dance halls like the "Dancing Populaire" in Toulon. Others kept address books with lists of sailors who were sexually available, and made their own contacts directly: "[the maître d'hôtel] was an active pederast and had a book with the names and addresses of sailors at the flight center in Fréjus-Saint-Raphaël."[435]

The police methods were based on a good knowledge of the homosexual rendezvous places and their tactics: in addition to making arrests in public places or hotels used by prostitutes, most were caught in the urinals, the traditional meeting place. "All these individuals were identified during round ups carried out on February 24 and March 11, inside the WC at the Champ-de-Mars, where homosexuals have been meeting each other for some time, their shameful conduct causing protests from the inhabitants of the district."[436]

One might be accosted inside or outside the urinals in various ways. Yvan Philip was surprised near a urinal in "intimate conversation with a notorious invert," which made him a suspect as well. Similarly, Joseph Barch was challenged caught in the urinal at the Champ-de-Mars. He had gone in there at 20:15 in the company of two civilians whose "hesitant step gave the impression that they were on their way to a rendezvous." At 21:10 the inspectors entered, but found the men in proper positions; their explanations were embarrassed, but they denied being homosexual.

Staying overlong in the urinal was certainly a tip-off for the police. For the two suspects who claimed to have gone in only to satisfy nature's call, they concluded that the visit was peculiarly late and at the very least abnormal in duration, approximately thirty minutes; plus there was the obvious immorality of those who were "assiduous" in their use of urinals." [437]

---

435. Report dated 2 December 1932 (Toulon).
436. Report dated 26 April 1932 (Toulon).
437. *Ibid.*

Sometimes people were stopped by chance; two police officers on bicycle making their rounds on the boulevard du Nord once stopped in front of a parked car and thus discovered two men going at it. They were arrested and sentenced to two months at the prison of Toulon.

Alternatively, they might pick up a known homosexual and track down his partners; thus "a very close watch is kept on [the] entourage [of Guilhot Lafitte]."[438] Some homosexuals were also identified by denunciation: one student denounced both a notary and a professor of Greek as pederasts.[439]

But the police also had an arsenal of supposed "psychological" data that would enable them to easily identify inverts. The reports dwell on physical characteristics: "Based on his looks and where he hangs out, he appears to be likely to engage in homosexuality."[440] "Effeminate, he softens the features of his face by clever use of make-up, depilation and correction of the eyebrows by an arched line using a soft lead pencil."[441] "Large, thin, effeminate face and gestures, [he] represents the typical passive homosexual."[442]

The police always guard against any question by taking a critical view: the acts are "shameful," "unnatural." The reports affect to use scientific terminology, which lends a certain air of legitimacy to the police surveillance. By adapting the current discourse, the police assign themselves a role in the fight against perversion. A report casts doubt on the word of Augustin Garnier, who denies having slept with a sailor, because he is "a homosexual fundamentally inverted [!] for which 'the blue collar' is a derivative of his morbid lasciviousness."[443] Very often homosexual themselves used medical terms: "I am a homosexual since birth and there is nothing I can do against this vice which is incurable for me, as it is for so many other individuals."[444] "[The suspect] says he is impotent, and is therefore inclined to take his pleasure with men."[445] The reports show a very close interest in suspects' sexual practices; they always emphasize whether they are "passive" or "active" homosexuals; they distinguish the type of act requested, but they are also aware of couples, of lasting relationships.[446]

---

438. Report dated 21 March 1932 (Toulon).

439. Report dated 18 March 1929 (Renseignements généraux, Paris).

440. Report dated 8 September 1930 (Toulon).

441. Report dated 17 June 1932 (Toulon).

442. Report dated 26 April 1932 (Toulon); the phrase "typical passive homosexual" comes up frequently.

443. *Ibid.*

444. Report dated 7 August 1930 (Toulon).

445. Report dated 11 May 1932 (Toulon).

The French police thus spoke very differently than the British: it goes beyond a discussion of criminal investigation to become a tool in the regulation of social life. The report from the chief of police of Toulon and the Seyne to the Director of General Security[447] is presented in the form of a virtual summary of all that was known (and of all the prejudices) in those days about homosexuality. It distinguishes the "native invert" from "perversion acquired by contact or frequentation," and notes that "the obscure though real causes lie in the morbid degeneracy of a considerable number of individuals." The author also claims that, "the actual invert, who generally comes from the well-to-do classes, has a medical problem and acts out of instinct, out of physiological need rather than vice." He is not dangerous, but effeminate and soft. They tend to have a circle of males around them whose perversion is acquired, former convicts, soldiers, "real public dangers," and various lowlifes. In support of this assertion, an article dated March 1929 in Number 3 of the Annals of Forensic Medicine is cited, and the testimony of an army medical officer on the question of tattooing.[448]

In addition to what one could call ordinary police reports, more serious affairs were discussed that more clearly reveal the links between the national navy and prostitution and that expose the circuit that existed between Paris and the French ports. In Brest, a survey was conducted among sailors who were engaging in prostitution in the capital. One sailor had gone to Paris several times on leave; he lived there with his lover, who fed him and gave him pocket money. He was also offered good money (200 francs) for his services by one of his lover's friends. That was the extent of his activities: "I also went to rue de Lappe, but I did not do anything there."[449]

Two of his friends were polled, too. They went to the Bousquet dance hall in Paris (on rue de Lappe); they were often approached by homosexuals who took them to a hotel where "they engaged in pederasty." Often networks were formed, starting with one sailor who became the friend of a Parisian. He would then recruit other sailors and bring them to Paris; walking into various bars, they

---

446. Report dated 7 June 1932 (Toulon).

447. Report dated 23 January 1932 (Toulon).

448. Some of them indicated homosexual practices in various ways: a tattoo of a boot on the foreskin, for homosexuals of the lowest classes, a tattoo of a star with five or eight points marked (or not) with one to three blue dots, sometimes with the word "Love," inscribed in the deltoid region, right or left; and different signs inscribed on body parts that are normally hidden, such as blue dots on the eyelid or blue spots on the hands where the thumbs meet the index fingers.

449. Report dated 23 April 1929 (Brest).

quickly discovered the advantages conferred by their uniforms. The sailor Roger Adrot went to Paris on leave and visited a popular dance hall; he met a man there and understood immediately that he was being flirted with. He accepted his advances, "expecting to get some money from him."[450] A more serious incident featured some apprentices from the training ship Armorique. In Paris, a pimp engaged minor sailors during their holidays for prostitution. The boys solicited at the Théo restaurant, 86 rue de Bondy, and at the Noaygues dance hall, rue de Lappe. They then took their customers to hotels. Several of the young sailors recruited new comrades. The reports says that "they thus propagate among the crews a vice that is already unfortunately far too widespread."[451] This all tainted the reputation of the navy and the army, and therefore the honor of France, and the public was upset.

The senator of the English Channel region submitted an article[452] under the heading, "Must we go on tolerating the scandals of Toulon?" He reported that several prefects had simultaneously warned the sailors in their areas about the frequent incidents of indecency and suggested that the public prosecutor's office would be taking up the matter. It is difficult to believe this was all just a coincidence; these actions must have been instigated by the Ministry of the Interior. The article ends by asking: "Is M. Tardieu aware of the repulsive excesses that dishonor Marseilles, Toulon, Nice and our other ports?" *La Croix* published an article on September 13, 1929, "Let's watch out for our sailors' moral well-being," warning that in Toulon "several night clubs, especially popular with foreigners, are the scene of orgies like those that the friends of the Kaiser were known for in Corfu, a few years before the war" and that "infamous touts, stationed at the unloading docks, pick up young sailors on leave and bring them there." The author of the article, Commander G. Mabille Duchesne, stressed the lack of police control and the inability of the maritime authorities to intervene in matters involving civilians, and asked for better cooperation between the various authorities.

These articles reflect a new awareness among the public of the problem of male prostitution related to military personnel. One might wonder whether these concerns led to the increased surveillance, or whether it was the new mea-

---

450. Report dated 14 March 1928 (Brest).

451. Report dated 11 December 1929 (Paris).

452. Regrettably, there is no traceable attribution or reference (report from 3 January 1930, Toulon).

sures that were being taken in the maritime regions that brought the problem to light.

There is insufficient documentary evidence to say for sure what caused the police surveillance, but for our purposes, it is enough to know that the special monitoring of homosexuals who went with sailors began in Toulon around 1925. Several reports refer to instructions from the prefect of Toulon dating from February 2, 1925. The city's chief of police, Mr. Fabre, in a report dated June 24, 1927 addressed to the prefect of Toulon, recalls that, since he had arrived on the job, he had noticed the rather large number of homosexuals existing in that city. He had therefore written a report on December 16, 1924 inviting counter measures. One may thus suppose that the prefectural directives of 1925 were direct consequences of this report. The police chief furthermore remarked that "in agreement with you" he had since then mounted "a very tight monitoring" of establishments frequented by homosexuals and provided, progressively as they were discovered, lists of the names of civilians and military men with their complete description. These details suggest that no particular monitoring had been conducted before then, and that it had not been customary to keep tabs on homosexuals, at least not in Toulon. Several homosexuals arrested by the police also complained about this new atmosphere, protesting against what they considered to be arbitrary and unprecedented persecution.

In his December 1, 1931 report, Mr. Fabre explained in detail how he understood his mission: "It is up to the public powers to limit the danger which threatens our young people and to stop it from spreading. Allowing it to run free would bring major and irreparable harm to every sector of society in our country." "Our role is to monitor, pursue, and indict homosexuals who show up in Toulon and Seyne." It seems that the new police chief was behind this change in tone and that the subject of homosexuality was a particular concern to him, personally. He noted for example that: "[his] attention had not been diverted from this situation for one minute." That is a surprising assertion since this wide scale police action was not supported by any legal basis: "Notwithstanding the absence of applicable regulations, I exerted a *semi-official pressure*, which was fairly effective, on the tenants of those houses where homosexuals were known to reside: seven out of eight were found to be involved"[453] (my emphasis). The police chief obviously regretted that he could not pursue the legal consequences of the discoveries made during these unauthorized searches in the homosexual

---

453. Report dated 24 June 1927 (Toulon).

circles of Toulon. He further remarked that no action could be taken against the very many civilian inverts and that the sailors could only be brought to the attention of the military authorities for disciplinary measures.

The question of homosexual bars came up on several occasions; for instance, the prefect of the Var wrote to the Minister of the Interior, saying: "I do not see how I can legally close the establishments on the list that has been provided to me."[454] The civil authorities settled for pressuring the tenants in some semi-official way so that they would do whatever they had to, to get rid of the homosexuals themselves. The military authorities on the other hand could assign soldiers and sailors to keep an eye on establishments known to be homosexual rendezvous points. The vice-admiral maritime prefect of Toulon also mentioned the "regrettable legislation" which made any efforts to crack down "inoperative." Except in very rare instances, cases against French civilians resulted in dismissals and acquittals. "It would be highly desirable that the texts in force be modified in order to allow an effective repression of homosexuality."[455] The available documents show that the only times civilians were convicted was in the context of public indecency and inciting minors to vice. The December 1, 1931 report gives a list of "inverts" that have been identified, then enumerates the convictions for public indecency: in 1929, there were 24 French civilian inverts, 12 foreigners, 35 sailors or quarter-masters, and one candidate in the marine reserves, for a total of 72 men. In 1930, 37 French civilian inverts were listed, with 3 foreigners, 19 sailors or quartermasters, a sergeant, and a soldier from the 8th regiment of Senegalese riflemen, or 61 total. From January to October, 1931, 28 French civilian inverts, 5 foreigners and 8 sailors were listed, a total of 41.

The sentences varied according to the circumstances. A first conviction for public indecency might merit two months in prison and a fine of 25 francs, with four months in prison and a 50-franc fine for a second offense. Sentences clearly went up for repeated offenses. First sentences might be four months in prison, suspended, or two months in prison, firm. The harshest sentence (six months in imprison) was given for molesting a ten-year-old child. Most sentences varied between two and six months with or without suspension, sometimes accompanied by fines. Various factors could enter into the calculation, including, for sailors, a record of insubordination in the service. One sailor was stripped of his rank twice, the second time for "propositions of a certain type that are unnatural

---

454. Report dated 30 June 1927 (Draguignan).
455. Note dated 6 May 1927.

and immoral." When he continued to entertain relations with a sixteen-year-old sailor, he was sentenced to three months in prison and discharged from the navy.[456] In Lorient, a lieutenant commander who became the object of too much gossip ended up admitting the facts and requested permission to retire. In fact, it was the military who were most affected by the surveillance. Civilians could not be convicted directly for their homosexuality. But when the police stopped anyone they could identify individuals and, if they were later incriminated in crimes or misdemeanors, they could be sure the judges would not be lenient.

Two conclusions can be drawn from these various reports. There was no concerted repression of homosexuality by the civil, military and police authorities. Nevertheless, it seems that in the harbor towns, special instructions were given by the security services to the prefects of the maritime departments to monitor homosexual activities.[457] These orders testify above all to an ongoing confusion between homosexuality and subversion.

This means that, among those listed as inverts, foreigners were subjected to special measures and decrees of expulsion would be delivered as soon as possible. Spaniards, Italians and others were among those caught. The consequences of such surveillance could be very serious. One Italian workman who was about to receive naturalized citizenship was expelled. It seems that the case of a foreign homosexual who had already been granted naturalization also came up, and the prefect of the Var deplored that, according to the laws then on the books, it was not possible to strip him of his new nationality. Once again we see that the civil authorities compensated, when they could, for the lack of legislation on homosexuality by eliminating wholesale those homosexuals who were most vulnerable.

The foreign homosexual was considered most dangerous, as he might be a spy: "I will most particularly endeavor to discover foreigners, *especially those of German nationality*, who strike up relationships with navy personnel."[458] In the same vein, reports from the Ministry of the Interior frequently expressed concern about "communist and antimilitarist propaganda," "communist and homosexual propaganda in the military ports," and "public establishments that are popular with sailors who are communists or homosexuals." In 1927, the Navy Ministry forwarded to the Ministry of the Interior "lists of bars, and communist

---

456. Report dated 24 April 1929 (Toulon).
457. De la pédérastie en la marine (7 December 1929, Paris).
458. Report dated 11 February 1929 (Nice). My emphasis.

and homosexual places of assignation." This continual association implies that the French authorities considered these two activities to be closely linked and liable to undermine discipline in the army and the navy. An excellent example is that of Joseph Dubois, who ran the Dubois dance hall in Toulon. The police report of December 12, 1928 described the dance hall as "a rendezvous point for all kinds of dubious individuals, homosexuals and fugitives from justice." The owner was an anarchist, an active protester who overtly preached antimilitarism. He would buy *L'Humanité* and leave it on the tables for customers to read.

Homosexuality was used for political ends by all sides. "Never mind the deleterious effects this may have particularly on the morals of young men, and especially Navy recruits — the blue collar apparently being a stimulus — we have to consider that it gives a boost to the Communists who use it for propaganda purposes."[459] In fact, on January 15 and 23, 1930, the socialist newspaper *Le Rappel du Morbihan* decried a homosexual scandal which incriminated a naval officer among others. The newspaper insinuated that attempts had been made to quash the story: "A scandal, certainly, but an even worse scandal if this affair were kept quiet for the sole reason that the accused is in a position of influence."[460] "If today we break the rule of silence which we have observed up to now, it is because of the efforts that have been made to keep a lid on this scandal."[461]

Homosexuality, in the communist as well as the socialist press, was regarded as a vice of the privileged classes, one means among many of exploiting the lower classes. However, as we have seen, it was mainly sailors who prostituted themselves, for obvious pecuniary reasons. But homosexuality within the navy was not limited to the lower ranks, as the Béarn affair shows. An article in the November 28, 1928 *L'Humanité* reveals a scandal on board the aircraft carrier Béarn; a sailor lodged a complaint against the officers for "special morals." It seems that he was attacked by "sixteen opium smokers." According to the newspaper, after eight days of maneuvers in the waters off Bizerte, the crew was ready for a break. The officers, aiming to provide some entertainment, decided to create "a jazz," which the crew dubbed a "pedo-jazz." After a wild evening, a sailor "was forced." The victim was arrested and locked up. The newspaper concluded: "Here is a cynical display of the morals of the degenerate bourgeois men

---

459. Report dated 1 December 1931 (Toulon).
460. *Le Rappel du Morbihan*, 15 January 1930.
461. *Ibid.*

who command our navy comrades..... Such acts are representative of the fascistic and reactionary bourgeoisie in action."

The few elements from the investigator's report place the event in context. The victim was a "notorious Communist," and the police report described him as an effeminate homosexual who wore cologne and was very concerned about his personal appearance. To the police, he was "a damaged and dangerous individual" and furthermore he had been sentenced in 1927 to one year in prison for desertion during peace times. In addition, it seems that this sailor had a relationship with a naval officer, who had already been tagged as a homosexual in 1924 and 1925. This officer, moreover, was a drug user. As far as the police were concerned, this report was highly dangerous from the national point of view; intimacy between an officer and a simple sailor was in itself damaging to the hierarchy and to internal discipline, and tarnished the honor of the navy. Moreover, relations between an officer who was a drug addict and therefore not very reliable, who was in fact perhaps too talkative, and a communist sailor would seem to be the very incarnation of the civil and military authorities' worst fears with regard to homosexual relations. The police report cite "the presence on board this ship of a veritable 'nest' of homosexual sailors ... who mutually appeased their disgusting passions in truly scandalous scenes."[462]

From all this it is easy to imagine that the jazz evening got out of hand; whether the sailor was a victim or not is more difficult to determine. For the police the issue was clear: the sailor was in contact with *l'Humanité* which represented him as a victim of the maritime authorities. This made it into a matter of "antimilitarist propaganda" under cover of pederasty. Homosexuals and Communists were working together, the latter using the former to disseminate their propaganda. On the other hand, for the Communists, the denunciation of homosexual abuses was an opportunity to cast aspersions on the officer ranks, who were only servicing their vices and exploiting their crew for sexual ends. Homosexuality is only a pretext under which to stigmatize an adversary.

What conclusions can we draw from these documents? The police reports give a concrete idea of the homosexual subculture in the port cities, which appears to have been quite organized. They also reveal various practices of surveillance that bordered on illegality. Beyond the ports, it is difficult to draw any conclusions as to police activities, since there is little documentary evidence covering the remainder of France.

---

462. Report dated 1 December 1928.

* * *

Thus, the 1920s may have been years of relative liberation for homosexuals, but they were not free from concern. A close look at the efforts that were made to control homosexuality eliminates any notion of "laxity" on the part of the authorities. In England, the controls were tightened and became more systematic in 1931. However, the British police, zealous as they were, could only prevail in the most obvious cases: those which occurred on the public thoroughfare and which violated morals, generally involving male prostitutes, soldiers of the Guard or unrepentant johns. There was little they could do about acts committed in private, between consenting adults, unless someone made a denunciation.

In Germany, under the Weimar Republic and contrary to the generally accepted view, the repression was indeed real. There was hardly a dip in the number of convictions, and the draft legislation attests to the weak current of sympathy for homosexuality. Even if the leftist parties were partly won over to the homosexual cause, homosexual lobbying efforts for the most part failed. Germany's reputation for tolerance in the 1920s can only be chalked up to specific cases like Berlin, where the police were benevolent, as the statistics attest, and where homosexual manifestations were tolerated. Once more, except in the case of denunciation, acts made between consenting adults and in private had little risk of leading to the courthouse.

Lastly, while France rightly enjoyed a reputation of tolerance in the absence of criminal laws, there were still some concerns. This impunity irritated many who sought other means of getting rid of homosexuals altogether, targeting those who were most vulnerable or who called attention to themselves by other "deviant" practices such as drug use. Homosexual propaganda remained severely restricted by the censor, while the close watch on "maritime and communist" areas legitimized a meticulous surveillance of homosexuals in the port cities.

These larger trends tend to be overlooked: homosexuals want to believe "the Roaring Twenties" were characterized by a great liberation of morals, and tolerance on the part of the masses. The Depression of the 1930s exposed the tensions that still lurked at the heart of society. Homosexuals saw their position brutally shaken. This came as a horrific shock for all those who believed in the infinite progress of human reason. The superficial tolerance, fragile and illusory, was of very limited duration. The backlash was all the more terrible.

CHAPTER EIGHT

THE END OF A DREAM: THE GERMAN MODEL BLOWS UP

In the 1920s, Germany's militant activism and its flamboyant homosexual scene had seemed like a model for European homosexuals. However, the tolerance was partial and never extended beyond certain large cities like Berlin. Thus, the Nazi policy with regard to homosexuals was not a complete break with what had gone before.

In this area as in others, Nazism exploited preexisting trends in the population. However, it considerably increased the repression, issuing hysterical rhetoric on homosexuality and giving concrete examples to reinforce a great number of the homophobic fantasies that may have been suggested in the previous years. We cannot present here an exhaustive assessment of homosexuality under the Nazi regime, many details of which remain obscure.[463] Nevertheless, a study of the years 1933-1939 will enable us to get at one particularly painful question: how could the country that symbolized homosexual liberation also be the site of such intense persecution, a reversal that took place in just a few years' time? Here, we will try to analyze the destruction of that model (rather than describing anti-homosexual repression under Third Reich as a whole, which

---

463. After the war, §175 was still in force. Most homosexuals had gone back in the closet during the war and were reluctant to drop their anonymity afterwards, given the unfavorable climate. Those homosexuals who had been deported were shy to complain, both because of the pain such recollections brought up and because they were considered the "least glorious" victims. Some of them kept the real reason for their internment secret even from their families and close friends.

extended beyond 1939), while showing how it affected neighboring countries.[464]

1933-1935: DESTRUCTION OF THE GERMAN MODEL

The Nazis came to power on January 30, 1933 and in the first few years the
German model was wiped out: the homosexual scene was destroyed, the organizations and the newspapers disappeared, and homosexuals slipped back into the
shadows. The repression increased day by day, without following any predeter-
mined plan. It was only after "The Night of the Long Knives" and the vast
homophobic public opinion campaign following it that the legislation was
updated to reflect the new attitude.

You're Fired

Hitler's advent to power was immediately followed by an anti-homosexual
repression campaign.[465] The Prussian Minister of the Interior, Hermann
Goering, enacted three decrees to fight public indecency. The first related to
prostitution and venereal diseases, the second one closed bars that were used for
indecent purposes. This definition included "bars frequented only or mainly by

464. For the period after 1939, see especially Rüdiger Lautmann, *Seminar: Gesellschaft und Homosexualität* (Frankfurt-am-Main, Suhrkamp Taschenbuch, 1977, 570 pages), Heinz-Dieter Schilling, *Schwule und Faschismus* (Berlin, Elefanten Press, 1983, 174 pages), Burckardt Jellonek, *Homosexuelle unter dem Hakenkreuz* (Paderborn, Schöningh, 1990, 354 pages), Claudia Schoppmann, *Nationalsocialistische Sexualpolitik und weibliche Homosexualität* (Berlin, Centaurus, 1991, 286 pages), and the collection of archives edited by Günther Grau, *Hidden Holocaust? Gay and Lesbian Persecution in Germany, 1933-1945* (1993; London, Cassell & Cie, 1995, 308 pages).
465. The Reichstag fire (27 February 1933) served as a pretext for the elimination of the regime's main opponents. The event came to be seen as providential. It has long been suspected that the national-socialists, and especially Goering, were behind it. Nonethe-less, there is no proof. Goebbels seems to corroborate in his journal the hypothesis that the culprit was just a simple pyromaniac from Holland, a communist sympathizer named Marinus van der Lubbe. It is possible that he was used by the Nazis to give Hitler a pretext for eliminating his communist adversaries. The Nazi leaders accused the commu-nists of having set fire to the Reichstag and arrested 4,000 KPD militants. The communist press was banned and the social-democrat press was shut down for 15 days. The fire also provided a pretext for the signing of a presidential decree on 28 February abrogating the constitutional guaranties of personal liberty. See Marlis Steinert, *Hitler*, Paris, Fayard, 1991, 710 pages.

people who practice unnatural sex acts."[466] The third decree prohibited kiosks, bookshops, and libraries from selling or lending books or any publications which, "either because they comprise illustrations of nudes, or by virtue of their title or their contents, are likely to produce erotic effects on those who vie them."[467] They risked a fine, or loss of their license or loan authorization. Obviously, the homosexual periodicals fell under this rubric.

These decrees were enough to dissolve the homosexual subculture, and quickly. In the first months following Hitler's arrival, most of the homosexual bars and clubs were closed in all the major towns of Germany. Goering's second decree, dated February 23, 1933, made the repression official.[468] It ordered the closing of brothels and other establishments of that genre as well as bars frequented by homosexuals: "Such establishments cannot be tolerated anymore. The revival of Germany depends, in the final analysis, on the moral revival of the German people."[469] Consequently, suspicious bars were watched closely; if any infraction were confirmed, their licenses were withdrawn.

The consequences were immediate. On March 3, 1933, *Berliner Tageblatt* published an article announcing the closing of the best-known homosexual and lesbian bars and clubs in Berlin.[470] However, the bars did not all disappear at once, and the police used some of them to continue their surveillance. Working class taverns, where homosexual prostitution had been frequent in the 1920s, either closed or changed their style. Christopher Isherwood testified to the evolution of his favorite bar, Cozy Corner, in 1933: — For the last few years, politics had more and more divided the boys in the bars. They joined one or another of the street gangs which were encouraged (although not officially recognized) by the Nazis, Communists or nationalists. From now on the non-Nazis were in danger but many of them changed camp and were integrated ... gay bars of all kinds were subject to raids henceforth and many were closed.[471]

466. Cited in *Hidden Holocaust?*, *op. cit.*, p.26.
467. *Ibid.*
468. Already in 1932, the chief of political police from the Berlin prefecture, Rudolf Diels (who, after 1933, became the first head of the Gestapo), had banned homosexual dance parties and gatherings.
469. Cited in *Hidden Holocaust?*, *op. cit.*, p.28.
470. Luisen Kasino, Zauberflote, Dorian-Gray, Kleist-Kasino, Nurnberger Diele, Internationale Diele, Monokel-Bar, Geisha, Mali und Igel, Boral (also called Moses), Kaffee Hohenzollern, Silhouette, Mikado, Hollandais.
471. Christopher Isherwood, *Christopher and His Kind* [1929-1939], London, Methuen, 1977, 252 pages, p.98.

Homosexuals had to turn to the urinals once again as the only place to meet. This recourse was, of course, fraught with danger because of the police surveillance.[472]

A new wave of raids in the bars took place after June 1934, in conjunction with Röhm's "putsch," as *The Times* said on December 11, 1934. On December 10, busloads of SS men armed with machine-guns raided three small bars in the western part of the city. The customers, some of whom wore SA uniforms, were arrested as were all the personnel and were taken along to police headquarters. According to the newspaper, these bars had "a specific reputation" and the raid was intended to complete "the clean-up" of June 30.

On December 19, *The Times* announced that raids had been going on all over Germany for a week, and that several hundred people had been arrested. This operation was touched off by a trivial accident: about fifteen days before, a private party was being held in an apartment in Berlin. The hostess was the only woman present. In the wee hours of the morning, two of the guests accidentally knocked a flowerpot from the balcony into the street. The object struck a passer by and attracted the attention of the police, who went up to the apartment and found many prominent Berliners, including several members of the NSDAP and Russian émigrés. The search of the apartment unearthed political documents concerning the events of June 30. This discovery impelled the authorities to re-start the "clean-up" of the milieux associated with the Brownshirts.

Goering's third decree, dated February 24, 1933, targeted obscene publications. Kiosks, newsstands, exhibits, libraries, or bookshops that held licentious books and periodicals were to be placed under surveillance. The owners had to certify to the police that they would not offer such publications to their clientele, on penalty of a fine, and the right to sell or lend publications could be withdrawn. The sixth point of the decree stressed that the police were in cooperation with the religious authorities in the fight against obscene publications. This was a continuation of the policy carried out by certain parties, like the DNVP, under Weimar, in the context of the campaign "against pornography and smut." This decree was welcomed in traditional circles, as an article in the *Deutsche Allgemeine Zeitung* (April 6, 1933) testifies: "The Vatican is pleased to see Germany's national fight against obscene material."[473]

---

472. To see how the Nazis arrival affected homosexuals in small towns, see Cornelia Limpricht, Jürgen Müller and Nina Oxenius, *"Verführte" Männer, das Leben der Kölner Homosexuellen im Dritten Reich*, Cologne, Volksblatt Verlag, 1991, 146 pages.
473. Cited in *Hidden Holocaust?, op. cit.*, p.30.

Following the decree, all homosexual magazines were put out of business. A report from August 26, 1933, concerning "the manufacture, distribution and use of Marxist and erotic literature,"[474] attests that as of that date all the homosexual periodicals ceased to exist. Significantly, they were lumped together with Marxist and affiliated literature and periodicals (concerning the youth movements, the trade unions, sports, fashion), heterosexual pornography and erotic literature, "the so-called scientific literature on sexuality," literature on abortion and contraception, and everything that was presented as art, especially the naturist publications.

To complete the destruction of the homosexual scene, the homosexual movements had to be broken up. "The decree on the protection of the people and the State" of February 28, 1933 suspended freedoms and allowed the elimination of opposition movements. Most of the homosexual movements disbanded. On May 6, 1933, Magnus Hirschfeld's Institut für Sexualwissenschaft was broken into and ransacked by the Nazis; documents and books from the library were publicly burned on May 10, as well as the works of Havelock Ellis, Freud and other sexologists. Magnus Hirschfeld was fortunate to be traveling abroad at the time.

Christopher Isherwood, who was present, reported emotionally on this display of brutality and savagery that marked the end of the great German homosexual movement:

> — On May 6, the Institute was plundered by a group of a hundred students. They arrived by truck, early in the morning, with a brass band. Hearing the music Erwin [Hansen, a communist employee of the Institute] looked out the window and — hoping to prevent the damage that obviously was imminent— politely asked them to wait one moment while he went down to open the doors. But the students preferred to enter as warriors; they broke down the doors and swarmed into the building. They spent the morning pouring ink on the carpets and the manuscripts and loading the trucks with books from the Institute's library, including those which had nothing to do with sex, history books, art journals, etc. In the afternoon a bunch of storm troopers arrived and did a more meticulous search, for they obviously knew what they were looking for. (It has been suggested, since then, that certain famous members of the Nazi party had been seen by Hirschfeld and that they were afraid records of their disease, revealing their homosexuality, could be used against them. But, if that were the case, they surely would have examined the Institute's files more discreetly.)

Christopher was later told that all the really important papers and books had been carried abroad by friends and envoys of Hirschfeld, not long before. A

---

474. GStA, I.HA, Rep.84a, n° 5343.

few days later, the books and papers that had been seized were burned, as well as a bust of Hirschfeld, on the square opposite the Opera. Isherwood was among the crowd of onlookers; he managed to utter the word "shame,"— but "not very loud."[475]

The report of the Nazi newspaper *Der Angriff* is more concise: "A team of German students yesterday occupied the Institut für Sexualwissenschaft run by the Jew Magnus Hirschfeld. This institute which has operated under the cover of scientific purposes and was protected for fourteen years by the Marxists was simply, as the search revealed clearly, a den of filth and smut."[476] The WhK dissolved in June 1933.[477] Hitler's advent also put an end to Gemeinschaft der Eigenen. Nazi troops ransacked Adolf Brand's house[478] and seized all his material, photographs, books, and articles. His publisher, who produced *Der Eigene*, had to close.[479] The Bund für Menschenrecht was also a victim and seems to have gone out of existence in March 1933.[480]

The homosexuals all had to find strategies to survive. Some emigrated, others married. Bruno Balz, who wrote for several homosexual newspapers, married in 1936 after having served a prison sentence. Günther Maeder, a former associate of WhK, married in 1940. Certain artists managed to survive, more or less protected by the regime, like the directors Rolf Hansen and Hans Deppe.

---

475. Christopher Isherwood, *Christopher and His Kind, op. cit.*, p.101.

476. Cited in *Livre brun sur l'incendie du Reichstag et la terreur hitlérienne* [1933], Paris, Tristan Mage éditions, 1992, 2 vol.

477. After trying to re-establish the Institute in Paris, Magnus Hirschfeld took refuge in Nice, where he died 14 May 1935. His intimate friend Karl Giesen committed suicide in 1938. Richard Linsert died suddenly in early February 1933. Kurt Hiller had fled in March to Frankfurt-am-Main and was arrested 23 March 1933, but was released five days later. He went back to Berlin and was arrested again on 2 April, then was released — until he was sent to the Oranienburg concentration camp on 14 July. He got out nine months later; he left Germany and took refuge in Prague, then in London. He died in 1972. Helene Stöcker emigrated in 1933 and was a refugee in the United States, after passing through Switzerland and Sweden.

478. There were five perquisitions between 3 May and 24 November 1933.

479. His assistant Karl Meier managed to save a small amount of the material. Brand himself was not worried: unlike Magnus Hirschfeld and Kurt Hiller, he was neither a Jew nor a leftist. Besides, he had friends within the NSDAP. And finally, he was married. Brand died in 1945, at home, during an American bombing raid.

480. Its main newspapers, *Blätter für Menschenrecht, Die Freundin, Das Freundschaftsblatt*, went out of print at that time. The publishing house of Friedrich Radszuweit in Potsdam was ransacked. His adopted son was sent to the Orianenburg concentration camp, where he was assassinated. The magazine *Die Freundschaft* also disappeared at that time.

Certain homosexual artistic circles survived for a time, like that of Richard Schultz and that of the producer of the UFA films, Nikolaus Kaufmann. Traces of the homosexual scene could still be found. In Kassel, a circle of friends made up of former members of Bund für Menschenrecht still managed to function in 1938. In Wurzburg, a homosexual bookshop was found in the address book of an arrested clergyman; homosexual newspapers were also found in the possession of another clergyman. However, such discoveries were rare. In less than six months, the German homosexual scene had been reduced to zilch.

First Victims: "Corrupters of Youth" and Male Prostitutes

Before the adoption of the new §175, the fight against homosexuality con-centrated on certain particularly visible categories. On February 10, 1934, a decree of the Ministry of the Interior ordered the regular monitoring of "profes-sional criminals" and "habitual sex criminals." These measures affected homo-sexual pedophiles and male prostitutes, among others. The police were authorized to impose restrictions[481] on these criminals, and they could use "pre-ventive custody" in the event of not-cooperation.[482] The regional police were to file regular reports on these people to the regional office of the criminal police. Files on these individuals, with their photographs and their fingerprints, were to be kept up to date.

Following these measures, a meeting was held in Hamburg on October 5, 1934, to discuss cooperation between the Office of Youth and the Hitler Youth to address the problem of Hamburg's main rail station, which was a center of homosexual prostitution. At this meeting there were clearly two ways of looking at homosexuality. The two Hitler Youth representatives drew an alarmist picture and called for energetic measures to be taken; the Hamburg police took a more traditional view, in which the fight against homosexuals was not a priority, did not require large-scale operations and need not be the subject of hysteria. The report provided a list of hotels, youth hostels, and pensions that young sus-pects used as refuges, a list of the principal gathering places and a list of people who had homosexual activities in October 1934.[483]

---

481. In particular, the following were forbidden: change of residence without police authorization, going out at certain hours (11:00 pm to 5:00 am in summer, 11:00 to 6:00 in winter), driving or using cars or motorcycles, entering certain public places, walking in the parks and woods. See *Hidden Holocaust?, op. cit.*, p.38-39.

482. In the case of sexual criminals, these limitations applied only to those who had been convicted twice.

Soon these measures were widened. The excitement that followed the elimination of Röhm served as a pretext for the creation of a special office charged with handling homosexual matters (Sonderdezernat Homosexualität) under the Gestapo.[484] At the end of the year, all the regional offices of the criminal police were required to provide a list of the people who were known to be homosexuals, especially those who were members of any Nazi organization. These lists were to arrive at the Gestapo offices before December 1, 1934.[485] According to a report made for Reichsführer SS Himmler, of the 1170 men in "preventive custody" in June 1935, 413 were homosexuals, 325 of them interned in the Lichtenburg concentration camp.[486]

By this date, anti-homosexual repression already entailed inhuman conditions and "preventive custody" was a pretext for serious abuse, as testified by an anonymous letter from a German homosexual, addressed to Ludwig Müller, bishop of the Reich, in June 1935.[487] According to the letter, raids organized by the Gestapo and carried out by young SS soldiers, for the most part from southern Germany, were being conducted in Berlin and all over the country. Prisoners were brought to the Gestapo buildings where they were kept waiting, standing against the wall, for twelve hours or more without anything to drink or eat. They were not allowed to go to the toilet for six hours. The SS, members of the Adolf-Hitler regiment, beat and insulted them.[488] The operation was supervised by Obersturmführer Josef Meisinger.[489] Then, they either were let go or were sent to Kolumbia-Haus, in Berlin-Tempelhof, a center detention especially for homosexuals. The prisoners were under constant torture there, physical as well as mental.

The next stage was the concentration camp of Lichtenburg. There too, the prisoners were tortured. They had to do "sports" in the morning until they dropped from exhaustion. The punishment was public, and some were sent to

---

483. Cited in *Hidden Holocaust?, op. cit.*, p.43.

484. *Sonderdezernat* II 1 S.

485. *Hidden Holocaust?, op. cit.*, p.46.

486. *Ibid.*, p.60-61.

487. *Ibid.*, p.55-58.

488. This testimony is corroborated by a report from a member of the Adolf-Hitler regiment who described the raids, *ibid.*, p.51-53.

489. Head of Division II 1 H1, in the Gestapo. From 1936 to 1940, he was the Reich's Bureau Chief for the repression of homosexuality and abortion. It was he who organized the actions against homosexuals, especially the political scandals (Röhm, von Fritsch). Meisinger was a brutal man who was feared even within the SS.

the Bunker. The author of the letter insisted that the prisoners had not been tried. A few hundred had already gotten out of Lichtenburg, but many in a very alarming state. The author protested against these actions and called for the Church to intervene. He was persuaded that these abuses were unauthorized and that the Führer would condemn them if he were informed of what was going on. He asked for an investigation at Kolumbia-Haus and Lichtenburg, saying that the culprits should be brought to justice.

Beefing Up the Legislation

Legislative reforms marked a new stage in the Nazis' fight against homosexuality. Until September 1935, only isolated and badly coordinated measures were taken. The Nazi State first wiped out all organized forms of homosexual life, striving to eliminate any sign of homosexual activity and community. The essential structures having been destroyed, the next step was to do away with individual homosexual activity. The object of the Nazi "ire" should be well defined: it was not the homosexual himself, but the homosexual act, and homosexual desire. Homosexuals did not represent a separate category of individuals and could, at least it was hoped, be reinstated in the community. The homosexual was not targeted by the regime unless he engaged in homosexual activity (sex acts, seduction, propaganda, meeting) and his culpability varied according to a scale of definite criteria. However, he was a victim in any case, since he could survive only by disavowing his essential nature.

In October 1933, on Hitler's orders, the Reich Minister of Justice Gürtner had created a Commission on Criminal Law (Strafrechtskommission) to draft a new penal code. Count Wenzeslaus von Gleispach, a specialist in criminal law, from Vienna, was in charge of the section on "Sex crimes." In June 1935, the sixth amendment to the penal code was adopted; it considerably reinforced the repression of male homosexuality. On the other hand, it left out lesbianism entirely.

The new §175

The Nazis did not advance any new arguments for making stronger laws against homosexuality. They mostly relied on medical theories that described homosexuality as a form of degeneracy. There was a need to prevent the contamination of innocent people, especially young people, who could fall under the influence of homosexuals.

Judge Oyen[490] considered that homosexuality might be an innate predisposition, but that the fact that there were cases of seduction justified making it a criminal act. The mere fact that homosexuals felt no attraction whatsoever for the female sex was not a sufficient reason to spare them. Oyen ridiculed the proposition: would one acquit a man guilty of rape on the pretext that no woman would have him? Added to that were the arguments of public morality and political pragmatism: "Moreover, there is no question that the healthy moral sense of the vast majority of the population would find it completely incomprehensible that the current government 'recognized,' so to speak, the legitimacy of homosexual conduct by abolishing the threat of punishment."

The deliberations of the Commission on Criminal Law were also unambiguous. Gürtner, the Minister for Justice, noted: "The question of removing homosexuality from the rubric of criminal law is not on the table." Pr. Gleispach, who reported on the Commission's work, noted that the idea of de-criminalizing it was popular among "certain sex pathologists who were mostly not of Aryan stock." He asked that criminality not be limited to "acts resembling coitus," because "for the most part, sexual relations between homosexuals do not take the form of acts resembling coitus." Dr. Lorenz, director of the County Court and co-rapporteur, summarized the dangers of male homosexuality: "It is a danger to the State, for it damages men's character and their civic life in the most serious way, disrupts healthy family life and corrupts young males." Finally the Justice Minister of Saxony, Thierack, elaborated on the varieties of the homosexual threat. He distinguished "three categories: young men, male prostitutes and, most dangerous of all, descendants of degenerate families or older men who no longer enjoy normal relations. The last group seduces young people, often by offering them money." These various considerations led to the adoption of a considerably reinforced §175.

The new §175 came into effect on September 1, 1935, in accordance with the amendment to the German criminal code, article 6, adopted on June 28, 1935.[491]

---

490. To see where the 1935 law came from, we may consult the instructions of Judge Oyen, who published a complete history of anti-homosexual measures. He also expounded his own point of view and called for reinforced legislation. We can also consult the deliberations of the Commission for Penal Rights (Strafrechtskommission) which touched on the reform of §175, during its 45th session, on 18 September 1934. BAB, R 22/973. This document is not dated, but is anterior to the reform of the Criminal Code, which took place in June 1935, and is posterior to 1933.

491. See the text in the Appendices.

It presented several innovations. First the term "unnatural sex acts" (wider-natürliche Unzucht) was replaced by "sex acts" (Unzucht), which widened considerably the scope of application of the law. As of 1935, any act inspired by sexual desire with regard to another man fell under the jurisdiction of the law: that included masturbation and any contact with a sexual intent, for example caresses or naked wrestling. Ejaculation was not necessary to prove that a crime had taken place. There was a very clear intent to cover every possible form of homosexuality.

Since the end of the 19th century, doctors and lawyers had struggled to define homosexuality as precisely as possible. The new law was the result of this obsession. The Nazi legislation carries to an extreme the judiciary's desire to exercise control. For that power to be total, the homosexual act has to become vague, and thus largely a fantasy.

§175a, in comparison, was not very original. It repeated the innovations that had been tried out in several of the 1920s legislative drafts. Aggravated "homosexual acts" (prostitution, use of the force or authority) had been targeted with specific penalties in all the drafts since 1909. In fact, the principal innovation of the June 28, 1935 amendment was the great freedom it allowed judges in sentencing. They were invited to take into account not only the law but also "the guiding principles of criminal law," "general healthy sense" and "the unwritten sources of the law." That meant that the principle, "no penalty where there is no law," was abrogated and that the judge was free to condemn an act if he considered it immoral.

Lesbians

Lesbians found themselves in a very special situation.[492] The Nazi ideology accorded Aryan women a very limited place, and confined them to the roles of mother and guardian of the hearth. When the Nazis came to power they immediately excluded women from any influential positions they may have occupied.[493] Moreover, the feminist movements were called upon to dissolve or be incorporated into National-Socialist organizations (Gleichschaltung).[494] "The Order in Council for the protection of the people and the State" of February 28, 1933 eliminated all opponents, and especially feminist associations that were

---

492. See Claudia Schoppmann, *Nationalsozialistische Sexualpolitik...*, *op. cit.*
493. As of 7 April 1933, women could no longer work as bureaucrats; as of May 1934, they were no longer allowed to practice medicine, or dentistry after February 1935. From that point on, women who worked could only fill unskilled positions.

politically active, like the International League of Women for Peace and Freedom (Internationale Frauenliga für Frieden und Freiheit) led by Helene Stöcker. On May 10, 1933, Robert Ley, Nazi leader of the Labor Front, announced the creation of a Women's Front and asked Lydia Gottschewsky to integrate the 230 female civic and religious organizations into it.

As of November 1933, no new women's groups were to be formed.[495] The Deutsches Frauenwerk (DFW) was founded on October 1, 1933 as a rallying point of all Aryan women; Gertrud Scholtz-Klink became its leader in February 1934. She was also leader of NS-Freundschaft (NSF), an elite organization. In 1941, the two organizations had 6 million members, a third of them in the NSF. As a whole, the Nazi women's organizations had 12 million members.[496]

The question of lesbianism never became a priority. However, during the debate on the reform of §175, some people did speak out in favor of applying criminal penalties,[497] using the old arguments that "normal women" were in danger of being seduced by lesbians, and the risk of depopulation. The president of the Reichsrat, Klee, intervened on this point during the 45th session of the Commission on Criminal Law, in September 1934. However, most specialists agreed that sapphism was not very dangerous, as seduced women could always

---

494. *Gleichschaltung* was the name given to the national-socialist revolution: the term could be translated as "uniformization," "coordination" or "mise au pas." The plan was to make the Reich conform to one standard, according to the motto *"Ein Volk, ein Reich, ein Führer"* ("One people, one empire, one leader") and to install totalitarianism.

495. Numerous conservative associations, like the *Königin-Luise Bund* (Queen Louise League) and the *Frauenbund der DNVP* (DNVP Women's League), were accepted on the basis of certain conditions, such as the exclusion of Jews and adherence to the principles of Nazism. The BDF (*Bund Deutscher Frauenvereine*, Federation of German Women's Associations), which brought together sixty organizations and had 500,000 members, was dissolved, as was the General Association of German Teachers. The Association of German Catholic teachers and the Association of German protestant Teachers refused to disband. Many women from educated families considered that their social position put them above the police terror.

496. In order to understand why so many women were willing to follow a party whose ideology was clearly misogynist, see Claudia Koonz, *Les Mères-patries du Troisième Reich*, Paris, Lieu Commun, 1989, 553 pages.

497. The question is particularly sharp in comparison with Austria where, since 1852, homosexual acts between men and between women had been punishable by five years in prison. After the Anschluss, this situation created insolubles problems. It was never definitively decided whether an Austrian committing a homosexual act in Germany should be sentenced according to the Austrian law or let go, according to the law of the Reich.

be led back to the correct path. Thierack, who became a Minister for Justice in 1942 noted, "Unlike men, women are always ready for sex."[498] Moreover, women being excluded from power, it was superfluous to condemn lesbians. The criminologist E. Mezger noticed that the repression of lesbianism did not arise naturally from the condemnation of male homosexuality, but that it was a question "of weighing two different evils."[499] It was to be also feared that such a law would not lead to judgments in chain, in particular with regard to prostitutes and abusive denunciations against innocent women. Again, here are the same arguments that prevented the condemnation of lesbianism in England in the early 1920s.

This position never was completely accepted by certain lawmakers. Rudolf Klare became an ardent partisan in the fight against lesbianism. In his book *Homosexualität und Strafrecht* (1937),[500] he expresses approval of the 1935 law, but wishes that more could be done to eradicate lesbianism; according to him, female homosexuality was just as alarming a phenomenon as male homosexuality, and it ought to be repressed to the same degree.[501] Jurist Ernst Jenne published an article in *Deutsches Recht* in 1936 entitled: "Soll §175 auf Frauen ausgedehnt werden? " ("Should §175 be broadened to include women?"). In his view, women like men must have a healthy sexual life. The fact that evidence is difficult to gather or that false charges may be brought was true for men as well as for women, and that was not a valid argument against extending §175.

It is impossible to calculate how much lesbians were affected by retaliatory measures. Like the men, they saw their bars closed and their newspapers banned. However, most lesbians managed to survive under Nazism by adopting various strategies. Some conformed to the system, like Gertrud Baümer; others chose to make an unconsummated marriage with a homosexual; others, like Charlotte Wolff, emigrated. Many lesbians let their hair grow and wore feminine clothing to avoid calling attention to themselves.

Some sought to dissimulate their recent activities. Elsbeth Killmer, formerly a writer for *Die Freundin*, Selma Engler, editor of *BIF*, and Ruth Margarete Röllig, author of the book *Les Lesbiennes de Berlin*, managed to camouflage their

---

498. BAB, R 22/973.

499. *Ibid.*

500. In 1937, in *Deutsches Recht*, he ran an article in which he recalled that ancient German laws had imposed the death penalty for homosexuality.

501. See also "Zum Problem der weiblichen Homosexualität," *Deutsches Recht*, December 1938.

homosexuality and continued their careers as writers or artists.[502] The Jewish painter Gertrude Sandmann faked a suicide in order to escape the Gestapo, was hidden in an apartment for years by her friends and managed to survive. The risk of denunciation was grave. Two dancers accused the ballet mistress Sabine R., from the Theater am Nollendorfplatz in Berlin,[503] of indecent activities with certain ballerinas. They sent a letter to the Ministry for Propaganda in February 1934. Their charges were made in retaliation for a non-renewed contract. The director of the theater supported the defendant, however, and she was not prosecuted. The two dancers were convicted of calumny.

Certain lesbians were, however, prosecuted, most of the time for reasons other than their sexuality. Burbot Hahm, the president of the lesbian club Violetta, was arrested for seduction of a minor. She was thrown in prison, then sent to a concentration camp. She came out of there half paralyzed. Hilde Radusch was condemned as a Communist. Others were arrested for being "asocial," or prostitutes. In the category of political prisoners, the name list for the convoy to Ravensbrück on November 30, 1940, shows the name of Elli S. 26 years, "lesbian."[504]

Legal sources almost never mentioned lesbians. Still, it was possible to convict women in certain quite specific cases, under the terms of $174 which carried a sentence of more than six months in prison and up to five years of forced labor. This applied to "teachers who commit indecent acts with their pupils, adoptive parents or nursemaids with their children, churchmen, professors, teachers with their minor students and pupils."

Lesbians were sometimes pursued by the police, but it is not clear for what aim and with what consequences. Thus a report from the secret service for the Office on Racial Policy of the NSDAP noted on June 20, 1938: "Sufficient material is now available on the extent and the distribution of homosexuality. In order to fight female homosexuality (lesbianism) also, we urgently ask for information on the observations made by our colleagues themselves or external reports given to our colleagues. To this end, the addresses of people known as lesbians must be provided to us as soon as possible. The reports must be sent to the Office of Racial Policy (Rassenpolitisches Amt) — Reichsleitung — Rechtsstelle Berlin W8, Wilhelmstr. 63."[505]

---

502. See Claudia Schoppmann, *Nationalsozialistische Sexualpolitik...*, *op. cit.*
503. BAB, R 55/151.
504. Cited by Claudia Schoppmann, in *Hidden Holocaust?*, *op. cit.*, p.13.
505. *Hidden Holocaust?*, *op. cit.*, p.81. BAB, NSD 17/12.

A report from the security services of Frankfurt-am-Main, addressed to the offices of the State police on January 9, 1936, mentions the case of the "blonde Heidi" and "Mrs. K": "Mrs. K has a homosexual (lesbian) dependent relationship with the "blonde Heidi." Mrs. K was the former wife of an SS officer, whom she divorced. She works in an office, but it could not be established where she lived. "Heidi" was a young woman of 22 or 23 years, very elegant, from Langen, in Hesse. Her father was a hotelier, but before that he was an influential member of the SPD and police chief in Krefeld. In 1933, he spent a year in a concentration camp. Heidi received many people in her two-room flat in Frankfurt, all of suspicious appearance: Bolsheviks, artists and intellectuals. It was said that sexual orgies were held there. Heidi went to the Café Bettina, in Bettinastrasse, and Bauernschänke, which was also a homosexual locale.[506]

Generally speaking, however, it is fair to say that lesbians were not subjected to persecutions comparable to those of homosexuals. If they agreed to abdicate their personality and conform to the prevailing standards, they had little reason to be worried.

1935-1939: THE ORGANIZATION OF THE ANTI-HOMOSEXUAL TERROR

The new legislation was used as a basis for beefing up the fight against homosexuality. Under the impetus of the Reichsführer SS and police chief Himmler,[507] the campaign against homosexuality was centralized. Great political battles were waged against the Catholic clergy and General Werner von Fritsch, and the party redoubled its vigilance with regard to homosexuality in the SS and Hitlerjugend.

One question remained: what to do with the homosexual who were arrested? There were two thoughts on that: eradication and "rehabilitation." Both approaches dehumanized homosexuals, and set them up to be treated like numbers or, at best, guinea pigs.

Stronger Repression

The period from 1935 to 1939 saw an abrupt acceleration of the repression. What was unique in the Nazi treatment of homosexuality, compared to that of

---

506. *Hidden Holocaust?, op. cit.*, p.80-81.
507. Himmler became chief of police in 1936.

Weimar or England at the same time, was its totalitarian impulse: all homo-sexual acts must be listed, recorded, and repressed. Nothing must escape the control of the State.

Centralization and rationalization of the campaign against homosexuality

There was a pause in the pressure against homosexuals in 1936. On the occasion of the Olympic Games in Berlin, Himmler gave the following order (on July 20, 1936): "In the coming weeks, I prohibit any measures being taken against foreigners in the name of $175, including interrogations or summonses to appear, without my personal authorization."[508] And the repression began again as soon as autumn fell.

From that point on, the fight against homosexuality was highly organized and systematic.[509] A secret directive from Himmler on October 10, 1936 regarding "the fight against homosexuality and abortion" was used its basis.[510] A special office was created within the Office of Criminal Police of the Reich (Reichskriminalpolizeiamt, RKPA).[511] The activities of the Reich Central Office for the Combating of Homosexuality and Abortion (Reichszentrale zur Bekämpfung der Homosexualität und der Abtreibung) were first to record, file and classify every case of homosexual that was reported to it. In 1940, the files of the Central Office counted 41,000 names of convicted or suspected homo-sexuals.[512] Special files were kept on male prostitutes and pedophiles ($174 and 176). The files were used to provide various institutions, especially the German Institute for Psychological Research and Psychotherapy led by Pr. Matthias Hei-

---

508. Heinz-Dieter Schilling, *Schwule und Faschismus*, *op. cit.*, p.28.

509. Himmler had just reorganized the criminal police (*Kripo*) on 17 June 1936.

510. *Hidden Holocaust?*, *op. cit.*, p.88-91. The secret directive dated 10 October 1936 was then covered up. On 9 February 1937, it was specified that it would be preferable to use "special agents" to fight homosexuality. This comment seems to indicate that the policemen responsible for dealing with homosexuals needed to have special training. That seems likely, since Himmler himself expressed that view several times to a police audi-ence.

511. The RKPA was founded on 20 September 1936. In 1939, it was merged with the RSHA (*Reichssicherheitshauptamt*, Central Security Service for the Reich). The various departments of the Reich then came under Bureau V for fighting crime (the former RKPA), and the Reich Bureau for combatting homosexuality and abortion became Group B, division 3: Immorality.

512. For example, in 1938, statistics show 28,882 registered homosexuals of which 7,472 were "corrupters of youth" and 587 were prostitutes. See *Hidden Holocaust?*, *op. cit.*, p.116.

nrich Goering, with selected individuals on whom research on homosexuality could be conducted. The creation of the Central Office did not mean the disappearance of the special Gestapo office in charge of these matters.[513] Both were headed by the same person, Obersturmführer Josef Meisinger.[514]

At a conference given April 5 and 6, 1937 for experts and doctors in his service, Meisinger explained the goals and the tasks of the campaign against abortion and homosexuality.[515] In his words, homosexuals were not to be merely punished, they were also to be rehabilitated. This task accorded with the assimilation of abortion and homosexuality. Both inhibited reproduction, and therefore lessened German power. Homosexuals not only had to be prevented from attracting any followers, but redirected toward "normal," i.e. procreative, sexuality.

The work of the Central Office rested above all on cooperation with the local police. They were to report any incidents and even cases that were merely suspicious, for violations related to §174 (sex crimes with dependents), §176 (children forced to commit sex crimes), §253 (blackmail related to homosexuality), §175 (sex crimes between men), §175a (aggravated cases of §175). In the latter two instances, a report was necessary only if the person concerned was a member of the NSDAP or of one of its organizations, occupied a position of command, belonged to the armed forces, was member of a religious order, a civil servant, a Jew, or occupied an important post before the change of regime.[516] These details illustrate a desire to be selective. They seem to indicate that the "average" homosexual was not the chief concern of the Central Office, and that they would let the local police handle them. The homosexuals who were regarded as dangerous were the pedophiles, the "corrupters of youth" and people who took advantage of a position of power or a position within the party. This selection reflected Himmler's phobias, as he was particularly worried about

---

513. In October 1934, the *Sonderdezernat Homosexualität* became the *Sonderreferat* II S1. In May 1935, it took the designation II 1 H 3, under the direction of Commissar Kanthack, who was replaced in 1939 by Commissar Schiele.

514. In 1940, Meisinger was replaced as head of the "Central" by Erich Jakob, who had been heading up the police anti-abortion service in Berlin since 1935. In June 1943, Dr. Carl-Heinz Rodenberg, a proponent of castration for homosexuals, was named scientific director.

515. *Hidden Holocaust?, op. cit.*, p.110-115.

516. This also applied to prostitutes. Cases involving people under the age of 25 were to be specially marked. See *Hidden Holocaust?, op. cit.*, p.87.

homosexuals' harmful influence at their work places, and their capacity to form coteries.

In fact, there were always differences in how homosexuals were treated. Some, like repeat offenders, received very stiff sentences; others were arbitrarily sheltered. Special measures were taken in favor of actors and artists.[517] Himmler gave a decree on October 29, 1937, addressed to the Gestapo,[518] the local offices of the State police, the Office of the Criminal Police of the Reich and the local offices of the criminal police, stipulating that "any detention of an actor or an artist for unnatural acts requires prior approval, unless he is caught in the act." A memorandum from the criminal police in Dresden, dated September 8, 1938, relating to an arrest that had taken place, proves that this decree was effective:[519] "But the arrest cannot be sustained without the approval of the Reichsführer SS — because it concerns actors." Conversely, in a directive from December 14, 1937, the Minister of the Interior toughened up the terms of detention for other categories of homosexuals.[520] "Preventive custody" in reform camps or labor camps was now applied to recidivists and male prostitutes. Such detention was to last "as long as necessary." The need for this detention was to be reviewed after not more than two years, but not sooner than twelve months.

Tighter sentencing (1935-1939)

When §175 was modified in 1935 and repression was increase, it led to a significant rise in convictions. If one compares the statistics of the period 1935-1939 with those of the period 1919-1934,[521] one notes that 1935-1939 saw the greatest repression of homsexuality in Germany between the two wars.

In 1934, the number of people tried for homosexuality was 872. In 1935, it was 2,121, and in 1936, 5,556. In other words, between 1934 and 1935 there was an

517. The most famous case was that of the actor Gustaf Gründgens, a notorious homosexual, whom Goering named to as director of the State Theater. In 1936, Klaus Mann did a portrait of him in *Méphisto*.

518. *Hidden Holocaust?, op. cit.*, p.137-138.

519. *Ibid.*, p.137.

520. *Ibid.*, p.138-144.

521. In order to be able to make valid comparisons, I have used as my source the *Statistik des Deutschen Reichs*, vol.577, published in 1942, which offers the avantage of being both reliable and detailed. It distinguishes between homosexuality crimes under §175 and those related to bestiality. This is an important distinction as the numbers are considerable. In 1933, 778 persons were tried for homosexuality and 213 for bestiality. Unfortunately, after 1937, the statistics no longer distinguish between the two. See tables in the Appendices.

increase of 143%, and between 1935 and 1936 an increase of 162%! The number of convictions also increased: 1901 in 1935, 5,097 in 1936. For 1937 we have only the number convicted (including for bestiality), 8,271 people; that is an increase of 62%. In 1938, 9,479 people were tried (bestiality included) and 8,562 convicted. Finally, in 1939, 8,274 people were tried (bestiality included) and 7,614 were convicted. The shift in 1939 can, in my view, be attributed to the war, for the following years also mark a very significant decline: 3,773 convictions in 1940, 3,739 in 1941, and 2,678 in 1942.[522] Going to war and a drop-off in convictions, no doubt because the fight against homosexuality could no longer be a priority and the forces of the country were mobilized around other goals. Moreover, a number of homosexuals could have enrolled in the army as a form of cover.

The apogee of repression then was the year 1938, with 9,479 people tried and 8,562 convicted. The average number of trials between 1919 and 1934 was 704; but between 1935 and 1939 it was above 6,000. The number of convictions also increased. In 1933, 86% of those tried were convicted. In 1935, the proportion convicted was 89%; in 1936, 91%; 1938, 90%, and 1939, 92%.

We have detailed statistics only for the years 1935 and 1936. In 1935, 1,901 were convicted, 12 to forced labor, 1,703 to a prison sentence, 129 to a fine, 108 to the loss of civic rights. In 1936, 5,097 were convicted: 192 to forced labor, 4,617 to prison, 183 to a fine, 291 the loss of civic rights. The fine and the loss of civic rights could be tacked onto another sentence. In 1935, more than 90% of those convicted had to do prison time or forced labor. In 1936, 94% did. In 1933, only 85% of those convicted received a prison sentence — but in 1919, it was 97%. That means that this was a return to very severe repression, a return to the rates that prevailed at the beginning of the period.

The sentences also reflected a harsher repression, since more and more of the sentences were for more than three years of forced labor. In 1936, 12 sentences of forced labor were given for misdemeanors against §175, of which five were for more than three years. There were 180 sentences for crimes against §175a, including 46 that were higher than three years. Fines accounted for only 6.7% of the sentences in 1935, and 3.6% in 1936, showing clearly that the judges wanted to punish homosexuality in other ways. By comparison, fines accounted for 30% before 1925 and still 12% in 1931. The loss of civic rights also increased, from an average of 2.5% of convictions to approximately 5.6%.

---

522. After 1943, there are gaps in the statistics.

These statistics confirm the intensification of homophobic policies, which were already quite visible in any event. But they were still far below the figures recorded by the Reich Central Office for the Combating of Homosexuality and Abortion and the special office of the Gestapo, which would amass nearly 90,000 homosexual files between 1937 and 1940.[523] This discrepancy reflects very different situations. The monitoring of homosexuals was extreme and meticulous; the files covered every suspect and not only cases that were tried or proven. Even so, probably not every case appears in the legal statistics. Indeed, it has been seen that recidivists, "corrupters of youth," and male prostitutes were subjected to special treatment.[524] They could be sent to labor camp before being tried, and perhaps without ever being tried. Some prisoners could be let go if their conduct was considered to be satisfactory, i.e. if they testified to an attraction for women; but they also could die as a result of the torture, malnutrition or medical experiments — homosexuals being particularly in demand in this field. For these reasons, it is hard to say how many homosexuals were actually victims of Nazi repression.

Practices of the police and the judiciary

To determine whether National Socialism made any significant changes to the "traditional" way of handling homosexuality and to find out about the police practices, the directives issued by local police headquarters are helpful. The criminal police in Kassel, on May 11, 1937,[525] call homosexuals "enemies of the State," saying that: "they are constantly seducing and contaminating young people." Male prostitutes are described as particularly dangerous but not all

---

523. *Hidden Holocaust?*, *op. cit.*, p.131. The military psychiatrist Otto Wuth, who published a memorandum on homosexuality in the Wehrmacht in 1943, noted that cases recorded throughout all the police organizations of the Reich reached 32,360 (including 308 in the military) en 1937, 28882 (including 102 in the military) in 1938 and, for the first half of 1939, 16,748 (including 327 in the military). The statistics after that are incomplete. During the first half of 1942, 4,697 homosexuals were registered (including 332 in the military).

524. As of 1940, homosexuals who had seduced more than one partner were also sent directly to the concentration camps. Otto Wuth counted 7,452 corrupters of youth and 800 prostitutes for 1937; in 1938, 7472 corrupters and 587 prostitutes; and for the first half of 1939, 4,162 corrupters and 300 prostitutes; for the first half of 1942, 1257 corrupters and 114 prostitutes. All these numbers refer to people who were *charged*, not *convicted*, which makes it difficult to do any calculations.

525. *Hidden Holocaust?*, *op. cit.*, p.95-96.

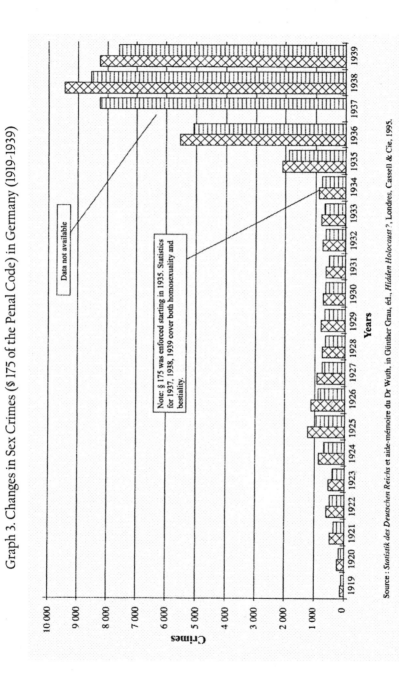

Graph 3. Changes in Sex Crimes (§ 175 of the Penal Code) in Germany (1919-1939)

Data not available

Note: § 175 was enforced starting in 1935. Statistics for 1937, 1938, 1939 cover both homosexuality and bestiality.

Years

Crimes

Source : *Statistik des Deutschen Reichs* et aide-mémoire du Dr Wuth, in Günther Grau, éd., *Hidden Holocaust ?*, Londres, Cassell & Cie, 1995.

homosexual. Therefore it is decided to keep a constant watch on the roads, the stations, parks, urinals, labor exchanges, and bars "to eradicate male prostitutes completely." Hotel doormen, porters, taxi drivers, medical employees, hair-dressers and bath attendants are to be questioned about their customers. Schools, youth movements, military institutions and monasteries will be subject to investigation. Pupils and members of these organizations will be questioned about their leaders and their comrades. All the known homosexuals must be on file, with their photograph and their fingerprints. If one cannot prove the crime, the suspect must not be let go. A search must be conducted in order to find letters from friends or other homosexuals. If the search does not turn up any material, the suspects must receive a detailed warning, be kept under surveil-lance and "monitored more and more closely." The interrogations must be carried out with tact, in particular in the case of minors and victims of black-mailers: "Somebody who is being made to talk must lose his inhibitions when he testifies to the police. He must be convinced that without his cooperation, he will never get rid of his 'tormentor,' and that the police will treat his declarations with understanding and the greatest discretion."

These directives are very instructive. They illustrate first of all the means used and the importance attached to the fight against homosexuality. The city was divided up in a rational way, and all the places where homosexuals were likely to be were placed under surveillance. The surveillance was not left to the police alone; the population was mobilized in order to watch or identify sus-pects. Certain traditionally homophile organizations were favorite targets, like schools and youth movements, or the monasteries which were at the center of the homophobic campaign of 1937. "Psychological" methods were popular. "The homosexual is not a normal criminal. To apprehend him, one must use tact and, if possible, gain his confidence, so that he gives you information. If the defendant shows any desire for 'redemption,' his rehabilitation should be facilitated." This attitude reflects the particular status of the homosexual and the nuances of treatment. The "corrupter of youth" is a danger, a monster for whom one may have no pity, for he spreads evil and undermines the morals of the German people. Seen as incurable, he is beyond any rehabilitated. On the other hand, the male prostitute is not necessarily homosexual and can be reintegrated into society, just like the young man who was seduced. Homosexuality is not in itself a criterion for social rejection: it is the practice of homosexuality, and its repeated practice, that makes the homosexual an "enemy of the State."

These nuances required unusual psychological talents on the part of the policemen and it seems that the complexity of the orders sometimes led to "mistakes." Summoned to stamp out homosexuality, while integrating the psychology of the criminal, certain police officers missed the point of their mission. A major scandal erupted in Frankfurt-am-Main in September 1937 when the president of the County Court (Oberlandesgericht) of Frankfurt wrote to Gürtner, Justice Minister of the Reich, to let him know that abuses had been committed in certain events concerned with §175. These errors were a consequence of the Reichsführer SS Himmler's trip to Frankfurt, where he gave a particularly vibrant speech against homosexuality before an audience of policemen, enjoining them to fight homosexuality with all their strength. Some of them seem to have badly misinterpreted the message.

Gürtner passed the files on to Himmler on January 24, 1938. All of them concerned cases of entrapment by the police.[526] Officer Wildhirt used a seventeen-year-old boy to trap a homosexual on April 7, 1937; a sergeant allowed a certain fellow to give him fellatio in order to establish proof of his culpability (June 25, 1937). The Minister for Justice concluded: "Although I do not deny that a merciless campaign against homosexuality is urgently required to maintain the strength of the German people, I find it intolerable for the reputation of the police that officers be permitted to offer their own body in order to trap homosexuals. Leaving aside the question of whether senior police officers are allowed to encourage others to make themselves accessory to illegal acts committed by homosexuals, one cannot in any event justify the use of young people, who are easily influenced and who face a particularly grave danger of corruption, in order to trap criminals in the way described in the first case." Himmler responded that he, too, deplored the use of such measures to trap homosexuals and that "[he] had had the officers in question informed that their behavior is unacceptable, and that in the future such methods of trapping homosexuals are not to employed any more." This dossier illustrates the confusion that the anti-homosexual campaign could cause in certain minds. It also shows that the police methods were not so different from those used in England at the same time.

Specific of Germany Nazi, on the other hand, were the sweeps carried out by special mobile units of the Gestapo in certain cities. They might go after one particular site, like a school, and might be based on a denunciation. In Hamburg, on August 28, 1936, a clean up of the bars was launched in. Several hundred men

---

526. BAB, R 22/1460.

were arrested. On December 23, 1937, an operation was launched at Halle, in Saxony.[527]

The Nazi system encouraged denunciations. By abundantly distributing anti-homosexual propaganda in the newspapers, the population was incited to take part in the fight; the State encouraged the baser instincts and transformed the average citizen into a dispenser of vigilante justice. In 1934, the carpenter Josef Holl denounced the Benedictine father Wilhelm Dutli (Pater Nokter II) to the Bavarian police.[528] Holl, who was working on the joinery of the monastery of Schäftlarn since 1933, accused the father of a crime against §175 and of subversive political activities. The father was Swiss and he subscribed to foreign news-papers, which according to Holl contained anti-national articles. Furthermore, Holl had a 21-year-old colleague, Ludwig Weigelsberger. Since July 11, 1934, "relations between Weigelsberger and Pater Nokter became very intimate." Dutli regretted his acts deeply and promised not to do it again. Appended to the file, a police report from November 28, 1934 notes that a search was conducted but that no seditious newspapers were found. There does not appear to have been any follow-up with regard to father Dutli: since he was of Swiss nationality, he could not be sentenced anyway.

Foreign nationality was not always a safeguard, however. People from the territories annexed by Germany were not shielded like the Swiss. After Czecho-slovakia was dismembered on March 15, 1939 and the Sudetenland was annexed by the Reich, inhabitant of the Sudetenland could be sentenced according to the laws of the Reich. Worse yet, the laws were retroactive!

As a most dramatic example we may consider Anton Purkl, who was imprisoned in Dresden in 1939 for unnatural crimes. Purkl was born in 1887; he was married and father of a child. In 1913, he was kicked out of the Wandervogel. During the war, he was taken prisoner in Russia. In 1923, he joined the youth movement led by the architect Heins Rutha, who professed the theories of Blüher. He had never been convicted before. He was charged with engaging in indecent contacts with one of his minor pupils (§174), and a variety of other indecent acts involving men (§175a) and boys. The counts of indictment read like a virtual sexual biography of the defendant. In this enumeration the will of the Nazi regime is clear: it was not enough to condemn Purkl for the charges against him. Purkl was both "a corrupter of youth" and a recidivist. On December 22,

---

527. *Hidden Holocaust?, op. cit.*, p.133.
528. BAB, NS 19/889.

1939, Purkl and several others were sentenced to three years in prison and six months' deprivation of civil rights.[529] It is specified that the fact that these acts occurred in the Sudetenland prior to February 28, 1939 does not in any way prevent the execution of the sentence. Purkl filed many appeals, but all were rejected.

Some Specific Cases

While the Reich police were in charge of routine cases, the Gestapo was used for specific cases. The Reichsführer SS and chief of the police Himmler was worried from the start about what role homosexuality might play within the party. The SS was of particular concern. Himmler feared that homosexuality could take root there, corrupting young recruits and encouraging the formation of cliques, which he had specifically denounced in the SA. And the Hitler Youth, like all the youth groups, had a tendency to attract homosexuals. Himmler also tried to "purify" the Wehrmacht, without much success. Lastly, two big homophobic campaigns with a political subtext were launched between 1935 and 1938. Both were failures, but they contributed to fanning the public's fears of homosexual contamination in every level of society.

Homosexuality in the "Hitlerjugend" and the SS

Homosexuality within the NSDAP or the organizations subordinate to it was a subject of concern to the Nazi leadership very early on.[530] Röhm's elimination served as a pretext for purging the party.[531] Hitler himself announced that every mother could send "her son to the SA, the Party and the Hitler Youth" "without any fear that he would be corrupted there in mores and morals." On

---

529. He was sentenced to one year and four months in prison and one year and one month in prison for the two incidents involving the schoolboy; one year in prison for the case with Oswald, six months for Weinmann, four months for Hetz and three months for the unnamed person. As one can see, acts with minors were punished far more severely. This was not an exception under the Nazis; even under Weimar, the judges could not find strong enough words against pedophiles.

530. For testimony as to homosexuality in the party organizations, see Joachim S. Hohmann (ed.), *Keine Zeit für gute Freunde, Homosexuelle in Deutschland, 1933-1969*, Berlin, Foerster Verlag, 1982, 208 pages; in particular, Konstantin Orloff's testimony: in 1930, he was 17. A member of the Hitler Youth, he made love with his group leader. He left in 1931 and joined Otto Strasser's *Schwarze Front*. According to him, most of his members were homosexuals. In 1932, he met Röhm, who propositioned him and wanted to take him to the hotel.

July 30, 1934, a letter was addressed to the Dresden police, asking them to provide the names of people convicted under the terms of §175 or suspected of homosexual activities, who were members of the NSDAP or who, without belonging to the party, might be members of the youth organization.[532] In August 1934, a report from the leadership of the NSDAP of Saxony required the various gendarmeries of the district of Chemnitz to list the people in the party, with their names and their ranks, "whose way of life contravened §175 of the penal code."

In 1936, the Reich Central Office for the Combating of Homosexuality gathered information on homosexuals. It asked regional police offices to forward the files concerned with §175 and 175a but, as mentioned above, a report was necessary only for significant cases, especially the members of the NSDAP or one of its organizations.

Himmler was particularly worried about homosexual activities within the SS. In his speech at Bad Tölz on February 18, 1937, addressing the generals of the SS, he raised the problem. He became particularly vehement when discussing exemplary measures: "Every month a case of homosexuality in the SS is presented. We have eight to ten cases per annum. I have thus decided the following: in every case, these individuals will be officially demoted, removed from the SS and taken before a court. Having served the sentence set by the court, they will be sent on my order to a concentration camp and will be executed during "an attempt to escape." In each case, the corps from which this individual came will be informed of the matter by my order. I thus hope to extirpate these people from the SS, to the last one: I want to preserve the noble blood that we receive in our organization and the work of racial cleansing which we continue in Germany."[533]

The measures were certainly radical. The eradication of homosexuality in the SS was a clearly expressed intention. A pretense of legality was preserved — the trial, the official sentence — but, in fact, the homosexual SS was condemned

---

531. The Gauleiter of Silesia, Helmut Brückner, was destitute after the putsch; Dr. Achim Gercke, a bisexual, party member since 1925, was an expert in racial research for the Minister of the Reich for moving Jews out of the country. In 1935 he was under Gestapo surveillance for a homosexual adventure that went on for a year; he managed to evade the suspicions, but had to quit his job. Ernst vom Rath, a homosexual, party member since 1932, was able to carry on his career at in Foreign Affairs; in 1938, he was secretary of the legation to the German embassy in Paris.

532. *Hidden Holocaust?, op. cit.*, p.44-45.

533. *Ibid.*, p.87.

to death.[534] The charge of homosexuality thus became one of most serious that could be levied against anyone.

Thus the lawyer Ludwig Lechner, SS-Obersturmführer and a friend of Himmler, was accused in 1938 of touching a girl of sixteen and a half years; he was pardoned at Himmler's own request. A little later he was convicted of a crime against §175 on the person of a fourteen-year-old boy. He was sentenced to one year and three months of forced labor and three years loss of civic rights.[535]

The case of the SS-Gruppenführer (a general, a very high position within the Nazi hierarchy) Wittje stands out.[536] Wittje was thrown out of the SS for alcoholism in 1938. The affair was quite complicated and Himmler played an important role. In his report of June 17, 1938, Himmler established a chronology of the events and, what is extremely rare, explained how he came to have the inward conviction that SS-Gruppenführer Wittje was guilty. In June 1934, after the elimination of Röhm, Hitler telephoned to inform him that General von Blomberg, then Minister for War, had said to him that within the SS there was a man who had been turned out of the Reichswehr for homosexuality: Wittje. Himmler declared himself to be very surprised and was astonished that, under these conditions, Wittje was still authorized to wear the uniform and moreover to receive a pension from the army. Himmler asked to meet General von Blomberg and his chief of staff von Reichenau. Wittje had entered the SS in 1930 at a low level (einfacher SS-Mann), but had distinguished himself and rose quickly. However, twice while he was in the Reichswehr, Wittje had, in a state of intoxication, put his arm around, hugged and kissed a warrant officer. The following day, he did not recall the incident. Himmler called Wittje in and questioned him; Wittje immediately tendered his resignation. Himmler refused it, for he had never done anything wrong in the SS. On the other hand, he did ask him to stop drinking henceforth, and warned him against homosexuality. For a year, nothing else happened. In 1935, SS-Gruppenführer Lorenz, who had replaced Wittje in Hamburg, announced that he had had to discharge two men from Wittje's former staff for homosexuality. In 1934-1935 also, Wittje went back to drinking. Rumors began to spread about misconduct. In 1937, Wittje's former driver confirmed the rumors of homosexuality but when he had to reiterate his charges before the court, he retracted. He was convicted of calumny, discharged

---

534. This decision was formalized by the confidential decree dated 15 November 1941 for "cleaning up [*Reinhaltung*] the SS and the police" (BAB, R 58/261). See postface.

535. BAB, NS 19/1087. It is not known what became of him afterwards.

536. BAB, NS 19/3940.

from the SS and sent to the concentration camp at Sachsenhausen. Himmler heard further echoes of Wittje's behavior in Hamburg in 1937 and 1938. He was drinking again and always organizing "evenings of camaraderie." Himmler charged the Gestapo in Hamburg with clearing up these rumors but, according to him, they did not handle the matter well. Two new cases came up. Himmler concluded his report by noting that his "experience" showed that it was very possible for a man to be wrongfully accused of homosexuality. It was also possible that an intoxicated man might accidentally embrace another man. It was also possible that on one or two occasions, a man might be wrongfully accused by others seeking reprisals, because they knew that homosexuality is punished by the law. But it was not possible that witnesses of different backgrounds, far apart and upset by their own suspicions, could deliver identical testimonies and describe systematically that the man put his arms around, hugged and kissed his companion. Must one then conclude that the charges of homosexuality levied against Wittje were well founded? He was inclined to say yes. Could Wittje fill the position of Gruppenführer in the SS? No. It seems however that the business was even further complicated, probably because of the defendant's rank. Witnesses for the prosecution and for the defense were heard; Himmler accused the court of showing too much indulgence. The transcript of the trial is not available, which makes any interpretation difficult. Nevertheless, in a letter of June 17, 1938 Himmler noted that "the suit against Gruppenführer Wittje must be used as an example." Wittje was demoted and discharged from the SS. The charge of alcoholism, although well founded, seems to have been a pretext for getting rid of an individual who had become too much of a liability, legitimating at the highest level the rumors of homosexuality, which Himmler wanted to avoid at all costs.

Another of the party's concerns was the fate of the younger generation. Since 1936, the Hitler Youth had fought vigorously against the older youth groups, which had been prohibited. Many lawsuits were launched, accusing the leaders of crimes relating to §175.[537] The most famous was the one that started in Düsseldorf September 18 and 19, 1936 against the old Nerother Bund or Rheinische Jugendburg Bund. Its leader, Robert Oelbermann, was sentenced to

---

537. It is hard to say whether some of these trials were fabricated. These movements had a reputation that made this type of accusation plausible and they could be used to discredit them in the eye of the public.

twenty-one months of forced labor. After eighteen months, he was sent to the concentration camp at Sachsenhausen and he died in Dachau on March 28, 1941.

However, at the very heart of the Hitler Youth, homosexuality was spreading and the leadership of the Reich Youth, with Baldur von Schirach at its head, was keen to put an end to these practices. Since they came to power, strict measures of control had been instituted and, since 1936, it was obligatory to denounce homosexual acts.[538] At the first hint of suspicion, the boy in question lost any leadership function; if the suspicions were confirmed, the prosecutor was informed. The sentences were recorded by the Reich Central Office for the Combating of Homosexuality.

The Hitler Youth also kept files. In 1938, it was decided that every year when boys were promoted to higher ranks, the leaders of each troop or company would receive instruction on questions concerning §174 and 176.[539] On the other hand, it was up to the parents to inform young people about sexual matters.

There are several files pointing a finger at members of the Hitler Youth.[540] In 1934, one Friedrich Schorn, Unterbannführer of the Hitler Youth, was reported for sex crimes under §174.1. He was an instructor of apprentices in a mechanical weaving company in Halbau. He gave a complete confession. Schorn was then placed in preventive custody in the prison of Sagan. On November 3, 1934, the Attorney General sent in a list of charges. He had been abusing minors since 1929 but was never convicted. Until 1923, he was an officer in the army; he had to leave because he had made advances to an orderly. He had engaged in indecent acts with several boys between 1930 and 1933. Schorn was sentenced to five years in prison, as the acts he was charged with had been committed before he became a member of the Hitler Youth.[541]

On November 7, 1934 the chief of the Reich Youth (Reichjugendführer) sent the Minister of the Interior a list of the members of Hitler Youth and Jungvolk who had been convicted for misdemeanors under §175 and expelled.[542] In five months, at least eleven leaders in the Hitler Youth and Jungvolk had been

---

538. These measures were made considerably tougher during the war. See postface.

539. BAB, R 22/1176.

540. GStA, HI, Rep.84a, n° 17298.

541. The same file contained the accusation filed against another member of the Hitler Youth. Hans Müller, a salesman from Cologne, was a team leader (*Fähnleinführer*) in the Jungvolk. In April 1933, he and his group took part in an educational trip to Köttingen. During the trip, as during a trip at Easter in 1934 and at Pentecost in the same year, he fondled several of the boys he was chaperoning. On 22 September 1934, he was placed in preventive detention in prison in Cologne. That is all that is known about this case.

convicted and expelled. The fight against homosexuality within the party orga-nizations was apparently conducted vigorously; but given the lack of statistics, it is difficult to assess whether it was a success.

Homosexuality in the Wehrmacht

Until the beginning of the war, the Wehrmacht took its own approach to homosexuality. Those cases that came up might relate to either §175 or 175a, just like for civilians. However, one might suppose that the authorities were espe-cially concerned lest the Wehrmacht become a center of homosexual propa-gation.[543] Wehrmacht kept a special file on homosexuals, which in 1940 counted 5,000 names. A questionnaire was to be filled out for each homosexual and sent to the Reich Central Office, and the Reich Central Office sent the army recruitment center a list of "corrupters of youth" and male prostitutes.

The cooperation between the army and the Reich Central Office did not always go smoothly. On September 5, 1938, the High-Command returned the list of pedophiles and male prostitutes, saying that there was no point in forwarding them to the recruitment offices, either because they were not kept up to date or because the men had not been tried yet, and they were young and likely "to be hounded all their lives for a youthful indiscretion often caused by seduction, without ever being convicted for it in a court of law." Lastly, "Even if the lists were to be kept up to date, recording them would in itself mean an additional burden for the recruitment offices, and the recruitment offices have more important matters to attend to; the result would by no means justify the amount of work required."[544]

In fact, homosexuality cases did not reach a peak in the Wehrmacht before the war. In 1940 the number of indictments increased, probably because of the many homosexuals who signed up.[545] In cases judged to be based on "an incorri-

---

542. Otto Rosenberg, Horst Gehrke, Gerhard Schewinski, Kurt Zipprik, al from Bartenstein, were kicked out of the Hitler Youth on 25 November 1934. *Fähnleinführer* Hans-Jürgen Puzig from Flatow was kicked out on 23 April 1934. *Scharführer* Düwel of Cologne was kicked out on 25 August 1934. The former *Oberbannführer* Ernst Erdelt of Liegnitz was kicked out on 25 July 1934, former *Fähnleinführer* Küppenbender on 25 October 1934, and Schorn and Hans Müller as well. Lückenbach, the former *Fähnlein-führer* of *Jungvolk* was kicked out on 25 November 1934.

543. Obligatory military service was reintroduced in 1935 for all men aged 18 to 45, and up to 60 for officers. In 1936, the army already had 500,000 men; in August 1939, it had 2.6 million soldiers.

544. *Hidden Holocaust?, op. cit.*, p.127.

gible predisposition," the sentence was prison and, in serious cases, forced labor and detention in a camp. If it were a matter of homosexuality of "circumstance," or "seduction," the defendants could be reinstated in the army after having served their sentences. This was construed as a favor, to enable them to prove their virility before the enemy. Nevertheless, crimes concerned with §175 were regarded as incompatible with the exercise of command.

Homosexuality as a way of eliminating opponents

The Nazi regime was pragmatic in the elimination of its opponents. To identify its enemies for prosecution and punishment it used a few overarching themes, and homosexuality was one of the best options, as the Röhm incident proved. In 1937, a new homophobic campaign was launched, this one aimed at the Catholics and in particular the religious orders. A hundred monks and nuns were charged with various misdeeds before the German courts, mostly relating to homosexuality. Many members of the Catholic clergy had already been prosecuted for trafficking in currencies or communist conspiracies, without much success. The purpose of these persecutions was to discredit the religious orders and the Catholic Church and to justify canceling their rights as educational establishments. Hitler hoped by this means to put pressure on the Vatican and the German episcopate and to get them to end their protests. The Gestapo had conducted investigations and held the information in reserve to be used at the right moment. The last straw was the papal encyclical *Mit brennender Sorge* (With Burning Anxiety) of March 14, 1937, which warned against the ideological bases of Nazism.

The first target of the Gestapo was a small community of lay brothers in Waldbreitbach, a village close to Trier, in the Palatinate. They were supervised rather loosely by the Franciscans and took care of the handicapped in local hospitals. They had not been particularly selected nor trained, and the Church authorities admitted to some negligence. Even so, the court case was a failure. The Gestapo brought as a witness one of the mentally-retarded patients. The prosecutor asked him whether he could point out to the court any person who had tried to seduce him and lure him into committing indecent acts. The witness pointed to the president of the court. The case was dismissed.[546]

---

545. This explanation was offered as early as 1943 by the military psychiatrist Otto Wuth, who penned a report on homosexuality in the army. In total, from 1 September 1939 to 30 June 1944, 7000 were convicted; that is a small number, given the size of the armed forces.

In the Rhenish lands, nearly a thousand judicial inquests had been launched against the lay brothers. Nearly 300 were dead ends, for 150 of them were forewarned and got away, and 150 had some immunity. On May 22, 1937, 300 suits were filed and others were in preparation against the Franciscans of Waldbreitbach, the Alexians of Neuss and Cologne-Lindenthal, the brothers of Mercy of Montabour, and the Capuchin and Benedictine lay orders.[547]

A Gestapo memorandum dated April 8, 1937[548] shows how the smear campaign developed under Josef Meisinger, Regierungsrat Haselbacher and SS-Sturmbannführer Hartl. Concrete details on each suit were shared with the public in order to stir up popular outrage, and propaganda articles based on scientific assertions were published. Altogether, 100,000 copies of a pamphlet entitled *You Must Recognize Them and Their Acts* were distributed. An anticlerical work by Burghard Assmuss, entitled *Klosterleben, Enthüllungen über die Sittenverderbnis in den Klöstern* ("Life in the Monasteries and Revelations on the Depravity of Morals in the Monasteries"), was published in 1937; it was full of slander on the sex life of monks. The climax of the campaign was Goebbels' speech at Berlin's Deutschlandhalle in front of 25,000 people on May 30, 1937, answering the charges of the cardinal archbishop of Chicago. According to him, the lawsuits reflected "a frightening and revolting phenomenon of moral decadence whose equivalent could not be found in all of the history of humanity." "The criminal aberrations of the Catholic clergy threaten the physical and moral health of our young people. I declare before the German people that this plague will be radically extirpated and, if the Church is too weak, the State will to it."[549] The speech skillfully exploited the popular instincts, presenting the members of the clergy not only as homosexuals but as "corrupters of youth" and abusers of the handicapped. Goebbels and the Nazi leaders posed by contrast as paragons of family virtues.

---

546. Cited by Richard Plant, *The Pink Triangle*, New York, Holt & Cie, 1986, 257 pages, p.133. Other examples suggest that most of the accusations were trivial. The court in Paderborn acquitted a Catholic priest, Abbot Sommer, curé of Siddessen, who was charged with indecency. The witnesses retracted their statements while on the stand. The prosecutor had asked for nine months in prison. In Münster, Westphalia, Abbot Deitmaring, curé of Hoetmear, charged with indecency, was also acquitted due to lack of evidence. In his case, the prosecutor had asked for between three and five years in prison (*Le Temps*, 16 May 1937).

547. *Le Temps*, 22 May 1937.

548. *Hidden Holocaust?*, op. cit., p.135-136.

549. *Le Temps*, 30 May 1937.

The speech was interrupted several times by the crowd, shouting: "Hang them! ... Massacre them! ..."

The anti-Catholic campaign continued until 1941. By 1936, all the Catholic youth organizations had been closed down. The monks had been expelled from more than 35 monasteries. In 1941, Goebbels banned all Catholic magazines and newspapers. Between 1937 and 1945, more than 4,000 clerics died in the concentration camps from torture, disease or starvation.[550]

Still, while the homophobic campaign cast a pall on the Catholic clergy, it was on balance a failure. Of approximately 20,000 German priests, only 57 were convicted; of 4,000 members of the regular clergy, only 7 were convicted. Lastly, of 3,000 lay brothers, 170 were convicted, mostly Franciscans.[551] Between 1933 and 1943, less than 0.5% of the 22.4 million German Catholics left the Church.

Another campaign was launched in 1937 with the aim of destabilizing the army. General von Blomberg and General von Fritsch had warned Hitler against attacking Czechoslovakia, fearing it would bring France and Great Britain into the war. The crisis between the generals and Hitler came to a head in 1938.[552] Circumstances facilitated the elimination of von Blomberg, who had recently remarried — to a young woman whose mother had run a massage parlor. Goering discovered that the young woman had posed for pornographic photographs and that she had been registered as a prostitute. Goering showed the photographs to von Blomberg, who offered his resignation.

He should have been replaced by General Werner von Fritsch, the very model of the Prussian officer, a confirmed bachelor, a shy, religious man who lived only for the army. He was admired by his officers and his troops, and was beyond any criticism. But his independence, his mistrust of the Nazi leaders — with whom he did not associate — had earned him some enemies, in particular among the Himmler-Heydrich-Goering triumvirate. While Hitler recognized von Fritsch's professional qualities, he hardly liked him. Then Goering intervened: he dug up a sordid affair dating to 1936. One Otto Schmidt, a thief and blackmailer, had accused von Fritsch of homosexuality. The case had been taken

---

550. Richard Plant, *The Pink Triangle, op. cit.,* p.136.

551. On this subject, see Hans Günther Hockerts, *Die Sittlichkeitsprozesse gegen katholische Ordensangehörige und Priester, 1936-1937,* Mayence, Mathias Grünewald Verlag, 1971, 224 pages.

552. Several works present the elimination of the generals as a coup arranged by Hitler in order to place himself at the head of the armed forces. Marlis Steinert suggests, rather, that the events were unexpected and Hitler used them to his own advantage.

up by section II H in the Gestapo. In an interrogation conducted by Josef Meis-inger, Schmidt gave a deposition swearing to have seen General von Fritsch go to the toilets with one of his acquaintances, the homosexual Josef Weinberger, at the Potsdamer Platz subway station in Berlin on November 22, 1933. According to him, they engaged in indecent acts, and then the general gave Weinberger some money. Otto Schmidt then popped up, presented himself as a member of the SA, and extorted 500 RM in order to keep quiet. (It is not clear whether, at this point, Meisinger knew that this whole story related to Captain Achim von Frisch, not General Werner von Fritsch.) Meisinger reported to Himmler, but Hitler ordered them to burn the file. The outside pressures were great enough, in 1936, and there was no need to start a homosexual scandal at the top of the mil-itary hierarchy. Nevertheless, Heydrich took Himmler's advice and kept a copy of the most important documents.[553] In 1937, Otto Schmidt was in prison again; he was released on condition that he become a state witness on sexual deviants. Hitler was alerted; he showed more interest than in 1936. He called in Hossbach, a colonel in the Wehrmacht, who gave little credit to the charges. Hossbach informed Fritsch, who was stunned. Otto Schmidt swore he recognized him; and von Fritsch was suspended from his functions. At the first hearing, the defense lawyer pointed out contradictions in Schmidt's testimony. The old captain, who had been beaten in prison, admitted to everything and Otto Schmidt admitted having given a false deposition. Von Fritsch was released, but was unable to regain his post office at the head of the army. He died in combat, in Poland, in September 1939, at the head of an obscure regiment. Schmidt was sent to Sach-senhausen concentration camp for four years; he was liquidated there on orders from Goering.[554]

Hitler then took command of the Wehrmacht. The path was clear for the Anschluss. Once again, the charge of homosexuality, even completely unfounded, had done its job.

"Rehabilitation" or "Eradication"?

The Nazi regime was energetic in conducting its campaign against homo-sexuality. However, not all homosexuals were considered in the same way, and there was never any question of exterminating homosexuals as a whole.

---

553. In Friedrich Koch, *Sexuelle Denunziation, die Sexualität in der politischen Auseinanderset-zung*, Frankfurt-am-Main, Syndikat, 1986, 223 pages.
554. Richard Plant, *The Pink Triangle, op. cit.*, p.140-143.

Only the "incorrigible" homosexuals were to be eliminated, particularly those who presented a danger to youth. As these were unofficial measures, it is impossible to gauge the exact number of those who were sent to the camps, how much time they spent there on average, or how many died there. For those whose homosexuality was regarded as "acquired," through vice or seduction, "rehabilitation" was considered. Internment in the concentration camps was based on the idea that homosexuals could be "rehabilitated" by labor. Now, it was a question of curing them. Several means were considered, from psychoanalysis to castration. These efforts did not produce the anticipated results and, just before the war, Himmler (who had been an ardent fan of the notion of "rehabilitation") was less and less inclined to waste time and money on the "abnormal." Camp became the customary treatment, and now it was extended to all homosexuals who had seduced more than one partner.

Elimination by Labor

The fate of homosexuals in the concentration camps is described in studies by Rüdiger Lautmann and Richard Plant.[555] Lautmann and a team of researchers studied thirteen or fourteen institutions that held imprisoned homosexuals; Richard Plant studied the situation of the homosexual in Buchenwald. In both cases, only to partial conclusions can be drawn. Indeed, many of the files are incomplete: some documents were destroyed when the camps were evacuated; others were not kept up to date. Certain files are still missing because they were dispersed in the former socialist countries. Among the officials, only Rudolf Hoess left his *Memoirs*. Lautmann and Plant succeeded in collecting very few interviews from old "pink triangles." Thus the analysis offered below is compartmental. It is focused on the years 1933-1939, since that is the period currently under discussion.

Shortly after the Nazis took over, homosexuals started being sent to concentration camps. Kurt Hiller, an activist from the WhK, was sent to Orianenburg. Himmler's order of December 14, 1937 and his decree of July 12, 1940 specifically designated "corrupters of youth" and male prostitutes; and as of 1940, recidivists too were to be placed in "preventive custody."[556] Not all homosexuals were sent to the camps after serving out their sentences, but arbitrary

---

555. Rüdiger Lautmann, *Terror und Hoffnung in Deutschland, 1933-1945*, Reinbek, Rowohlt, 1980, 570 pages; *Seminar: Gesellschaft und Homosexualität*, Frankfurt-am-Main, Suhrkamp Taschenbuch, 1977, 570 pages; Richard Plant, *The Pink Triangle, op. cit.*

internments did take place. The first camp opened was that of Dachau, on March 30, 1933. In June 1933, Himmler named Theodor Eicke to run the camp, which became the model for Sachsenhausen, Buchenwald and Mauthausen. Homosexuals were interned in each of these camps, but their exact number is not known. It seems, however, that they were the smallest minority in the camps, with émigrés, "profaners of the race" and transfers from the armed forces. Lautmann lists 150 homosexuals at Dachau between March and September 1938. According to him, an estimated 5,000–15,000 homosexuals were sent to concentration camps between 1933 and 1945, but these statistics cannot be refined further.

Like other prisoners, those who wore the pink triangle faced inhuman conditions of detention. It seems that they suffered particularly. One of Richard Plant's witnesses reports that on arrival in the camp of Buchenwald, homosexuals and Jews were beaten. Eugen Kogon reports that homosexuals at Flössenburg, Sachsenhausen, Buchenwald and Mauthausen were sent to work in the quarries in greater number than other groups. In Auschwitz and Sachsenhausen, they were sent to the camp brothel in order to be "rehabilitated."[557]

Homosexuals suffered special isolation. A letter from the Reich Justice Minister addressed to the Reichsführer SS on December 15, 1939[558] requested that homosexuals be separated from other prisoners, and not intermingled with them, in order to avoid any homosexual contact. In the Austrian camps (Ostmark), the prisoners were isolated at night. A special block contained individual cells, in particular in Rodgau. In the Ems and Rodgau camps, where such isolation could not be maintained, "the principle of dilution" was applied: "The principle consists in distributing homosexuals so that everywhere they go, they have to face a great majority of non-perverts who keep them under control, because of a healthy horror of homosexuality which is also very widespread among the [rest of the] prisoners." The system was reinforced by the way the blocks were managed: homosexuals were assigned to places where it was very easy to keep an eye on them and, where there were bunk beds, in the upper

---

556. On 12 May 1944, a secret decree from the chief of the security police ordered that homosexuals thrown out of the Wehrmacht, that is, those who showed a "predisposition or an acquired and clearly incorrigible urge," should be sent to concentration camps. They were to go to camp, either immediately upon being kicked out, or after serving their time.

557. Eugen Kogon, L'État SS [1947], Paris, Éditions du Seuil, coll. "Points histoire," 1993, 445 pages, p.290-291.

558. Hidden Holocaust?, op. cit., p.152-153.

bunks. Homosexuals were not to have any possibility of communicating individually during work: they were not assigned to the kitchens or the storehouses. In Auschwitz, Rudolf Hoess sequestered them in a hut.

Their special status deprived homosexuals of any external aid. Their friends did not dare to write to them, for fear of being regarded as homosexual themselves; and their families often abandoned them. The other groups of prisoners avoided them, and for the most part shared the prejudices against them. Everywhere, the SS like the prisoners themselves seemed to be convinced that homosexuals were obsessed with sex and that they had to be monitored closely.

Aggravating the situation was the fact that some of the SS guards were homosexual themselves and they took their favorites captive, especially Poles and Russians, as "dolly boys" (Pielpel). The SS competed with the Kapos for the "Pielpels" and that went over very badly with the rest of the prisoners.

Political leaders had nothing to gain by supporting decent treatment for the homosexuals; they were seen as unreliable and likely to divide the "antifascist" coalition. The favors granted to selected young men did not mean better treatment for homosexuals overall and the pink triangles as a group did not benefit from the special treatment. In fact, solidarity among homosexuals was very limited. They did not occupy decision-making positions in the prisoner hierarchy and they almost never became Kapos. In the hierarchy of the camp, the pink triangles were at the lowest level, right before the Jews.

Buchenwald has been studied in detail. The camp opened in 1937; in 1938, it held 28 prisoners bearing the pink triangle. There were 46 in 1939 and 51 in 1940. After Himmler's decree on recidivists, the number rose to 74 in 1942, 169 in 1943, and 189 in 1944. On the whole, homosexuals were a negligible presence, less than 1% of the total camp population. Until the autumn 1938, homosexuals were assigned to the political blocks.[559] In October 1938, they were sent in the disciplinary company to work under inhuman conditions, subjected to the arbitrary violence of the SS. They were then the lowest group in the camp. Proportionally to their number, they were also sent most frequently to the death camps of Nordhausen, Natzweiler and Gross-Rosen. The labor shortage brought some respite: by the summer of 1942, they were put to work with the other prisoners in the war industry. Then in January 1944, they were sent to Dora to produce V2 rockets. The working conditions, housing and sanitation were terrible: 96 homo-

---

559. *Ibid.*, p.266-270. Report from the spring of 1945.

sexual prisoners died between February 8 and 13, 1945, more than half of those who had been interned at Buchenwald as of that date.

According to prisoners' reports, most of the homosexuals at Buchenwald were castrated. Others were used for medical experiments on typhoid fever. Heinz Heger's testimony[560] is the best known of the rare direct records left by homosexuals who were sent to concentration camps, but it is probably not very representative of the general fate. In 1939 Heger, an Austrian, was twenty-two years old. He came from a bourgeois Catholic family, and his father was a high civil servant working in an embassy in Vienna.[561] In March 1939, Heger was sentenced to six months reclusion in a disciplinary house, then was sent to Sachsenhausen. His lover, the son of a Nazi dignitary, was not convicted, for he was regarded as "mentally disturbed."[562] Inside the camp, homosexuals were the most despised prisoners. He was placed in a block with other pink triangles. At night, he had to sleep in just a shirt, keeping his hands showing on top of the cover, for "you fags, you would still manage to take your pleasure."[563] He was not allowed to speak with other "triangles," in order not to seduce them. Most of the homosexuals were put to work in the clay pits under inhuman conditions. Heger managed to survive by becoming the dolly boy of a Kapo.

When the latter was sent to Flossenburg, the homosexual block was broken up. Heger had the good fortune to be chosen by the senior of the block. According to Heger, homosexual relations among the prisoners were accepted as a substitute for regular sex, but that was not tolerated between homosexuals themselves. The purpose of such a distinction was to preserve the myth of a "normal" and "virile" sexuality and transferred onto the homosexual the burden of the "flaw" and the charge of femininity.

Until 1940, the death penalty was applied for homosexual relations. It seems that thereafter, morals loosened up. Public torture was common and Heger saw that as a sign of suppressed homosexuality in certain of the SS, who appeased their impulses through voyeurism and sadism. Thanks to his sup-

560. Heinz Heger, *Les Hommes au triangle rose. Journal d'un déporté homosexuel, 1939-1945*, Paris, Éditions Persona, 1981, 160 pages.

561. His father committed suicide in 1942, unable to face his son's infamous arrest and the sarcastic comments of the neighbors.

562. Heger thinks that he was sent to concentration camp so that Fred's homosexuality would not come to light. That is plausible, but cannot be proved since there is no documentation. In fact, Heger was not in any of the categories of homosexuals that were liable to be sent to camp.

563. Heinz Heger, *Les Hommes au triangle rose, op. cit.*, p.48.

porters Heger managed to become Kapo; this appears to have been a very rare exception.

The case of Karl Willy A. appears, unfortunately, more standard. Born in 1914 in Rehau, in Bavaria, he was working as a mason near Leipzig. On May 17, 1943, he was sentenced to preventive custody as a recidivist. Between 1934 and 1940, he had been convicted four times for unnatural acts and, the two last times, had been sentenced to forced labor, for corruption of minors. At the end of his sentence, he was brought back to the Leipzig prison. "As the last case occurred shortly after his marriage, one can hardly count on his being cured." Willy A. was therefore sent to Buchenwald, where he arrived on June 10, 1943. He died on November 24, 1943 of "purulent pleurisy." "By order of the camp doctor, the body [could] not be viewed, for reasons of hygiene." He was incinerated and his wife was notified; she refused to accept the urn.[564]

It is very difficult to estimate the number of lesbians who were sent to concentration camps. Lesbianism was not punished by law and the lesbians who were arrested were often caught on some other pretext. Neither is it known whether lesbians wore a specific insignia. Isa Vermehren says that lesbians wore a pink triangle with LL (Lesbische Liebe) inside. She seems to have seen this insignia on a panel displaying the various emblems at Ravensbrück. Other witnesses said the pink triangle designated Jehovah's Witnesses, not lesbians. In addition, it seems that some lesbians were recorded as asocial (black triangle) or criminals (green triangle).

All the known cases of lesbians interned in camps were later than the years 1933-1939. Claudia Schoppmann[565] reports the case of Else, a waitress from Potsdam, who lived with a friend and who was sent to Ravensbrück, then to Flossenburg, as an "asocial." Erich, who also testified, was interned in Flossenburg and met Else in the brothel there in 1943. She had probably been forced to prostitute herself at Ravensbrück, where women were promised their freedom if they agreed to serve in the brothel for a certain period. Lesbians were sent there in particular, to put them on the right path. Else disappeared thereafter and it is not clear what became of her.

The desire to humiliate lesbians is also apparent in another example, from a later period but unconfirmed. The testimony is provided by a friend of Helene G., who was an assistant in the Luftwaffe in Oslo between 1943 and 1945. She

---

564. *Hidden Holocaust?, op. cit.,* p.275-279.
565. *Ibid.,* p.14.

was a Telex operator and handled secret messages and espionage. She lived in the Luftwaffe quarters with another assistant who, unfortunately, caught the eye of a lieutenant. She repelled his advances. The two women were arrested by the military secret police and were separated. Helene G. was convicted by the court martial for potential subversion of the military, was discharged from the Wehrmacht and sent to the concentration camp of Bützow, in Mecklenburg. She was placed in a special block with six other lesbians. They were separated from the other women and were guarded by men. When the Kapos led them near the SS guards, they would tell the prisoners of war: "These represent a lower form of life. You wouldn't even want to kiss them with the leg of a chair. If you do'em right, you'll each get a bottle of schnapps," and they brought forward the Russian and French prisoners first. Thereafter, the lesbians were kept apart from the other women and were set to labor. Two died of hunger. Helene G. survived one year beyond the end of the war, then died of tuberculosis. If this information is true, it certainly shows the contempt and the hatred for lesbians, and the hostility engendered by the very thought of such a thing as independent female sexuality. Moreover, it shows that the lesbian lost her rights as an "Aryan woman," since she was handed over to the foreign prisoners.[566]

There are only scattered traces showing the presence of lesbians in the camps. There were two among the victims of Doctor Friedrich Mennecke in Ravensbrück: Jenny Sarah S., Jewish, single, a saleswoman in Frankfurt-am-Main and an "instinctive lesbian, who only goes to such places"; and Erna Sara P., Jewish, from Hamburg, married, was a "very active lesbian." She "sought out the lesbian cafés that still were functioning and exchanged affections at the cafés."[567]

Female homosexual friendships were formed in the camps just as male ones were. Fania Fenelon, who gives her story in *Das Mädchenorchester in Auschwitz*, 1982, talks about the Kapo Hilde, a black triangle, who shamelessly flaunted her relationship with her friend Inge. Fania was part of the Auschwitz orchestra

---

566. Cited in *ibid.*, p.83. This is one of the best-known testimonies and it has been cited by numerous authors. Ilse Kokula produced it for the first time. Still, Claudia Schoppmann has pointed out some inconsistencies in it: Bützow was in a camp for prisoners of war that was not supposed to house women. And then, the POW camps were under the command of the Wehrmacht and not the SS. She concludes that in the absence of any documents on Bützow it is impossible to explain these contradictions, but thinks that it is plausible that they may be a result of the disorganization that was spreading in the final months of the war.

567. Cited by Claudia Schoppmann, *Nationalsozialistische Sexualpolitik...*, *op. cit.*, p.235.

that was invited in the summer of 1944 to play for a "ball" one night in the "asocial" block. This was the block where, for the most part, former prostitutes were collected, and according to Fania Fenelon 90% of them had become lesbians.[568] Krystina Zywulska, in *Wo früher Birken waren* (1980), says much the same. Margarete Buber-Neumann, a political prisoner at Ravensbrück, testifies in *Milena, Kafkas Freundin* (1977): "Passionate friendships were as widespread among the politicals as the asocials or the criminals. The only difference was that the political prisoners' friendships remained platonic, whereas the others very often were lesbian."[569]

Such relations were severely punished if they were discovered: the punishment could be the deprivation of food for one or more days, beating with a rod (25 to 100 strokes), restriction to the bunker or being sent to a disciplinary battalion, or even death. The punishments varied according to the camp and the year. The Communist Dory Maase reports that in Ravensbrück, before 1941, lesbian relations were punished by death. Rudolf Hoess also reported the existence of homosexual practices: "Even the harshest punishments, even assignment to a disciplinary battalion, cannot put an end to it."[570]

"Curing" and castrating

Himmler, ardent partisan of the fight against homosexuality that he was, still retained a sense that "rehabilitation" should be attempted. He was persuaded that only 2% of the cases of homosexuality were innate and that the rest must be the result of giving in to vice or seduction. The goal was to reinstate such people into the community at the end a period of punishment and rehabilitation.

Himmler himself was quite interested in medical research on the subject and encouraged it. Psychoanalysis was seen as the first likely form of rehabilitation.[571] In 1935, psychoanalysis had been "Aryanized." All the Jewish members had had to resign from the German Society of Psychoanalysis (DPG, Deutsche Psychoanalystiche Gesellschaft). Carl Müller-Braunschweig and Felix Boehm

---

568. *Ibid.*, p.237.
569. *Ibid.*, p.238.
570. *Ibid.*, p.247.
571. See Thierry Féral, *Nazisme et psychanalyse*, Paris, La Pensée universelle, 1987, 92 pages. The Nazis considered psychoanalysis to be on outgrowth of the Jewish mind, that would corrupt the German people. Freud's writings were burned on 10 May 1933 and many psychoanalysts were forced to go into exile. Some, like K. Landauer and J. Mittmeister, were assassinated.

reorganized the leadership. In 1936, the German Institute for Psychological Research and Psychotherapy (Deutsches Institut für psychologische Forschung und Psychotherapie) was created under the direction of Matthias Heinrich Goering, a cousin of Hermann Goering's. The DPG was integrated into the Institute in November 1938.

The Institute favored the treatment of homosexuals and claimed a success rate of 70%. Thus out of 510 homosexual patients, it said it had "cured" 341 of them. Several members of the Institute published articles on the treatment of homosexuality.[572] The Institute also set up a program to collaborate with the Luftwaffe. Matthias Goering tried to extend the influence of psychiatry in the field of combating homosexuality, in particular in the context of the campaigns carried out in the Wehrmacht and the Hitler Youth. A manuscript by Felix Boehm, Secretary of the Institute, dated February 28, 1938,[573] recommends that a post of "confidential doctor" be created in all the party organizations, and partic-ularly in the youth organizations, so that people would have someone to go to in the event anything risky came up. On December 6, 1939, Boehm sent around a circular for the members of Institute,[574] asking them to send him a report on the treatments carried out against homosexuality, so that he could evaluate them. Himmler himself charged several doctors with working on homosexuality. A December 5, 1936 letter from SS-Hauptsturmführer Werner Jansen was sent in the name of Himmler to the Science Ministry, the Instruction and the Education of the People[575] to ask whether research on left-handed persons and homo-sexuals had been conducted. SS-Hauptsturmführer Ulmann answered on December 8 in the affirmative: Dr. Creutzfeldt was soon to present the results of his research. The conclusions of this study are not known.

June 14, 1937, Pr. Karl Astel, president of the regional office for refining the race (Landesamt für Rassenwesen) in Thuringe wrote to ask Himmler for the names and addresses of at least 100 homosexuals in Thuringe so that he could conduct some research on the nature of homosexuality.[576] In its response of June 22, Himmler showed himself to be quite interested and promised to have the

---

572. Notably: Johannes Heinrich Schultz, director of the polyclinic of the Institute, Felix Boehm, Maria Kalau vom Hofe, Fritz Mohr, Werner Kamper. See Claudia Schopp-mann, *Nationalsozialistische Sexualpolitik...*, *op. cit.*
573. *Hidden Holocaust?*, *op. cit.*, p.129.
574. *Ibid.*, p.130.
575. BAB, NS 19/073.
576. BAB, NS 19/1838.

Gestapo get him the required names. What happened after that is not known; but doctors had to be very careful in drafting their conclusions, for the Reichs-führer SS had quite set ideas on the subject and did not tolerate experiments that cast any doubt on his certainty.[577]

In addition to psychoanalysis, more radical means were planned to "reha-bilitate" homosexuals. A law was adopted on July 14, 1933 "to prevent descen-dants afflicted with hereditary diseases" (Gesetz zur Verhütung erbkranken Nachwuchses).[578] It went into effect on January 1, 1934. Between 1934 and 1945, 200,000 men and 200,000 women were officially sterilized. Thousands of them died in the aftermath of the operation. It is not clear how many more were victims of attempted sterilization in the concentration camps.

The "law against dangerous recidivists and measures for security and improvement" (Gesetz gegen gefährliche Gewohnheitsverbrecher und über Massregeln der Sicherung und Besserung) of November 24, 1933 authorized cas-tration in certain cases,[579] in addition to punitive measures. This could be applied only in the event of rape, blasphemy, pedophilic acts, sex acts with con-straint, sex acts in public, murder and assassination with a sexual motive. Homosexuals fell into these categories only if they had had sexual intercourse with boys of less than fourteen years or were convicted of exhibitionism. The majority of homosexual convicted under the terms of §175 and 175a were not affected.

The option of "voluntary castration" was made possible by an amendment to the law "to prevent descendants afflicted with hereditary diseases" of June 26, 1935. Clause 2 of §14[580] authorized castration in the case of homosexual crimes, but only with the consent of the person. A doctor also had to give his consent. A directive dated January 23, 1936 explicitly stated that one could not force, even

---

577. For example, his relationship with the Berlin doctor Martin Brustmann was abruptly broken off. Brustmann was a member of the NSDAP, a colleague of Matthias Goering, personal doctor to Heydrich and Himmler's family, as well as medical consultant for national security (SD). In 1943, when the war effort was in highest gear, he was accused of being too lax. The "rehabilitation" of homosexuals was by then considered a waste of time.

578. This had to do mostly with cases of "congenital weakness," manic-depression, schizophrenia, epilepsy, "St. Vitus' Dance," and hereditary deafness, congenital deformi-ties and alcoholism.

579. The first sentence of castration was pronounced on 10 December 1933 in Berlin, by the court of Duisbourg, against a 33-year-old man who was sentenced to 20 months in prison and to castration for having raped a schoolboy.

580. *Hidden Holocaust?, op. cit.*, p.250.

indirectly, a criminal to give his assent to castration; but on May 20, 1939, Reichsführer SS Himmler cancelled this directive. No doubt in the previous years some of the homosexuals placed in camps had agreed to the operation anyway, in the hope of some liberation.[581] The number of homosexuals who underwent castration between 1935 and 1945 is unknown.[582]

Nevertheless, castration for the "treatment" of homosexuality was still under discussion as a viable option. A complete report on the "causes of homosexuality and the castration of homosexuals" shows that the question was studied very thoroughly.[583]

It becomes quite clear that the medical theories on homosexuality were radicalized after 1933. Whereas, during the previous period, homosexuality was presented as an innate abnormality or a natural occurrence, here was a return to the old theories of degeneracy (Wolf, Deussen, Lang, Jensch), to biological explanations stressing hormonal dysfunctions (Lemke, Habel), and even to the simplistic assertion that homosexuality is an acquired vice (Schröder). The links between homosexuality and degeneration of the race are particularly clear in Lothar Gottlieb Tirala, in *Rasse, Geist und Seele* ("Race, spirit and heart"), published in 1935: "Here were created, following the mixture of the Nordic and Near-Eastern races, Nordic and Oriental races, and Nordic and Western races, a category of male and female sexual intermediaries which one may constantly run into in the large cities."[584] The report goes on to study the position of each doctor on penal repression, then it considers the idea of castration. On this point the opinions are very divided. The doctors who think that homosexuality is innate oppose it. Others think that the likelihood of success is slim. Nevertheless, certain doctors had already conducted experiments and maintained that their attempts had been successful. The Swiss Dr. Wolf, the Dane Dr. Sand and the German Dr. Rodenberg each provided statistics.[585] Wolf castrated 22 homosexuals; he acknowledged one failure. Sand castrated 72, with one failure.

---

581. A decree from 23 September 1940, from the Reich Bureau of Criminal Police, established that preventive detention should no longer apply to recidivist homosexuals if the criminal had been castrated and if, according to the medical experts, there was no reason to fear a relapse.

582. Psychiatrist Nikolaus Jensch's study, *Untersuchungen an entmannten Sittlichkeitsverbrechern* ("Research on castrated sex criminals"), published in 1944, established that of the 693 castrated men in the study, 285 were homosexuals.

583. BAB, R 22/950, p.39 *sq.* no date or author given (1942?).

584. Lothar Gottlieb Tirala, *Rasse, Geist und Seele*, Munich, J.F. Lehmann Verlag, 1935, 256 pages, p.72-73.

Rodenberg conducted 88 operations, of which 6 had failed. The report thus notes that, out of 182 cases, there were only 8 failures, that is to say a success rate of 96%. Similarly, Boeters[586] maintained that castration almost always resulted in "sexual death." Lang, on the other hand, emphasizes the lack of perspective on these experiments; since they had only been tried in the last few years, it was impossible to know their long-term consequences. The report concludes on a moderate note. It emphasizes the short duration of the trial period and the limited number of experiments. It also speculates about the conditions of this castration: should it be voluntary or obligatory?

In fact, many reports had cast doubt on castration as a "remedy" for homosexuality. Arthur Kronfeld, in *Sexualpathologie*, had been completely frank on the subject: "The treatment of homosexuality, in the sense of a promising medical therapy, almost does not exist. The transplantation of the gonads, carried out by Lichtenstern and Mühsam, with or without preliminary castration, does not seem to have produced lasting results.... Even in my own experiments, I have never observed more than a temporary success. Insofar as psychological treatment intended to transform the homosexual impulse into a normal impulse, that also generally ends in failure." Günther Grau conveys the conclusions of Dr. Friedemann Pfäfflin, who studied 600 cases of castration, including 120 "volunteers" going back to 1934–1945, in *Hidden Holocaust?*[587] He distinguishes three kinds. The first group used castration as an alternative to execution. (A seventy-year-old man who was convicted twelve times for begging and six times under §176-3 was castrated on August 14, 1934; the man hanged himself immediately afterwards.) The second group consisted of cases where castration was presented as a lesser evil than custody. The beneficial and therapeutic effect of castration were emphasized. The third group chose castration with a therapeutic aim, after having weighed the chances of success, and after comparison with other measures.

---

585. *Die Kastration bei homosexuellen Perversionen und Sittlichkeitsverbrechen des Mannes* (Cited BAB, R 22/950); "Die gesetzliche Kastration; das dänische Sterilisationsgesetz vom 1.6.1929 und seine Resultate," *Mon. Krim. Biol.*, 1935, p.5-49 (*ibid.*); "Zur Frage des kriminaltherapeutischen Erfolges der Entmannung homosexueller Sittlichkeitsverbrecher," *DJ*, 1942, p.581 *sq.* (*ibid.*).

586. "Gedanken zum Problem der Homosexualität," *Mon. Krim. Biol.*, 1938, p.333 *sq.*; 1939, p.430 *sq.*; 1941, p.32 *sq.* and 248 *sq.*

587. This refers to files that were found in Hamburg amid a lot of 1137 and which correspond to the general files of forensic biology from the Hamburg prison.

By the end of 1937, these operations were being carried out in 73 research centers of forensic biology attached to prisons or concentration camps.[588] It was even projected to create a central organization for research on castration, but the war came first.[589] In fact, it was mostly after 1939 that castration came to be considered in a systematic way as a treatment for homosexuality. It was also during the war that Dr. Carl Vaernet's experiments were carried out, which intended to "cure" homosexuals by hormonal treatment.[590]

From 1933 to 1939, "rehabilitation" and "eradication" were both in vogue, but after the war began, "rehabilitation" fell out of favor. It was essential to get rid of the "asocials" who were undermining the health and the morality of the nation. More and more homosexuals were sent to concentration camps. There, the charade of "rehabilitation" continued: homosexuals were set to labor or were sent to a brothel in order to be cured. When the war became total and the shortage of manpower started to be felt, "castration" seemed an effective way to return homosexuals, now "cured," to the army.

THE LATE 1930S: FRENCH AND ENGLISH HOMOSEXUALS IN A TURMOIL

The late 1930s also meant a retreat for English and French homosexuals, although the situation was certainly not comparable with that of Germany. England stepped up the repression very clearly, but France was still relatively mild and now became the homosexual center of Europe. In both countries, there was an increase in reactionary rhetoric, which called homosexuality a proof of the decline of civilization.

Homosexuality Goes Out of Fashion

The Crash of 1929 was a major turning point in the public's perception of homosexuality. From now on, political and economic problems dominated the

---

588. *Hidden Holocaust?, op. cit.*, p.253-256.

589. A directive from the Reich's Central Security Service dated 2 January 1942 (cited *ibid.*, p.256) placed castrated men under the supervision of the police. They were required to give notice of any change of address. In cases where, despite being castrated, the individual by his conduct still represented a danger to the community, and in particular youth, the criminal police could send him directly to a concentration camp without any new trial.

590. See Appendices.

public discourse, and conformity became an important value again; minorities were singled out and accused of destroying national cohesion through their efforts to satisfy their separate interests. This was not a new phenomenon: there had been plenty of reactionary talk in the 1920s, but now, with the financial crisis, their cries fell on more receptive ears as the hunt for scapegoats got under way.

Depopulation

In the 1930s, governments became concerned with depopulation. In the United Kingdom, there was a sharp drop in the birth rate: it fell to 16.3 per thousand in 1930.[591] The situation was also alarming in France, where the birth rate fell from 21.4 per thousand in 1920 to 18 per thousand in 1930 and 14.6 per thousand in 1938. Since 1935, deaths outnumbered births. France was under-populated, and took in many foreign workers.[592]

Nevertheless, France did not actually practice any pro-birth policy, although some measures were taken. The Parliament had already approved laws against contraceptive propaganda on July 31, 1920, prohibiting the sale of contra-ceptive material and stiffening the penalties for abortion.[593] On March 11, 1932, it required the creation of compensation funds in each profession. By the end of the 1930s, public opinion was increasingly sensitive to the pro-birth propaganda, which presented population figures as a major asset in international compe-tition. The surplus of deaths was shocking. The medical and moral rhetoric lit into the immorality of youth and women who worked, and demanded that they reestablish family values. February 8, 1938 marked the opening of a conference in the Senate on "the crisis of the falling birth rate."[594] *Le Temps* launched a major investigation (July 4-22, 1938) entitled "The Distressing Problem of Depopu-lation." The Orders in Council of 1938 extended family benefits to new categories of workers, and the Family Code of July 29, 1939 marked a new stage in French demographic policy: it revisited and brought into alignment all the various mea-

---

591. Keynes, in an article in *Eugenics Review* from 1937, talks about the "suicide of the race." At that time, Hitler, in his exposé to the upper echelons of the State and the army, asserted that England was in the process of an irreversible decline (Hossbach protocol).

592. Foreigners made up 3.7 % of the population in 1919 and 7.1 % in 1931.

593. Abortion has been a crime in France since 1791. It is prohibited by the 1808 crim-inal code. The law of 23 March 1923 made the stipulations even stronger.

594. *Le Temps*, 10 and 17 February 1938.

sures regarding inheritance, taxes and family allowances. The laws against abortion were again reinforced.

Decadence and decline

In the satirical literature of the 1930s, homosexuality is presented as a growing threat. The National body and the human body were associated with each other in a disconcerting way and "inversion" was called a national cancer. In the face of economic difficulties, social upheavals, and the misery of everyday life, homosexuals (like other minority groups — Jews, foreigners, women who worked) were singled out for public abuse and were held responsible for all the evils of a society in decline. Some people already accused homosexuals in the 1920s of being directly responsible for the national "bankruptcy"; others only used them as a pretext for denouncing the democracy, parliamentarism, and liberalism that allowed such excesses.[595] George-Anquetil's book, *Satan conduit le bal* ("Satan leads the ball," 1925), which is set during the first government headed by Poincaré (1921-1922), is an excellent example of this genre.[596] It denounces a "century of neurosis that led the world and humanity astray, a century of hysteria, vice and lust, treacherously masked as virtue."[597] Orgies, bacchanalias and lubricious spectacles of every sort are seen as the daily fare of a democracy that has a "nervous problem."[598] All the talk about homosexuality was just one of many ways of sapping the foundations the democratic, liberal and parliamentary society that was responsible for the decline in morals, the economic crisis and the loss of influence on the international scene. "The first sign of the acuity of the crisis that has struck France ... is without question the physiological disorder, it is the expanding perversion and immorality. In every period of decline, as at the later days of the Roman Empire, an absolute madness rips through all the world and, as always, prevails most furiously among the leading and idle classes."[599]

Criticism of the regime didn't balk at calumny and insult. George-Anquetil associated the names of eminent figures with scenes of debauchery, endorsing

---

595. On this subject, see also Marc Simard, "Intellectuels, fascisme and antimodernité in la France des années trente," *XXe siècle*, April-June 1988, p.35-75.

596. Georges-Anquetil, *Satan conduit le bal* (a philosophical and opinioned novel of manners) [1925], Paris, Agence parisienne de distribution, 1948, 536 pages, p.226. Anquetil was a journalist who covered scandals, and used his periodical *Le Grand Guignol* to launch attacks against various public figures.

597. *Ibid.*, p.5.
598. *Ibid.*, p.27.
599. *Ibid.*, p.22.

the notion that France was being led to ruin by the very men who governed it. He slammed every political party and attacked politicians, bankers and the press with equal vigor, from *l'Humanité* (socialist) to *l'Action française* (royalist/nationalist). He attacked "the whoremonger George Clemenceau, who brought us victory [in the War] and prostitution," "Antonin Dubost, president of the Senate who was found dead in the most notorious brothel of Paris, poisoned by the police, they say, but in any case parading around at the age of seventy in the company of two young pederasts."[600] The corrupt elite was counter-balanced by a myth of France's deep roots, protected from all the bad new influences: "The pure air of our countryside protects our peasants from these miasmas, and the healthy fatigue of the workmen protects them from such temptations (if tempted they would be)."[601] Homosexuality becomes thus a perversion limited to the higher reaches of society: "This is a vice of luxury, it is not our humble citizens who practice it."[602]

In the 1930s, talk about a decline became commonplace. The disintegration of the political system, the fall in the birth rate, the penetration of society by foreign and Jewish influences were denounced as well as the liberalization of morals and homosexuality. Reactionary thought, especially from the far right, used homosexuality as a political foil. Roy Campbell wrote of the Spanish republicans in Oswald Mosley's journal *British Quarterly Union*, in January-April 1937: "The sodomites are on your side/ the cowards and the sickos."

For essayists of the decline, the (purely fantastic) rise in homosexuality was ascribed to "contagion," for the sole objective of the homosexual was "reproduction," which he could not achieve through normal means. In the same style, homosexuality was equated with modernity, this time interpreted in a pejorative sense. Philosophers of the decline entertained the myth of an ideal society resting on a moral consensus and guaranteeing the unity and the power of the nation.

Be they French, British or German, victorious or vanquished, all wished to regain the conditions of life of the pre-war period: economic stability, social conformity, and international domination. Rather than search out the principal causes of the crisis of the inter-war period, they preferred to designate scapegoats and blame them for everything. "This homosexual prurience... is only a

---

600. *Ibid.*, p.224.
601. *Ibid.*, p.229.
602. *Ibid.*

result of certain modern concepts, whose representatives ignore the tragic consequences of their own positions."[603] Industrialization and the increasing urbanization of society were among the causes of the propagation of evil, whereas triumphant individualism had led to the church's fall from influence and the rise of immorality.[604]

The goal of most of those denouncing the decline was to excite the general public so that it would react vigorously to the dangers menacing the fatherland. Dr. Albert Chapotin began his book *Les Défaitistes de l'amour* (1927) with the exhortation: "We hope that we will be able to increase the number of good citizens willing to found a family as soon as possible, instead of taking their time in unwarranted explorations. We will thus help to hold at bay the depopulation which is likely to lead our country to decline."[605] His chapter on homosexuality is entitled "Descent to hell: the monsters."

In a work entitled *For The Safety of The Race: Sex Education* (1931), Dr. Sicard de Plauzoles maintained that the availability of robust conscripts in good health was going down. On the other hand, the number of abnormal and degenerated men was going up, due to "civilization," i.e. alcohol, poverty, syphilis, tuberculosis, the loss of sexual standards. Likewise, Dr. Jean Pouÿ, in *Conseils à la jeunesse sur l'éducation sexuelle* ("Advice to young people on sex education," 1931), explains that "many young people whose energies depopulated France so urgently needs could be stopped on the slippery slope of perverse practices." There was only one solution: "the admirable act of procreation."

The same theme is taken up by T. Bowen Partington in *Sex and Modern Youth* (1931), which also blames the pernicious influence of bad books, plays and, especially, bad films purveying immorality.[606]

An increasing denunciation of female homosexuality is also heard. Charles-Noël Renard, in the introduction to his book *Les Androphobes* (1930), a fantastical novel, violently attacks lesbians. France, he says, is already under the

---

603. F.W. Foerster, *Morale sexuelle et pédagogie sexuelle*, Paris, Librairie Bloud & Gay, 1929, 270 pages, p.163-165.

604. See for example H.E. Timerding, *Sexualethik*, Leipzig, B.G. Teubner, 1919, 120 pages, and Max von Gruber, *Hygiene of Sex*, trans. from German, London, Tindall & Cox, 1926, 169 pages.

605. Dr. Albert Chapotin, *Les Défaitistes de l'amour*, Paris, Le Livre pour tous, 1927, 510 pages, p.9.

606. See also Waldo Franck, "Sex Censorship and Democracy," and Samuel D. Schmalhausen, "The Sexual Revolution," *in* V.F. Calverton and S.D. Schmalhausen (dir.), *Sex in Civilization*, London, Allen & Unwin, 1929, 719 pages.

spell of the homosexual mindset and any trace of virility and masculine courage has disappeared: "Our civilization is entirely, in its finest details, the result of a biological interpretation particular to eunuchs, doddering old men and uni- sexuals [lesbians]."[607] For Renard, the war was a useless sacrifice which left men the losers, while women took power and set out to destroy civilization. In his novel, he uses a group of girls in a train to illustrate all the permutations of female perfidy: "I had understood long ago what type of girls keep apart from men; I knew from their gestures, from their general demeanor, what cult these belonged to."[608] As they are described, the girls seem appalling hysterical, lubri- cious, sadistic and vicious. They all are, except one, intellectuals: one is a pro- fessor, another a pharmacist, two are government workers. Renard further observes: "In every prude lurks a lesbian, as in every emancipated woman."[609] Their professions enable them to spread their poison and to secretly take up the reins of society: "The Administration belongs to us ... Everything belongs to us ... And soon, the world..."[610] A gigantic international lesbian plot is underway. The man-haters recruit their victims as little girls: "It is not just for my own pleasure: I distract them from men before they have any right to think about it; I take them, I educate them, I make them into tigresses.... and then I release them into the arena ... Let the men try to pet that one! Ha!"[611]

Renard wants to warn people, but wavers between two methods. On the one hand, he delivers a systematic attack against women, who are supposedly stupid and reducible to their sexuality alone: "The woman is a phonogenic and an unstoppable genital apparatus,"[612] but he also enjoys giving vent to long dis- courses on the unhappy fate of the male genre. This turns into a striking inversion of the concept of the "double standard": "We forgive a man everything, EXCEPT THE USE OF HIS SEXUALITY; we forgive a woman everything BECAUSE OF HER SEXUALITY. One always finds extenuating circumstances for an assassination; never for a rape ... the husband who would dare to excuse himself for tapping his wife on the head for her faults would be covered with mud in court and tarred and feathered by any civilized crowd, while the woman

---

607. Charles-Noël Renard, *Les Androphobes*, Saint-Étienne, Imprimerie spéciale d'édition, 1930, 324 pages, p.59.

608. *Ibid.*, p.118.

609. *Ibid.*, p.224.

610. *Ibid.*, p.126.

611. *Ibid.*, p.142.

612. *Ibid.*, p.204.

assassin would only have to accuse the man she killed of unisexuality and she would be acquitted, and even congratulated.... But if she justified her action on the basis of fanatical tribadism, her triumph would be all the greater."[613]

This paranoiac delusion would be laughable if it did not reflect the state of mind of some part of the male population, in France as well as in England and Germany. Such flights of fancy resonated deeply among all the disappointed men in the post-war period, unemployed or losing ground, all those who might see women's entry into the workforce as an injustice, not to mention the success of even a small number of them. Charles-Noël Renard's final appeal sounds sinister in retrospect, like a premonition of the disaster to come: "The SAVIOR will be the one who will destroy the work of Woman. / Let us clear the way for him, forge him weapons, prepare the greatest revolution, the biggest war that ever drenched the Earth in blood."[614]

The anguish of a decline tied to homosexuality is summarized by Drieu La Rochelle. Drieu has a complex personal relationship with inversion. He doubts his virility, and has trouble with women.[615] Anything that casts doubt on his virility sends him into a panic. He is disgusted by inverts, although in his school days he had had several homosexual friendships; after suffering a bout of impotence at a brothel, he tries unsuccessfully to sleep with a man.[616] Like many men, he was both fascinated and repelled by the thought of female homosexuality.[617] Drieu identifies strength and virility, femininity and homosexuality. Obsessed by the idea of decadence and decline, he tends to confound sexual metaphors and political interpretation. Jean-Louis Saint-Ygnan, who analyzes the concept of decadence in Drieu, notes that for him Western civilization had been in decline since the Middle Ages. Symbolically, Drieu represents the Frenchman as an invert.[618] Sexual decadence, identified with sterility, is thus identified with the national decline and depopulation. The themes of homosexuality, the feminine body are equated to the disintegration of the social body, the symbol of a nation that has become effeminate and infected by foreign elements.

613. *Ibid.*, p.60-61.

614. *Ibid.*, p.63.

615. Cited in Pierre Drieu La Rochelle, *Journal 1939-1945*, Paris, Gallimard, coll. "Témoins," 1992, 519 pages, p.29.

616. This was probably the case in the army. The affair with Aragon remains unverified.

617. Pierre Drieu La Rochelle, *Journal 1939-1945*, *op. cit.*, p.31.

618. *La Suite dans les idées*, Cited by Jean-Louis Saint-Ygnan, *Drieu la Rochelle ou l'Obsession de la décadence*, Paris, Nouvelles Éditions latines, 1984, 260 pages, p.147.

Turning Inward

The 1930s rang the death knell for hedonism. In December 1931, the October Club was founded at Oxford and the university became an outpost of the "Reds," the communist and pacifist students who supported the workingmen on strike and went to Spain as volunteers in the war. That year, the repression of homosexuals was intensified in England, apparently due to the influence of the new chief of the London police, Sir Philip Game. Pub owners were informed that they were not to serve homosexual clients any more. The situation quickly became intolerable. A surveillance system was organized; overly apparent homosexuals were requested to leave, the same as drunks.

Quentin Crisp took the full brunt of this reaction: "The ostracism was complete: because of increased police vigilance, the owners of even the most scandalous cafés would not let me in."[619] Police raids were more and more frequent; the pubs of the West End were off limits and homosexuals retreated to Pimlico and Bloomsbury, where the artistic and literary atmosphere still maintained a certain tolerance for some time.[620] The public toilets were also subject to regular raids:

> — The police methods became increasingly sinister. The system of using *agents provocateurs* became a routine. The principal theatre of operations for this particular strategy was the dimly lit public toilets on the less traveled streets of London ... the police thought of homosexuals like the Indians of North America thought of bisons. They sought a means of exterminating them by the herd [sic. Crisp was not an American historian.]. Tipped off to the venue where great costume balls were being held, they would turn their focus there.... In one raid, a hundred or more boys, howling, bursting with laughter, punching and kicking in their plumed and bejeweled evening gowns with embroidered trains could be picked up and shoved or thrown into vans by a relatively small squad of police officers ... When these balls stopped being organized because they became more dangerous than fun, the police turned their wrathful eye to the homos clubs.[621]

In France the repression was less visible, but the heyday of the homosexual clubs was over. The promenades were no fun anymore, since the prefect of Chiappe ordered brighter lights be put into the passageways. Nevertheless, it seems that, compared to the destruction of the German scene and the lifelessness of the English scene, France again became the homosexual magnetic North.

---

619. Quentin Crisp, *The Naked Civil-Servant* [1968], London, Fontana, 1986, 217 pages, p.86.

620. See Gifford Skinner's testimony in *Gay News*, n° 135.

621. Quentin Crisp, *The Naked Civil-Servant*, *op. cit.*, p.82-83.

Hitler's arrival sounded the departure bell for the English homosexuals, whether intellectuals like Auden, Spender and Isherwood or anonymous homosexuals of other classes.[622] When René Crevel arrived in Munich in August 1933, he was struck by the change: "In Munich the atmosphere was suffocating, and the abundance of prostitution did nothing to relieve the sinister aspect of the Nazis faces (tight lips and creased brows)."[623] The shock was terrible; two visions of Germany collided head-on.

More unsettling must have been the discovery that the values that had symbolized the Weimar Republic were being retrieved and recycled to embody the fascist man. Stephen Spender confronted his vision of a radiant Germany with the new reality:

> — Christopher and I ... used to use Germany as a palliative for our personal problems; [we] became increasingly conscious that the carefree private lives of our friends were a façade covering an immense chaos. We had more and more the impression that this life was going to be swept away. While we spent our holidays on the island of Rügen, where naked bathers were stretched by the hundreds on the beach, under a brutal sun, sometimes we could hear the bark of orders, and even shots coming from the forest along the shore, where storm troops were training as executioners, waiting for the martyrdom of those who were naked and unarmed.[624]

Some began to ask themselves questions:

> — When I came to Germany for the first time, I came in a completely irresponsible way, for the thrill. I was the malicious boy who had got his foot in the apartment of Waldemar this afternoon and now wanted even more. However, once I had explored the Berlin nightlife entirely and I started to tire of it, I became puritanical. I severely criticized the debauched foreigners who came to Berlin looking for pleasure. They exploited the famished German working class and transformed them into prostitutes. My indignation was perfectly sincere, and was even justified; the Berlin nightlife, when it was seen from outside, was rather pathetic. But had I really changed? Wasn't I being just as irresponsible as before, running away from the consequences? Wasn't this a form of betrayal?[625]

Irresponsibility often gave way to love for a country which had brought them pleasure and freedom. The course chosen by the esthete Brian Howard is

---

622. See Norman, in *Between the Acts. Lives of Homosexual Men, 1885-1967*, edited by K. Porter and J. Weeks, London, Routledge, 1991, 176 pages.

623. Letter to Marcel Jouhandeau, cited by François Buot, *René Crevel*, a these presented at the university Paris-X Nanterre, under the direction of René Rémond, 1987, 395 pages.

624. Stephen Spender, *World within World* [1951], London, Faber & Faber, 1991, 344 pages, p.131.

625. Christopher Isherwood, *Down There on a Visit*, London, Methuen, 1962, 271 pages, p.56.

exemplary on this point. He was friendly in 1931 with Klaus and Erika Mann, who kept him current as to the political situation in Germany and the danger represented by the Nazis. Howard, hitherto relatively indifferent, became an ardent militant on the left and took a greater and greater interest in German politics. He contributed to the *New Statesman*, and was active in the Left Book Club. In 1934 he was in Bavaria with the Mann family and wrote several articles on the concentration camps. In Amsterdam, he found Christopher Isherwood and Klaus Mann, who was publishing the anti-Nazi magazine *Die Sammlung* at that time. He became Guy Burgess's friend in 1937 and joined the Independent Labour Party in 1938, when it had taken a position against the war. When the war broke out anyway, he was in France and his German companion was interned in a camp in Toulon. Thus, beyond the defense of personal interests — those of the homosexual, — he took part in a larger fight for the defense of freedoms in general and a certain idea of humanity.

Some homosexual intellectuals sought to become engaged by helping German émigrés. René Crevel was one of these who did; in July 1934, he joined an anti-Nazi group in Amsterdam and gathered support for intellectual émigrés, at the request of Klaus Mann.

For many English intellectuals the only solution was to go into the exile; deprived of a country that they had learned to love, and unable to see hope for any welcome in an England that was in full reaction, they chose to leave, mostly for the United States. Christopher Isherwood left London on March 26, 1934 to join his friend Heinz in Amsterdam. "Thus, he symbolically rejected the England of Kathleen [his mother]." That was only the beginning of a long peregrination. Heinz was finally arrested and sentenced to six months in prison and a year of forced labor, plus two years in the army. Isherwood was charged with having engaged in indecent activities "with the prisoner" in fourteen foreign countries and the Reich.[626]

The flight of homosexual pacifists was taken extremely badly in England. Auden and Isherwood were attacked for a long time: "Is my honourable friend conscious of the indignation caused by young men who leave the country, saying that they do not wish to fight? If they are not registered as conscientious objectors, are they mindful that they may be stripped of their nationality?" asked deputy Sir Jocelyn Lucas in the House of Commons on June 13, 1940.

---

626. Id., *Christopher and His Kind, op. cit.,* p.213.

Benjamin Britten and Peter Pears, who lived in the United States from 1939 to 1942, also had to face overt hostility; a letter from one their friends, Ralph Hawkes, who had returned to London in September 1940, noted that there was no doubt that they would have difficulties in playing [his] works, while caustic remarks are still being made in comment on [his] departure. Marjorie Fass wrote: "Bill [Ethel Bridge] tells me that there are many articles in various newspapers on Benji [Benjamin Britten] & Auden & Co.; it is quite possible that they will never be able to return to England."[627] In 1941, a controversy over Britten arose in *Musical Times*, when a letter from second lieutenant aviator E.R. Leavis entitled "An English composer leaves for the west" ignited a firestorm that went on from August through October.

Paradoxically, in the 1930s homosexuality became an increasingly public, increasingly political topic, while homosexuals themselves had to retreat to the private arena — "private faces in public places," W.H. Auden would write. Homophobia took over even in the most liberal circles, like those of the German émigrés.

German Exiles

According to Jean-Michel Palmier, an estimated 59,000 and 65,000 Germans emigrated after Hitler came to power.[628] They had many reasons for going into exile: some feared for their lives, others left Germany out of distaste or out of conviction, or in solidarity with others. Many political opponents and Jews were among the first to leave. Some German homosexuals also chose to go into exile. Among the more famous was the opera star and choreographer of the UFA, Jens Keith, who left Germany in 1937 after receiving a citation from the police, following a denunciation. He stayed in Paris until the Occupation; then he returned to Berlin and worked for the Metropol-Theater. Willi Tesch, cinema producer Nikolaus Kaufmann's friend, left Germany at the same time as he did; he joined the French Resistance. Among the politically active homosexuals, the writers Ludwig Renn and Hans Siemsen emigrated, in addition to Klaus Mann.

---

627. Cited *in* Donald Mitchell and Philip Reed (ed.), *Letters from a Life, Selected Letters and Diaries of Benjamin Britten*, vol.2, *1939-1945*, London, Faber & Faber, 1991, 1 403 pages, p.870.

628. See Jean-Michel Palmier, *Weimar en exil*, Paris, Payot, 1988, t.I and II, 533 and 486 pages.

Initially, the homosexual émigrés went to Austria or Hungary, or to Switzerland — especially Basel and Zurich, which had a homosexual subculture; but most went to Paris. Ferdinand Bruckner left Germany in 1933, for Vienna, then Paris; he went to the United States in 1936. The photographer Herbert List was also in Paris at that time.

Many lesbians also left Germany. Charlotte Wolff, a Jewish doctor, left Berlin in April 1933 for Paris, then for London. Christa Winsloe, the author of *Girls in Uniform*, left Germany in 1938 and took refuge in the south of France. She was assassinated with her friend in June 1944. Erika Mann, Therese Giese, and Annemarie Schwarzenbach followed more complex courses, wandering throughout Europe, the United States and even the Orient. The actress Salka Viertel described life in Paris in this period: "The hot nights of summer attracted great masses of strollers on the boulevards: young couples and not so young people of every color and from every possible country. After eleven years spent in the United States, the freedom of the love life in Paris impressed me, the bi- and homosexual mixture which had become unthinkable in Germany since the laws of Nuremberg."[629]

Klaus Mann's view of this forced exile was more bitter: "Spent a moment with Eddy, Bobby and two English aunts of good society. (Those aunties with whom one speaks only because that is what they are: just as, now, one often finds oneself obliged to speak to Jews or to émigrés, simply because they are Jews or émigrés)."[630]

For much, exile was a time for making assessments, reflecting on oneself and on politics. The magazine *Die Sammlung* tried to group together all the exiled writers who were against Nazism and wanted to defend real German literature. It was sponsored by Heinrich Mann, Aldous Huxley, and André Gide; it published articles by Thomas Mann, René Schickelé, Alfred Döblin, Hermann Hesse and Stefan Zweig. It was banned in Germany, and the writers who contributed to it were boycotted by German booksellers — Thomas Mann, Alfred Döblin and René Schickelé soon had to drop out.

Exile brought a new political and homosexual maturity to Klaus Mann. His novel *Volcano* (1939) is an allegory of émigré life, particularly their disastrous love affairs and their self-destructive tendencies. He protested the reigning

---

629. *100 Jahre Schwulenbewegung*, Berlin, Schwules Museum, 1997, 384 pages, p.171.
630. Klaus Mann, *Journal. Les années brunes, 1931-1936*, Paris, Grasset, 1996, 452 pages, 30 November 1936, p.377.

homophobia. Reading on an article on "homosexuality and Fascism" in *Zeitschrift für Sexualökonomie* on December 2, 1934, he decided to write about it himself. He noted that "they were not far from identifying homosexuality with Fascism" and criticized the new Soviet laws as well as the way the Röhm affair was being exploited by the socialist and communist newspapers. He questioned the attitude of the Nazis who were variously "trying to form homosexuals cliques, to lock up them, castrate them or slaughter them." René Crevel says this article reveals the impasse facing homosexuals; between Fascism and Communism, there was no more room for any demands about sex: "From the sexual point of view, it seems that the liberties that had been allowed and tolerated were now going to be denied by both sides."[631]

In fact, the German exiles were ambiguous on homosexuality. While homosexuals were stigmatized by the regime, opponents to Nazism could use homosexuality as a weapon in anti-Hitler propaganda. The Communist Party's new line was at the origin of this tendentious assimilation. In 1933, the International Committee to Assist Victims of Hitlerian Fascism published the Brown Book on the burning of the Reichstag and the Hitlerian terror. Van der Lubbe, the incendiary young Dutchman, is presented as a homosexual who betrayed the communist cause because of his sexual preferences: "Van der Lubbe is first of all a homosexual. He has an effeminate style; his reserve and timidity in the presence of women is testified by many witnesses; his taste for male company is notorious." These tendencies put him in contact with the Nazi leadership, in particular Dr. Bell, "Röhm's pimp." Van der Lubbe's material dependence "made him flexible and compliant."[632] After "The Night of the Long Knives," *Pravda* denounced both the Hitlerian plot and the morals of Röhm, which were represented as being typical of the whole regime. The proclamation signed by the SPD committee in exile in Amsterdam (clandestinely distributed in various German cities) is similar: "[Hitler] identified his honor with that of the assassins, torturers and debauchees. By accusing them today and by holding them up to the public's scorn, he convicts himself; for it was on these men, their crimes, and their shame, that all his system rested." [633]

Several works published by German writers in exile fed the myth that there was collusion between homosexuals and Nazis. One of the best-known

---

631. Cited by François Buot, *René Crevel, op. cit.*, p.346.
632. *Livre brun sur l'incendie du Reichstag..., op. cit.*
633. *Le Temps*, 3 July 1934.

texts is Bertolt Brecht's *Ballade vom 30. Juni*, which presents "The Night of the Long Knives" and suggests a homosexual relationship between Röhm and Hitler. One may also cite *Hitler's Youth*, by Hans Siemsen, published in London in 1940; or *Vor grossen Wandlungen* (1937), by Ludwig Renn, in which the Nazis and a sui-cidal aristocrat are homosexual, while the resistance were virile heterosexuals. There are also hints of homophobia in Vicky Baum's *Shanghai Hotel*, published in 1939, a novel featuring several clients of a hotel in Shanghai which is blown up. Among the clients are Dr. Emmanuel Hain, a half-Jew, whose son Roland was "a child of the war," and has sensitive nerves. He was sent to an experimental school, conducted in the open air. But "one of the professors was enamored of the young boy: too sensitive to Roland's strange charms, he committed suicide with his revolver." At the age of twenty, Roland entered the NSDAP, not knowing that he was partly Jewish, and slept with one of the leaders. His childhood friend, Kurt, a heterosexual and anti-Nazi, observes his evolution with sadness and distress: "He was, like him, part of that postwar generation that was not shocked by love between members of the same sex. Perhaps it was a holdover from wartimes when the men on their own together? or a distaste for procreating in an over-populated country? Some found it comic, some tragic, others inter-esting. Many tried it just out of snobbery, following a fashion."[634] Roland's life ends tragically. His comrades discover that he is Jewish, and he is assassinated.

* * *

For ten years, English and French homosexuals had been going to enjoy the liberty of Germany. Now the roles were reversed and it was the German homo-sexuals who went abroad to seek freedom and tolerance. And it was not just the police repression; there had been a remarkable change in public opinion: homo-sexuals were consigned to the dark corners or, worse, pointed out. And ironi-cally, at the very moment when homosexuals were suffering the worst persecutions in Germany, they were compared to their tormentors, as though they were all in one enemy camp.

It is very difficult to say how many homosexuals were victims of Nazism. Official statistics of the Reich, the remaining Nazi statistics and the notes of Dr. Wuth, suggest that 100,000 would be a rough estimate of the number of homo-sexuals recorded by the Reich Central Command for the Combat of Homosexu-

---

634. Vicky Baum, *Shanghai Hotel* [1939], Paris, Phébus, 1997, 669 pages, p.67 and 95.

ality. Of them, approximately 50,000 were convicted. Between 5,000 and 15,000 homosexuals were sent to concentration camps.[635] The German homosexual population is estimated to have been between 1.5 and 2 million at that time, so it appears that the great majority of homosexual must have succeeded in surviving under Nazism. That does not diminish the fact that they were constantly targeted by the regime and that they lived in anguish and infamy during this period.

Was Nazism unique in its treatment of homosexuals? The Nazis were unusual in the use of police terror, the dehumanization of victims, sentences disproportionate to acts, and the broad use of force. However, the methods had already been tested in England and under Weimar. Neither did Nazism invent the homophobic political campaign: it was the Socialists and the Communists who tried that, first. Medical abuses were made possible by the psychiatric will to control perverts, and castration was adopted on the basis of foreign (Danish and Swiss) research.

Wilhelm Reich saw Fascism as a consequence of the repression of natural sexual needs.[636] If this explanation, partial at best, is true, then it may be that the treatment of homosexuality under Nazism was merely an extension of traditional homophobia. Nazism and homosexual repression in Europe were part of one continuum, as Guy Hocquenghem noted. He saw this similarity as the reason for the silence that surrounded homosexual repression. "The Nazis had only gone a little further. But the elimination or, in any case, the restriction of homosexuals ... there was not one allied country that did not do it, too. All things considered, the massacre of homosexuals had to be kept secret especially since it would reveal a similarity between Nazism and those who claimed to be its judges and its mortal enemies."[637]

---

635. Certain authors estimate the number of victims at several hundred thousand, even up to a million, including Jean Boisson (*Le Triangle rose. La déportation des homosexuels [1933-1945]*, Paris, Robert Laffont, 1988, 247 pages). Such figures are have no serious basis. The desire to rehabilitate homosexual victims cannot be based on a historical aberration. To speak of a "final solution" or a "homocaust" for homosexuals is an absurdity that denigrates the homosexual cause

636. Wilhelm Reich, *La Psychologie de masse du fascisme* [1933], Paris, Payot, coll. "Petite bibl. Payot," 1972, 341 pages, p.92.

637. Guy Hocquenghem, preface to the book by Heinz Heger, *Les Hommes au triangle rose, op. cit.*, p.11-12.

POSTFACE

TOWARD HOMOSEXUAL LIBERATION

> But do not imagine we do not know,
> Nor that what you hide with such care won't show
> At a glance:
> Nothing is done, nothing is said.
> But don't make the mistake of believing us dead;
> I shouldn't dance [if I were you].[638]

The Second World War was just as much a shock in homosexual history as the First War. In Germany, it coincided with the apogee of Nazi repression. It was characterized by an extension of terror; more individuals were sent to concentration camps and more were castrated — in the interests of "re-education."

In 1940, homosexuals who had seduced more than one partner were also sent directly to the concentration camp. Hitler ordered stronger efforts to fight against homosexuality within the party and the Wehrmacht on August 18, 1941. On November 15, 1941 a confidential decree was published for "the cleansing (Reinhaltung) of the SS and the police."[639] The death penalty was instituted for any member of the SS or the police found guilty of homosexual acts. In less serious cases, the sentence could be commuted to a sentence of hard labor or prison, not less than six months. If the defendant was younger than twenty-one, the court could, in less serious cases, withhold sentencing.

---

638. W.H. Auden, "The Witnesses" (1932).
639. BAB, R 58/261.

Homosexuals found within the Hitler Youth were also at greater risk. A 1940 directive from the RSHA authorized sending minors to detention camps for young people, run by the police. This treatment was reserved for boys who were guilty of criminal or antisocial behavior, and it is possible that homosexuals were sent there.

Lastly, a confidential study was launched at the Reich Ministry of Justice, the Gestapo, the Office of Criminal Police and the Army Medical Inspectorate in order to determine what measures should be taken in the case of homosexuality in the Wehrmacht. The Ministry of Justice opposed giving any amnesty or rehabilitation. The Gestapo and the criminal police supported maintaining the old distinction between homosexuals by inclination and those who had been seduced. The military psychiatrist Otto Wuth, in February 1943, wrote a memorandum on the extent of the infection in the army. Finally, two series of measures were adopted: on May 19, 1943, the chief of the OKW, General Keitel, presented "Guidelines for Treating Criminal Cases of Unnatural Acts," and on June 7, 1944, the medical chief of the Luftwaffe, Schröder, presented a 14-page directive entitled: "Instructions for Doctors and How to Evaluate Cases of Homosexuality."

Other solutions were also proposed. On September 14, 1943, the legal branch of the SS proposed that people convicted for crimes under §175 be assigned to special units. Reichsführer SS Himmler had already decided that minor cases could be assigned to special units of the Waffen-SS. The most serious cases were to be sent to concentration camps. The proposal for intermediate cases suggested integrating them into the special unit of Waffen-SS Dirlewanger. On May 12, 1944, a secret decree from the chief the security police ordered that homosexuals turned out of the Wehrmacht (i.e. those who exhibited "a predisposition or an acquired and clearly incorrigible impulse") were to be sent to a concentration camp.

Lastly, castration was debated in many forums. There was draft legislation in 1943 dealing with "the treatment of outsiders to the community (Gemeinschaftsfremden)." This group, described as a burden on society, included specifically vagrants, beggars and homosexuals. The all-out war prevented its being put into operation; it would have meant obligatory castration for homosexuals. In addition, a secret order of November 14, 1942, from the economic and administrative service of the SS gave the green light to camp commanders to order castration in special cases that were not covered by the law. This decree "legalized" the castration of homosexual in the camps. After the war, homosexual survivors of the concentration camps had trouble getting their testimony heard.

After the war, S175 remained in force and homosexual deportees were often treated with contempt. Finally, on June 25, 1969, West Germany (FRG) decided that homosexual acts between consenting men over the age of 21 no longer came under the jurisdiction of the law. East Germany (DRG) had reformed S175 in 1968, legislating that homosexual acts between consenting men over the age of 18 were no longer punished. By the early 1970s, homosexual rights movements were created, often on the American model. On June 7, 1973, the Bundestag of West Germany lowered the age of consent to eighteen years. (For heterosexuals, the age of sexual majority was fourteen). On December 14, 1988, the East German Volkskammer abolished S151, which punished homosexuality between adults and adolescents aged sixteen to eighteen years. After the reunification of Germany, on June 11, 1994, S175 was definitively abolished.

In England, it seems that the war years saw a certain relaxation of police surveillance and a resuscitation of the homosexual scene. The plug would be pulled on this resuscitation in the early 1950s, which were marked by conformity, and homophobia was encouraged by the fears of the cold war. In England, the Cambridge spy scandal (Guy Burgess, Donald Maclean and Anthony Blunt) revived the myth of the homosexual traitor. In the 1950s, the number of convictions for homosexuality reached a new zenith: on average 2,000 people per year; and scandals accusing public personalities of homosexual were rife.

The subject was discussed in the House of Lords and, in 1954, the Minister of the Interior charged Sir John Wolfenden with studying the question. In 1957, his committee recommended the depenalization of homosexuality (except in the navy and the army); this was finally voted into law only ten years later. The age of consent for male relations remained set at twenty-one years; it was lowered to eighteen in 1994. In November 1970, the Gay Liberation Front was created, on the model of the American movement.

Meanwhile, even if Paris attracted homosexuals, the repression in France was also reinforced. The law of August 6, 1942, article 1st, subparagraph 1 of article 334 of the modified penal code encompassed "impudic or unnatural" homosexual and lesbian acts committed with minors less than twenty-one years of age. The 1950s and 1960s were also marked by mixed signals. Writers like Roger Peyrefitte and Jean Genet published openly homosexual novels, and a homosexual review, *Arcadie*, was created by André Baudry, but at the same time the Miguet amendment, in July 1960, defined homosexuality as "a social plague." In March 1971, the FHAR (Front for Homosexual Revolutionary Action) was created; but the law of August 6, 1942 remained in force and was repealed only in 1982.[640]

---

640. See Frédéric Martel, *Le Rose et le Noir. Les homosexuels in France depuis 1968*, Paris, Éditions du Seuil, 1996, 456 pages.

Conclusion

Progress or Increased Repression?

The inter-war period was crucial in homosexual history, far more than just a transitional phase between the profusion of medical opinions of the turn of the century and the protest movements of the 1960s. These years sum up the entire battle over homosexuality, the conflicting tendencies that shaped public opinion and the ideological implications of "deviance."

National Interactions, Convergences and Distinctions

Many phenomena were common in the three countries studied, both in terms of homosexual behavior and in terms of the public's attitudes. There was an overall liberalization of morals in the 1920s, which went hand in hand with increased tolerance. That was characterized by the rapid formation of the homosexual scene and also by the constitution of a homosexual culture that went beyond common references in the field of literature or theater. There were two opposing models around which the sense of identity formed: that of exclusion, articulated by Adolf Brand and André Gide, and that of integration, asserted by Magnus Hirschfeld and Bloomsbury. Homosexual tourism was a novel expression of this new identity, inaugurated at the end of the 19th century by the fad for traveling in Italy and in Capri. Berlin was affirmed as the new capital of the homosexual microcosm in the 1920s. But for those who were part of it, this process of establishing an identity, of carving out an identity for oneself as a homosexual and for homosexuals collectively was only in the preliminary phase. It would be misleading to make too much of it; there was no real solidarity among homosexuals as such.

In all three countries studied, tolerance did increase; maybe not in every milieu, but it became widespread in the upper classes, intellectual circles and in the large cities. Homosexuality also related directly to the working class, but more by means of prostitution. The theme of the working-class lover was symbolic of the inter-war period and contributed to bridging the gap between upper-crust homosexuals and the workers. It was the middle class, the petite bourgeoisie, and small-town families that seemed most mired in traditional prejudices and morality. There was a major shift in the 1930s, but perhaps the change was not as dramatic as has sometimes been thought. Indeed, it should not be forgotten that the reactionary forces were already in evidence in the 1920s, even if they found fewer opportunities for expression. The economic crash, political turmoil and international tensions would create an opening for all the old criticisms to come back, showing that the wave of tolerance had been largely superficial. In ten years, it had not had time to take root in the public mindset, anyway.

In spite of these similarities, fine observation of the behaviors and attitudes allows us to define three specific national and interactive models. Germany was the standard of reference for homosexuality in the inter-war period. Two things made it special: first, it was the locus of the communal model for homosexuals, characterized by the creation of homosexual movements. The homosexual identity was reflected there as a wake-up call, an assertion of rights, a political position. Lesbians, neither coerced by repression nor encouraged by any real mobilization, mostly stayed out of these struggles. The German model was open to outsiders: the homosexual movements were in constant dialogue with the political, legal and religious authorities, and also with the public. But German homosexuality was also open to foreigners: the German model was exported and was imitated in England and France. There were frequent and beneficial interactions: English and French homosexuals visited Germany and took back ideas for founding movements, a new sexual freedom and a feeling of membership in one community.

The other characteristic that is specific to Germany was negative. Germany, having been the center of homosexual freedom in the 1920s, became that of repression in 1933. It was the only country to actually toughen up its anti-homosexual laws. The persecution was organized by the Nazi regime, which clearly designated homosexuals as one of the groups to be eliminated from the society. This policy ended up signifying that they would be sent to concentration camps, where thousands of them died. Here again, the interactions with other countries are obvious: the beginning of German repression coincided with the retreat of English homosexuals, the gradual disappearance of the homosexual subculture in England and the aggravation of police practices in that country. The end of the blissful interlude in Germany was marked by the exile of many German intellectuals, including some homosexuals, who perpetuated in their memoirs the remembrance of Berlin in the "Roaring Twenties."

The French model seems quite different. France was outstanding in the inter-war period in that it did not condemn homosexuality under the law. In contrast to Germany, there as no clear break between the 1920s and the 1930s: the laws were not changed and the stepped up police activity remained relatively moderate. France was above all a symbol for the lesbians who chose Paris rather than Berlin as their capital. Sapphism also made headway in literature, where the theme of the "New Woman" was gradually being elaborated: liberated, adventurous, often lesbian. Interactions with England were visible: many English lesbians would visit with their English-speaking friends. That was true for Vita Sackville-West, Radclyffe Hall and Una Troubridge, among others. Violet Trefusis even chose to settle in France after her relationship with Vita Sackville-West ended.

However, France was not much affected by the homoerotization of society (defined as the worship of the male body) that was detectable during the same period in Germany and England. Moreover, the French model of homosexuality was adamantly individualistic. The homosexual scene was just a place to meet and have a good time; it was not part of an emerging community structure and did not stimulate an awakening identity. The heralds of homosexuality were mostly intellectuals, like Marcel Proust and André Gide, who were most interested in their own personal expression. In fact, the French model turned out not to be very exportable. They were not militant, and looked only for limited improvements in the situation. However, the lack of ambition explains why French homosexuals suffered less than the others from the moral crisis of the 1930s.

To conclude, the English model seems particularly innovative; in England homosexuality took a new direction, building on the example of its neighbors but maintaining its own characteristics. As in Germany, homosexuality in England remained a misdemeanor; homosexuals were still under threat, and that encouraged the development of a homosexual identity. As in France, however, the homosexual community remained concentrated around an intellectual and artistic elite. The homosexual identity was therefore not exerted through militant organizations (except for the timid BSSP), but neither did it take the form of an individual struggle. In fact, the English model of homosexuality was neither communal nor individualistic, rather, it was cultural and social. Certain institutions like the public schools, the universities, the secret service and the literary circles turned out to be particularly open to homosexuals. One can even speak of a "homosexualization" of the leading classes, explained by the prevalence of single-gender structures (homosociality) and the emphasis on the value of relationships among men.

That also explains why the lesbians were the target of conservative groups in England more than in other countries. Castrating bitches, vampires, opium addicts, degenerate and louche, lesbians came to incarnate the very worst fantasies about feminism.

The English difference did not mean there was greater tolerance. There was a dichotomy between thought and action, between practice and morals, more than elsewhere. The English model was thus both interactive and distinctly national: the British homosexuals took the French and German examples as a starting point from which to build their identity; at the same time, they had a common culture that was specific to Britain, nonexportable.

The 1930s saw the militants back off — after just getting started in the 1920s — and the retreat of institutional homosexuality. The figure of the homosexual faded into the shadows and gradually, retroactively, was blended into the Wildean myth. However, unlike in Germany, most homosexuals did not feel the direct impact of the repression but were able to blend back into the rest of society.

Questions: The Nature and Style of Homosexuality in the Inter-war Period

The topic of homosexuality in the inter-war period is rich in meaning. Through it, we can explore many aspects of popular attitudes having to do with the most intimate fears and fantasies of the societies. The First World War called into question the patriarchal, puritanical and authoritarian society based on the superiority of the father in the family structure and on male domination at the institutional level. The war confirmed the failure of the masculine principle as the principle around which society was organized, showing the limits violence, arrogance, and physical force. They had led humanity to disaster. Man was humiliated, crushed, reduced. The period following the First World War built on opposite values, feminine values: peace, pleasure, harmony. That did not mean the victory of women, not at all: despite real victories, like winning voting rights in England and Germany and better access to the world of employment, women's emancipation remains largely illusory. Nevertheless, men felt affronted by this new freedom in women, and many perceived it as a loss and a defeat for men, and an attack on their virility.

Homoerotization was a way of reacting to the situation: young people rejected the parental model as a symbol of the war and chose androgyny. Young men accentuated their femininity, like England's Bright Young People; they celebrated estheticism, beauty and the knack like the new fashion values. Women flaunted their emancipation by adopting more practical haircuts and clothing, which played down the traditional symbols of femininity and testified to their lack of concern about appealing to men. Artistic representations faithfully echoed these tendencies and the youthful body — flexible, slender, muscular, bronzed, and androgynous — became the social ideal. This homoerotic image was laden with heavy fantasies: it replicated the image of the sacrificed generation, all the youth mowed down on the battlefields whose beauty had stirred such a troubling homosexual attraction. The new generation sought both to deny death and at the same time affirm the triumph of life, embodied in the perfect man/woman who was sufficient in and of itself and could serve as a basis for a new society. Homosexuality became an attribute of youth, a sign of permanent adolescence, a society that did not want to grow up any more, which did not want to face the world as an adult. In the inter-war period, behaviors were modeled on those of teenagers: forgetfulness, pleasure and irresponsibility became the mainstays of social organization.

The worship of homosexuality associated with a myth of adolescence was used by the forces of progress as well as by the forces of reaction: the Aryan version was only one variation among others on the notion of the androgynous body. Whereas the Weimar Republic had stressed the feminine values conveyed by homosexuality (androgyny, softness, conciliation), Nazism focused on its virile qualities (misogyny, Männerbund, cult of the man). In fact, while the left supported homosexuals out of opportunism and a commonality of interests, it was quick to turn against them as soon as the political situation required it. Homosexuality was then denounced as a "fascistic perversion." Equally equivocal, while fascists and Nazis condemned homosexuals in the most insulting terms and then set out to persecute them in an organized way, they also built their movements around a homoerotic mythology and esthetics. Homosexuals could only come out losers, wither way. With no real support, left behind by a homoerotic fad that did not really relate to them, they became the prey of various parties and were among the first victims of the crisis of the 1930s.

One must add to these sets of themes the visceral antifeminism of the period, which explains why lesbians always seem to have kept themselves apart from events. The homoerotization of the society may have included the revival of feminine values, but it did not mean a feminization of society. On the contrary the period was marked by the revival of male social structures (public schools, university, youth movements, the Männerbund). In fact, lesbians were victims twice over: as women, they were part of a social minority that had only a negligible and recently acquired influence; as homosexuals, they were seen as attacking the bases of society and as a threat to family unity (the last refuge of morality). To affirm their own identity, they had to fight on two fronts: the campaign for rights, as women, and the campaign to affirm their sexual rights, as lesbian. Meanwhile, the feminists refused to consider the special needs of lesbians and the homosexual movements disregarded the female cause. The repression of lesbianism is explained, finally, by the patriarchal State's will to regain control of society: and for that, first of all, it had to tackle problem of the family, center of authority and a small-scale model of the society as a whole. But belief was so strong in male superiority, and it was so apparent that female sexuality could be contained, that no specific laws should be needed; social pressure alone would be enough to drive women back to their proper places.

From these various observations, it seems reasonable to conclude that homosexuality in the inter-war period affected the whole of society and not merely a small fraction of the population. That hypothesis will give rise to controversy and debate. One of the greatest revelations of this study is, finally, the extraordinary abundance of research material: homosexuality, far from being a taboo subject, was everywhere. It was analyzed, and romanticized, throughout the period. It was praised and insulted, celebrated and decried it, but it certainly was talked about. But as they gained public attention, homosexuals lost their last hope of autonomy. The fight for homosexuals failed because it rested on the laurels of its first victories. Lulled by the successes of the immediate post-war period, conscious that attitudes were shifting in their favor, homosexuals believed that their acceptance and their final integration were only a question of time. They took advantage of their new freedom, the opportunities presented by the homosexual scene and the relaxation — or absence — of repression, rather than focusing on the political and legal battles that still had to be fought. They overlooked the alarms sounded by the homosexual organizations, which recalled that in Germany and England homosexuality was still a crime punished by the law and that calls for a crackdown, far from disappearing, were increasing.

For those who were promoting the theory of decadence, the lead up to the war needed to include the elimination of the weak, the degenerate, the parasites. Homosexuals were first in line. Things had gone full circle; from one war to the next, man regained his lost virility. The younger generations which had not been able to prove their virility as combatants in the First World War now had to take up the torch again and give up the ideals and the models of the 1920s. There was no more place for the androgynous and solar homosexual myth. Conformity and the black of night were back, for at least thirty years.

APPENDIX I. STATISTICS

ENGLAND: CHANGES IN HOMOSEXUAL CRIMES BETWEEN 1919 AND 1940

1. Police statistics

Crimes	1919	1920	1921	1922	1923	1924	1925	1926	1927	1928
U	47	71	43	59	68	70	67	91	67	58
A	92	192	187	221	221	265	345	354	345	336
I	138	156	168	170	201	185	166	155	197	141
Total	277	419	398	450	480	520	578	600	609	535

2. Number of persons tried

Crimes	1919	1920	1921	1922	1923	1924	1925	1926	1927	1928
U	38	34	30	35	35	33	23	44	38	20
A	81	164	134	137	157	159	159	202	256	234
I	112	126	129	124	156	133	113	81	109	105
Total	231	324	293	296	348	305	295	327	403	359

3. Number of persons tried in circuit court (court of appeals)

Crimes	1919	1920	1921	1922	1923	1924	1925	1926	1927	1928
U	37	33	29	34	33	33	22	43	32	20
A	41	83	58	66	63	56	54	75	88	72
I	106	124	127	119	147	123	104	78	107	98
Total	184	240	214	219	243	212	180	196	227	190

4. Number of persons tried in criminal court

Crimes	1919	1920	1921	1922	1923	1924	1925	1926	1927	1928
U	1	1	1	1	2	0	1	1	3	0
A	40	89	76	71	94	103	105	127	168	162
I	6	2	2	5	9	10	9	3	2	7
Total	47	92	79	77	105	113	115	131	173	169

1929	1930	1931	1932	1933	1934	1935	1936	1937	1938	1940
102	47	73	46	82	64	78	125	102	134	97
364	398	391	487	554	581	535	690	703	822	808
191	203	178	258	210	192	227	352	316	320	251
657	548	642	791	846	837	840	1167	1121	1276	1156

1929	1930	1931	1932	1933	1934	1935	1936	1937	1938	1940
46	31	43	26	44	39	36	62	60	74	51
227	226	221	243	260	287	261	317	290	413	349
108	125	99	129	112	133	114	139	194	203	111
381	382	363	398	416	459	411	518	544	690	511

1929	1930	1931	1932	1933	1934	1935	1936	1937	1938	1940
45	28	39	25	39	33	32	55	48	67	44
65	59	80	63	62	59	64	74	65	104	88
108	116	92	119	104	116	101	119	175	178	96
218	203	211	207	205	208	197	248	288	349	228

1929	1930	1931	1932	1933	1934	1935	1936	1937	1938	1940
1	3	4	1	5	6	4	7	12	7	7
162	167	141	180	198	228	197	243	225	309	261
0	9	7	10	8	17	13	20	19	25	15
163	179	152	191	211	251	214	270	256	341	283

U : Unnatural Offences.
A : Attempt to Commit Unnatural Offences
I : Indecency with Males.
Source: Parliamentary Papers, Judiciary Statistics.

5. Police statistics by district (U + A + I)

Districts	1919	1933	1937
Bedfordshire	0	1	3
Berkshire	1	6	14
Buckinghamshire	7	6	34
Cambridgeshire	2	6	8
Cheshire	10	13	105
Cornwall	0	12	1
Cumberland	2	0	1
Derbyshire	1	4	12
Devon	9	65	53
Dorset	0	3	2
Durham	7	9	1
Essex	5	15	47
Gloucestershire	1	21	13
Hereford	0	1	3
Hertfordshire	1	4	2
Huntington	0	0	0
Kent	12	30	66
Lancashire	51	140	114
Leicestershire	3	7	2
Lincoln	7	18	22
Metropolitan Police	62	149	185
London City	0	2	3
Normouth	5	11	11
Norfolk	3	30	3
Northamptonshire	0	3	5
Northumberland	2	10	9
Nottingham	1	14	15
Oxfordshire	2	1	18
Rutland	1	0	0
Salop	0	6	17
Somerset	3	6	34
Southampton	19	56	98
Staffordshire	5	4	25
Suffolk	2	8	25
Surrey	2	'9	35
Sussex	4	38	63
Warwick	2	20	83
Westmorland	0	0	0
Wiltshire	3	2	7
Worcester	5	10	23
York (East Riding)	1	2	8
York (North Riding)	4	3	4
York (West Riding)	16	111	88

England, 1919

1. Cases and outcomes, Crown (circuit) courts

Crimes	U	A	I
Total	37	33	106
Men	37	33	106
Case dropped	0	0	0
Mentally ill	0	1	0
Acquitted	13	7	40
Guilty but mentally ill	0	0	1
Total convicted	29	25	65
Hard labor	11	5	0
Prison	9	20	54
Reformatory	0	0	0
Warning + probation	0	0	0
Warning	3	0	20
Others	1	0	0

2. Length of sentences, Crown (circuit) courts

Crimes	U	A	I
Total prison sentences	16	32	63
14 days or less	0	0	1
1-3 months	0	3	9
3-6 months	1	6	27
6-9 months	1	3	10
9 months - 1 year	2	10	13
1 year - 18 months	5	4	2
18 months - 2 years	7	6	1
Total hard labor	17	7	1
3 years	6	3	1
4 years	5	1	0
5 years	4	3	0
5-7 years	2	0	0
7-10 years	0	0	0
10+ years	0	0	0

3. Gender and age of convicts

Crimes	U	A	I
Total	24	32	65
Men	24	32	65
Ages 14-16	0	0	2
Ages 16-21	1	0	2
Ages 21-30	6	5	9
Ages 30-40	5	10	17
Ages 40-50	4	6	10
Ages 50-60	8	8	18
Age 60 +	0	3	1

4. Cases and outcomes, criminal court

Crimes	A
Total	197
Charges withdrawn	25
Guilty	172
Acquitted	2
Warning	11
Warning + probation	28
Asylum	3
Total prison	98
14 days - 1 month	10
1-2 months	12
2-3 months	37
3-6 months	39
Fines	28

England, 1933

1. Cases and outcomes, Crown (Circuit) Courts

Crimes	U	A	I
Total	39	42	104
Men	39	42	104
Not prosecuted	0	0	0
Mentally ill	0	0	1
Acquitted	4	8	25
Guilty but mentally ill	0	0	0
Total convicted	35	34	78
Hard labor	6	3	2
Prison	21	25	47
Reformatory	3	0	0
Warning + probation	2	4	9
Warning	1	2	18
Others	2	0	2
Preventive detention	0	0	0
Recidivist	10	27	29
Prison	7	17	22
Other sentences	0	0	0

2. Length of sentences Crown (circuit) courts

Crimes	U	A	I
Total hard labor	11	5	0
3 years	0	0	0
4 years	0	0	0
5 years	0	0	0
5-7 years	4	0	0
7-10 years	2	0	0
10+ years	5	5	0
Total prison	9	20	54
14 days or less	0	2	1
14 days - 1 month	1	2	6
1-3 months	0	4	10
3-6 months	3	2	5
6-9 months	4	7	19
9 months - 1 year	1	3	11
1 year- 18 months	0	0	1
18 months - 2 years	0	0	1

3. Gender and age of convicts

Crimes	U	A	I
Total	35	48	78
Men	35	47	78
Less than 14 years	0	0	0
Ages 14-16	0	2	1
Ages 16-21	12	3	25
Ages 21-30	6	10	19
Ages 30-40	11	14	10
Ages 40-50	6	11	11
Ages 50-60	0	4	10
Ages 60+	0	3	3

4. Cases and outcomes, criminal court

Crimes	A
Total arrested	38
Charges withdrawn	3
Case dropped	1
Warning	2
Warning + probation	2
Asylum	2
Total convicted	28
Prison	22
Reformatory	2
Fines	4

England, 1937

1. Cases and outcomes, Crown (circuit) courts

Crimes	U	A	I
Total	48	54	175
Not prosecuted	2	0	0
Acquitted	5	8	23
Convicted	42	45	152
Hard labor	17	7	1
Prison	16	32	63
Reformatory	2	1	1
Warning + probation	4	4	24
Warning	2	1	56
Other	1	0	2

2. Length of sentences, Crown (circuit) courts

Crimes	U	A	I
Total prison sentences	21	25	47
14 days or less	0	0	2
14 days - 1 month	0	0	1
1-3 months	1	1	4
3-6 months	5	6	19
6-9 months	2	2	7
9 months - 1 year	4	6	13
1 year - 18 months	6	9	1
18 months - 2 years	3	1	0
Total hard labor	6	3	2
3 years	3	2	2
4 years	1	0	0
5 years	2	1	0
5-7 years	0	0	0
7-10 years	0	0	0
10+ years	0	0	0

3. Gender and age of convicts

Crimes	U	A	I
Total	42	51	152
Under 17	0	0	0
Ages 17-21	8	4	17
Ages 21-30	8	7	39
Ages 30-40	10	12	38
Ages 40-50	8	15	28
Ages 50-60	3	10	13
Over 60	4	3	13

4. Cases and outcomes, criminal court

Crimes	A
Total arrested	198
Charges withdrawn	26
Prosecuted	172
Warning	7
Warning + probation	11
Reformatory	23
Preventive detention	2
Asylum	0
Total convicted	123
Prison	96
Less than 14 days	2
14 days - 1 month	7
1-2 months	8
2-3 months	27
3-6 months	5
Reformatory	7
Whipping	1
Fines	16
Others	3

GERMANY: CHANGES IN HOMOSEXUAL CRIMES BETWEEN 1919 AND 1939

Convictions under $ 175

1. Homosexuality convictions, adult

ADULTS	1919	1920	1921	1922	1923	1924	1925
Indicted	110	237	485	588	503	850	1226
Convicted	80	169	357	493	416	689	1019
Acquitted	26	65	126	94	87	160	203
Non-lieu	4	3	2	1	0	1	4
Foreigners	4	6	9	10	7	10	9
Recidivists	27	39	65	100	93	174	272
Prison	78	162	346	336	308	528	803
Less than 3 months	53	118	260	21	178	375	529
3 months - 1 year	18	34	76	102	113	128	246
more than 1 year	7	10	10	13	17	25	28
Loss of civic rights	2	3	9	14	8	20	16
Fines	?	7	3	151	102	150	202

Source: Statistik des Deutschen Reichs.

2. Homosexuality convictions, minors (ages 12 to 18)

MINORS	1919	1920	1921	1922	1923	1924	1925
Indicted	33	51	103	105	90	126	128
Convicted	24	10	63	83	64	102	104
Acquitted	9	3	40	22	26	24	24

of the Criminal Code (1919 - 1934)

1926	1927	1928	1929	1930	1931	1932	1933	1934
1126	911	731	786	732	618	721	778	872
927	761	636	653	625	508	625	674	771
196	141	92	131	105	102	94	96	99
3	9	3	2	2	8	2	8	2
15	9	7	8	8	7	6	9	7
259	263	225	270	332	210	239	269	290
730	583	480	490	485	392	464	575	635
800	401	326	340	341	270	340	378	290
195	163	140	132	100	110	111	167	252
35	19	14	18	14	12	13	30	93
14	16	10	10	9	5	8	17	40
177	161	131	149	151	100	140	86	110
1926	1927	1928	1929	1930	1931	1932	1933	1934
124	104	98	89	92	69	93	82	99
100	84	82	71	81	57	79	74	?
24	20	16	18	11	12	14	8	?

3. Statistics by Länder (1925-1926)

Years	Prussia		Bavaria		Saxe		Wurtemberg		Baden	
	A	C	A	C	A	C	C	A	C	A
1925	730	572	207	187	139	123	69	54	46	45
1926	617	481	195	170	130	110	91	78	74	70

Thuringia		Hesse		Hamburg		Mecklenburg		Oldenburg		Brunswick	
A	C	A	C	A	C	A	C	A	C	A	C
28	28	28	25	48	36	21	17	8	7	9	9
13	11	23	18	67	57	32	28	8	6	7	7

A = Arrested
C = Convicted

4. Statistics by age (1928)

Adults & minors	under 16	16-18	18-21	21-25	25-30	30-40	40-50	50-60	60-70	over 70
804	39	80	153	103	104	123	106	61	33	2

5. Statistics by socio-professional category (1928)

	Agriculture workers, hunters, fishermen		Industrial workers, craftsman		Trade, transport		Civil servants, liberal professions, health care workers	Household help	Salaried workers	No career, unemployed
	P	W	P	W	P	W				.
	18	134	15	306	37	146				
Total	152		321		183		54	6	54	30

P = Proprietors, supervisors
W = Workers, employees

6. Statistics by city (1930)

1930	Berlin	Düsseldorf	Frankfurt/M	Cologne	Konigsberg	Munich
I	732	41	41	45	43	31	75
C	625	30	39	32	39	29	65

	Dresden	Stuttgart	Karlsruhe	Hamburg	Bremen	Lübeck	
I	98	59	66	24	33	0	
C	84	47	64	23	33	0	

I = Indicted
C = Convicted

Germany: Homosexuality crimes (1935-1939), $175 of the Criminal Code

1. Homosexuality convictions (1935-1936)

	1935	1936
Indicted	2121	5556
Convicted	1901	5097
Youths	236	466
Acquitted	220	459
Hard labor	12	192
Prison	1703	4622
Prison - more than one year	419	1388
Prison - between 3 months and 1 year	825	2389
Prison - less than 3 months	459	845
Fines	129	183
Loss of civic rights	108	291

Source : *Statistik des Deutschen Reichs, vol. 577.*

2. Homosexuality convictions (1937-1939)

	1937	1938	1939
Indicted (§ 175 : homosexuality and bestiality)	?	9479	8274
Condvicted (§ 175 : homosexuality and bestiality)	8271	8562	7614
Youths	973	974	689

Source : *Notes of Dr Wuth, in* Hidden Holocaust ?, *G. Grau (ed.), London, Cassell & Cie, 1995*

3. Specific sentences

	1937	1938	1939
Coprrupting young people	7452	7472	4162
Prostitutes	800	587	114

Source : *Aide-memoire du Dr Wuth, in Hidden Holocaust ?, op. cit.*

4. Homosexuals on file with the Gestapo and the Kripo, and those convicted for homo-sexuality

	Gestapo (national secret police)	Kripo (criminal police)	Convicted (for homosexuality or bestiality)
1937	32,360	12,760	8,271
1938	28,882	10,638	8,562
1939	33,496	10,456	7,614
Total	**94,738**	**33,854**	**24,447**

Source: H.-G. Stmke, Homosexuelle in Deutschland, eine politische Geschichte, Munich, Verlag, C. H. Beck, 1989.

APPENDIX II. SONGS

THE "LILA LIED," GERMANY'S LESBIAN ANTHEM[641]

Was will man nur
Ist das Kultur
Dass jener Mensch so verspönt ist,
Der klug und gut,
Jedoch mit Mut
Und eigner Art durchströmt ist
Das grade die
Kategorie
Vor dem Gesetz verbannt ist
Und dennoch sind die Meisten stolz
Dass Sie von anderem Holz.

Refrain

Wir sind nur einmals anders als die andern,
Die nur im Gleichschritt der Moral geliebt,
Neugierig erst durch tausend Wunder wandern
Und für die's nur noch das Banal gibt
Wir aber wissen nicht wie das Gefühl ist,
Denn wir sind alle anderer Weltur Kind:
Wir lieben nur die Lila Nacht, die schwül ist,
Weil wir ja anders als die Andern sind!

Wozu die Qual,
Uns die Moral
Der Andern aufzudrängen?
Wir, hört geschwind,
Sind wie wir sind,
Selbst wollte man uns hängen.
Wer aber denkt
Dass man uns hängt
Den sollte man beweinen,
Dem bald, gebt Acht,
Wir über Nacht
Auch unsere Sonne scheinen.
Dann haben wir das gleiche Recht erstritten!
Wir leiden nicht mehr, sondern sind gechitten!

Refrain

---

641. Published in a bilingual edition in *Cahiers Gai-Kitsch-Camp*, n° 16, 1992, 140 pages.

FRANCE'S "LAVENDER SONG, " LA "CHANSON MAUVE"

Peut-on bien conclure
Que c'est ça la culture,
Si chaque être est réprouvé,
Qui possède sagesse
Bonté, hardiesse
Et singularité,
Si ces mêmes gens
Précisément
Sont dans l'illégalité
La plupart sont fiers pourtant
D'être différents.

    Refrain

C'est comme ça: des autres nous sommes différents,
Ils marchent au pas de, au pas de la morale
A travers mille premiers émerveillements,
Puis pour eux tout devient si banal, si banal
Ils ne sont pas tellement étrangers, ces sentiments
Car de tout autre monde nous sommes les enfants:
Nous aimons la nuit en mauve au parfum suffocant
C'est comme ça: des autres nous sommes différents!

C'est un mal que la morale
Des autres sur nos têtes,
Car nous sommes
Ce que nous sommes
Même si on nous arrête.
La corde au cou
Ce n'est pas nous,
On en conviendra
Car bientôt
Très bientôt
Notre heure viendra
Alors nous serons sans souffrance!
Égaux! Finie l'intolérance!

    Refrain

APPENDIX III. GERMAN LEGISLATION ON HOMOSEXUALITY

§175 OF THE CRIMINAL LAW CODE

Unnatural sexual intercourse [Unzucht widernatürliche] whether perpetrated between persons of the male sex or between men and animals, is punishable by prison; it may also entail a loss of civic rights.

DRAFT LEGISLATION OF 1909

§250: Unnatural sexual intercourse committed with a person of the same sex is punishable by prison. If the act was perpetrated by taking advantage of a relationship of dependence by an abuse of power or authority, or something similar, then a sentence of hard labor, of up to five years or, in case of extenuating circumstances, a prison sentence of not less than six months, is incurred. The same penalty applies to anyone who conducts commerce in unnatural acts on a professional basis. The sentence mentioned in paragraph 1 also applies to unnatural acts with animals.

§255: Envisioned for those cases falling under §250 al.3, where §42 (reformatory) and §53 (limitation of sejour) apply.

ALTERNATIVE DRAFT LEGISLATION OF 1911

§245: A person of the male sex who commits unnatural acts with a minor of the same sex, or with an adult of the same sex, by taking advantage of a relationship of dependence by an abuse of power or authority or similar, or by luring him with an offer of pecuniary benefits, is punishable by a sentence of up to five years' hard labor.

DRAFT LEGISLATION OF THE COMMISSION OF 1913

§322: Sexual intercourse between men.

Commission of acts similar to coitus between persons of the male sex is punishable by a prison sentence.

Anyone who commits such an act by taking advantage of a relationship of dependence by an abuse of power or authority, or who as an adult corrupts an adolescent, is punishable by a sentence of up to five years' hard labor or, in case of extenuating circumstances, a prison sentence of not less than six months.

The same sentence (al.2) applies to those who commit the act on a professional basis.

Offering oneself on a professional basis or declaring oneself ready to do so shall be incur a sentence of up to two years in prison.

In cases falling under al.3 and 4, the defendant may also be banned from the city/region, independently of the jail sentence.

§323: Any man committing acts similar to coitus with an animal shall be sentenced to prison.

DRAFT LEGISLATION OF 1919

§325: Sexual intercourse between men.

Men who together commit an act similar to coitus shall be sentenced to prison.

A man who has reached majority who commits the act by corrupting an adolescent shall be sentenced to up to five years' hard labor.

The same sentence applies to any man who commits the act by exploiting a relationship of dependence based on an abuse of power or authority.

The same sentence (al.2) applies to anyone who commits the act on a professional basis.

Any man who offers himself for such an act or declares himself ready to do so in an effort to make a profession of the commerce in unnatural acts shall be sentenced to up to two years in prison.

In cases falling under al.2 to 4, local banishment may be pronounced independently of the jail sentence.

§326: Sexual intercourse with animals.

Any man committing an act similar to coitus with an animal shall be sentenced to prison.

DRAFT LEGISLATION OF 1925 (THE REICHSRAT VERSION)

§267: Sexual intercourse between men.

Any man committing an act similar to coitus with another man shall be sentenced to prison.

An adult man who seduces a male adolescent in order to commit a sexual act shall be sentenced to prison for not less than six months. Any man committing sexual intercourse with another man on a professional basis or by exploiting his dependence due to a work relationship or other position of authority shall be sentenced likewise. In particularly serious cases the sentence may be as high as five years of hard labor.

GOVERNMENT BILL OF 1927 (REICHSTAG VERSION)

§295 Sexual intercourse with animals.

Any man committing unnatural sexual acts with an animal shall be sentenced to prison.

§296 sexual intercourse between men.

Any man committing an act similar to coitus with another man shall be sentenced to prison.

§297 Grave instances of sexual intercourse between men.

The following shall be sentenced to not less than six months' imprisonment:

1– A man who obliges another man, by force or by imminent threat to life or limb, to commit a sexual act with him or to allow himself to be used for that purpose.

2– A man who obliges another man, by exploiting his dependence due to a work relationship or other position of authority, to commit a sexual act with him or to allow himself to be used by him for that purpose.

3– Any man committing a sexual act with another man on a professional basis.

4– A man of more than 18 years of age who corrupts a male adolescent in order to commit a sexual act with him or in order that he allows himself to be used by him for that purpose.

In the first case, even the attempt is punishable. In particularly serious cases, the sentence may go up to ten years of hard labor.

Draft Legislation of 1933

§295 Sexual intercourse with animals.

Any man committing an act similar to coitus with an animal shall be sentenced to prison.

§296 sexual intercourse between men.

Any man committing an act similar to coitus with another man shall be sentenced to prison.

§297 Grave sexual acts between men.

The following shall incur a sentence of not less than six months:

1– A man who obliges another man, by exploiting his dependence due to a work relationship or other position of authority, to allow himself to be used for a sexual act.

2– An adult man who seduces a male minor so that he allows himself to be used for a sexual act.

3– Any man committing a sexual act with another man on a professional basis or who offers himself for that purpose.

In particularly serious cases, the sentence may go up to ten years of hard labor.

Law of 1935

§175: Any man who commits a sexual act with another man or who allows himself to be used by him for that purpose shall be sentenced to prison.

In the case of defendants who, at the time of the act, had not yet attained the age of 21 years, in the least severe cases the court may waive the sentence.

§175 a: The following shall incur a sentence of up to ten years of hard labor; in case of extenuating circumstances, a prison sentence of not less than three months:

1– Any man who obliges another man, by force or by imminent threat to life or limb, to commit a sexual act with him or to allow himself to be used for that purpose.

2– Any man who convinces another man, by exploiting his dependence due to a work relationship or other position of authority or subordination, to commit a sexual act with him or to allow himself to be used by him for that purpose.

3– Any man of more than 21 years of age who seduces a minor male of less than 21 years, so that he commits a sexual act with him or allows himself to be used by him for that purpose.

4– Any man committing a sexual act with men on a professional basis or who allows himself to be used by men for the purpose of such an act or who offers himself for that purpose.

$175 B: An unnatural sexual act that is committed by men with animals shall incur a prison sentence; civic rights may also be withheld.

APPENDIX IV. DR. CARL VAERNET'S EXPERIMENTS AT BUCHENWALD (1944)

The experiments conducted by Dr. Carl Vaernet at Buchenwald were posterior to the period studied in this work. Nevertheless, the author has judged it useful to present them in an appendix as they represent the results of two policies in particular: that of the physicians who were anxious to obtain absolute control over the homosexuals and to prove that they had an "illness" that was "curable'; and that of the Nazi leaders, who sought to re-integrate the homosexuals into the national community (that is to say, into the army as a crucial element in the total war) by "rehabilitating" them. These cases are particularly well documented.[642]

These experiments, intended to "cure" homosexuals, were conducted at Buchenwald. They were spearheaded by the Danish physician Carl Peter Jensen, alias Carl Vaernet, who abandoned the office he had kept in Copenhagen since 1934 and arrived in Germany in 1942. In Denmark, he was in contact with the head of the Danish Nazi party Fried Clausen. It was the physician of the Reich, Dr. S.S. Grawitz, informed Himmler of Vaernet's research on hormones. Himmler was very interested in his "recovery" program for homosexuals and asked that he be treated with the "utmost generosity," and he gave him a chance to conduct his research in Prague.[643]

In July 1944, he began his human experiments. With Schiedlausky, the garrison physician of the Waffen-SS in Weimar-Buchenwald, he chose six convicts from Buchenwald, and then ten more.[644]

The first six detainees (operated on, September 13):
N° 33463/3 (homos.) Sonntag, Johann, born 24.2.1912 in Lugau
N° 43160/3 (SV[645]) castrated. Kapelski, Philipp, born 1.9.1908 in Duisburg-Hamborn (selected, but in the end not retained)
N° 21686/4 (homos.) Steinhof, Bernhard, born 6.8.1889 in Oelde

---

642. BAB, NS 4/50, NS 3/21.

643. Günther Grau, *Hidden Holocaust? Gay and Lesbian Persecution in Germany, 1933-1945* [1993], London, Cassell & Cie, 1995, 308 pages, p.282-283: Himmler's order to the Reich Physician Dr. SS Grawitz, 3 December 1943. Himmler also asked for a 3- or 4-page monthly report, as he was "very interested in these things."

644. *Hidden Holocaust?*, op. cit., p.284.

645. SV: *Sittlichkeitsverbrecher* ("sex criminal").

N° 22584/4 (homos.) Schleicher, Gerhard, born 13.3.1921 in Berlin

N° 21912/4 (homos.) Sachs, Karl, born 21.9.1912 in Falkenau

N° 7590/4 (homos. castrated), Lindenberg, Ernst, born 10.3.1895 in Heinde

The other ten convicts (operated on, December 8):

Six were castrated (it is not clear whtether they were homosexual):

N° 9576/4, Ledetzsky

N° 21526/4 Reinhold

N° 31462/4 Schmidt

N° 20998/56 Henzes

N° 29941/56 Boecks

N° 21957/56 Kösters

Four were homosexual:

N° 779/4 Vosses, Wilhelm

N° 6169/4 Parths, Franz

N° 6186/47 Kerentzes, Friedrich

N° 41936/3 Mielsches, Fritz

Of the sixteen men, Vaernet operated on twelve: he made an incision in the groin and implanted a hormonal preparation, contained in a capsule. Blood tests and urine tests were used to follow the results of the experiment. On October 30, 1944, Vaernet sent a report to Dr. Grawitz. On September 13, 1944, five homosexuals were operated on: two were castrated, one was sterilized, two were not operated on. The goal was to determine whether the implantation of an "artificial male sexual gland" could normalize homosexuals' sexual orientation, to establish the necessary dose, and to test the standardization of the gland -- which was implanted with different levels of hormone (1a, 2a, 3a). According to the preliminary results, dose 3a transformed homosexuality into a normal sexual impulse; dose 2a awakened a normal sexual impulse in a person who was castrated seven years before. Dose 1a revived the erectile function in a castrated person, but not his sexual impulse. Furthermore, all three doses transformed severe depression and tension into optimism, calm and self-confidence. They all produced a sense of physical and psychological well-being. On October 28, 1944, the temporary results were as follows: in all three patients the homosexual impulse has been converted into a heterosexual impulse. The patients are more optimistic. Their physical strength is better and they are less subject to fatigue. Their sleep has improved. They seem to be in better shape. The other convicts have noticed this, as well. Patient n°5 asked to be operated on so "he could do as well as the others." Vaernet qualified the operation as a big success. However, if the patients answered his questions in a satisfactory manner, we may suppose that they did so at least in part so that they could be declared "cured," and be released. The fate of the men who underwent these experiments is not known. On December 21, 1944, convict Henze died of cardiac problems associated with infectious enteritis and a general physical decline.

Vaernet presents a brief biography of one of the homosexuals operated on, n° 21686, Bernhard Steinhof. "Born in 1889, a theologian and a member of a religious order, he was always sickly, very uncommunicative, but good natured and helpful. Pubescent at 18 years. Between 1911 and 1912 made attempts to get close to a girl, but failed to arrive at the sex act because of his anxiety. At school, he was initially a mediocre pupil because of unstable living conditions, then became a good pupil. From 1924 to 1928, sexual intercourse with young men, intracrural sexual intercourse, no anxiety. From 1932 to 1935, again with men, then normal sexual intercourse with a girl. Same satisfaction. Last pollution in February 1944. 8 years of hard labor; nothing to report on that."

On 16.9.1944, implantation of an "artificial male sexual gland" (dose 3a).

After the operation:
    16.9.44: pain – no neurological sensation
    17.9.44: no pain
    18.9.44: erection
    19.9.44: stronger erection in the morning
    20.9.44: stronger erection several times
    21.9.44: another erection
    22.9.44: erection, but weaker – no pain
    23.9.44: erection in the evening and in the morning
    24.9.44: idem
    26.10.44: the wound from the operation is healing without any [adverse] reaction. No reaction to the "artificial gland" implanted. Feeling better and dreams about women. Outlook has improved considerably. Seems younger; his features are softer. Today, he came for testing laughing and without inhibition – the first time he was tested, he was taciturn and answered only

direct questions, but today, he spoke freely and in detail about his past life and the changes that have occurred since the implantation.

The patient reported:

Sleep improved shortly after the operation. Before, he felt tired and had no interest in anything; he was depressed and he thought only about life in the camp.

The depression disappeared: he is looking forward to the moment of his recovery; he is making some plans for the future; now he handles everything better, even psychologically, and feels free in every respect.

Other convicts have told him that he has changed and that he seems younger and more fit.

His erotic imagination has also changed completely. Before, all his thoughts and erotic fantasies related to young males, but now they feature women. He doesn't like life in the camp: he thinks about the women in the whorehouse, but he cannot go there for "religious" reasons.

Rate of cholesterol in the blood 12.10.44: 190%.
Rate of cholesterol in the blood 24.10.44: 210%.

What became of these victims is not known. These experiments were not explicitly mentioned during the Nuremberg trials, and Vaernet escaped to South America.

APPENDIX V. ABBREVIATIONS AND ACRONYMS

ADGB   Allgemeiner Deutscher Gewerkschaftsbund: General Confederation of German Trade Unions
AN   Archives nationales (French National Archives, Paris)
BAB   Bundesarchiv Berlin: Federal Archives of Berlin
BDF   Bund Deutscher Frauen: German Women's Union
BfM   Bund für Menschenrecht: Union for the Rights of Man
BSSP   British Society for the Study of Sex Psychology
BVP   Bayerische Volkspartei: Bavarian People's Party
DDP   Deutsche demokratische Partei: German Democratic Party
DFV   Deutscher Freundschaftsverband: German Friendship Association
DNVP   Deutschnationale Volkspartei: National Party of the German People
DVP   Deutsche Volkspartei: German People's Party
Gestapo Geheime Staatspolizei: State Secret Police (political police)
GStA   Geheimes Staatsarchiv Preussischer Kulturbesitz (Berlin): Secret State Archives on the Prussian Cultural Patrimony
HJ   Hitlerjugend: Hitler Youth
KPD   Kommunistische Partei Deutschlands: German Communist Party
Kripo Kriminalpolizei: Criminal police, judiciary police
KZ   Konzentrationslager: Concentration camp
NSDAP Nationalsozialistische Deutsche Arbeiterpartei: National Socialist German Workers Party
OKW   Oberkommando der Wehrmacht: Wehrmacht High Commandement
PRO   Public Record Office: British archives (London)
RKPA   Reichskriminalpolizeiamt: Criminal Police of the Reich
RSHA   Reichssicherheitshauptamt: Security Service of the Reich
SA   Sturmabteilung: Storm troopers
SD   Sicherheitsdienst: Security Service
SPD   Sozialdemokratische Partei Deutschlands: German Social-Democratic Party
SS   Schutzstaffel: Protective Forces
USPD   Unabhängige Sozialdemokratische Partei Deutschlands: Independent German Social-Democratic Party
WhK   Wissenschaftlich-humanitäres Komitee: Scientific-Humanitarian Committee
WLSR   World League for Sex Reform: World League for Sexual Reform

ANNOTATED BIBLIOGRAPHY

This bibliography, detailed as it is, can hardly pretend to be exhaustive. Naturally, I've given preference to sources relating specifically to homosexuality, those that are little known, and I have settled for giving fellow researchers a basic bibliographic orientation as to more general works that allow one to establish the political economoic and social context of the era.

PRIMARY SOURCES

A. *Archives*

1– France
National Archives
F7 13960 (2): Pederasty, especially in the navy (1927-1932).
F 7 14663: Morality police.
F 7 14836: Narcotics trade.
F 7 14837: Narcotics usage.
F 7 14840: Narcotics usage.
F 7 14854: Women.

BB 18 6172: 44 BL 228.
BB 18 6173.
BB 18 6174: 44 BL 303.
BB 18 6175: 44 BL 340.

BB 18 6175: 44 BL 386.

BB 18 6178: 44 BL 402.

BB 18 6178: 44 BL 403.

BB 18 6186.

2- England

The Public Record Office

HO 45/12250: Criminal Law Amendment Bill (1921).

HO 45/24867: Sexual Offences Committee Action (1926).

HO 45/24955: Sexual Offenders Treatment.

HO 45/25033: Norman Haire (1937).

MEPO 2/2470: Criminal Law Amendment Bill

MEPO 3/946: Nudism.

MEPO 3/982: Hugh A. Chapman (1934-1935).

MEPO 3/989: Urinals.

MEPO 3/990: Plain-Clothes Officers.

MEPO 3/994: Mitford Brice.

MEPO 3/995: G.H. Buckingham.

MEPO 3/997: John Henry Lovendahl.

3- Germany

a) The Bundesarchiv, Berlin

Reichsministerium des Innern:

R 18/5308.

Reichsjustizministerium:

R 22/850 /854 /943 /950 /970 /973 /1175 /1176 /1197 /1460 /3062 /5006.

R 22/FB 21764 (5774 /5775 /5776 /5777).

Reichsministerium für Volksaufklärung und Propaganda:

R 55/151 /1219.

Reichssicherheitshauptamt:

R 58/239 /261 /473 /483 /1085 /1127.

Rasse-und Siedlungshauptamt:

NS 2/41 fol.1.

Konzentrationslager:

NS 3/21.

NS 4/21 /50.

Persönlicher Stab-Reichsführer SS:

NS 19/889 /897 /1087 /1270 /1838 /1916 /2075 /2376 /2673 /2957 /3030 /3392 / 3579 /3940 /4004.

Nachlässe Reinhard Mumm:

90 MU 3 506 /507 /508 /509 /510 /511 /512 /513 /514 /515 /526 /527 /528 /529 /530 /531 /532.

b) The Geheimes Staatsarchiv Preussischer Kulturbesitz, Berlin

Reichsjustizministerium:

I. HA, Rep.84a, n° 5339 /5340 /5341 /5342 /5343 /8100 /8101 /8104 /17209 / 17214 /17224 /17245 /17257 /17263 /17272 /17275 /17276 /17298 /17355 /17347.

Ministerium des Innern:

I.HA, Rep.77, Tit.435, n° 1, vol.1, vol.2.

c) Collections of archives

Günther GRAU (ed.), *Hidden Holocaust? Gay and Lesbian Persecution in Germany, 1933-1945*, London, Cassell & Cie, 1995, 308 p.; trans. from German., Homosexualität in der NS-Zeit: Dokumente einer Diskriminierung und Verfolgung, Frankfurt-am-Main, Fischer Taschenbuch Verlag, 1993.

B.   *Print Sources*

1– Periodicals

a) Dailies

Berliner Tageblatt, 1919-1921, 1931, 1934.

Deutsche Zeitung, 1919-1929.

Das schwarze Korps, various articles.

Le Temps, 1919-1939.

The Times, 1919-1939.

Völkischer Beobachter, various articles.

b) Light or satirical reviews

Fantasio, 1919-1937.

Punch, 1919-1939.

Simplicissimus, 1919-1939.

La Vie parisienne, 1920, 1924, 1934, 1938.

2– Homosexual periodicals

Only bits and pieces of the homosexual press of the Twenties and Thirties remain. It is unusual to come across a complete series. Most of the German magazines have been preserved in Berlin, at the Schwules Museum and at Spinnboden.

L'Amitié.
Das dritte Geschlecht.
Der Eigene, 1919-1933.
Eros, 1928.
Frauenliebe und Leben, 1928.
Die Freundin, 1924-1933.
Die Freundschaft, 1928.
Das Freundschaftsblatt, 1926, 1932.
Der Hellasbote, 1923.
Die Insel, 1930.
Inversions.
Jahrbuch für sexuelle Zwischenstufen, 1919-1923.
Mitteilungen des WhK, 1926-1933.
Die Tante, 1925.
Zeitschrift für Sexualwissenschaft, 1919-1931.

3– Legal stastistics

These allow analysis of how sentencing for homosexuality shifted over time in England and in Germany.

Parliamentary Papers, "Accounts and Papers," années 1919, 1922-1939.
Judicial Statistics, England and Wales, 1920 (1921), BS 18/4.
Statistik des Deutschen Reichs, Kriminalstatistik, vol.301, 311, 320, 328, 335, 346, 354, 370, 384, 398, 429, 433, 448, 478, 507, 577.

4– Medical works

Sexology played an important role in defining homosexuality. Here are the principal works on the question.

Alfred ADLER, Das Problem der Homosexualität, Leipzig, S. Hirzel, 1930, 110 p.

Henri ALLAIX, De l'inversion sexuelle à la détermination des sexes, Le Chesnay, Imprimerie moderne de Versailles, 1930, 10 p.

W.M. BECHTEREV, Über die Perversion und die Abweichungen des Geschlechtstriebe vom reflexologischen Standpunkt aus, Stuttgart, Verlag von Ferdinand Enke, 1928, 20 p.

André BINET, La Vie sexuelle chez la femme, Paris, L'Expansion scientifique française, 1932, 240 p.

Dr J.R. BOURDON, Traitement de la froideur chez la femme, Paris, Librairie "Astra," 1931, 221 p.

Edward CARPENTER, Selected Writings, vol.1, Sex, reprinted., London, Gay Men Press, 1984, 318 p.

Dr CAUFEYNON (pseud. Jean FAUCONNEY), La Perversion sexuelle, Paris, Bibliothèque populaire des connaissances médicales, 1932, 108 p.

Jean Martin CHARCOT and Victor MAGNAN, "Inversion du sens génital et autres perversions sexuelles," in Archives de neurologie, n°s 7 and 12, 1882.

Havelock ELLIS and J.A. SYMONDS, Sexual Inversion [1897], New York, Arno Press, 1975, 299 p.

Otto EMSMANN, Zum Problem der Homosexualität, Berlin, Verlag der vaterländischen Verlags- und Kunstanstalt, 1921, 100 p.

Sigmund FREUD, Névrose, psychose et perversion [1894-1924], Paris, PUF, coll. "Bibl. de psychanalyse," 1992, 303 p.

–,Trois Essais sur la théorie de la sexualité [1905], Paris, Gallimard, 1987, 211 p.

–,La Vie sexuelle [1907-1931], Paris, PUF, coll. "Bibl. de psychanalyse," 1992, 159 p.

Alfred FUCHS, Die konträre Sexualempfindung und andere Anomalien des Sexuallebens, Stuttgart, Verlag von Ferdinand Enke, 1926, 129 p.

Max von GRUBER, *Hygiene of Sex*, trans. from German, London, Tindall & Cox, 1926, 169 p.

René GUYON, *Sex Life and Sex Ethics*, London, John Lane The Bodley Head Ltd, 1933, 386 p.

Angelo HESNARD, L'Individu et le Sexe. Psychologie du narcissisme, Paris, Stock, 1927, 227 p.

–,*Psychologie homosexuelle*, Paris, Stock, 1929, 208 p.

–,Traité de sexologie normale et pathologique, Paris, Payot, 1933, 718 p.

Magnus HIRSCHFELD, *Die Homosexualität des Mannes und des Weibes* [1914], Berlin, Walter de Gruyter, 1984, 1067 p.

–,*Perversions sexuelles*, traduit et adapté par le Dr P. Vachet, Paris, Les Éditions internationales, 1931, 333 p.

–,*Le Sexe inconnu*, Paris, Éditions Montaigne, 1936, 224 p.

Magnus HIRSCHFELD (dir.), *Zur Reform des Sexualstrafrechts*, vol.IV, Sexus, Monographien aus dem Institut für Sexualwissenschaft in Berlin, Berlin, Verlag Ernest Birchner, 1926, 186 p.

Pierre HUMBERT, *Homosexuality et psychopathies, étude clinique*, Paris, G. Doin et Cie éditions, 1935, 139 p.

Josef KIRCHHOFF, *Die sexuellen Anomalien*, Frankfurt-am-Main, Verlag Oswald Quass, 1921, 132 p.

Sacha NACHT, Psychanalyse des psychonévroses et des troubles de la sexualité, Paris, Librairie Alcan, 1935, 324 p.

–, Pathologie de la vie amoureuse: essai psychanalytique, Paris, Denoël, 1937, 198 p.

Bertram POLLENS, *The Sex criminal*, London, Putnam, 1939, 211 p.

Dr RIOLAN, *Pédérastie et homosexuality*, Paris, F. Pierre, 1909, 108 p.

Dr Georges SAINT-PAUL, *Invertis et homosexuels, thèmes psychologiques* [1896], preface by Émile Zola, Paris, Éditions Vigon, 1930, 152 p.

René de SAUSSURE, *Les Fixations homosexuelles chez les femmes névrosées*, Paris, Imprimerie de la Cour d'appel, 1929, 44 p.

Richard SCHAUER, *Désordres sexuels*, Paris, Éditions Montaigne, 1934, 254 p.

–,*Sexualpathologie, Wesen und Formen der abnormen Geschlechtlichkeit*, Vienna-Leipzig-Berne, Verlag für Medizin, Weidmann & Co, 1935, 272 p.

Oswald SCHWARZ, Über Homosexualität: ein Beitrag zu einer medizinische Anthropologie, Berlin, Georg Thieme Verlag, 1931, 122 p.

–,*Sexualität und Persönlichkeit*, Vienna-Leipzig-Berne, Verlag für Medizin, 1934, 205 p.

Max SENF, *Homosexualisierung*, Bonn, A. Marcus und E. Weber's Verlag, 1924, 74 p.

Ambroise TARDIEU, *La Pédérastie* [1857], Paris, Le Sycomore, 1981, 247 p.

Kenneth WALKER and E.B. STRAUSS, *Sexual Disorders in the Male*, London, Hamish Hamilton Medical Books, 1939, 248 p.

Dr A. WEIL (dir.), Sexualreform und Sexualwissenschaft, Vorträge gehalten auf der ersten internationalen Tagung für Sexualreform auf sexualwissenschaftlicher Grundlage in Berlin, Berlin, Julius Püttmann, 1922, 286 p.

World League for Sexual Reform, Sexual Reform Congress, Copenhagen, 1-5 July 1928, Copenhagen, Levin & Munksgaard, 1929, 307 p.

–,Sexual Reform Congress, London, 8-14 september1929, London, Kegan Paul, 1930, 670 p.

–,Sexual Reform Congress, Vienna, 16-23 september1930, Vienna, Elbemühl, 1931, 693 p.

5– Sex education manuals

Of all the works on sex education, those listed below refer more or less directly to homosexuality.

René ALLENDY and Hella LOBSTEIN, *Le Problème sexuel à l'école*, Paris, Aubier, 1938, 253 p.

Rudolf ALLERS, *Sexualpädagogik*, Salzburg-Leipzig, Verlag Anton Postet, 1934, 270 p.

Anonyme, *The Education of Boys in the Subject of Sex*, London, Student Christian Movement, 1927, 115 p.

Eugène ARMAND, L'Émancipation sexuelle, l'Amour en camaraderie et les Mouvements d'avant-garde, Paris, Éditions de l'En-dehors, 1934, 23 p.

Association du mariage chrétien, *L'Église et l'Éducation sexuelle*, Paris, Aubin, 1929, 201 p.

Mary Everest BOOLE, *What One Might Say to a Schoolboy*, London, C.W. Daniel, 1921, 24 p.

T. BOWEN PARTINGTON, *Sex and Modern Youth*, London, Athletic Publication Ltd, 1931, 136 p.

Dorothy BROMLEY and Florence BRITTEN, *Youth and Sex. A Study of 1300 College Students*, New York and London, Harper & Brothers Publishers, 1938, 303 p.

Adolf BUSEMANN, *Das Geschlechtsleben der Jugend und seine Erziehung*, Berlin, Union Deutsche Verlagsgesellschaft, 1929, 57 p.

V.F. CALVERTON and S.D. SCHMALHAUSEN (dir.), *Sex in Civilization*, London, Allen & Unwin, 1929, 719 p.

Dr Jean CARNOT, *Au service de l'amour*, Paris, Éditions Beaulieu, 1939, 256 p.

Reginald CHURCHILL, *I Commit to Your Intelligence*, London, J.M. Dent & Sons Ltd, 1936, 137 p.

Gladys M. COX, Youth, *Sex and Life*, London, Arthur Pearson, 1935, 229 p.

E. DEDERDING, *Schützt unsere Kinder vor den Sexualverbrechern!*, Berlin, Deutscher Volksverlag, 1931, 47 p.

Henri DROUIN, *Conseils aux jeunes gens*, Paris, Librairie Garnier frères, 1926, 185 p.

Havelock ELLIS, *Études de psychologie sexuelle*, t.VII, L'Éducation sexuelle, Paris, *Mercure de France*, 1927, 220 p.

Violet FIRTH, *The Problem of Purity*, London, Rider & Co, 1928, 127 p.

F.W. FOERSTER, *Morale sexuelle et pédagogie sexuelle*, Paris, Librairie Bloud & Gay, 1929, 270 p.

Sigmund FREUD, "Les explications sexuelles données aux enfants" [1907], in *La Vie sexuelle*, Paris, PUF, 1992, 159 p.

R.P.S.J. de GANAY, Dr Henri ABRAND and abbé Jean VIOLLET, *Les Initiations nécessaires*, Paris, Éditions familiales de France, 1938, 47 p.

Brian GREEN (Rev.), *Problems of Human Friendship*, London, The "Pathfinder" Papers, 1931, 37 p.

Heinrich HANSELMANN, *Geschlechtliche Erziehung des Kindes*, Zurich-Leipzig, Rotapfel Verlag, 1931, 69 p.

Magnus HIRSCHFELD and Ewald BOHM, *Éducation sexuelle*, Paris, Éditions Montaigne, 1934, 271 p.

William Lee HOWARD, *Confidential Chats with Boys*, London, Rider & Co, 1928, 144 p.

Kenneth INGRAM, *An Outline of Sexual Morality*, London, Cape, 1922, 94 p.

R.H. INNES, *Sex from the Standpoint of Youth*, London, The New World Publishing Cie, 1933, 16 p.

N.M. IOWETZ-TERESHENKO, *Friendship-Love in Adolescence*, London, Allen & Unwin Ltd, 1936, 369 p.

Dr LAIGNEL-LAVASTINE, *Vénus et ses dangers*, Paris, Ligue nationale française contre le péril vénérien, 1925, 14 p.

Jean LÉONARD, *Le Lever de rideau ou l'Initiation au bonheur sexuel*, Paris, Jean Fort éditeur, 1933, 219 p.

Rennie MACANDREW, *Approaching Manhood, Healthy Sex for Boys*, London, The Wales Publishing Co, 1939, 95 p.

–,*Approaching Womanhood, Healthy Sex for Girls*, London, The Wales Publishing Co, 1939, 93 p.

R. MACDONALD LADELL, *The Sex Education of Children*, Birmingham, Cornish Brothers Ltd, 1934, 24 p.

T. MILLER NEATBY, *Personal: To Boys*, London, The Alliance of Honour, 1934, 27 p.

–,*Youth and Purity*, London, British Christian Endeavour Union, 1937, 27 p.

Friedrich NIEBERGALL, *Sexuelle Aufklärung der Jugend: ihr Recht, ihre Wege und Grenzen*, Heidelberg, Evangelischer Verlag, 1922, 25 p.

Dr Jean POUŸ, Conseils à la jeunesse sur l'éducation sexuelle, Paris, Maloine, 1931, 29 p.

Preussisches Ministerium für Wissenschaft, Kunst und Vorbildung (dir.), *Sittlichkeitsvergehen an höheren Schulen und ihre disziplinäre Behandlung*, Leipzig, Verlag von Quelle & Mener, 1928, 141 p.

C. Stanford READ, *The Struggles of Male Adolescence*, London, Allen & Unwin, 1928, 247 p.

George RILEY SCOTT, Sex Problems and Dangers in War-Time. A Book of Practical Advice for Men and Women on the Fighting and Home-Fronts, London, T. Werner Laurie Ltd, 1940, 85 p.

Gerhard Reinhard RITTER, *Die geschlechtliche Frage in der Deutsche Volkserziehung*, Berlin-Cologne, A. Marcus und E. Weber's Verlag, 1936, 397 p.

Robert RITTER, *Das geschlechtliche Problem in der Erziehung*, Munich, Verlag von Ernst Reinhardt, 1928, 88 p.

Père S.V.D. SCHMITZ, *A la source pure de la vie*, Mulhouse, Éditions Salvator, 1937, 48 p.

Dr Heinrich SCHULTE-HUBBERT, *Um Sittlichkeit und Erziehung an höheren Schulen*, Münster, Aschendorffsche Verlagsbuchhandlung, 1929, 62 p.

Oswald SCHWARZ, *The Psychology of Sex and Sex Education*, London, New Education Fellowship, 1935, 33 p.

J.S.N. SEWELL, The Straight Left, Being Nine Talks to Boys Who Are about to Leave their Public-School, London, Society for Promoting Christian Knowledge, 1928, 64 p.

Eddy SHERWOOD, *Sex and Youth*, London, Student Christian Movement, The Garden City Press, 1928, 150 p.

F.H. SHOOSMITH, *That Youth May Know. Sex Knowledge for Adolescents*, London, Harrap & Co, 1935, 117 p.

–,The Torch of Life. First Steps in Sex Knowledge, London, Harrap & Co, 1935, 150 p.

Dr SICARD DE PLAUZOLES, *Pour le salut de la race: éducation sexuelle*, Paris, Éditions médicales, 1931, 98 p.

F.V. SMITH, *The Sex Education of Boys*, London, Student Christian Movement Press, 1931, 15 p.

J.P. STEFFES (dir.), *Sexualpädagogische Probleme*, Münster, Münster Verlag, 1931, 231 p.

Erich STERN (dir.), *Die Erziehung und die sexuelle Frage*, Berlin, Union Deutsche Verlagsgesellschaft, 1927, 381 p.

Marie STOPES, *Sex and the Young*, London, The Gill Publishing Co, 1926, 190 p.

Heinrich TÖBBEN, *Die Jugendverwahrlosung und ihre Bekämpfung*, Münster, Aschendorffsche Verlagsbuchhandlung, 1922, 245 p.

Tihamer TOTH, *Reine Jugendreife*, Freibourg, Herder & Co, 1931, 140 p.

A. TREWBY, *Healthy Boyhood*, London, The Alliance of Honour, Kings & Jarcett, 1924, 63 p.

Theodore F. TUCKER and Muriel POUT, *Sex Education in Schools*, London, Gerald Howe Ltd, 1933, 144 p.

Edwin WALL, *To the Early Teens or Friendly Counsels to Boys*, London, The Portsmouth Printers Press, 1931, 120 p.

W.J. WATSON, *Ce que tout jeune homme doit savoir à l'âge de la puberté*, Paris, Éditions Prima, 1932, 94 p.

Leslie D. WEATHERHEAD, *The Mastery of Sex through Psychology and Religion*, London, Student Christian Movement Press, 1931, 249 p.

Erich ZACHARIAS, *Die sexuelle Gefährdung unserer Jugend*, Berlin, Buch-druckerei des Waisenhauses, 1929, 38 p.

Alfred ZEPLIN, Sexualpädagogik als Grundlage des Familienglücks und des Volkswohls, Rostock, Carl Hinstorff Verlag, 1938, 117 p.

6– Other works on homosexuality

a) Surveys, journalistic debates, news reports

René ALLENDY, "Le crime et les perversions instinctives," in *Le Crapouillot*, May 1938

–,"Les conceptions modernes de la sexualité," in *Le Crapouillot*, september1937.

Maurice BAUMONT, L'Affaire Eulenburg et les Origines de la Première Guerre mondiale, Paris, Payot, 1933, 281 p.

Robert BOUCARD, *Les Dessous des prisons de femmes*, Paris, Les Éditions de France, 1930, 236 p.

Francis CARCO, *Prisons de femmes*, Paris, Les Éditions de France, 1933, 244 p.

Maryse CHOISY, *Un mois chez les filles*, Paris, Éditions Montaigne, 1928, 254 p.

Maryse CHOISY and Marcel VERTÈS, *Dames seules*, Lille, Cahiers Gai-Kitsch-Camp, n° 23, reprinted. 1993, 53 p.

Michel du COGLAY, *Chez les mauvais garçons. Choses vues*, Paris, R. Saillard, 1938, 221 p.

Anne de COLNEY, *L'Amour aux colonies*, Paris, Librairie "Astra," 1932, 214 p.

Alexis DANAN, *Mauvaise graine*, Paris, Éditions des Portiques, 1931, 249 p.

Gabriel GOBRON, *Contacts avec la jeune génération allemande*, Toulouse, Éditions la Lanterne du Midi, 1930, 284 p.

Ambroise GOT, *L'Allemagne à nu*, Paris, La Pensée française, 1923, 248 p.

John GRAND-CARTERET, *Derrière "lui": l'homosexuality en Allemagne [1907]*, Lille, Cahiers Gai-Kitsch-Camp, 1992, 231 p.

"L'homosexuality en littérature," *Les Marges*, 15 March 1926, n° 141, t.35.

Joseph KESSEL, *Bas-fonds de Berlin*, Paris, Les Éditions de France, 1934, 224 p.

Peter Martin LAMPEL, *Jungen in Not*, Berlin, G. Kiepenheuer, 1928, 240 p.

Theodor LESSING, *Haarmann. The Story of a Werewolf* [1925], in *Monsters of Weimar*, London, Nemesis Books, 1993, 306 p.

Oscar METENIER, *Vertus et vices allemands*, Paris, Albin Michel, 1904, 281 p.

Hilary PACQ, *Le Procès d'Oscar Wilde*, Paris, Gallimard, 1933, 263 p.

Eugène QUINCHE, *Haarmann, le boucher de Hanovre*, Paris, Éditions Henry Parville, 1925, 182 p.

Marcel REJA, "La révolte des hannetons," in *Mercure de France*, 1 March 1928, p.324-340.

Louis-Charles ROYER, *L'Amour en Allemagne*, Paris, Éditions de France, 1936, 225 p.

b) Homosexual movements; judical reforms

Albrecht BÖHME, "Soziale Medizin und Hygiene: die neuen Gesetze über Kastration und Homosexualität," in *Münchener medizinische Wochenschrift* (MMW), 16 August 1935, n° 33, p.1330-1331.

Adolf BRAND (dir.), *Die Bedeutung der Freundsliebe für Führer und Völker*, Berlin, Adolf Brand, 1923, 32 p.

Fritz DEHNOW, *Sittlichkeitsdelikte und Strafrechtsreform*, Berlin, Julius Püttmann, 1922, 22 p.

Documents of the Homosexual Rights Movement in Germany, 1836-1927, New York, Arno Press, reprinted. 1975, no page numbers.

Isaac GOLDBERG, Havelock Ellis. A Biographical and Critical Survey, London, Constable, 1926, 359 p.

Kurt HILLER, *§ 175: die Schmach des Jahrhunderts!*, Berlin, Paul Steegeman Verlag, 1922, 132 p.

–,"Die homosexuelle Frage," in *Die neue Generation*, cahiers 7/8, July-August 1927, p.223.

–,"Das neue Sexualstrafrecht und die schwarze Gefahr," in *Die Weltbühne*, 5 August 1930, n° 32, p.191-196; 12 August 1930, n° 33, p.224-229; 19 August 1930, n° 34, p.266-270.

Magnus HIRSCHFELD, *Les Homosexuels de Berlin [1908]*, Paris, Cahiers Gai-Kitsch-Camp, 1993, 103 p.

–,*Von einst bis jetzt [1923]*, Berlin, Verlag Rosa Winkel, 1986, 213 p.

–,"Der neue § 175, ein Gesetz für Erpresser," in *Die Weltbühne*, 20 January 1925, n° 3, p.91-95.

Magnus HIRSCHFELD (dir.), *Sittengeschichte des ersten Weltkriegs*, Berlin, Müller & Kiepenheuer, 1929, 607 p.

Hans HYAN, "§ 175," in *Die Weltbühne*, 22 June 1926, n° 25, p.969-973.

Joseph ISHILL (dir.), *Havelock Ellis in Appreciation*, Berkeley Heights, Oriole Press, 1929, 299 p.

Kartell für Reform des Sexualstrafrechts (dir.), Gegenentwurf zu den Strafbestimmungen des Amtlichen Entwurfs eines allgemeinen deutschen Strafgesetzbuchs über geschlechtliche und mit dem Geschlechtsleben in Zusammenhang stehende Handlungen, Berlin, Verlag der neuen Gesellschaft, 1927, 99 p.

Botho LASERSTEIN, "§ 175," in *Die Weltbühne*, 20 July 1926, n° 29, p.91.

H. LENZ, Verbrechen und Vergehen wider die Sittlichkeit, ein kritischer Beitrag zur Strafrechtsreform, Trier, Paulinus-Druckerei, 1928, 72 p.

Richard LINSERT, *§ 297, Unzucht zwischen Männern*, Berlin, Neuer Deutscher Verlag, 1929, 130 p.

Hansjörg MAURER, § 175, eine kritische Betrachtung des Problems der Homosexualität, Munich, Willibald Drexler, 1921, 62 p.

"Neueste Entscheidungen von grundsätzlicher Bedeutung," in *Deutsche Juristen Zeitung*, 1 september1935, 40, volume 17, p.1047-1048.

"§ 175 StGB," in *Juristische Wochenschrift*, 28 september1935, p.2732-2734.

Houston PETERSON, *Havelock Ellis, Philosopher of Love*, United States, Houghton Miffin Inc., 1928, 432 p.

PFORR, "Die widernatürliche Unzucht," in *Preussische Polizeibeamtenzeitung*, 4 October 1924, n° 40, p.408-410.

"Reichsgericht. § 175 StGB," in *Juristische Wochenschrift*, 22 January 1938, p.167.

Botho SCHLEICH, "Die Bekämpfung der Homosexualität und die Rechtssprechung," in *Deutsches Recht*, 1937, vol. 13/14, p.299-300.

SIEGFRIED (pseudonym for Viktor CATHREIN), *Im Zeichen der Zeit! § 175*, Berlin, Verlag der vaterländischen Verlags- und Kunstanstalt, 1920, 14 p.

St Ch. WALDECKE (pseud. Ewald TSCHECK), *Das WhK: warum ist es zu bekämpfen und sein Wirken schädlich für das deutsche Volk?*, Berlin, Adolf Brand, Gemeinschaft der Eigenen, 1925, 18 p.

Johannes WERTHAUER, "§ 175," in *Die Weltbühne*, 5 October 1926, n° 40, p.525-526.

"Wissenschaftlich-humanitäres Komitee," in *Die Weltbühne*, 14 février 1933, n° 7, p.253.

c) Party literature

Eugène ARMAND, *L'Homosexualité, l'Onanisme et les Individualistes*, Paris, Éditions de l'En-dehors, 1931, 32 p.

Eugène ARMAND, Gérard de LACAZE-DUTHIERS and Abel LÉGER, *Des préjugés en matière sexuelle*, Paris, Éditions de l'En-dehors, 1931, 32 p.

Eugène ARMAND, Vera LIVINSKA and C. de ST HÉLÈNE, *La Camaraderie amoureuse*, Paris, Éditions de l'En-dehors, 1930, 32 p.

Burghard ASSMUS, Klosterleben, Enthüllungen über die Sittenverderbnis in den Klöstern, Berlin, A. Bock Verlag, 1937, 102 p.

Curt BONDY, *Die Proletarische Jugendbewegung in Deutschland*, Lauenburg, Adolf Saal Verlag, 1922, 152 p.

Carl Christian BRY, *Verkappte Religionen, Kritik des kollektiven Wahns [1924]*, Munich, Ehrenwirth Verlag, 1979, 253 p.

Karl August ECKHARDT, "Widernatürliche Unzucht ist todeswürdig," in *Das schwarze Korps*, 22 June 1935, p.13.

Friedrich ENGELS, *L'Origine de la famille, de la propriété privée et de l'État* [1884], Paris, Éditions sociales, 1971, 364 p.

Felix HALLE, "Die Reform des Sexualstrafrechts und das Proletariat," in *Die Internationale*, 1 November 1926, p.666-668.

Institut zum Studium der Judenfrage (dir.), *Die Juden in Deutschland*, Munich, Verlag Franz Eher Nachf., 1936, 416 p.

Rudolf KLARE, *Homosexualität und Strafrecht*, Hamburg, Hanseatische Verlagsanstalt, 1937, 172 p.

–,"Die Bekämpfung der Homosexualität in der deutschen Rechtsgeschichte" in *Deutsches Recht*, 15 July 1937, cahiers 13/14, p.281-285.

Alexandra KOLLONTAI, *Marxisme et révolution sexuelle*, Paris, Maspero, 1973, 286 p.

Livre brun sur l'incendie du Reichstag et la terreur hitlérienne [1933], Paris, Tristan Mage éditions, 1992, 2 vol.

Klaus MANN, "Homosexualität und Faschismus" [1934-1935], in *Heute und morgen. Schriften zur Zeit*, Munich, Nymphenburger Verlagshandlung, 1969, 364 p.

Wilhelm REICH, *La Lutte sexuelle des jeunes* [1932], Paris, Maspero, 1972, 148 p.

–,*La Psychologie de masse du fascisme* [1933], Paris, Payot, coll. "Petite bibl. Payot," 1972, 341 p.

–,*La Révolution sexuelle* [1936], Paris, Christian Bourgois éditeur, 1982, 340 p.

Alfred ROSENBERG, *Le Mythe du xxe siècle* [1930], Paris, Éditions Avalon, 1986, 689 p.

–,Der Sumpf, Querschnitte durch das "Geistes-" Leben der November-Demokratie, Munich, Verlag Franz Eher Nachf., 1930, 237 p.

Lothar Gottlieb TIRALA, *Rasse, Geist und Seele*, Munich, J.F. Lehmann Verlag, 1935, 256 p.

Ignaz WROBEL (pseudonym of Kurt TUCHOLSKY), "Röhm," in *Die Welt-bühne*, 26 April 1932, n° 17, p.798-799.

d) Public schools, youth movements

Hans BLÜHER, *Die deutsche Wandervogelbewegung als erotisches Phänomen* [1914], Frankfurt-am-Main, Verlag Frankfurt am Main, 1976, 190 p.

–,*Die Rolle der Erotik in der männlichen Gesellschaft*, Iena, Eugen Diederichs, 1919, 2 vol., 248 and 224 p.

–,*Der Charakter der Jugendbewegung*, Lauenburg, Adolf Saal Verlag, 1921, 56 p.

Richard COMYNS CARR (ed.), *Red Rags, Essays of Hate from Oxford*, London, Chapman & Hall, 1933, 291 p.

P.H. CRAWFURTH SMITH, *Oxford in the Melting-Pot*, London, The White Owl Press, 1932, 24 p.

Terence GREENIDGE, *Degenerate Oxford?*, London, Chapman & Hall, 1930, 245 p.

T.E. HARRISSON, *Letter to Oxford*, Reynold Bray, The Hate Press, 1933, 98 p.

Lucien MIALARE, *La Criminalité juvénile*, Paris, Les Presses modernes, 1926, 254 p.

Hans MUSER, *Homosexualität und Jugendfürsorge*, Paderborn, Verlag Ferdinand Schöningh, 1933, 184 p.

Siegfried STURM, Das Wesen der Jugend und ihre Stellung zu Blüher und Plenge zu Sexualtheorie und Psychoanalyse, Wurzbourg, Hannes Wadenklee, 1921, 20 p.

Edward THOMAS, *Oxford*, London, Black A. & C. Black, 1932, 265 p.

Alec WAUGH, *Public-School Life. Boys, Parents, Masters*, London, Collins Sons & Co, 1922, 271 p.

Gustav WYNEKEN, Die neue Jugend, ihr Kampf um Freiheit und Wahrheit in Schule und Elternhaus, in Religion und Erotik, Munich, Steinicke Verlag, 1914, 60 p.

–,*Revolution und Schule*, Leipzig, Klinkhardt Verlag, 1921, 74 p.

–,*Wickersdorf*, Lauenburg, Adolf Saal Verlag, 1922, 152 p.

–,*Eros*, Lauenburg, Adolf Saal Verlag, 1924, 72 p.

Kurt ZEIDLER, *Vom erziehenden Eros*, Lauenburg, Freideutscher Jugendverlag Adolf Saal, 1919, 39 p.

e) Essays, pamphlets, manifestos

Egan BERESFORD, *The Sink of Solitude*, London, The Herness Press, 1928, no page numbers.

Paul BUREAU, *L'Indiscipline des mœurs*, Paris, Librairie Bloud & Gay, 1920, 608 p.

GEORGES-ANQUETIL, *Satan conduit le bal* [1925], Paris, Agence parisienne de distribution, 1948, 536 p.

André GIDE, *Corydon* [1924], Paris, Gallimard, 1991, 149 p.

–,*Retour de l'URSS*, Paris, Gallimard, 1936, 125 p.

Pierre LIÈVRE, "André Gide," in *Le Divan*, July-August 1927.

Thomas MANN, *Sur le mariage* [1925], bilingual edition, Paris, Aubier-Flammarion, 1970, 191 p.

François NAZIER, *L'Anti-Corydon, essai sur l'inversion sexuelle*, Paris, Éditions du Siècle, 1924, 126 p.

Ernst Erich NOTH, La *Tragédie de la jeunesse allemande*, Paris, Grasset, 1934, 261 p.

François PORCHÉ, *L'Amour qui n'ose pas dire son nom*, Paris, Grasset, 1927, 242 p.

WILLY, *Le Troisième Sexe*, Paris, Paris-Édition, 1927, 268 p.

f) Feminism and lesbianism

E.F.W. EBERHARD, *Die Frauenemanzipation und ihre erotischen Grundlagen*, Vienna-Leipzig, Wilhelm Braumüller, 1924, 915 p.

J.M. HOTEP, Love and Happiness, Intimate Problems of the Modern Woman, London, Heinemann, 1938, 235 p.

Laura HUTTON, *The Single Woman and Her Emotional Problems*, London, Tindall & Cox, 1937, 173 p.

Mathilde von KEMNITZ, *Erotische Wiedergeburt*, Munich, Verlag von Ernst Reinhardt, 1919, 212 p.

RACHILDE, *Pourquoi je ne suis pas féministe*, Paris, Éditions de France, 1928, 87 p.

Alice RILKE, "Die Homosexualität der Frau und die Frauenbewegung," in *Deutsches Recht*, 15 février 1939, vol. 3/4, p.65-68.

Ruth Margarite RÖLLIG, *Les Lesbiennes de Berlin* [1928], Lille, Cahiers Gai-Kitsch-Camp, 1992, 140 p.

Anton SCHÜCKER, *Zur Psychopathologie der Frauenbewegung*, Leipzig, Verlag von Curt Kabitzsch, 1931, 51 p.

Clara ZETKIN, *Batailles pour les femmes*, Paris, Éditions sociales, 1980, 444 p.

g) Others

ANOMALY (pseudonyme), *The Invert and His Social Adjustment*, London, Baillein, 1927, 159 p.

Archives du surréalisme, *Recherches sur la sexualité*, January 1928-August 1932, Paris, Gallimard, 1990, 212 p.

Association for Moral and Social Hygiene, *The State and Sexual Morality*, London, Allen & Unwin, 1920, 78 p.

Floyd BELL, *Love in the Machine Age*, London, Routledge & Sons, 1930, 428 p.

Paul BROHMER, *Biologie-Unterricht und völkische Erziehung*, Frankfurt-am-Main, Verlag Moritz Diesterweg, 1933, 84 p.

François CARLIER, *La Prostitution antiphysique* [1887], Paris, Le Sycomore, 1981, 250 p.

Albert CHAPOTIN, *Les Défaitistes de l'amour*, Paris, Le Livre pour tous, 1927, 510 p.

Louis ESTÈVE, *L'Énigme de l'androgyne*, Paris, Les Éditions du monde moderne, 1927, 161 p.

Theodore de FELICE, *Le Protestantisme et la Question sexuelle*, Paris, Librairie Fischbacher, 1930, 80 p.

Remy de GOURMONT, *Physique de l'amour* [1903], Paris, Les Éditions 1900, 1989, 236 p.

Alexandre PARENT-DUCHÂTELET, *La Prostitution à Paris au xixe siècle* [1836], collected and annotated by Alain Corbin, Paris, Éditions du Seuil, 1981, 217 p.

Siegfried PLACZEK, *Freundschaft und Sexualität*, Berlin-Cologne, A. Marcus und E. Weber's Verlag, 1927, 186 p.

Paul PROVENT, *La Criminalité militaire en temps de paix*, Paris, Marchal et Billard, 1926, 340 p.

Heinz SCHMEIDLER, *Sittengeschichte von heute*, die Krisis der Sexualität, Dresde, Carl Reissner Verlag, 1932, 372 p.

Camille SPIESS, *Pédérastie et homosexualité*, Paris, Daragon, 1917, 68 p.

–,*L'Inversion sexuelle*, Paris, Éditions de l'En-dehors, 1930, 5 p.

–,*Éros ou l'Histoire physiologique de l'homme*, Paris, Éditions de l'Athanor, 1932, 280 p.

H.E. TIMERDING, *Sexualethik*, Leipzig, B.G. Teubner, 1919, 120 p.

Hans von TRESCHKOW, *Von Fürsten und anderen Sterblichen, Erinnerungen*, Berlin, Fontane, 1922, 240 p.

Harvey WICKAM, *The Impuritans*, London, Allen & Unwin, 1929, 296 p.

7– Fiction, novels, collections of poetry

W.H. AUDEN, *Collected Shorter Poems, 1927-1957*, London, Faber & Faber, 1966, 351 p.

Djuna BARNES, *L'Almanach des dames* [1928], Paris, Flammarion, 1972, 165 p.

Natalie BARNEY, *Aventures de l'esprit* [1929], Paris, Persona, 1982, 215 p.

–,Nouvelles pensées de l'Amazone, Paris, Mercure de France, 1939, 215 p.

Vicky BAUM, *Shanghai Hôtel* [1939], Paris, Phébus, 1997, 669 p.

André BEAUNIER, *La Folle Jeune Fille*, Paris, Flammarion, 1922, 282 p.

Pierre BENOÎT, *Monsieur de la Ferté*, Paris, Albin Michel, 1934, 314 p.

E.F. BENSON, *Snobs*, Paris, Salvy, 1994, 217 p.

Gustave BINET-VALMER, *Lucien*, Paris, Flammarion, 1921, 283 p.

–,*Sur le sable couchées*, Paris, Flammarion, 1929, 246 p.

André BIRABEAU, *La Débauche*, Paris, Flammarion, 1924, 246 p.

Édouard BOURDET, *La Prisonnière, comédie en trois actes* (first staged on 6 March 1926 at the Fémina), Paris, Les Œuvres libres, 1926, 116 p.

Joseph BREITBACH, *Rival et rivale* [*Die Wandlung der Suzanne Dasseldorf*], Paris, Gallimard, 1935, 389 p.

André BRETON, *Nadja* [1928], Paris, Gallimard, coll. "Folio," 1982, 190 p.

Arnold BRONNEN, *Septembernovelle* [1923], Stuttgart, Klett-Cotta, 1989, 65 p.

Rupert BROOKE, *The Poetical Works*, London, Faber & Faber, 1990, 216 p.

Ferdinand BRUCKNER, *Le Mal de la jeunesse* [1925], Amiot-Lenganey, 1993, 108 p.

Francis CARCO, *Jésus-la-caille*, Paris, Mercure de France, 1914, 250 p.

CHARLES-ÉTIENNE, *Notre-Dame-de-Lesbos*, Paris, Librairie des Lettres, 1919, 309 p.

–,*Les Désexués*, Paris, Curio, 1924, 267 p.

–,*Le Bal des folles*, Paris, Curio, 1930, 255 p.

CHARLES-ÉTIENNE and Albert NORTAL, *Les Adolescents passionnés*, Paris, Curio, 1928, 253 p.

Jean de CHERVEY, *Amour inverti*, Paris, Chaubard, 1907, 212 p.

Jean COCTEAU, *Le Livre blanc* [1928], Paris, Éditions de Messine, 1983, 123 p.

–,*Les Enfants terribles* [1929], Paris, Grasset, 1990, 130 p.

COLETTE, *Le Pur et l'Impur* [1932], Paris, Hachette, 1971, 189 p.

–,*Œuvres complètes*, Paris, Gallimard, coll. "Bibl. de la Pléiade," 3 vol., 1984, 1986, 1991.

René CREVEL, *La Mort difficile*, Paris, Simon Kra, 1926, 202 p.

–,*Mon corps et moi*, Paris, Éditions du Sagittaire, 1926, 204 p.

Clemence DANE (pseud. Winifred ASHTON), *Regiment of Women* [1917], London, Greenwood Press, 1978, 345 p.

Lucien DAUDET, *Le Chemin mort*, Paris, Flammarion, 1908, 382 p.

Henri DEBERLY, *Un homme et un autre*, Paris, Gallimard, 1928, 220 p.

Lucie DELARUE-MARDRUS, *L'Ange et les Pervers*, Paris, Le Livre moderne illustré, 1930, 159 p.

Robert DESNOS, *La Liberté ou l'Amour!* [1924], Paris, Gallimard, 1962, 160 p.

Jean DESTHIEUX, *Figures méditerranéennes: "Femmes damnées,"* Paris-Gap, Ophrys, 1937, 135 p.

Alfred DÖBLIN, L'Empoisonnement [Die beiden Freundinnen und ihr Giftmord, 1924], Arles, Actes Sud, 1988, 108 p.

André du DOGNON, *Les Amours buissonnières*, Paris, Éditions du Scorpion, 1948, 286 p.

René ÉTIEMBLE, *L'Enfant de chœur*, Paris, Gallimard, 1937, 251 p.

E.M. FORSTER, *Maurice* [written in 1914], Paris, Christian Bourgois, 1987, 279 p.

–,Un instant d'éternité et autres nouvelles [The Life to Come, and Other Stories, 1972], Paris, Christian Bourgois éditeur, 1988, 306 p.

Michel GEORGES-MICHEL, *Dans la fête de Venise*, Paris, Fayard, 1923, 256 p.

André GIDE, *L'Immoraliste* [1902], Paris, Gallimard, coll. "Folio," 1996, 182 p.

–,*Les Nourritures terrestres* [1917], Paris, Gallimard, coll. "Folio," 1997, 246 p.

–,*Les Faux-Monnayeurs*, Paris, Gallimard, 1926, 499 p.

Ernst GLÄSER, *Classe 22*, Paris, V. Attinger, 1929, 317 p.

Ivan GOLL, *Sodome et Berlin*, Paris, Émile-Paul frères, 1929, 250 p.

Julien GREEN, *Œuvres complètes*, Paris, Gallimard, coll. "Bibl. de la Pléiade," 7 vol.

Daniel GUÉRIN, *La Vie selon la chair*, Paris, Albin Michel, 1929, 281 p.

Amédée GUIARD, *Antone Ramon*, Paris, J. Duvivier, 1914, 390 p.

James HANLEY, *The German Prisoner*, London, éd. part., 1930, 36 p.

Max-René HESSE, *Partenau*, Paris, Albin Michel, 1930, 323 p.

Christopher ISHERWOOD, *Mr Norris Changes Train* [1935], London, Chatto & Windus, 1984, 190 p

–, *Adieu à Berlin* [*Goodbye to Berlin*, 1939], Paris, Hachette, 1980, 288 p.

–, *Down there on a Visit*, London, Methuen, 1962, 271 p.

Hans Henny JAHNN, *Perrudja* [1929], Paris, José Corti, 1995, 802 p.

Marcel JOUHANDEAU, *De l'abjection*, Paris, Gallimard, 1939, 156 p.

–,*Mémorial IV. Apprentis et garçons*, Paris, Gallimard, 1953, 161 p.

Eric KÄSTNER, *Fabian*, Paris, Balland, 1931, 308 p.

Jacques de LACRETELLE, *La Bonifas* [1925], Paris, Gallimard, 1979, 338 p.

D.H. LAWRENCE, *Le Paon blanc* [1911], Paris, Calmann-Lévy, 1983, 413 p.

–,*Women in Love* [1921], London, Penguin, 1960, 541 p.

–,*Kangourou* [1923], Paris, Gallimard, 1996, 668 p.

T.E. LAWRENCE, *Les Sept Piliers de la sagesse* [1926], Paris, Payot, 1989, 820 p.

Rosamund LEHMANN, *Dusty Answer* [1927], London, Collins, 1978, 355 p.

Wyndham LEWIS, *The Apes of God* [1930], London, Penguin, 1965, 650 p.

Compton MACKENZIE, *Vestal Fire* [1927], London, The Hogarth Press, 1986, 420 p.

–,*Extraordinary Women* [1928], London, The Hogarth Press, 1986, 392 p.

Klaus MANN, *La Danse pieuse* [1925], Paris, Grasset, 1993, 272 p.

–,*Le Tournant* [1949], Paris, Solin, 1984, 690 p.

Thomas MANN, *Tonio Kröger* [1903], Paris, Stock, 1923, 124 p.

–,*La Mort à Venise* [1912], Paris, Fayard, 1971, 189 p.

–,*La Montagne magique* [1924], Paris, Le Livre de poche, 1977, 2 vol., 509 p.

Victor MARGUERITTE, *La Garçonne* [1922], Paris, Flammarion, 1978, 269 p.

Roger MARTIN DU GARD, *Le Cahier gris*, in *Œuvres complètes*, Paris, Gallimard, coll. "Bibl. de la Pléiade," 1981, t.I, 1 403 p.

–,*Un taciturne*, in *Œuvres complètes*, ibid., 1983, t.II, 1 432 p.

Henry MARX, *Ryls, un amour hors la loi*, Paris, Ollendorff, 1923, 252 p.

MÉNALKAS (pseud. Suzanne de CALLIAS), *Erna, jeune fille de Berlin*, Paris, Éditions des Portiques, 1932, 254 p.

Francis de MIOMANDRE, *Ces Petits Messieurs*, Paris, Émile-Paul frères, 1922, 258 p.

Henry de MONTHERLANT, *Les Garçons*, Paris, Gallimard, 1973, 549 p.

Robert MUSIL, *Les Désarrois de l'élève Törless* [1906], Paris, Éditions du Seuil, 1960, 250 p.

Beverley NICHOLS, *Patchwork*, London, Chatto & Windus, 1921, 305 p.

OLIVIA (pseud. Dorothy BUSSY), *Olivia*, Paris, Stock, 1949, 148 p.

Wilfred OWEN, *The Poems of Wilfred Owen*, ed. by Jon Stallworthy, London, The Hogarth Press, 1985, 200 p.

Fortuné PAILLOT, *Amant ou maîtresse, ou l'androgyne perplexe*, Paris, Flammarion, 1922, 283 p.

Liane de POUGY, *Idylle saphique* [1901], Paris, Lattès, 1979, 272 p.

Marcel PROUST, *A la recherche du temps perdu*, Paris, Gallimard, coll. "Bibl. de la Pléiade," 4 vol., 1987-1989.

Adela QUEBEC (pseudonyme), *The Girls of Radclyffe Hall*, "printed for the author for private circulation only," London, 1935, 100 p.

RADCLYFFE HALL, *The Well of Loneliness* [1928], London, Virago Press, 1982, 447 p.

Ernest RAYMOND, *Tell England: A Study in a Generation*, London, Cassell & Cie, 1922, 320 p.

Paul REBOUX, *Le Jeune Amant*, Paris, Flammarion, 1928, 289 p.

Charles-Noël RENARD, *Les Androphobes*, Saint-Étienne, Impr. spéciale d'édition, 1930, 324 p.

Maurice ROSTAND, *La Femme qui était en lui*, Paris, Flammarion, 1937, 127 p.

Alain ROX, *Tu seras seul*, Paris, Flammarion, 1936, 403 p.

Naomi ROYDE-SMITH, *The Tortoiseshell Cat*, London, Constable, 1925, 310 p.

–,The Island, *A Love Story*, London, Constable, 1930, 328 p.

Maurice SACHS, *Alias* [1935], Paris, Éditions d'Aujourd'hui, 1976, 220 p.

–,*Le Sabbat* [written in1939, published in1946], Paris, Gallimard, 1960, 298 p.

Vita SACKVILLE-WEST, *Ceux des îles* [1924], Paris, Salvy, 1994, 360 p.

SAGITTA (J.H. MACKAY), *Der Puppenjunge* [1926], Berlin, Verlag E.C.H., 1975, 367 p.

Ernst von SALOMON, *Les Réprouvés* [1930], Paris, Plon, 1986, 378 p.

–,*Les Cadets* [1933], Paris, Correa, 1953, 277 p.

Siegfried SASSOON, *Collected Poems*, 1908-1956, London, Faber & Faber, 1984, 317 p.

Dorothy SAYERS, *L'autopsie n'a rien donné* [*Unnatural Death*, 1927], Paris-London, Morgan, 1947, 253 p.

Stephen SPENDER, *Le Temple* [*The Temple*, 1929], Paris, Christian Bourgois, 1989, 310 p.

Violet TREFUSIS, *Broderie anglaise* [1935], Paris, UGE, coll. "10/18," 1986, 185 p.

Bruno VOGEL, *Alf*, Berlin, Gilde freiheitlicher Bücherfreunde, 1929, 349 p.

Alec WAUGH, *Pleasure*, London, Grant Richards Ltd, 1921, 320 p.

Evelyn WAUGH, *Retour à Brideshead* [*Brideshead Revisited*, 1947], Paris, UGE, coll. "10/18," 1991, 429 p.

–,*Ces corps vils*, Paris, UGE, coll. "10/18," 1991, 245 p.

A.E. WEIRAUCH, *Der Skorpion*, Berlin, Crest Book, 1964, 192 p.

WILLY et MÉNALKAS, *L'Ersatz d'amour*, Amiens, Librairie Edgar Malfère, 1923, 206 p.

–,*Le Naufragé*, Amiens, Librairie Edgar Malfère, 1924, 181 p.

Christa WINSLOE, *Manuela ou Jeunes filles en uniformes*, Paris, Stock, 1934, 253 p.

Virginia WOOLF, *Mrs Dalloway* [1923], Paris, Stock, 1988, 220 p.

–,*Orlando* [1928], Paris, Stock, 1974, 351 p.

Francis Brett YOUNG, *White Ladies*, London, Heinemann, 1965, 693 p.

Marguerite YOURCENAR, *Alexis ou le Traité du vain combat* [1929], Paris, Gallimard, 1971, 248 p.

–,*Le Coup de grâce* [1939], Paris, Gallimard, 1971, 248 p.

Stefan ZWEIG, *La Confusion des sentiments* [1926], Paris, Le Livre de poche, 1991, 127 p.

C.   *Testimonies*

1– Memoirs, autobiographies, personal journals, interviews

J.R. ACKERLEY, *My Father and Myself* [1968], London, Penguin, 1971, 192 p.

Valentine ACKLAND, *For Sylvia: An Honest Account*, London, Chatto & Windus, 1985, 135 p.

Harold ACTON, *Memoirs of an Aesthete* [1948], London, Hamish Hamilton, 1984, 416 p.

Noel ANNAN, Our Age: English Intellectuals between the Wars: A Group Portrait, New York, Random House, 1991, 479 p.

Natalie BARNEY, *Souvenirs indiscrets*, Paris, Flammarion, 1960, 234 p.

Simone de BEAUVOIR, *Mémoires d'une jeune fille rangée* [1958], Paris, Gallimard, 1995, 503 p.

Claude CAHUN, *Aveux non avenus*, Paris, Éditions du Carrefour, 1930, 238 p.

Jean COCTEAU, *Portraits-Souvenir 1900-1914*, Paris, Grasset, 1935, 253 p.

Quentin CRISP, *The Naked Civil-Servant* [1968], London, Fontana, 1986, 217 p.

Pierre DRIEU LA ROCHELLE, *Journal 1939-1945*, Paris, Gallimard, coll. "Témoins," 1992, 519 p.André GIDE, *Journal*, 1887-1925, Paris, Gallimard, coll. "Bibl. de la Pléiade," 1996, 1 840 p.

–, *Journal, 1889-1939*, Paris, Gallimard, coll. "Bibl. de la Pléiade," 1951, 1374 p.

–,*Si le grain ne meurt* [1926], Paris, Gallimard, coll. "Folio," 1986, 372 p.

Daniel GUÉRIN, *Autobiographie de jeunesse*, Paris, Belfond, 1972, 248 p.

–,Le Feu du sang: autobiographie politique et charnelle, Paris, Grasset, 1977, 286 p.

Cecily HAMILTON, *Life Errant*, London, J.M. Dent & Sons Ltd, 1935, 300 p.

Heinz HEGER, Les Hommes au triangle rose. Journal d'un déporté homosexuel, 1939-1945, Paris, Éditions Persona, 1981, 160 p.

Christopher ISHERWOOD, *Christopher and His Kind* [1929-1939], London, Methuen, 1977, 252 p.

–,*Lions and Shadows* [1938], London, Methuen, 1985, 191 p.

Marcel JOUHANDEAU, *Chronique d'une passion* [1949], Paris, Gallimard, 1964, 223 p.

Violette LEDUC, *L'Affamée*, Paris, Gallimard, 1948, 197 p.

–,*La Bâtarde*, Paris, Gallimard, 1964, 462 p.

Ella MAILLART, *La Voie cruelle* [1947], Paris, France Loisirs, 1987, 369 p.

Golo MANN, *Une jeunesse allemande*, Paris, Presses de la Renaissance, 1988, 412 p.

Klaus MANN, *Kind dieser Zeit* [1938], Munich, Nymphenburger Verlagshandlung, 1965, 264 p.

–,Journal. Les années brunes, 1931-1936, Paris, Grasset, 1996, 452 p.

Robin MAUGHAM, *Escape from the Shadows* [1940], London, Cardinal, 1991, 472 p.

Walter MUSCHG, *Entretiens avec Hans Henny Jahnn*, Paris, José Corti, 1995, 203 p.

Suzanne NEILD and Rosalind PARSON, *Women Like Us*, London, The Women's Press, 1992, 171 p.

Nigel NICOLSON, *Portrait d'un mariage* [1973], Paris, Stock, 1992, 319 p.

Ernst Erich NOTH, *Mémoires d'un Allemand*, Paris, Julliard, 1970, 506 p.

Dennis PROCTOR (ed.), *The Autobiography of G. Lowes Dickinson*, London, Duckworth, 1973, 287 p.

Francis ROSE (Sir), *Saying Life*, London, Cassell & Cie, 1961, 416 p.

Maurice SACHS, *Au temps du "Bœuf sur le toit"* [1939], Paris, Grasset, 1987, 235 p.

Annemarie SCHWARZENBACH, *La Mort en Perse* [written in1935], Paris, Payot, 1997, 161 p.

Pierre SEEL, *Moi Pierre Seel, déporté homosexuel*, Paris, Calmann-Lévy, 1994, 198 p.

Nicolaus SOMBART, *Chroniques d'une jeunesse berlinoise, 1933-1943*, Paris, Quai Voltaire, 1992, 369 p.

Stephen SPENDER, *World within World* [1951], London, Faber & Faber, 1991, 344 p.

Charlotte WOLFF, *Hindsight*, London, Quartet Books, 1980, 312 p.

Virginia WOOLF, *Instants de vie* [1976], Paris, Stock, 1986, 273 p.

T.C. WORSLEY, Flannelled Fool. A Slice of Life in the Thirties, London, Alan Ross, 1967, 213 p.

Marguerite YOURCENAR, *Quoi? L'éternité*, Paris, Gallimard, 1988, 340 p.

2- Correspondence

Cyril CONNOLLY, A Romantic Friendship, The Letters of Cyril Connolly to Noel Blakiston, London, Constable, 1975, 365 p.

Correspondance André Gide/Dorothy Bussy, Jan. 1925-Nov.1936, Paris, Gallimard, Cahiers André Gide, 1981, t.II, 650 p.

Klaus MANN, *Briefe und Antworten*, vol.1, 1922-1937, Munich, Spangenberg, 1975, 405 p.

Donald MITCHELL and Philip REED (ed.), *Letters from a Life, Selected Letters and Diaries of Benjamin Britten*, vol.1, 1923-1939, vol.2, 1939-1945, London, Faber & Faber, 1991, 619 and 1 403 p.

Louise de SALVO and Mitchell A. LEASKA (ed.), *The Letters of Vita Sackville-West to Virginia Woolf*, London, Hutchinson, 1984, 473 p.

Violet TREFUSIS, *Lettres à Vita, 1910-1921*, Paris, Stock, 1991, 509 p.

Virginia WOOLF, *Paper Darts, The Illustrated Letters*, London, Collins, 1991, 160 p.

3– Oral testimonies

The following works are based on oral testimony given by gays and lesbians who lived during the period under discussion.

Gay Men's Oral History Group, *Walking after Midnight. Gay Men's Life Stories*, Hall-Carpenter Archives, London, Routledge, 1989, 238 p.

Joachim S. HOHMANN (ED.), Keine Zeit für gute Freunde, Homosexuelle in Deutschland, 1933-1969, Berlin, Foerster Verlag, 1982, 208 p.

Lesbian Oral History Group, *Inventing Ourselves. Lesbian Life Stories*, Hall-Carpenter Archives, London, Routledge, 1989, 228 p.

Kevin PORTER and Jeffrey WEEKS (ed.), *Between the Acts. Lives of Homosexual Men, 1885-1967*, London, Routledge, 1991, 153 p.

SECONDARY SOURCES

A. France, England and Germany in the Twenties and Thirties: reference works

The following works provide the political, economic and social context in which the hisroty of homosexzuality evolved. Of course, there are thousands of books onthe history of Germany, England and France during the 1920s and 1930s; in a somewhat arbitraty manner I have selected a certain number of works that seemed indispensible in developing an understanding of the era, with a preference for synthetic works and those research works that contribute to an understanding of the history of sexuality and public atitudes.

1– Epistemology
A few works that indicate the value of a history of sexuality, of atitudes and behaviors.

Guy BOURDE and Hervé MARTIN, *Les Écoles historiques*, Paris, Éditions du Seuil, coll. "Points histoire",1989, 413 p.

Alain BOUREAU, "Propositions pour une histoire restreinte des mentalités," in *Annales ESC*, November-December 1989.

Maurice HALBWACHS, *La Mémoire collective*, Paris, PUF, 1950, 170 p.

Pierre LABORIE, "De l'opinion publique à l'imaginaire social," in *XXe siècle*, n° 18, April-June 1988.

Jacques LE GOFF (dir), *La Nouvelle Histoire*, Bruxelles, Complexe, 1988, 334 p.

Bernard LEPETIT, Les Formes de l'expérience, une autre histoire sociale, Paris, Albin Michel, 1995, 337 p.

Denis PESCHANSKI, Michael POLLACK and Henri ROUSSO, *Histoire politique and sciences sociales*, Bruxelles, Complexe, 1991, 285 p.

2– History of sexuality

These were groundbreaking works in the history of sexuality and which provide a broader context within which to consider the history of homosexuality in the between-war era. These works also suggest new angles to be researched and suggest an approach to the endeavor.

Amour et sexualité en Occident, Paris, Éditions du Seuil, coll. "Points histoire," 1991, 335 p.

Alain CORBIN, Les Filles de noce. Misère sexuelle et prostitution au xixe siècle, Paris, Flammarion, 1978, 496 p.

Jean-Louis FLANDRIN, *L'Église et le Contrôle des naissances*, Paris, Flammarion, 1970, 133 p.

–,*Le Sexe et l'Occident*, Paris, Éditions du Seuil, coll. "Points histoire," 1981, 375 p.

–,*Familles, parenté, maison, sexualité dans l'ancienne société*, Paris, Éditions du Seuil, coll. "Points histoire," 1984, 332 p.

–,Les Amours paysannes, XVIe-xixe siècle, Paris, Gallimard, 1993, 334 p.

Michel FOUCAULT, *Histoire de la sexualité*, t.I, La Volonté de savoir, Paris, Gallimard, 1976, 211 p.

Philippe PERROT, *Le Corps féminin, xviiie-xixe siècle*, Paris, Éditions du Seuil, coll. "Points histoire," 1984, 279 p.

Anne-Marie SOHN, Du premier baiser à l'alcôve, la sexualité des Français au quotidien (1850-1950), Paris, Aubier, 1996, 310 p.

3– Politics

Fabrice ABBAD, *La France des années vingt*, Paris, Armand Colin, 1993, 190 p.

L'Allemagne de Hitler, 1933-1945, Paris, Éditions du Seuil, coll. "Points histoire," 1991, 420 p.

Jean-Pierre AZÉMA and Michel WINOCK, *La Troisième République*, Paris, Calmann-Lévy, 1976, 520 p.

Hannah ARENDT, *Les Origines du totalitarisme*, t.III, Le Système totalitaire, Paris, Éditions du Seuil, coll. "Points politique," 1972, 313 p.

Pierre AYCOBERRY, *La Question nazie*, Paris, Éditions du Seuil, coll. "Points histoire," 1979, 314 p.

Jean-Jacques BECKER, *La France en guerre (1914-1918)*, Bruxelles, Complexe, 1988, 221 p.

Jean-Jacques BECKER and Serge BERSTEIN, *Victoire et frustrations, 1914-1929*, Paris, Éditions du Seuil, coll. "Points histoire," 1990, 455 p.

Serge BERSTEIN, *La France des années trente*, Paris, Armand Colin, 1993, 186 p.

Serge BERSTEIN and Pierre MILZA, *Histoire du xxe siècle*, Paris, Hatier, 1987, t.I, 433 p.

–,*Histoire de l'Europe*, Paris, Hatier, 1992, t.V, 378 p.

–,*L'Allemagne, 1870-1991*, Paris, Masson, 1992, 278 p.

Dominique BORNE and Henri DUBIEF, *La Crise des années trente, 1929-1938*, Paris, Éditions du Seuil, coll. "Points histoire," 1989, 322 p.

Martin BROSZAT, *L'État hitlérien: l'origine et l'évolution des structures du IIIe Reich*, Paris, Fayard, 1985.

Jacques DROZ (dir.), *Histoire générale du socialisme*, t.III, 1919-1945, Paris, PUF, 1977, 714 p.

Eugen KOGON, *L'État SS* [1947], Paris, Éditions du Seuil, coll. "Points histoire," 1993, 445 p.

Jean MAITRON, *Le Mouvement anarchiste en France*, t.II, De 1914 à nos jours, Paris, Maspero, 1983, 435 p.

Roland MARX, *L'Angleterre de 1914 à 1945*, Paris, Armand Colin, 1993, 175 p.

François-Charles MOUGEL, *Histoire du Royaume-Uni au xxe siècle*, Paris, PUF, 1996, 600 p.

Norman PAGE, *The Thirties in Britain*, London, Macmillan, 1990, 147 p.

Detlev J.K. PEUKERT, *La République de Weimar*, Paris, Aubier, 1995, 301 p.

René RÉMOND, *Notre siècle, 1918-1988*, Paris, Fayard, 1988, 1 012 p.

Marlis STEINERT, *Hitler*, Paris, Fayard, 1991, 710 p.

Rita THALMANN, *La République de Weimar*, Paris, PUF, coll. "Que sais-je?," 1986.

David THOMSON, *England in the Twentieth Century*, London, Penguin, 1981, 382 p.

Jean TOUCHARD, *Histoire des idées politiques* [1958], Paris, PUF, 1985, t.II, 865 p.

4– Society, economics, culture

Années trente en Europe: le temps menaçant, 1929-1939, catalogue from the 20 February-25 May 1997 exposition, Paris, Paris Musées, 571 p.

André ARMENGAUD, *La Population française au xxe siècle* [1965], Paris, PUF, 1992, 127 p.

Jean-Pierre AZÉMA, *De Munich à la Libération*, Paris, Éditions du Seuil, coll. "Points histoire," 1979, 412 p.

Stéphane AUDOIN-ROUZEAU, *14-18, les combattants des tranchées*, Paris, Armand Colin, 1986, 223 p.

Christine BARD, *Les Filles de Marianne. Histoire des féminismes en France, 1914-1940*, Paris, Fayard, 1995, 528 p.

Olivier BARROT and Pascal ORY (dir.), *Entre-deux-guerres*, Paris, François Bourin, 1990, 631 p.

Jean-Jacques BECKER and Stéphane AUDOIN-ROUZEAU, *Les Sociétés européennes and la Guerre de 1914-1918*, Nanterre, Publications de l'université de Nanterre, 1990, 495 p.

François BÉDARIDA, *La Société anglaise du milieu du xixe siècle à nos jours*, Paris, Éditions du Seuil, coll. "Points histoire," 1990, 540 p.

Hans Peter BLEUEL, *La Morale des seigneurs*, Paris, Tallandier, 1974, 247 p.

Renate BRIDENTHAL, Atina GROSSMANN and Marion KAPLAN, *When Biology Became Destiny, Women in Weimar and Nazi Germany*, New York, Monthly Review Press, 1984, 364 p.

Renate BRIDENTHAL, Claudia KOONZ and Susan STUARD, *Becoming Visible, Women in European History*, Boston, Houghton Mifflin Cie, 1987, 579 p.

Asa BRIGGS, *A Social History of England*, London, Weidenfeld & Nicolson, nouvelle éd., 1994, 348 p.

Claude CAHUN, *Photographie*, exhibition catalogue from the 23 June-17 September 1995 show, Paris, Paris Musées, 169 p.

Jean-Louis CRÉMIEUX-BRILHAC, *Les Français de l'an quarante*, Paris, Gallimard, 1990, 2 vol., 647 and 740 p.

Dominique DESANTI, *La Femme au temps des années folles*, Paris, Stock, 1984, 373 p.

Yvonne DESLANDRES and Florence MULLER, *Histoire de la mode au xxe siècle*, Paris, Somogy, 1986, 404 p.

Georges DUBY and Michelle PERROT (dir.), *Histoire des femmes en Occident*, Paris, Plon, 1992, t.V, 647 p.

Modnis EKSTEINS, *"Le Sacre du Printemps," la Grande Guerre et la Naissance de la modernité*, Paris, Plon, 1989, 424 p.

André ENCREVÉ, *Les Protestants en France de 1800 à nos jours*, Paris, Stock, 1985, 276 p.

Norbert FREI, *L'État hitlérien and la Société allemande*, 1933-1945, Paris, Éditions du Seuil, 1994, 369 p.

Paul FUSSELL, *The Great War and Modern Memory*, Oxford, Oxford University Press, 1975, 363 p.

Peter GAY, *Le Suicide d'une république, Weimar 1918-1933*, Paris, Gallimard, 1993, 268 p.

Richard GRUNBERGER, *A Social History of the Third Reich*, London, Weidenfeld & Nicolson, 1971, 535 p.

Pierre GUILLAUME, *Médecins, Église et foi*, Paris, Aubier, 1990, 267 p.

Guerres et cultures (1914-1918), a collective work, Paris, Armand Colin, 1994, 445 p.

Samuel HYNES, *A War Imagined, The First War World and English Culture*, New York, Atheneum, 1991, 514 p.

Claudia KOONZ, *Les Mères-patries du IIIe Reich*, Paris, Lieu Commun, 1989, 553 p.

Sergiusz MICHALSKI, *Nouvelle objectivité*, Cologne, Taschen, 1994, 219 p.

Jean-Pierre NORDIER, *Les Débuts de la psychanalyse en France, 1895-1926*, Paris, Maspero, 1981, 274 p.

Jean-Michel PALMIER, *Weimar en exil*, Paris, Payot, 1988, t.I and II, 533 and 486 p.

Antoine PROST, *Histoire de l'enseignement en France, 1800-1967*, Paris, Armand Colin, 1968, 524 p.

-,*Les Anciens Combattants et la Société française, 1914-1939*, Paris, Presses de la FNSP, 1977, 3 vol., 237, 261 and 268 p.

Lionel RICHARD, *La Vie quotidienne sous la République de Weimar*, Paris, Hachette, 1983, 322 p.

Paul ROAZEN, *La Saga freudienne*, Paris, PUF, 1976, 474 p.

Marcel SCHEIDHAUER, *Le Rêve freudien en France, 1900-1926*, Paris, Navarin, 1985, 227 p.

Jean-François SIRINELLI, *Génération intellectuelle,* Paris, PUF, 1994, 720 p.

Rita THALMANN, *Être femme sous le IIIe Reich*, Paris, Robert Laffont, 1982.

Françoise THÉBAUD, *La Femme au temps de la guerre de 1914*, Paris, Stock, 1986, 314 p.

John WILLETT, *L'Esprit de Weimar. Avant-gardes et politique, 1917-1933*, Paris, Éditions du Seuil, 1991, 287 p.

Robert WOHL, *The Generation of 1914*, London, Weidenfeld & Nicolson, 1980, 307 p.

Théodore ZELDIN, *Histoire des passions françaises, ambition et amour, 1845-1945*, Paris, Payot, reprinted. 1994, 1 278 p.

B. History of Homosexuality

The history of homosexuality has only just begun; nonetheless, there is already a plethora of bibliographic sources, mainly for the post-World War II period. These works are of very uneven quality (some do not follow the norms of scholarly research, and some are too biased); I will indicate a few of those which I found most useful. I have also listed some of the better-known works, noting those I consider to be flawed).

1- Bibliographies

There are many bibliographies on homosexuality, but rarely do they touch on the period anterior to the Second World War. The following titles may help guide further research.

Vern L. BULLOUGH, *An Annotated Bibliography of Homosexuality*, New York, Garland, 1976, 2 vol.

Claude COUROUVE, *Bibliographie des homosexualités*, Paris, Nouvelles Éditions, 1978, 27 p.

Waynes R. DYNES, *Homosexuality: A Research Guide*, New York, Garland, 1987, 853 p.

Manfred HERZER, *Bibliographie zur Homosexualität*, Berlin, Verlag Rosa Winkel, 1982, 255 p.

2- General works

These works are good background for a general approach to homosexual history between the wars. Most of them emphasize the homosexual movements.

Barry D. ADAM, *The Rise of a Gay and Lesbian Movement*, Boston, Twaynes Publishers, 1987, 203 p.

Jean BOISSON, *Le Triangle rose. La déportation des homosexuels (1933-1945)*, Paris, Robert Laffont, 1988, 247 p. [à éviter, peu fiable; se rapporter à l'historiographie allemande].

Richard DAVENPORT-HINES, *Sex, Death and Punishment*, London, Fontana Press, 1990, 439 p. [très utile].

Martin DUBERMAN, Martha VICINUS and George CHAUNCEY Jr (dir.), *Hidden from History*, London, Penguin Books, 1991, 579 p. [an especially valuable series of articles].

Waynes R. DYNES (dir.), *Encyclopedia of Homosexuality*, New York-London, Garland, 1990, vol.1 and 2, 1484 p. [the articles are for the mos part on homosexual figures and the important dates in homosexual history; very useful].

Eldorado, homosexual Frauen und Männer in Berlin, 1850-1950, Geschichte, Alltag und Kultur, Berlin, Fröhlich und Kaufmann, 1984, 216 p. [catalogue from the exposition on homosexuality under Weimar; indispensible].

Günther GRAU (ed.), *Hidden Holocaust? Gay and Lesbian Persecution in Germany, 1933-1945*, London, Cassell & Cie, 1995, 308 p., trans. from German: *Homosexualität in der NS-Zeit: Dokumente einer Diskriminierung und Verfolgung*, Frankfurt-am-Main, Fischer Taschenbuch Verlag, 1993 [fundamental: collected from archives on the persecution of homosexuals in Nazi Germany].

Joachim S. HOHMANN, *Der unterdrückte Sexus*, Lollar, Achenbach, 1977, 627 p.

–,*Der heimliche Sexus*, Frankfurt-am-Main, Foerster Verlag, 1979, 330 p.

100 Jahre Schwulenbewegung, Berlin, Schwules Museum, 1997, 384 p.

Burckhard JELLONNEK, *Homosexuelle unter dem Hakenkreuz*, Paderborn, Schöningh, 1990, 354 p. [indispensible].

John LAURITSEN and David THORSTAD, *The Early Homosexual Rights Movement (1864-1935)*, New York, Times Changes Press, 1974, 91 p. [un ouvrage pionnier].

Rüdiger LAUTMANN, *Seminar: Gesellschaft und Homosexualität*, Frankfurt-am-Main, Suhrkamp Taschenbuch, 1977, 570 p. [this is a fundamental work, much of which has been borrowed by later writers].

–,*Terror und Hoffnung in Deutschland, 1933-1945*, Reinbek, Rowohlt, 1980, 570 p.

Salvatore J. LICATA and Robert P. PETERSEN, *The Gay Past: A Collection of Historical Essays*, New York, Harrington Park Press, 1985, 224 p.

Neil MILLER, *Out of the Past, Gay and Lesbian History from 1869 to the Present*, London, Vintage, 1995, 657 p. [a synthetic work, with excerpts from period documents].

Harry OOSTERHUIS and Hubert KENNEDY (dir.), *Homosexuality and Male Bonding in Pre-Nazi Germany*, New York, The Haworth Press, 1991, 271 p.

Richard PLANT, *The Pink Triangle*, New York, Holt & Cie, 1986, 257 p. [indispensible].

A.L. ROWSE, *Les Homosexuels célèbres*, Paris, Albin Michel, 1980, 310 p. [ouvrage très connu and à éviter: anecdotique and complaisant].

Heinz-Dieter SCHILLING (dir.), *Schwule und Faschismus*, Berlin, Elefanten Presse, 1983, 174 p. [très utile].

James D. STEAKLEY, *The Homosexual Emancipation Movement in Germany*, New York, Arno Press, 1975, 121 p. [a pioneering work that offersa solid approach to the question].

Hans-Georg STÜMKE, *Homosexuelle in Deutschland, eine politische Geschichte*, Munich, Verlag C.H. Beck, 1989, 184 p. [very rich].

Hans-Georg STÜMKE and Rudi FINKLER, *Rosa Winkel, Rosa Listen, Homosexuelle und "gesundes Volksempfinden" von Auschwitz bis heute*, Reinbeck, Rowohlt, 1981, 512 p.

Jeffrey WEEKS, *Coming Out. Homosexual Politics in Britain from the 19th Century to the Present*, London, Quartet Books, 1979, 278 p. [indispensible resource on homosexuality in Great Britain].

–,*Sex, Politics and Society*, London, Longman, 1989, 325 p. [larger than the preceding work but very useful].

3– Homosexual and lesbian theory

Simone de BEAUVOIR, *Le Deuxième Sexe*, Paris, France Loisirs, 1990, 1059 p.

Evelyn BLACKWOOD, *The Many Faces of Homosexuality, Anthropological Approaches to Homosexual Behavior*, New York, Harrington Park Press, 1986, 217 p.

Vern L. BULLOUGH, *Sin, Sickness and Sanity*, New York, Garland, 1977, 276 p.

Susan CAVIN, *Lesbian Origins*, San Francisco, Ism Press, 1989, 288 p.

Susan FALUDI, *Backlash*, Paris, Des femmes, 1993, 743 p.

Gay Left Collective (dir.), *Homosexuality, Power and Politics*, London, Allison & Busby, 1980, 223 p.

David F. GREENBERG, *The Construction of Homosexuality*, Chicago, The University of Chicago Press, 1988, 635 p.

Daniel GUÉRIN, *Essai sur la révolution sexuelle*, Paris, Belfond, 1969, 247 p.

–,*Homosexualité et révolution*, Paris, Utopie, coll. "Les Cahiers du vent du ch'min," 1983, 66 p.

Guy HOCQUENGHEM, *Le Désir homosexuel*, Paris, Éditions universitaires, 1972, 125 p.

Sheila JEFFREYS, *The Lesbian Heresy: A Feminist Perspective on the Lesbian Sexual Revolution*, New York, Spirifex Press, 1993, 262 p.

Leeds Revolutionary Feminist Group, *Love your Enemy? The Debate between Feminists and Political Lesbianism*, Leeds, Only Feminist Press, 1981, 68 p.

Kate MILLETT, *La Politique du mâle*, Paris, Stock, 1971, 463 p.

Kenneth PLUMMER (dir.), *The Making of the Modern Homosexual*, London, Hutchinson, 1981, 380 p. [the best, it presents the different theses and conflicting perspectives].

4– Works on lesbians

Marie-Jo BONNET, *Les relations amoureuses entre les femmes du XVIe au XXe siècle*, Paris, Odile Jacob, 1995, 416 p.

Claudine BRECOURT-VILLARS, *Petit glossaire raisonné de l'érotisme saphique, 1880-1930*, Paris, La Vue, 1980, 123 p.

Terry CASTLE, *The Apparitional Lesbian, Female Homosexuality and Male Culture*, New York, Columbia University Press, 1993, 307 p.

Lillian FADERMAN, *Surpassing the Love of Men*, New York, Morran & Cie, 1981, 496 p. [indispensible; une étude novatrice].

Sheila JEFFREYS, *The Spinster and Her Enemies: Feminism and Sexuality, 1880-1930*, London, Pandora, 1985, 282 p. [très utile].

Ilse KOKULA, *Weibliche Homosexualität um 1900 in zeitgenössischen Dokumenten*, Berlin, Frauenoffensive, 1981, 288 p.

Lesbian History Group, *Not a Passing Phase. Reclaiming Lesbians in History, 1840-1985*, London, The Women's Press, 1989, 264 p. [intéressant].

Claudie LESSELIER, *Aspects de l'expérience lesbienne en France, 1930-1968*, from the post-graduate dept. of sociologie, Paris-VIII, under the direction of R. Castel, November 1987, 148 p. [very useful on France].

Das Lila Wien um 1900, zur Ästhetik der Homosexualitäten, Vienna, Promedia, 1986, 127 p. [a reference on decadent Vienna].

Jane RULE, *Lesbian Images*, New York, Doubleday & Cie, 1975, 246 p.

Claudia SCHOPPMANN, *Der Skorpion, Frauenliebe in der Weimarer Republik*, Berlin, Frühlings Erwachen, 1984, 81 p.

–,*Nationalsozialistische Sexualpolitik und weibliche Homosexualität*, Berlin, Centaurus, 1991, 286 p. [fondamental].

Kristine von SODEN and Maruta SCHMIDT (dir.), *Neue Frauen, die zwanziger Jahre*, Berlin, Elefanten Presse, 1988, 176 p.

Eric TRUDGILL, *Madonnas and Magdalens*, London, Heinemann, 1976, 336 p.

Catherine VAN CASSELAER, *Lot's Wife, Lesbian Paris, 1890-1914*, Liverpool, The Janus Press, 1986, 176 p.

5– Specific works

These works deal with an aspect of the situation of homosexuality in the between-war period or shed light on certain points in the history of homosexuality.

Jean-Paul ARON and Roger KEMPF, *Le Pénis et la Démoralisation de l'Occident*, Paris, Grasset, 1978, 306 p.

Gilles BARBEDETTE and Michel CARASSOU, *Paris gay 1925*, Paris, Presses de la Renaissance, 1981, 312 p. [one of the few French works].

Hans Peter BLEUEL, *Strength through Joy, Sex and Society in National-Socialist Germany*, London, Pan Books, 1973, 352 p.

John BOSWELL, *Christianisme, tolérance sociale et homosexualité. Les homosexuels en Europe occidentale des débuts de l'ère chrétienne au XVIe siècle*, Paris, Gallimard, 1985, 521p.

–,*Les Unions du même sexe dans l'Europe antique et médiévale*, Paris, Fayard, 1996, 537 p.

BRASSAI, *Le Paris secret des années trente*, Paris, Gallimard, 1976, 190 p.

Vern L. BULLOUGH, "Challenges to Societal Attitudes towards Homosexuality in the Late Nineteenth and Early Twentieth Centuries," *Social Science Quarterly*, June 1977, vol.58, n° 1, p.29-41.

Peter COLEMAN, *Christian Attitudes to Homosexuality*, London, SPCK, 1980, 310 p. [a very useful synthesis on the Church's attitudetoward homosexuality].

Emmanuel COOPER, *The Sexual Perspective: Homosexuality and Art in the Last 100 Years in the West*, London, Routledge & Kegan, 1986, 324 p. [excellent].

Anthony COPLEY, *Sexual Moralities in France, 1780-1980. New Ideas on Family, Divorce and Homosexuality, An Essay on Moral Change*, London, Routledge, 1989, 283 p. [very rich].

Claude COUROUVE, *Les Homosexuels et les Autres*, Paris, Éditions de l'Athanor, 1977, 155 p.

–,*Les Origines de la répression de l'homosexualité*, Paris, C. Courouve, coll. "Archives des homosexualités," 1978, 19 p.

–,*Vocabulaire de l'homosexualité masculine*, Paris, Payot, 1985, 248 p.

Jean DANET, *Discours juridique et perversions sexuelles (xixe-xxe siècle)*, Nantes, University of Nantes, 1977, vol.6, 105 p. [a remarkable work, indispensible for an understanding of France's legal position on homosexuality].

W.U. EISSLER, *Arbeiterparteien und Homosexuellenfrage zur Sexualpolitik von SPD und KPD in der Weimarer Republik*, Berlin, Verlag Rosa Winkel, 1980, 142 p. [indispensible, on the atttitude of the German leftist parties toward homosexuality].

Thierry FÉRAL, *Nazisme et psychanalyse*, Paris, La Pensée universelle, 1987, 92 p.

Hubert FICHTE, *Homosexualität und Literatur*, Frankfurt-am-Main, S. Fischer, 1987-1988, t.I et II, 502 et 359 p. [complexe].

Lain FINLAYSON, "Gay Dress," in *Gay News*, n° 60, p.19.

John GATHORNE-HARDY, *The Public-School Phenomenon, 1597-1977*, London, Hodder & Stoughton, 1977, 478 p. [the best work on this question, and contains personal testimonies].

Ulfried GEUTER, *Homosexualität in der deutschen Jugendbewegung*, Frankfurt-am-Main, Suhrkamp, 1994, 373 p.

Arthur N. GILBERT, "Conception of Homosexuality and Sodomy in Western History," in *Journal of Homosexuality*, vol.6, nos 1-2, fall-winter 1980-1981.

Günther GOLLNER, *Homosexualität, Ideologiekritik und Entmythologisierung einer Gesetzgebung*, Berlin, Duncker und Humblot, 1974, 264 p.

Heide GÖTTNER-ABENDROTH, *Das Matriarchat I*, Stuttgart-Cologne-Berlin, Verlag W. Kohlhammer, 1989, 192 p.

Kurt HILLER, "Against Injustice," in *Gay News*, n° 98, p.15-16.

Hans Günther HOCKERTS, *Die Sittlichkeitsprozesse gegen katholische Ordensangehörige und Priester, 1936-1937*, Mayence, Mathias Grünewald Verlag, 1971, 224 p. [a good synthesis on the Nazi trials against the Catholic Church].

Joachim S. HOHMANN, *Sexualforschung und -aufklärung in der Weimarer Republik*, Berlin, Foerster Verlag, 1985, 300 p. [very useful].

Homosexualität und Wissenschaft, collective work, Berlin, Verlag Rosa Winkel, 1992, 287 p.

Ronald HYAM, *Empire and Sexuality: The British Experience*, Manchester, Manchester University Press, 1990, 234 p.

H. Montgomery HYDE, *A Tangled Web, Sex Scandals in British Politics and Society*, London, Constable, 1986, 380 p. [anecdotique, à éviter].

James W. JONES, *"We of the Third Sex," Literary Representations of Homosexuality in Wilhelmin Germany*, New York, Peter Lang, 1990, 346 p.

Philippe JULLIAN, Montmartre, Bruxelles, Séquoia, 1979, 206 p.

Friedrich KOCH, *Sexuelle Denunziation, die Sexualität in der politischen Auseinandersetzung*, Frankfurt-am-Main, Syndikat, 1986, 223 p.

Thomas KOEBNER, Rolf-Peter JANZ and Frank TROMMLER (dir.), *"Mit uns zieht die neue Zeit." Der Mythos Jugend*, Frankfurt-am-Main, Suhrkamp, 1985, 621 p. [very rich on the youth myth in Germany].

Rüdiger LAUTMANN (dir.), *Männerliebe im alten Deutschland*, Berlin, Verlag Rosa Winkel, 1992, 268 p.

Cornelia LIMPRICHT, Jürgen MÜLLER and Nina OXENIUS, *"Verführte" Männer, das Leben der Kölner Homosexuellen im Dritten Reich*, Cologne, Volksblatt Verlag, 1991, 146 p. [a rare work on homosexuality outside the cities].

Andrew LUMSDEN, "Censorship in Britain," in *The European Gay Review*, vol.1, 1986, p.75-81.

J.A. MANGAN and James WALVIN, *Manliness and Morality: Middle-Class Masculinity in Britain and America, 1800-1940*, Manchester, Manchester University Press, 1988, 278 p.

Hans MAYER, *Les Marginaux: femmes, juifs et homosexuels dans la littérature européenne*, Paris, Albin Michel, 1994, 535 p. [très discutable; hétérosexiste].

Jörn MEVE, *"Homosexuelle Nazis," ein Stereotyp in Politik und Literatur des Exils*, Hamburg, Männerschwarmskript, 1990, 111 p. [very useful].

George L. MOSSE, *Nationalism and Sexuality, Respect and Abnormal Sexuality in Modern Europe*, New York, Howard Fertig, 1985, 232 p. [polémique].

Rictor NORTON, "One Day They Were Simply Gone," in *Gay News*, n° 82, p.13-15.

Detlev PEUKERT, *Inside Nazi Germany, Conformity, Opposition and Racism in Everyday Life*, London, Batsford Ltd, 1987, 288 p.

Bertrand PHILBERT, *L'Homosexualité à l'écran*, Paris, Henri Veyrier, 1984, 181 p.

Klaus THEWELEIT, *Male Fantasies [Männerphantasien, 1977]*, Minneapolis, The University of Minnesota Press, 1987-1989, 2 vol., 517 p. [très contesté].

Achim THOM (dir.), *Medizin unterm Hakenkreuz*, Berlin, Verlag Volk und Gesundheit, 1989, 503 p.

Joseph WINTER, "The Law that Nearly Was," in *Gay News*, n° 79, p.11.

C. STUDIES ON INTELLECTUALS AND PROMINENT HOMOSEXUALS OF THE PERIOD

There are a great many monographs concerning homosexual intellectuals. The multiplicity of biographies and literary analyses provide a more personal history of homosexuality, allowing for a comparison of the paths chosen, the manners by which an identity was forged. Of couse, that can only offer clues on one facet of the question and still leaves us almost completely in the dark as to the daily life of the anonymous homosexuals.

1– General works

Quentin BELL, *Bloomsbury* [1968], London, Weidenfeld & Nicolson, 1986, 127 p. [a good synthesis, by someone who was close to the group].

Shari BENSTOCK, *Women of the Left Bank, Paris 1900-1940*, Austin, University of Texas Press, 1986, 518 p. [indispensible work on the "lost generation " of American lesbians in Paris].

Bernard BERGONZI, *Reading the Thirties*, London, Macmillan Press, 1978, 157 p.

Alexandra BUSCH, *Ladies of Fashion, Djuna Barnes, Natalie Barney und das Paris der 20er Jahre*, Bielefeld, Haux, 1989, 229 p. [in German].

John CAREY, *The Intellectuals and the Masses, Pride and Prejudice among the Literary Intelligentsia, 1880-1939*, London, Faber & Faber, 1992, 246 p.

Jon CLARK, Margot HEINEMANN, David MARGOLIES and Carole SNEE (dir.), *Culture and Crisis in Britain in the Thirties*, London, Lawrence & Wishart, 1979, 279 p.

Valentine CUNNINGHAM, *British Writers of the Thirties*, Oxford, Oxford University Press, 1988, 530 p. [indispensible].

Timothy D'ARCH SMITH, *Love in Earnest, Some Notes on the Lives and Writings of English "Uranian" Poets from 1889 to 1930*, London, Routledge & Keagan, 1970, 280 p. [on the little group of "Uranian" poets].

Paul FUSSELL, *Abroad, British Literary Travellers between the Wars*, Oxford, Oxford University Press, 1980, 246 p.

GALILEO, "The Gay Thirties," in *Gay News*, n° 54, p.11-12.

Martin GREEN, *Children of the Sun: A Narrative of Decadence in England after 1918*, London, Constable, 552 p. [on Brian Howard and Harold Acton; very useful].

Christopher HOLLIS, *Oxford in the Twenties, Recollection of Five Friends*, London, Heinemann, 1976, 136 p.

Samuel HYNES, *The Auden Generation*, London, Faber & Faber, 1976, 427 p. [très utile].

Incognito (George MALLORY), "Gay in the Twenties," in *Gay News*, n° 30, p.9.

Youri Ivanovitch MODINE, *Mes camarades de Cambridge*, Paris, Robert Laffont, 1994, 316 p. [sur les espions de Cambridge].

S.P. ROSENBAUM (ed.), *The Bloomsbury Group: A Collection of Memoirs, Commentary and Criticism*, London, Croom Ltd, 1975, 444 p.

Gifford SKINNER, "Cocktails in the Bath," in *Gay News*, n° 135, p.21-24.

Françoise du SORBIER (dir.), *Oxford 1919-1939*, Paris, Éditions Autrement, série "Mémoires," n° 8, Paris, 1991, 287 p. [a colection of articles and interviews; presenting a comparison between the "aesthetes" and the "athletes"].

George STAMBOLIAN and Elaine MARKS (dir.), *Homosexualities and French Literature*, London, Cornell University Press, 1979, 387 p.

Lewis D. WURGAFT, *The Activist Kurt Hiller and the Politics of Action on the German Left, 1914-1933*, Philadelphie, The American Philosophic Society, 1977, 114 p.

2– Monographs

Anthony ALPERS, *The Life of Katherine Mansfield*, New York, The Viking Press, 1980, 466 p.

Deirdre BAIR, *Simone de Beauvoir*, Paris, Fayard, 1991, 854 p.

Michael BAKER, *Our Three Selves: A Life of Radclyffe Hall*, London, Hamish Hamilton, 1985, 386 p.

Vincent BROME, *Havelock Ellis, Philosopher of Sex*, London, Routledge & Kegan, 1979, 271 p.

Robert CALDER, Willie. *The Life of Somerset Maugham*, London, Heinemann, 1989, 429 p.

Humphrey CARPENTER, *W.H. Auden, a Biography*, London, Allen & Unwin, 1981, 495 p.

–,The Brideshead Generation, Evelyn Waugh and his Friends, London, Weidenfeld & Nicolson, 1989, 523 p.

–,Benjamin Britten, a Biography, London, Faber & Faber, 1992, 680 p.

René de CECCATTY, Violette Leduc, éloge de la Bâtarde, Paris, Stock, 1994, 256 p.

Jean CHALON, Liane de Pougy, Paris, Flammarion, 1994, 389 p.

John COLMER, E.M. Forster, The Personal Voice, London, Routledge & Kegan, 1975, 243 p.

Emmanuel COOPER, The Life and Work of H.S. Tuke, 1858-1929, London, Gay Men Press, 1987, 72 p.

Michael de COSSART, Une Américaine à Paris. La princesse de Polignac et son salon, 1865-1943, Paris, Plon, 1979, 245 p.

Paul DELANY, The Neo-Pagans: Friendship and Love in the Rupert Brooke Circle, London, Macmillan, 1987, 170 p.

Éric DESCHODT, Gide, le contemporain capital, Paris, Perrin, 1991, 335 p.

Lovat DICKSON, Radclyffe Hall at the Well of Loneliness, London, Collins, 1975, 236 p.

Richard ELLMANN, Oscar Wilde, London, Hamish Hamilton, 1987, 632 p.

Michel ERMAN, Marcel Proust, Paris, Fayard, 1994, 286 p.

Andrew FIELD, Djuna Barnes, Paris, Rivages, 1986, 303 p.

Noel Riley FITCH, Sylvia Beach and the Lost Generation, New York-London, W.W. Norton & Co, 1983, 447 p.

Penelope FITZGERALD, Charlotte Mew and her Friends, London, Collins, 1984, 240 p.

Gillian FREEMAN, The Schoolgirl Ethic. The Life and Work of Angela Brazil, London, Allen Lane, 1976, 159 p.

Burdett GARDNER, The Lesbian Imagination (Victorian Style): A Psychological and Critical Study of Vernon Lee, New York, Garland, 1987, 592 p.

Victoria GLENDINNING, Edith Sitwell, a Unicorn among Lions, London, Weidenfeld & Nicolson, 1981, 391 p.

–,Vita, la vie de Vita Sackville-West, Paris, Albin Michel, 1987, 437 p.

Richard Perceval GRAVES, A.E. Housman, the Scholar-Poet, London, Routledge & Kegan, 1979, 304 p.

–,Robert Graves, The Heroic Assault, 1895-1925, London, Weidenfeld & Nicolson, 1986, 432 p.

Dominique GRENTE and Nicole MÜLLER, L'Ange inconsolable, Annemarie Schwarzenbach, Paris, Lieu commun, 1989, 274 p.

Manfred HERZER, *Magnus Hirschfeld, Leben und Werk eines jüdischen, schwulen und sozialistischen Sexologen*, Frankfurt-am-Main/New York, Campus, 1992, 189 p.

Philip HOARE, *Serious Pleasures: The Life of Stephen Tennant*, London, Penguin, 1992, 463 p.

−,*Noel Coward: A Biography*, London, Sinclair-Stevenson, 1995, 605 p.

Michael HOLROYD, *Lytton Strachey, a Biography*, London, Penguin, 1979, 1 144 p.

Christopher ISHERWOOD, "A Figure-Head, not a Leader," in *Gay News*, n° 126, p.17-19.

Francis KING, *E.M. Forster*, London, Thames & Hudson, 1978, 128 p.

Friedhelm KREY, *Hans Henny Jahnn und die mannmännliche Liebe*, Berlin, Peter Lang, 1987, 458 p.

Marianne KRÜLL, *Les Magiciens. Une autre histoire de la famille Mann*, Paris, Éditions du Seuil, 1995, 398 p.

Monique LANGE, *Cocteau, prince sans royaume*, Paris, Jean-Claude Lattès, 1989, 347 p.

James LEES-MILNE, *Harold Nicolson, a Biography (1886-1929)*, London: Chatto & Windus, 1980, vol.1, 429 p.

Herbert LOTTMAN, *Colette*, Paris, Gallimard, coll. "Folio," 1990, 496 p.

Irmela von der LÜHE, *Erika Mann, eine Biographie*, Frankfurt-am-Main/New York, Campus, 1994, 350 p.

Brenda MADDOX, *The Married man: A Life of D.H. Lawrence*, London, Sinclair-Stevenson, 1994, 652 p.

Joy MELVILLE, *Ellen and Edy: A Biography of Ellen Terry and her Daughter Edith Craigh, 1847-1947*, London, Pandora, 1987, 293 p.

Wendy MULFORD, *This Narrow Place, Sylvia Townsend Warner and Valentine Ackland, Life, Letters and Politics, 1930-1951*, London, Pandora, 1988, 276 p.

George D. PAINTER, *Marcel Proust* [1959], Paris, *Mercure de France*, 1985, 2 vol., 464 and 515 p.

Peter PARKER, *A Life of J.R. Ackerley*, London, Constable, 1989, 465 p.

Norman PITTENGER, "Wystan & Morgan," in *Gay News*, n° 156, p.23-24.

Henri RACZYMOW, *Maurice Sachs ou les Travaux forcés de la frivolité*, Paris, Gallimard, 1988, 503 p.

J.E. RIVERS, *Proust and the Art of Love*, New York, Columbia University Press, 1980, 327 p.

Jean-Louis SAINT-YGNAN, *Drieu La Rochelle ou l'Obsession de la décadence*, Paris, Nouvelles Éditions latines, 1984, 260 p.

Josyane SAVIGNEAU, *Marguerite Yourcenar, l'invention d'une vie*, Paris, Gallimard, 1990, 790 p.

W.I. SCOBIE, "Christopher Isherwood," in *Gay News*, n° 93, p.16-17.

Meryle SECREST, *Between Me and Life: A Biography of Romaine Brooks*, London, Macdonald & Jane's, 1976, 432 p.

Kenneth SIMCOX, *Wilfred Owen, Anthem for Doomed Youth*, London, Woburn Press, 1987, 166 p.

Pierre SIPRIOT, *Montherlant sans masque, t.I, L'Enfant prodigue, 1895-1932*, and t.II, *Écris avec ton sang, 1932-1972*, Paris, Robert Laffont, 1980-1990, 500 and 505 p.

Robert SKIDELSKY, *J.M. Keynes, Hopes Betrayed, 1883-1920*, London, Macmillan, 1983, 447 p.

Charles SOWERWINE and Claude MAIGNIER, *Madeleine Pelletier, une féministe dans l'arène politique*, Paris, Éditions ouvrières, 1992, 250 p.

Gillian TINDALL, *Rosamund Lehmann: An Appreciation*, London, Chatto & Windus, 1985, 201 p.

Hugo VICKERS, *Cecil Beaton*, London, Weidenfeld & Nicolson, 1985, 656 p.

Françoise WERNER, *Romaine Brooks*, Paris, Plon, 1990, 334 p.

George WICKES, *The Amazon of Letters. The Life and Loves of Natalie Barney*, London, W.H. Allen, 1977, 286 p.

Jeremy WILSON, *Lawrence d'Arabie*, Paris, Denoël, 1994, 1 288 p.

Brenda WINEAPPLE, *Genêt, a Biography of Janet Flanner*, London, Ticknore Fields, 1989, 361 p.

Charlotte WOLFF, *Magnus Hirschfeld: A Portrait of a Pioneer in Sexology*, London, Quartet Books, 1986, 494 p.

3– Specific works

Eva AHLSTEDT, *La Pudeur en crise: un aspect de l'accueil d' "A la recherche du temps perdu" de Marcel Proust, 1913-1930*, Paris, Jean Touzot, "Acta Universitatis Gothoburgensis," 1985, 276 p.

–,*André Gide et le Débat sur l'homosexualité*, Paris, Jean Touzot, "Acta Universitatis Gothoburgensis," 1994, 291 p.

Karl Werner BÖHM, *Zwischen Selbstsucht und Verlangen, Thomas Mann und das Stigma Homosexualität*, Wurzbourg, Königshausen & Neumann, 1991, 409 p.

Henri BONNET, *Les Amours et la Sexualité de Marcel Proust*, Paris, Librairie A.G. Nizet, 1985, 101 p.

Lilian FADERMAN and Ann WILLIAMS, "Radclyffe Hall and the Lesbian Image," in *Conditions*, n° 1, April 1977.

Barbara FASSLER, "Theories of Homosexuality as a Source of Bloomsbury's Androgyny," in *Signs*, vol.5, n° 2, winter 1979.

Serge GINGRAS, *L'Homosexualité dans la prose d'Henry de Montherlant*, thèse Calgari, 1985, 90 p.

Gerhard HÄRLE, *Die Gestalt des Schönen*, Königstein/Ts, Hain, 1986, 165 p. [on Thomas Mann].

−,*Männerweiblichkeit, zur Homosexualität bei Klaus und Thomas Mann*, Frankfurt-am-Main, Athenäum Verlag, 1988, 412 p.

Marita KEILSON-LAURITZ, *Von der Liebe die Freundschaft heisst*, Berlin, Verlag Rosa Winkel, 1987, 159 p. [sur Stefan George].

Hédi KHELIL, *Sens, jouissance. Tourisme, exotisme, argent dans deux fictions coloniales d'André Gide*, Tunis, Éditions de la Nef, "Passerelles" 1, 1988, 172 p.

Rebecca O'ROURKE, *Reflecting on the Well of Loneliness*, London, Routledge & Kegan, 1989, 146 p.

Arthur King PETERS, *Jean Cocteau and André Gide, an Abrasive Friendship*, New Brunswick, Rutgers University Press, 1973, 426 p.

Patrick POLLARD, *André Gide, Homosexual Moralist*, New Haven, Yale University Press, 1991, 498 p.

Jean RAISON, "Publish and Be Banned," in *Gay News*, n° 148, p.17-18.

Katrina ROLLEY, "Cutting a Dash: The Dress of Radclyffe Hall and Una Troubridge," in *Feminist Review*, n° 35, été 1990.

Sonja RUEHL, "Inverts and Experts: Radclyffe Hall and the Lesbian Identity," in Brunt and Rowan (dir.), *Feminism, Culture and Politics*, Lawrence & Wishart, 1982, 190 p., p.15-37

Stefan ZYNDA, *Sexualität bei Klaus Mann*, Bonn, Bouvier Verlag, 1986, 156 p

INDEX

K

L

M

Wolf, Dr., 244
Wolfenden, Sir John, 263
Wolff, Charlotte, 166, 213, 257
Woolf, Leonard, 153
Woolf, Virginia, 81, 96, 99, 154–156
Wusche, Ernst, 66
Wuth, Otto, 220, 231, 259, 262
Wyneken, Gustav, 40–41, 108, 116

Y

Young, Francis Brett, 34, 36, 121, 269

Z

Zacharias, Erich, 38
Zeidler, Kurt, 39
Zetkin, Clara, 24, 28, 102
Zola, Émile, 42
Zweig, Stefan, 53, 257
Zywulska, Krystina, 241

Printed in the United States
24106LVS00001B/263

9 780875 862781